Legal Issues of Services of General Interest

Series editors

Johan Willem van de Gronden
Markus Krajewski
Ulla Neergaard
Erika Szyszczak

More information about this series at http://www.springer.com/series/8900

Andrea Gideon

Higher Education Institutions in the EU: Between Competition and Public Service

Andrea Gideon
Liverpool Law School
University of Liverpool
Liverpool
UK

and

Centre for Law and Business
National University of Singapore
Singapore
Singapore

Legal Issues of Services of General Interest
ISBN 978-94-6265-167-8   ISBN 978-94-6265-168-5   (eBook)
DOI 10.1007/978-94-6265-168-5

Library of Congress Control Number: 2016957144

Published by T.M.C. ASSER PRESS, The Hague, The Netherlands www.asserpress.nl
Produced and distributed for T.M.C. ASSER PRESS by Springer-Verlag Berlin Heidelberg

Printed on acid-free paper

This Springer imprint is published by Springer Nature
The registered company is Springer Science+Business Media B.V.
The registered company address is: Van Godewijckstraat 30, 3311 GX Dordrecht, The Netherlands

Series Information

The aim of the series *Legal Issues of Services of General Interest* is to sketch the framework for services of general interest in the EU and to explore the issues raised by developments related to these services. The Series encompasses, inter alia, analyses of EU internal market, competition law, legislation (such as the Services Directive), international economic law and national (economic) law from a comparative perspective. Sector-specific approaches will also be covered (health, social services). In essence, the present Series addresses the emergence of a European Social Model and will therefore raise issues of fundamental and theoretical interest in Europe and the global economy.

Series Editors

Ulla Neergaard
Faculty of Law
University of Copenhagen
Studiestræde 6
1455 Copenhagen K
Denmark
e-mail: ulla.neergaard@jur.ku.dk

Johan Willem van de Gronden
Faculty of Law
Radboud University
Comeniuslaan 4
6525 HP Nijmegen
The Netherlands
e-mail: j.vandeGronden@jur.ru.nl

Erika Szyszczak
Sussex Law School
University of Sussex
Brighton, BN1 9SP
UK
e-mail: E.Szyszczak@sussex.ac.uk

Markus Krajewski
Fachbereich Rechtswissenschaft
Universität Erlangen-Nürnberg
Schillerstraße 1
91054 Erlangen
Germany
e-mail: markus.krajewski@fau.de

This work is dedicated to my grandfather, Viktor Albert Benedikt Walther Titius, who always encouraged me very strongly in the pursuit of my academic career.

Preface

This book is based on my Ph.D. project 'European Higher Education Institutions under EU Law Constraints—An interdisciplinary analysis of the position of European higher education institutions between directly applicable EU law and their public service mission'. It has been revised and developed further and contains additional new research. I started the project as I craved an academic challenge after having worked outside of academia in Indonesia for a year. At the time of thinking about a research project, a new field of research was emerging: the tensions between the economic and the social in EU law and policy. When I began the research project, I discovered my passion for competition law, a field in which I now feel firmly anchored and in which I am currently researching new exciting topics with a focus on ASEAN. Without the Ph.D. project, I would never have discovered this interest. Since the Ph.D. new developments have taken place within the topics investigated in this book. In particular, the recent developments in UK higher education policy and the adoption of the new Research Framework and General Block Exemption Regulation make the book timely and I hope to be able to make a modest contribution to the relevant debates.

Along the way, there were many people without whom this journey would have never been possible and to whom I would like to express my gratitude. First and foremost I would like to thank my primary Ph.D. supervisor Prof. Dagmar Schiek, who not only provided invaluable feedback and encouragement for my Ph.D., but was also a supportive superior in my work for various research projects and as a teaching assistant for EU law. Even beyond this, she has always been an approachable mentor for any other questions I have had concerning my academic career and progress and I would not be where I am without her.

I would also like to thank my second supervisor Ann Blair for her insights and comments on my work, especially for the interesting discussions about the English higher education system. Professor Susanne Karstedt has very kindly advised me on the empirical part of my work. I am very grateful to all of them.

I would like to thank the School of Law of the University of Leeds for funding my tuition fees with the William Harrison Scholarship and providing travel assistance for presenting my work at conferences. Furthermore, I would like to sincerely thank the interviewees and their universities for the time and invaluable information the interviewees have given me.

I am also very grateful to my examiners of the Ph.D. project Prof. Michael Dougan and Prof. Michael Cardwell for their feedback and the collegial atmosphere during the viva (even if it was interrupted by a fire alarm). Michael Cardwell has also subsequently been a very keen supporter of my work and suggested the Ph.D. thesis as the University of Leeds contribution for the Jean Blondel Ph.D. prize for which it indeed has been subsequently submitted and shortlisted among the top five theses. I have to thank him and Prof. Alastair Mullis for making this possible.

When it comes to turning the Ph.D. thesis into a book, I have to express my deepest gratitude to Prof. Erika Szyszczak. Not only has she suggested publication in the series, but also stayed with the project. During the process of rewriting of the Ph.D. as a monograph, she has been a very helpful, encouraging and, especially, patient editor. I am sincerely grateful for all her support. I would, of course, also like to thank the other editors of the series (Prof. Johan Willem van de Gronden, Prof. Markus Krajewski and Prof. Ulla Neergaard) for accepting the book as part of the series.

Furthermore, I would like to thank Dr. Albert Sanchez-Graells for his thorough and extremely helpful feedback on the initial draft and for his general encouragement. Useful feedback has also been given by Dr. Mike Gordon and by the members of the ECPR Standing Group on Politics of Higher Education, Research and Innovation (formerly the European Research Area Collaborative Research Network) at various conferences where I have presented parts of this work.

Finally, I would like to thank all my friends, family and colleagues for their encouragement, practical and moral support and their patience. In particular, I owe thanks to Dr. John Mellors, Sam Theisens, Dinnia Joedadibrata, Dr. Jule Mulder, Christiane and Helmut Gideon, Dr. Janna Köke, Beatrice Weihert, Christine Thevissen, Sarah and Jenny Mellors, Dr. Lena Kruckenberg and Dr. Ulrike Vieten for giving feedback on my work or providing practical support such as letting me stay at their homes during the empirical phase of my work. I am deeply grateful to all these as well as to my other friends, family members and colleagues.

Singapore   Andrea Gideon

Contents

Abbreviations

ABA	American Bar Association
Abs.	Absatz (German for paragraph)
AiF	Arbeitsgemeinschaft industrieller Forschungsgemeinschaften (Industrial Research Associations)
BBC	British Broadcasting Corporation
BEIS	Department for Business, Energy and Industrial Strategy (new UK department)
BERs	Block exemptions regulations
BGH	Bundesgerichtshof (German Federal Court)
BIS	Department for Business, Innovation and Skills (previous name of UK government department)
BMBF	Bundesministerium für Bildung und Forschung (Federal Ministry of Education and Research)
BV	Besloten vennootschap (private limited liability company in the Netherlands)
BVerfGE	Bundesverfassungsgerichtsentscheidung (decision of the German constitutional court)
CE	Common Era
CESifo	Umbrella organisation of the 'Center for Economic Studies' and 'Information und Forschung'
Charter	Charter of Fundamental Rights of the European Union
CHEPS	Center for Higher Education Policy Studies, University of Twente
CHERPA	Consortium for Higher Education and Research Performance Assessment
CJEU	Court of Justice of the European Union
CMA	Competition and Markets Authority (UK)
C.M.L. Rev.	Common Market Law Review
COM	Commission
CöV Heft	Rechnungswesen und Controlling in der öffentlichen Verwaltung (Publication on controlling in public administration)
CUP	Cambridge University Press

DFG	Deutsche Forschungsgemeinschaft (German Research Foundation)
DG	Directorate General (of the European Commission)
EACEA	Education, Audiovisual and Culture Executive Agency
EC	European Community
ECI	European Citizen Initiative
ECJ	European Court of Justice (previous name and abbreviation of the CJEU)
ECTS	European Credit Transfer System
ed/eds	Editor/s
edn	Edition
EEC	European Economic Community
e.g.	Exempli gratia (for example)
EHEA	European Higher Education Area
EIoP	European Integration online Papers
ELJ	European Law Journal
ERA	Education Reform Act 1988
EStAL	European State Aid Law Quarterly
Et al.	Et alii (and others)
Etc.	Et cetera (and so forth)
ETSGIs	Education and training services of general interest
EU	European Union
EUA	European University Association
EuZW	Europäische Zeitschrift für Wirtschaftsrecht (academic journal)
EZ	Ministerie van Economische Zaken (Ministry of Economic Affairs, the Netherlands)
fEC	Full Economic Costing (English full costing methodology)
FHEA	Further and Higher Education Act 1992 (UK)
FQS	Forum: Qualitative Social Research
fte	Full-time equivalent
GBER	General block exemption regulation
GDP	Gross Domestic Product
GERD	Gross domestic expenditure on R&D
GG	Grundgesetz (German Constitution)
GRUR	Gewerblicher Rechtsschutz und Urheberrecht (journal)
HE	Higher education
HEFCE	Higher Education Funding Council for England
HEIF	Higher Education Innovation Fund
HEIs	Higher Education Institutions
HMRC	Her Majesty's Revenue and Customs
HRG	Hochschulrahmengesetz (Framework Act for Higher Education)
HSGIs	Health services of general interest
i.e.	Id est (that is)
Ibid	Ibidem (at the same place)
IJELP	International Journal for Education Law and Policy
IP/R	Intellectual property/rights

JCMS	Journal of Common Market Studies
JGIM	Journal of General Internal Medicine
KNAW	Koninklijke Nederlandse Akademie van Wetenschappen (Royal Netherlands Academy of Arts and Sciences)
KU Leuven	Katholieke Universiteit Leuven (Catholic University Leuven)
LSE	London School of Economics and Political Sciences
M	Million
MEP	Member of the European Parliament
MIT	Massachusetts Institute of Technology
n	Note
N8	Eight universities in the North of England
NCAs	National competition authorities
NHS	National Health Service (UK)
NMa	Nederlandse Mededingsautoriteit (Netherlands Competition Authority)
No.	Number
NWO	Nederlandse Organisatie voor Wetenschappelijk Onderzoek (Netherlands Research Council)
OCW	Ministerie van Onderwijs, Cultuur en Wetenschap (Ministry for Education, Culture and Sciences)
OECD	Organisation for Economic Co-operation and Development
OFT	Office of Fair Trading (former UK Competition Authority)
OJ	Official Journal
OMC	Open Method of Coordination
Ors	Others
OUP	Oxford University Press
p/pp.	Page/s
PACEC	Public and Corporate Economic Consultants
para	Paragraph
Ph.D.	Doctor of Philosophy
PI	Principal investigator
PPPs	Public–private partnerships
QAA	Quality Assurance Agency (UK)
QR	Quality-related research funding
QS	Quacquarelli Symonds
R&D(&I)	Research and development (and innovation)
RCUK	Research Councils UK
REF	Research Excellence Framework
RIO	Research and Innovation Observatory
RVO	Rijksdienst voor Ondernemend Nederland (Netherlands Enterprise Agency)
s	Section
seq	Sequentes (following)
SGEIs	Services of general economic interest
SGIs	Services of general interest
SMEs	Small and medium sized enterprises

SNIP	Small but significant and non-transitory increase in price
SSGIs	Social services of general interest
SSRN	Social Science Research Network
STEM	Science, technology, engineering and maths
STW	Stichting voor de Technische Wetenschappen (Technology Foundation)
TEF	Teaching Excellence Framework
TEU	Treaty on European Union
TFEU	Treaty on the functioning of the European Union
THE	Times Higher Education
TKI	Topconsortia voor Kennis en Innovatie (Top Consortia for Knowledge and Innovation)
TRAC	Transparent Approach to Costing
TUD	Technische Universiteit Delft
UCAS	Universities and Colleges Admission Service
UCU	University and College Union
UIFZ	Universitäts-Industrie-Forschungs-Zentren (University-industry research centres)
UK	United Kingdom
UKRI	United Kingdom Research and Innovation
US/USA	United States (of America)
UUK	Universities UK
UvA	Universiteit van Amsterdam
VAT	Value added tax
VSNU	Vereniging van universiteiten (Association of universities in the Netherlands)
VVDstRL	Veröffentlichungen der Vereinigung der Deutschen Staatsrecht-slehrer (publication series)
WHW	Wet op het hoger onderwijs en wetenschappelijk onderzoek (Higher Education and Research Act)

Cases

CJEU

General Court

Commission Decisions

National Cases

Legislation

Treaties

Treaty establishing the European Economic Community (EEC Treaty)

Single European Act OJ [1987] L 169/1

Treaty of Maastricht on European Union OJ [1992] C 191/01

Treaty on European Union, together with the complete text of the Treaty establishing the European Community OJ [1992] C 224/01 (EU Treaty and EC Treaty)

Treaty of Amsterdam amending the Treaty on European Union, the Treaties establishing the European Communities and related acts OJ [1997] C 340/01

Treaty of Nice amending the Treaty on European Union, the Treaties Establishing the European Communities and certain related acts OJ [2001] C 80/01

Treaty establishing a Constitution for Europe OJ [2004] C 310/01 (European Constitution)

Treaty of Lisbon amending the Treaty on European Union and the Treaty establishing the European Community OJ [2007] C 306/01

Charter of Fundamental Rights of the European Union OJ [2010] C 83/02

Treaty on the Functioning of the European Union (Consolidated version 2012) OJ [2012] C 326/01

Secondary Legislation

Commission Communications

Commission Communication 'Towards a European Research Area' COM (2000) 6 final

Commission Communication 'Services of general interest in Europe' OJ [2001] C 17/04

Commission Communication 'Guidelines on the application of Article 81(3) of the Treaty' OJ [2004] C 101/08

Commission Communication Community framework for state aid for research and development and innovation OJ [2006] C 323/01 (referred to as previous Research Framework)

Commission Communication 'Implementing the Community Lisbon Programme: Social Services of General Interest in the European Union' COM(2006) 177 final

Commission Communication 'Guidance on the Commission's enforcement priorities in applying Article 82 of the EC Treaty to abusive exclusionary conduct by dominant undertakings' OJ [2009] C 45/02

Commission Communication on the application of the European Union State aid rules to compensation granted for the provision of services of general economic interest OJ [2012] C 8/02

Commission Communication 'European Union framework for State aid in the form of public service compensation' OJ [2012] C 8/03

Commission Communication concerning the prolongation of the application of the Community framework for State aid for research and development and innovation OJ [2013] C 360/1

Commission Communication Criteria for the analysis of the compatibility with the internal market of State aid to promote the execution of import projects of common European interest OJ [2014] C 188/44

Communication from the Commission Framework for State aid for research and development and innovation OJ [2014] C 198/01 (referred to as Research Framework)

Communication from the Commission on the European Citizens' Initiative "Water and sanitation are a human right! Water is a public good, not a commodity!" COM(2014) 177 final

Communication from the Commission to the European Parliament, the Council, the European Economic and Social Committee and the Committee of the Regions 'Research and innovation as sources of renewed growth' COM/2014/0339 final

Commission Notices

Commission Notice on the definition of the relevant market for the purposes of Community Competition law OJ [1997] C 372/5

Commission Notice on agreements of minor importance which do not appreciably restrict competition under Article 101(1) of the Treaty on the Functioning of the European Union (De Minimis Notice) OJ [2014] C 291/1

Commission Notice 'Guidelines on the effect on trade concept contained in Articles 81 and 82 of the Treaty' OJ [2004] C 101/81

Commission Notice on the notion of State aid as referred to in Article 107(1) of the Treaty on the Functioning of the European Union OJ [2016] C 262/1

Conclusions

Presidency Conclusions, Lisbon European Council 23./24.03.2000

Presidency Conclusions, Brussels European Council, 22 and 23 March 2005

Conclusions, Brussels European Council, 17 June 2010, EUCO13/10 CO EUR 9 CONCL 2

Decisions

Decision 1982/2006/EC concerning the Seventh Framework Programme of the European Community for research, technological development and demonstration activities (2007–2013) OJ [2006] L 412/01

Decision 2012/21/EU on the application of Article 106(2) of the Treaty on the Functioning of the European Union to State aid in the form of public service compensation granted to certain undertakings entrusted with the operation of services of general economic interest OJ [2012] L 7/3

Directives

Directive 77/388/EEC on the harmonization of the laws of the Member States relating to turnover taxes-Common system of value added tax: uniform basis of assessment OJ [1977] L 145/1

Directive 2000/60/EC 'establishing a framework for Community action in the field of water policy' OJ [2000] L 327/1

Directive 2004/38/EC on the right of citizens of the Union and their family members to move and reside freely within the territory of the Member States amending Regulation (EEC) No 1612/68 and repealing Directives 64/221/EEC, 68/360/EEC, 72/194/EEC, 73/148/EEC, 75/34/EEC, 75/35/EEC, 90/364/EEC, 90/365/EEC and 93/96/EEC OJ [2004] L 158/77

Directive 2005/36/EC on the recognition of professional qualifications OJ [2005] L 255/22

Directive 2006/111/EC on the transparency of financial relations between Member States and public undertakings as well as on financial transparency within certain undertakings OJ [2006] L 318/17

Directive 2008/6/EC amending Directive 97/67/EC with regard to the full accomplishment of the internal market of Community postal services OJ [2008] L 52/3

Directive 2014/24/EU on public procurement and repealing Directive 2004/18/EC OJ [2014] L 94/65

Directive 2014/104/EU on certain rules governing actions for damages under national law for infringements of the competition law provisions of the Member States and of the European Union OJ [2014] L 349/1

Regulations

Regulation 4064/89/EEC of 21 December 1989 on the control of concentrations between undertakings OJ [1989] L 395/01

Regulation 1/2003/EC on the implementation of the rules on competition laid down in Articles 81 and 82 of the Treaty OJ [2003] L 1/1

Regulation 139/2004/EC on the control of concentrations between undertakings (the EC Merger Regulation) OJ [2004] L 24/1

Regulation 330/2010/EU on the application of Article 101(3) of the Treaty on the Functioning of the European Union to categories of vertical agreements and concerted practices OJ [2010] L 102/1

Regulation 1217/2010/EU on the application of Article 101(3) of the Treaty on the Functioning of the European Union to categories of research and development agreements OJ [2010] L 335/36

Regulation 1218/2010/EU on the application of Article 101(3) of the Treaty on the Functioning of the European Union to certain categories of specialisation agreements OJ [2010] L 335/43

Regulation 492/2011/EU on freedom of movement for workers within the Union Text with EEA relevance OJ [2011] L 141/01

Regulation 360/2012/EU on the application of Articles 107 and 108 of the Treaty on the Functioning of the European Union to de minimis aid granted to undertakings providing services of general economic interest OJ [2012] L 114/12

Regulation 531/2012 on roaming on public mobile communications networks within the Union OJ [2012] L 172/10

Commission Regulation 1407/2013/EU on the application of Articles 107 and 108 of the Treaty on the Functioning of the European Union to de minimis aid, OJ [2013] L 352/1

Commission Regulation 316/2014/EUC on the application of Article 101(3) of the Treaty on the Functioning of the European Union to categories of technology transfer agreements OJ [2014] L 93/17

Commission Regulation 651/2014/EU declaring certain categories of aid compatible with the internal market in application of Articles 107 and 108 of the Treaty (General Block Exemption Regulation) OJ [2014] L 187/1

Other Acts

Framework Programme for Research 1984–87 COM(83) 260 final information from the Commission Community framework for State aid for research and development OJ [1996] C 45/5

Commission White Paper on the modernisation of the rules implementing Articles 85 and 86 of the EC Treaty Programme No. 99/027 OJ [1999] C 132/01

Guidelines on the assessment of horizontal mergers under the Council Regulation on the control of concentrations between undertakings OJ [2004] C 31/03

Guidelines on the assessment of non-horizontal mergers under the Council Regulation on the control of concentrations between undertakings OJ [2008] C 265/07

Paper of the services of DG Competition containing a draft framework for state aid for research and development and innovation of 19 December 2013

Bologna

Sorbonne Joint Declaration on harmonisation of the architecture of the European higher education system by the four Ministers in charge for France, Germany, Italy and the United Kingdom, 25 May 1998

Bologna Joint Declaration of the European Ministers of Education, 19 June 1999

Leuven and Louvain-la-Neuve Communiqué of the Conference of European Ministers Responsible for Higher Education, 28–29 April 2009

Budapest-Vienna Declaration on the European Higher Education Area, 12 March 2010

Yerevan Communiqué of the EHEA Ministerial Conference of 14–15 May 2015

National Legislation (in alphabetical order)

Germany

Bayerisches Hochschulgesetz (Bavarian Higher Education Act)
Berliner Hochschulgesetz (Berlin HEI Act)
Bremisches Hochschulgesetz (Bremen HEI Act)
Deutsches Gesetz über Arbeitnehmererfindungen, short *Arbeitnehmererfindungsgesetz* (Employee Invention Act)
Gesetz über die Hochschulen in Baden-Württemberg (Act on HEIs in Baden-Württemberg)
Gesetz über Urheberrecht und verwandte Schutzrechte (Copyright Act)
Gesetz zur Flexibilisierung von haushaltsrechtlichen Rahmenbedingungen außeruniversitärer Wissenschaftseinrichtungen, short *Wissenschaftsfreiheitsgesetz* (Freedom of Research Act)
Grundgesetz (Constitution) English translation available on: http://www.gesetze-im-internet.de/englisch_gg/
Hochschulrahmengesetz (Framework Act for Higher Education)

Netherlands

Kader financieel beheer rijkssubsidies (Subsidy Framework for Public Subsidies)
Kaderbesluit EZ-subsidies (Framework Act for EZ-Subsidies)
Regeling nationale EZ-subsidies (National EZ-Subsidies Regulation)
Uitvoeringsbesluit WHW 2008 (WHW Executing Act 2008)
Wet op het hoger onderwijs en wetenschappelijk onderzoek (Higher Education and Research Act, WHW)
Wet Versterking Besturing (Strengthening Administration Act)

UK

Competition Act 1998
Education Act 2011
Education Reform Act 1988
Further and Higher Education Act 1992
Higher Education Act 2004
Higher Education and Research Bill (currently debated in parliament)
Patents Act 1977
Teaching and Higher Education Act 1998

Other

Sherman Act (US American Competition Act)

Chapter 1
Introduction: An Interdisciplinary Analysis of the Mission of European Higher Education Institutions and Potential External Constraints

Abstract The aim of this book is to provide an in-depth appreciation of the impact of EU law and policy on the Member States' higher education institution (HEI) sectors with a particular emphasis on the exposure of research in universities to EU competition law. This introductory chapter delineates the topic, research questions, methods and outline of the book. It then proceeds to explore the historical and theoretical background for studying EU law constraints on HEIs. It will be shown how HEIs moved away from their traditional mission to become more economic in nature. Employing approaches from European integration theory, it will be seen that this can increase the likelihood of potential spill-over from the (economic) provisions of EU law potentially requiring further commodification of HEI activity.

Keywords Tension between the economic and the social in the EU · Mission/idea of higher education institutions · History of universities · Commodification of higher education institutions · European integration theory · Neo-functionalism · Spill-over

Contents

© T.M.C. ASSER PRESS and the author 2017
A. Gideon, *Higher Education Institutions in the EU: Between Competition and Public Service*, Legal Issues of Services of General Interest, DOI 10.1007/978-94-6265-168-5_1

1.1 Introduction

The position of higher education institutions (HEIs) in the European integration project mirrors tensions between EU economic integration and the wider mission of the EU and its Member States, which are frequently discussed as tensions between economic and social integration. On the one hand, the EU does not use the supranational method of integration in this field but employs soft law measures (Open Method of Coordination (OMC) and the extra-EU Bologna Process). On the other hand, the main activities of HEIs, namely higher education and research, constitute yet another field where the forces of directly applicable Treaty provisions, such as Union citizenship, the free movement provisions and provisions on competition law and state aid, may deconstruct some national policy concepts. At the same time, HEIs in many Member States have been subjected to national policies, partly influenced by EU policy, that force them to commodify their 'products', making HEIs more vulnerable to the economic provisions of EU law and potentially forcing further commercialisation which could endanger the traditional non-economic mission of European HEIs. This book explores how EU law and policy impact on the HEI sector with a specific focus on the exposure of HEI research to EU competition law and draws the conclusion that an alternative approach may be indicated.

Whilst tensions between the economic and the social have generally received increasing awareness over the last decade,[1] HEIs have received less attention in this respect and work which has investigated the influences of EU law on HEIs has mainly focussed on citizenship and the free movement provisions.[2] The consequences of EU competition law have only been tentatively investigated by few authors[3] and almost exclusively with regard to the education aspect of HEIs.[4] Furthermore, the discussion on the position of HEIs in Europe which takes place more widely in other disciplines[5] has received only limited attention from an EU legal studies perspective.[6]

This book aims to fill these gaps, by linking the debates and situating (European) HEI policy within the context of European integration theories. It will, furthermore,

---

[1] See, for example, the contributions in de Búrca and De Witte 2005; Dougan and Spaventa 2005; Neergaard et al. 2009; Mossialos et al. 2010; Schiek et al. 2011; Bruun et al. 2012; Burroni et al. 2012; Cantillon et al. 2012; Whyman et al. 2012; Neergaard et al. 2013 and Schiek 2013a.

[2] See, for example, Van der Mei 2005; Dougan 2008; Garben 2008; Reich 2009 and Damjanovic 2012.

[3] In addition to the author's own work (Gideon 2012, 2015a), the main commentators are: Steyger 2002; Swennen 2008/2009; Amato and Farbmann 2010 and Greaves and Scicluna 2010.

[4] Aside from the author's own work (Gideon 2015b), the exception are Huber and Prikoszovits 2008.

[5] See, for example, Van der Ploeg and Veugelers 2007; Cardoso et al. 2008; Koch 2008; Wissema 2009; Corbett 2012 or the contributions to Enders and De Weert 2009; McKelvey and Holem 2009; Palfreyman and Tapper 2009a and Chou and Ulnicane 2015.

[6] Most prominently by Garben 2010, 2011.

conduct an in-depth legal doctrinal analysis of potential EU competition law constraints on HEIs. This analysis is further specified for HEI research in three Member States (the United Kingdom (England), the Netherlands and Germany), whose HEI systems have been commercialised to different degrees. A qualitative empirical study will illustrate even more specifically how research in universities may be impacted upon by EU competition law (as an example of exposure to economic constraints) and in how far pivotal actors in universities are aware of this impact. The book will, thus, not only expand the knowledge about European (legal) integration and its effects on national HEI policies, but will also offer practical insights which can serve as guidance for policymakers and professionals in the national HEI sectors, allowing them to address potential problems and identify best practices.

1.2 Examining EU Law Constraints on HEIs

HEIs are investigated as a field where Member States avoid establishing supranational law, but where HEIs, nevertheless, can come within the ambit of directly applicable EU law. This could especially be the case if Member States pursue national policies of commercialisation thereby increasing the likeliness of applicability of the economic provisions of directly applicable EU law. Therefore, provisions of EU law seemingly unrelated to HEIs such as those on citizenship, the fundamental freedoms, competition and state aid can 'spill over' and might lead to unintended consequences for national policy choices. This may even trigger further commercialisation of the sector, which, in turn, may endanger the traditional non-economic missions of European HEIs. The book provides an in-depth appreciation of how EU law and policy (could) impact on the HEI sector with a specific focus on potential constraints from EU competition law on research in HEIs as an example of exposure to economic constraints.

This question is investigated from political and social science perspectives as well as through legal doctrinal analysis of legislation and case law, culminating in a qualitative empirical study covering ten universities in three Member States. Research in publicly funded research intense universities has been chosen as the field for the empirical study, since market structures are increasingly being introduced in this area and HEIs thus compete with each other and with other research providing actors. Research, therefore, has the potential to fall into the ambit of the more economic provisions of EU law and thus lends itself as an illustrative example of the constraints that may arise for the sector. EU competition law has been chosen, not only because there is little research on its potential impact, but also because this impact has the potential to demand significant changes in HEI practice, as already evident in the previous Research Framework's[7] requirement to introduce full costing for research in publicly funded research organisations in

---

[7] Community framework for state aid for research and development and innovation OJ [2006] C 323/01 (previous Research Framework).

Europe, including HEIs. The doctrinal and empirical investigation of competition law implications will demonstrate that even more demands for commercialisation of public universities may derive from EU competition law.

The book is structured into six chapters (including this introductory chapter). The remainder of this chapter will be dedicated to illuminating the historical and theoretical background. It will be shown how HEIs moved away from their traditional mission to become more economic in nature; increasing the likeliness of potential spill-over from the economic provisions of EU law. Chapter 2 will explore the current EU and extra-EU policies showing that Member States were reluctant to use the supranational method of integration in relation to HEIs. It will then demonstrate in overview the potential of spill-over from directly applicable EU law, namely from Union citizenship, the free movement provisions and competition law.

Chapter 3 continues this study in more detail in the area of EU competition law. It will first assess the concept of 'undertaking' and services of general economic interest (SGEIs) to determine how far HEIs might fall under the competition law provisions in the first place. It will be shown that this becomes increasing likely the more commercial elements an HEI system adopts. The second part of Chap. 3 then conducts an in-depth legal-doctrinal analysis of potential constraints on HEIs arising from competition and state aid law. We will see that, whilst the application of the competition rules might occasionally aid 'consumers' (students) or HEIs themselves, there are situations where they might have a detrimental social effect (e.g. when tuition fees are fixed at a low level to allow broader access) or more generally clash with national or university policies (e.g. they might require the opening of bodies distributing study places to foreign and commercial providers or require full costing and pricing at full cost plus levels for research).

Chapter 4 prepares the groundwork for the empirical study by setting out which countries have been chosen for the study and introducing a common approach to discussing their research systems. Each country is then explored in a separate subchapter after which a section provides a tentative overview of potential conflicts with EU competition law. Chapter 4 finds that the systems investigated differ in a variety of ways from the general national expenditure on research and the overall character of the system to the importance of individual sectors and the extent to which the recent trend of commodification has influenced the research systems. As regards research in HEIs, the importance of competitive factors in funding allocation has increased in all three systems, but it plays by far the most significant role in England where competitive factors even play a major role in generic research funding allocation. The growing importance in non-generic funding is associated with a variety of concern, most significantly with threats to academic freedom and budget constraints due to matching requirements as non-generic funding is not always provided at full cost levels. From a competition law perspective, we will see that differentiation between non-economic research, which does not fall under competition law, and research services, which do, is more difficult than it may appear, since this line can be fluid. If an activity does fall under competition law potential tensions in all three systems could arise from this with national research policies on HEIs. However, the more economically oriented the system, the more frequently this may happen.

The empirical study itself is contained in Chap. 5. In its first subchapter the methodology of the empirical study is explained showing, inter alia, how the universities under scrutiny have been chosen and how the interview questions have been drafted as well as how the interviews will be analysed; namely by employing a framework developed on the basis of the results of Chaps. 3 and 4. This is followed by a subchapter on each country discussing the economic constraints in the relevant system as experienced by interviewees, their awareness of and the potential constraints arising from EU competition law. In all three countries interviewees expected the commodification tendencies to continue and there was some criticism for this development. However, the more detailed sentiments about the research systems as well as the awareness of competition law of the interviewees differed between the countries which seems to correspond with the general character of the research systems. On the basis of the information received from the interviewees, a more in-depth appreciation than in Chap. 4 of the question in how far competition law becomes applicable is then provided in Chap. 5. Yet, as will be seen, this remains a difficult question. While some potential tensions with competition law discussed in previous chapters do not materialise based on the empirical information gathered, some in fact could cause concerns and others have been detected. Of course, there may still be the possibility of the application of exemptions, but these might not capture every situation and, in any case, might make the conduct of HEIs increasingly complicated from a legal/administrative perspective. Given the current situation, HEIs are thus advised to pay increasing attention to competition law.

Chapter 6 will connect the results of the empirical study with the previous chapters thereby assessing how applying the EU's economic constitution to HEIs may lead to unforeseen consequences including further commodification which could endanger the traditional non-economic mission of European HEIs. The constraints faced by the sector are then contextualised in the wider debate and some recent attempts by the Commission to align EU research policy with competition law are critically discussed. It is concluded that these attempts seem equally insufficient, as they do not necessarily clarify the legal position, are still fragmented, are decided upon entirely by the Commission and do not appear to necessarily reflect the views of the general public or stakeholders in HEIs. Therefore, an outlook is given of potential alternative strategies, as unlikely as their realisation in the current Eurosceptic climate may be, for a more coherent EU level policy on HEIs which moves away from the current tendency towards commodification and truly clarifies the legal position of HEIs under EU law, though the details of such approaches will have to be left to future research.

1.3 Historical and Theoretical Background

The remainder of this chapter will outline the development of HEIs in the EU to explain their character and current influences upon them (Sects. 1.3.1–1.3.3). To examine HEIs in the EU requires an understanding of the nature of European HEIs more widely. The idea of HEIs has been a manifold concept since the establishment of the first European universities in the narrower sense about 850 years ago which changed over time with emphasis being set on different aspects of their activities according to the general historical development of that time. Thus the 'mission' of the European university is best explained from a historical perspective. Further, the remainder of this chapter will position the book within the approaches of European integration theory to illuminate the theoretical background (Sect. 1.3.4).[8]

1.3.1 The Original Non-economic Purpose of European HEIs

The first HEIs[9] in Europe developed in the Middle Ages[10] and have since undergone two significant periods of change.[11] Originally European HEIs were bodies widely autonomous from the church and state.[12] This, despite the Bible being regarded as the ultimate truth, allowed HEIs to question current doctrine (the scholastic method) which is considered to be the beginning of the concept of academic freedom.[13] Whilst the medieval universities' main focus was to teach students recognising 'divine truth', professors also conducted experiments and knowledge transfer activities such as serving as advisors or judges.[14] As HEIs developed under pre-nation-state conditions and Latin served as the *lingua franca*, they were international institutions engaged in lively mutual exchange.[15]

The first period of change occurred in early modernity.[16] Corresponding to the rise of nation states in Europe, the previously international HEIs with free moving

---

[8] A shortened version of Sect. 1.3 is contained in Gideon 2015a.

[9] The terms HEI and university are used interchangeably here as in most literature on the subject (see Allen 1988, p. 14). This phenomenon, might be based on the fact that for many centuries the university was the most important HEI in the meaning of the term today. Where differentiation is essential this has been made clear.

[10] See Farrington and Palfreyman 2012, p. 11 who trace the earliest forerunner HEI in Europe back to the Pandidakterion in what is now Istanbul in 425 CE. The first universities in the narrower sense in Europe then developed in the High Middle Ages starting with the University of Bologna in 1158. See also Koch 2008, p. 20 seq; Cowan et al. 2009, p. 278; Wissema 2009, pp. 3, 9.

[11] The features of universities in different periods are elaborated upon here in an ideal-typical manner in the Weberian sense by describing the archetype extracted from common appearances (Weber 2005, p. 4 seq). Such an analysis thus explicitly does not entail that every situation is exactly in accordance with the archetype, instead it is more a trend becoming apparent.

[12] See Scott 2006, p. 7; Neave 2009, p. 19; Stichweh 2009, p. 2; Wissema 2009, p. 6 seq, 10.

[13] See Allen 1988, p. 16; Scott 2006, p. 2 seq, 8 seq; Wissema 2009, p. 5.

[14] See Allen 1988, p. 16; Scott 2006, p. 6 seq; Clark 2006, p. 4 seq; Wissema 2009, p. 4 seq, 9 seq; Neave 2009, p. 24.

[15] See Scott 2006, p. 7 seq; Wissema 2009, p. 10; Stichweh 2009, p. 2.

[16] Early 16th until late 18th century. See Erbe 2007, p. 11.

academics became national institutions. At the same time, societal developments such as the exploration of (to Europeans) hitherto unknown parts of the world, discoveries in the natural sciences by Copernicus, Galileo and, later, Newton and the rise of humanist philosophy nourished HEIs.[17] In the 19th century, the Prussian Minister of Education Wilhelm von Humboldt triggered the second period of change by establishing a new concept which integrated a stronger research focus into the nationalised HEIs.[18] Accordingly, research was conducted for the sake of acquiring new knowledge with no applications in mind,[19] was chiefly mono-disciplinary with increasing specialisation and was supposed to inform teaching. Furthermore, the ideas of allowing students to choose their courses freely and to guarantee professors freedom of choice regarding the directions of research and teaching, strengthened the academic freedom.[20]

By the end of the 19th century European universities had thus developed into research intensive institutions which, despite being nationalised, retained a high degree of academic freedom and autonomy. They served the public purpose in the national interest by teaching and conducting research for knowledge's sake rather than towards a particular, commercially exploitable aim and were funded mainly by the state.[21]

1.3.2   The Republican University in the United States

HEIs across the Atlantic developed differently; influenced by the spirit of establishing a democratic republic, the US HEI model focussed on equality of access (which, however, did not initially include gender and race equality) and equality between academic subjects. This led to the establishment of a vast variety of HEIs and was the basis for the beginning of mass higher education.[22] Two sets of ideas

---

[17] See Allen 1988, pp. 16, 21; Clark 2006, p. 6 seq; Scott 2006, p. 10 seq; Koch 2008, p. 74 seq; Wissema 2009, p. 9 seq, 14; Cowan et al. 2009, p. 279.

[18] See Denninger 2001, p. 10; Clark 2006, p. 3 seq; Scott 2006, p. 19 seq; Wissema 2009, p. 13 seq; Cowan et al. 2009, p. 279; Neave 2009, p. 24. Further on Humboldt's writings about the university see Koch 2008, p. 143 seq.

[19] Applied research as well as some research in the very expensive 'big science' thus developed mainly outside HEIs. See further Scott 2006, p. 21 seq.

[20] See Röhrs 1995, p. 124; Denninger 2001, p. 10 seq; Connell 2004, p. 19; Clark 2006, p. 3 seq; Scott 2006, p. 20 seq; Wissema 2009, p. 13 seq; De Weert 2009, pp. 135, 140; Neave 2009, p. 31.

[21] In the following, the term HEIs when used in the European context refers to these (usually public) institutions which combine research and tertiary education, since, despite the fact that there are now also other forms of HEIs, these classical European HEIs, for which the term 'university' could almost be used interchangeably, are the focus of this research.

[22] See Röhrs 1995, pp. 104, 116 seq, 121 seq; Scott 2006, p. 14 seq, 17.

shaped a second trend in US HEIs; the philosophy of the Progressive Era (late 19th until mid 20th century) which aimed at the refinement of big business and government towards their use for the public and economic efficiency[23] and the Wisconsin Idea which promoted that HEIs should be of service to the public through, inter alia, a focus on applied research, vocational education as well as knowledge exchange and facility sharing.[24] As a result, HEIs were expected to serve society more directly, for example, through providing vocational education, conducting applied research and cooperating with businesses and government.[25] This also led to an increase in external funding for, as well as influences on the directions of, research.[26]

These HEIs, while serving the public good, were susceptible to commercialisation of academic life. As early as in the 1970s, critical observers noticed a changing process in US HEIs towards creating something potentially tradable on a market rather than for ideal purposes for which the term 'commodification' has been applied.[27] This term, though of Marxist origin,[28] is used here to describe market-like behaviours even if they are not actually for profit.[29] On the basis of this business-like re-conceptualisation, US universities started to compete with each other and to reach out to international markets of education, arguably creating a world-wide market for higher education and academic research dominated by industrial centres of the world.[30]

1.3.3 Gradual Commodification of European HEIs

European HEIs did not go through an idealistic phase of orienting themselves on how to serve the public good more directly in the same way as their US counterparts. However, from the second half of the 20th century onwards universities

---

[23] The Progressive Era with its high time from 1890 to 1916 was a movement of various interest groups, however, with some major influences from the white US middle classes who, next to the mentioned focus, promoted a broad variety of other issues such as women's suffrage, restriction of immigration and prohibition. See Link 1959; Sklar 1992, p. 38, Jaycox 2005, preface and introduction.

[24] The Wisconsin Idea started in Wisconsin and was originally focussed on the state's university. See further Hoeveler 1976.

[25] See Allen 1988, p. 21 seq; Röhrs 1995, pp. 108, 115 seq, 123; Scott 2006, p. 23 seq.

[26] See Röhrs 1995, p. 107 seq; Scott 2006, p. 27 seq. The external influences on universities have later been criticised in the student protests of the 1960s (Scott 2006, p. 24).

[27] Shumar 2013.

[28] Ibid p. 15 seq.

[29] See also Radder 2010, p. 4 seq who perceives the interpretation and assessment of processes on the basis of economic criteria as the main characteristic of commodification. Similar Slaughter and Leslie 1997 p. 11 and Marginson 2007.

[30] See Choon Fong 2008, p. 79 seq who predicts that Asia will be this centre in the future.

were gradually re-structured in congruence with the demands of increasingly complex economies demanding qualified employees. Governments aimed at expanding access to higher education, opening existing HEIs to more students and creating a number of new HEIs. Dwindling public resources[31] seemed to require the end of free university education and the introduction of study fees. The increased numbers of institutions competed for public and private resources and also for being perceived as offering the most competitive education and highest levels of employability. The influence of the global successes of US universities contributed to the acceleration of internationalisation; together with new information technologies, it incited the national European HEIs to re-internationalise, using English as the new *lingua franca* and supporting student and researcher mobility[32] as well as international research collaborations.[33]

While all this did not necessitate turning the activities of HEIs into marketable services, it certainly facilitated this development. The concept of commodification, mentioned in the context of the United States' HEIs, which describes a process by which an activity (such as higher education or research) is changed in order to become a service tradeable on markets, seems equally suitable to describe the recent developments of European HEIs. This process turns education and research from a public good into a commodity. As has been seen, European public HEIs are national institutions. They are publicly funded, containing elements of national identity and culture and are tasked with accumulating and disseminating knowledge and providing higher education (without a particular, commercially exploitable aim) for all.[34] Public higher education can be regarded especially as belonging to the welfare state as wider access to HEIs is seen as a precondition of participation in complex economies and thus increasingly constitutes an element of social policy. Therefore, in Europe, where higher education and research can

---

[31] Former Higher Education Minister for England, David Lammy, for example, declared that 'any pressures on spending should be seen against the background of a long-term increase in student numbers [...] with "more students than ever before in our history"'. See Richardson H (2010) University budget cuts revealed. BBC, 1 February 2010 http://news.bbc.co.uk/1/hi/education/8491729.stm. Accessed 2 February 2010.

[32] As we will see in Chap. 2, the free movement of knowledge is now also a part of EU research policy (Sect. 2.2.1.3) and the free movement of citizens as part of Union citizenship allows for free movement and equal treatment (at least as regards access to HEIs) of EU students (Sect. 2.3.1.1).

[33] See Röhrs 1995, p. 109 seq, 115; Connell 2004, p. 17 seq, 22 seq; Scott 2006, p. 30 seq; Konsortium Bildungsberichterstattung 2006, p. 101; Choon Fong 2008, p. 80 seq; Cowan et al. 2009, p. 278 seq, 290 seq; Deiaco et al. 2009, p. 329 seq; De Weert 2009, p. 143 seq; Hubig 2009, p. 51; Neave 2009; Palfreyman and Tapper 2009b, p. 205 seq, 209 seq; Steinfeld 2009; Stichweh 2009, p. 2; Wissema 2009, p. 17 seq, 31 seq; Smith 2015.

[34] Teichler 2007, p. 105; Walkenhorst 2008, pp. 567, 574 seq.

widely be comprehended as a public good, commodification of HEIs also inverts the process of de-commodification characteristic for public services in the welfare state.[35]

The following trends are seen as characteristic for the commodification of European HEIs: public funding is reduced which leads to the introduction of business style administration of HEIs as well as competitive parameters for public funding and the need to look for alternative sources. Private providers start offering degree courses and organising research projects in the HEI 'market'. Academic research not only becomes more interdisciplinary, but also more applied.[36] Furthermore, universities start to focus on such fields of research where demand by business and public funders is greatest. HEIs also increasingly cooperate with industry and commercially exploit the results of their own research.[37]

As will be explored further in the rest of this book (in particular in Chap. 6 Sect. 6.4), such commodification gives rise to certain problems. Mass higher education, though desirable from an equality point of view, can threaten quality unless funding is increased. Otherwise, fees might need to be introduced, which again threatens the equality achieved by providing mass higher education in the first place. Mass teaching can also interfere with research commitments which led to a separation of teaching and research.[38] Changes in governance and funding

---

[35] Esping-Andersen coined the term 'de-commodification' to explain the purpose of welfare systems as a means to create independence for individuals of their capacity to engage in the market. See Esping-Andersen 1990, p. 21 seq, 35 seq; Esping-Andersen 1999, 43 seq.

[36] The following definition used by the OECD in its Frascati Manual will be used throughout this book: 'Basic research is experimental or theoretical work undertaken primarily to acquire new knowledge of the underlying foundation of phenomena and observable facts, without any particular application or use in view. Applied research is also original investigation undertaken in order to acquire new knowledge. It is, however, directed primarily towards a specific practical aim or objective. Experimental development is systematic work, drawing on existing knowledge gained from research and/or practical experience, which is directed to producing new materials, products or devices, to installing new processes, systems and services, or to improving substantially those already produced or installed' OECD 2002.

[37] For more on commodification trends see, Röhrs 1995, p. 106 seq; Connell 2004, p. 17 seq, 21 seq; Konsortium Bildungsberichterstattung 2006, p. 101 seq; Jongbloed and van der Meulen 2006; Choon Fong 2008, p. 78 seq, 82 seq; Deiaco et al. 2009, p. 330 seq; Palfreyman and Tapper 2009b; Steinfeld 2009; Stichweh 2009, p. 2; Cowan et al. 2009; De Weert 2009; Hubig 2009 p. 50 seq, 57, p. 28 seq; Kempen 2009; Neave 2009; Thornton 2012. In favour of these trends see Van der Ploeg and Veugelers 2007, p. 26 seq; Wissema 2009, p. 17 seq, 31 seq, 38 seq.

[38] See further Röhrs 1995 p. 106 seq; Connell 2004, p. 17 seq, 21 seq; Cowan et al. 2009, p. 292 seq; Deiaco et al. 2009, p. 330 seq; De Weert 2009, p. 134 seq (who also elaborates on case studies which explore the effects teaching and research have on each other), 140, 146; Neave 2009 pp. 18, 23 seq, 29 seq; Palfreyman and Tapper 2009b p. 203 seq, 210 seq.

structures threaten to destroy the spirit of cooperation in HEIs, as management becomes more top-down and individuals have to experience performance related job insecurity.[39] The conduction of increasingly applied, interdisciplinary and international research contributes to making research more expensive which, in turn, contributes to the increasing importance of external (non-generic public as well as private) research funding.[40] This can threaten 'blue sky' research which could improve the knowledge base in the long-term as well as academic freedom since governmental and business' policy aims are increasingly intertwined with the HEIs' letting them be influenced by the fashions of the time and short term political goals.[41] Yet, as has been seen, it is the traditional mission of the university to conduct such research and there is no other institution which could fill this role. Furthermore, this tendency can also lead to ethically problematic research.[42] In addition, preparing funding applications and other administrative work requires valuable time and money being spent on this which could have been used for teaching and research.[43]

---

[39] Indeed in July 2015 a letter by over 100 UK (United Kingdom) academics was published in The Guardian (newspaper) calling for the Parliament's Education Committee to investigate the 'deprofessionalisation and micro-management of academics [which] is relentlessly eroding their ability to teach and conduct research effectively and appropriately' as well as the 'unprecedented levels of anxiety and stress among both academic and academic-related staff'. See The Guardian (2015) Let UK universities do what they do best—teaching and research. The Guardian, 6 July 2015 http://www.theguardian.com/education/2015/jul/06/let-uk-universities-do-what-they-do-best-teaching-and-research. Accessed 15 July 2015.

[40] Smith 2015.

[41] For example, Peter Higgs who researched the well reported so-called 'god particle' and received the Nobel Prize for it recently expressed the view that he 'wouldn't be productive enough for today's academic system' and that the current system would prevent breakthroughs as his, as it would not allow the researchers the necessary time for research. See Aitkenhead D (2013) Peter Higgs: I wouldn't be productive enough for today's academic system. The Guardian, 6 December 2013 http://www.theguardian.com/science/2013/dec/06/peter-higgs-boson-academic-system. Accessed 21 April 2014. Similarly, Thomas Suedhof who recently won the Nobel Prize in medicine, expressed that funding for basic research is in danger and that this 'worries [him] tremendously'. See Conger K (2013) Thomas Südhof wins Nobel Prize in Physiology or Medicine. Stanford News, 7 October 2013 http://news.stanford.edu/news/2013/october/sudhof-nobel-prize-100713.html. Accessed 21 April 2014.

[42] For example, in the US universities were required to contribute with their research to the war goals during the Second World War and the Cold War, as the federal government (rather than state governments which provide generic funding) had become the most important funder. See Röhrs 1995, p. 107 seq; Scott 2006, p. 27 seq.

[43] Smith 2015. In light of the high costs of the Research Excellence Framework in the UK, even the UK government itself has raised concerns in this regard. See BIS 2015 p. 72.

1.3.4 HEIs in the EU in the Context of European Integration Theory

The two recent, though not necessarily linked,[44] tendencies of commercialisation and internationalisation have not gone unnoticed at the European level, where HEIs did not originally play a role. It was deemed necessary by European leaders to react and attempts have begun to be made to establish European policies on HEIs which will be explored in Chap. 2. However, as will be seen there, the supranational method of integration was largely avoided. Instead Member States decided to apply EU and extra EU soft law approaches. The negative connotation of these approaches[45] and (particularly since the economic crisis) of the EU in general,[46] might make further integration into the hard law frame unlikely at present.

This latter assumption is based on social constructivist conceptions of the EU integration project. Social constructivism is an approach in European integration theory[47] which employs a societal notion of the European project by focussing on all agents rather than just on Member States. According to social constructivism, reality is created by agents which are both influenced by and simultaneously influencing the social space.[48] Therefore, if the agents are negative, or even hostile,

---

[44] Internationalisation was, for example, also a feature of the medieval university model (see above) and there were tendencies towards commodification in the US American model in recent decades before re-internationalisation. See Röhrs 1995, p. 107 seq; Scott 2006, p. 27 seq.

[45] See Chap. 2 below on criticism of the Lisbon/Europe 2020 Strategy and, especially, the Bologna Process. Although the latter is not an EU mechanism, it might negatively influence supranational integration, since the general public often does not differentiate between EU and extra EU measures at the European level. As an example for the latter see the statement by a journalist in a German weekly news magazine; '[...] die seit zwei Jahren anhaltenden Bemühungen der 27 Bologna-Bildungsminister, die "Grundfreiheit des Wissens" in die EU-Verträge aufzunehmen [...]' (... the for two years continuing efforts of the 27 Bologna education ministers to integrate the fundamental freedom of knowledge into the EU Treaties ...). Dreisbach S, 'Studienreform - Gleichberechtigung sieht anders aus' (English Translation: Higher education reform—Equality looks differently) *FOCUS-Online* (4 August 2010) http://www.focus.de/wissen/campus/tid-18713/studienreform-gleichberechtigung-sieht-anders-aus_aid_521074.html Accessed 12 December 2013.

[46] For example, as expressed in the UK Prime Minister's speech on UK-EU relations (available on http://s3.documentcloud.org/documents/560654/cameron-europe-transcript.pdf) urging renegotiation of this Member State's status in the EU and promising the referendum on exiting the EU which subsequently led to a majority voting for exit. See further on the rise of euroscepticism Schiek 2013b, p. 11 seq with further references.

[47] European integration theory evolved in the interdisciplinary subject of EU studies and aims at explaining changes in the political reality in the EU. See Cichowski 2007, p. 3; Chryssochoou 2009, p. 14; Diez and Wiener 2009, p. 1 seq. The approaches in European integration theory differ in a variety of ways, for example, as to their assumption of the end state and the importance given to the process of integration (Schmitter 2004, p. 47 seq with a useful diagram on p. 48) or as to how far they consider non-state-actors (Schiek 2011, p. 19 seq). For an overview of varying approaches of European integration theory see Wiener and Diez 2009, 243 seq, 250 seq.

[48] For more on social constructivism see Risse 2009.

towards the social space (in a certain policy area) this can limit further development of the area. In respect of HEI policy at the European level, Member States appear to have already decided to keep this area out of the supranational EU frame and, as other important agents in this space, such as students and academics, are critical towards measures at the EU and wider European level, a coherent EU supranational policy seems unlikely to develop in the near future.

While HEI policies are thus likely to remain the main responsibility of the Member States for the foreseeable time,[49] HEIs are not immune to EU law[50] since EU law enjoys primacy over national law[51] and certain provisions have direct effect.[52] If HEIs fall within the ambit of constitutionalised elements of EU integration,[53] these elements thus apply to HEIs and can 'spill over' into HEI policies and have an influence upon them. Spill-over is a concept of neo-functionalism, another approach in European integration theory which, eventually, expects an ever closer Union as the outcome of European integration. However, neo-functionalism is more concerned with the process itself.[54] Regarding this process, neo-functionalism assumes that a certain policy can only, with difficulty, be integrated in itself, since policy areas tend not to be completely separable. It is, therefore, likely that an integrated area will spill over (functional spill-over) into other areas potentially fostered by European institutions (cultivated spill-over).[55] Such spill-over could cause unforeseen legal issues for HEIs which will be outlined in overview in Chap. 2.

On a more general level, this is also problematic since spill-over is often triggered by individuals relying on rights derived from EU law[56] and is therefore not necessarily coherent, or in the general interest. This can also be seen through the prism of social constructivism because agents are altering the social space by enforcing their rights, in turn leading the social space to expand by spilling over into other areas. Furthermore, with regard to the economic areas of EU law, the

---

[49] Despite the mainly redistributive policy developments at the EU level which will be explored in Chap. 2.

[50] Similar Beerkens 2008, p. 407.

[51] 6/64 *Costa* (Judgment of 15 July 1964, EU:C:1964:66).

[52] 26/62 *Van Gend* (Judgment of 5 February 1963, EU:C:1963:1).

[53] On the constitutional character of EU law see further Schiek 2012, p. 64 seq.

[54] It can be regarded as the antipode of liberal intergovernmentalism which assumes the Member States to remain the sole masters. See further on liberal intergovenmentalism Moravcsik and Schimmelfennig 2009.

[55] However, newer versions of neo-functionalism also acknowledge other outcomes in certain scenarios. On neo-functionalism see Schmitter 2004; de Búrca 2005; Hooghe and Marks 2006; Niemann and Schmitter 2009; Sandholtz and Stone Sweet 2012. With a focus on competition law, which arguably is one of the most integrated areas with extensive powers of the Commission, see McGowan 2007, pp. 3, 5 seq.

[56] The important role of individuals in enforcing EU law can be seen in the high number of preliminary ruling procedures; with the exception of 2003, preliminary ruling procedures have been the most common kind of new cases to come before the Court every year since 1994 with 428 new cases in 2014. See Court of Justice 2015, pp. 1113/114.

recent commodification of HEIs increases the likeliness of applicability of some of these norms. The potential legal consequences, can, in turn, drive HEIs towards even further commodification. However, the main activities of HEIs, namely teaching and research, are not only of a heightened social relevance,[57] but the de-commodification of these 'services' (i.e. the provision as public service to allow for a certain independence from market forces) is socially important in itself, as it, inter alia, allows to uphold academic freedom as regards the direction of research and teaching and equality in access to higher education for students.[58]

Such tensions between economic EU law and the social areas of public policy have received increasing attention generally over the last decade.[59] Since the European integration project started out as an economic integration endeavour (as this was assumed to be the best way to rebuild the war damaged economies of the Member States),[60] economic integration is at the current stage of European integration, more constitutionalised than social integration.[61] The latter is here understood in a wider sense as areas with a social purpose which empower the individual through de-commodification and thus includes areas such as health care and education, rather than just social policy in the narrower sense. Given the general turn towards neoliberalism of the European integration project in recent decades,[62] many policy areas previously provided by the state in the general interest, such as utilities and later health care, have been subjected to the regime of constitutionalised economic EU law,[63] while social integration has only developed slowly to balance this. Now, education and research in public HEIs may only be the latest public service with a social aim threatened to face constraints arising from EU economic integration as will be investigated in the following chapters.

---

[57] Lange and Alexiadou 2010, p. 235.

[58] See Geis 2010, p. 390 as regards independence in research and Collini 2010, as regards problems for teaching, inter alia inequality of access and dependence on market forces in a market system.

[59] See Sect. 1.1, especially those cited in n 1.

[60] Cafruny and Ryner 2009 who rely on critical political economy (an approach in European integration theory which explains integration with economic reasoning). See also Article 2 EEC Treaty: 'The Community shall have as its task, by establishing a common market and progressively approximating the economic policies of the Member States, to promote throughout the Community a harmonious development of economic activities, […] an accelerated raising of the standard of living and closer relations between the states […].'

[61] Schiek 2012, p. 74.

[62] According to critical political economy, a shift from the post-war 'European Social Model' towards a more neoliberal endeavour began after the Bretton Wood crisis which took place in the early 1970s. See Cafruny and Ryner 2009, p. 224 seq, 237 seq.

[63] See, for example, on the incorporation of the utility sector into the ambit of competition law and offering an explanation in neo-functionalism McGowan 2007, pp. 11, 13. He also points to external factors (p. 12) in line with generally more neo-liberal thinking as explained by critical political economy.

1.4 Conclusion

This introductory chapter has delineated the topic of the book and set out the research question. It has described the methods to be used and outlined the structure of the book. It has then explained the historical and theoretical background for studying HEIs under EU law constraints. In this it has been shown that European HEIs are traditionally widely autonomous institutions funded by the state which provide higher education for knowledge's sake and research with a strong focus on curiosity driven, basic research. Recently, these HEIs have tended towards commodification and internationalisation. Having employed approaches from European integration theory, it has been shown that directly applicable EU law can spill-over into the sphere of HEIs potentially requiring further commodification. In so far a pragmatic approach (as outlined in Sect. 1.3.4) is followed for studying European integration in the field of HEIs which mainly draws on neo-functionalism, but also includes social constructivist thoughts and explanations from critical political economy.

The aim of this book is to explore this potential spill-over further by, first, situating HEIs in the context of EU policy and law and then conducting an empirical study focussing on exposure of HEI research to EU competition law as an under-researched example of exposure to economic constraints in order to obtain a more in-depth appreciation of the constraints HEIs may face in a specific field. The next chapter will commence this exploration by providing a discussion of EU policy on HEIs and the potential of spill-over from directly applicable EU law in overview.

References

Allen M (1988) The Goals of Universities. Milton Keynes, Philadelphia

Amato F, Farbmann K (2010) Applying EU competition law in the education sector. IJELP 6:7–13

Beerkens E (2008) The Emergence and Institutionalisation of the European Higher Education and Research Area. Eur J Educ 43:407–425

BIS (2015) Fulfilling our potential. Her Majesty's Stationery Office, London

Bruun N et al (2012) The Lisbon Treaty and social Europe. Hart, Oxford/Portland

Burroni L et al (2012) Economy and society in Europe: a relationship in crisis. Edward Elgar, Cheltenham/Northampton

Cafruny AW, Ryner JM (2009) Critical political economy. In: Wiener A, Diez T (eds) European integration theory, 2nd edn. OUP, Oxford, pp 221–240

Cantillon B et al (2012) Social inclusion and social protection in the EU: interactions between law and policy. Intersentia, Cambridge/Portland

Cardoso AR et al (2008) Demand for higher education programs: the impact of the Bologna Process. CESifo Economic Studies 54:229–247

Choon Fong S (2008) The global challenge for universities. In: Marginson S, James R (eds) Education, science and public policy—ideas for an Education Revolution. Melbourne University Press, Carlton, pp 78–86

Chou M-H, Ulnicane I (2015) Special issue: New Horizons in the Europe of Knowledge. J Contemp Eur Res 11:1–152

Chryssochoou DN (2009) Theorizing European integration, 2nd edn. Routledge, London/New York

Cichowski RA (2007) The European Court and Civil Society. CUP, Cambridge

Clark W (2006) Academic Charisma and the origins of the research university. University of Chicago Press, Chicago

Collini S (2010) Browne's Gamble. London Rev Books 32:23–25

Connell H (2004) The growing significance of the research mission to higher education institutions. In: Connell H (ed) University Research Management. OECD, Paris, pp 17–25

Corbett A (2012) Education and the Lisbon Strategy. In: Copeland P, Papadimitriou D (eds) The EU's Lisbon Strategy: evaluating success, understanding failure. Palgrave MacMillan, Basingstoke, pp 149–167

Court of Justice of the European Union (2015) Annual report 2014. Publications Office of the European Union, Luxembourg

Cowan WB et al (2009) Running the marathon. In: McKelvey M, Holem M (eds) Learning to compete in European Universities. Edward Elgar, Cheltenham/Northampton, pp 278–299

Damjanovic D (2012) "Reserved areas" of the Member States and the ECJ: the case of higher education. In: Micklitz H-W, De Witte B (eds) The European Court of Justice and the Autonomy of the Member States. Intersentia, Cambridge, pp 149–174

de Búrca G (2005) Rethinking law in neo-functionalist theory. J Eur Policy 12:310–326

de Búrca G, de Witte B (2005) Social Rights in Europe. OUP, Oxford

De Weert E (2009) Organised contradictions of teaching and research: reshaping the academic profession. In: Enders J, de Weert E (eds) The changing face of academic life. Palgrave Macmillan, Basingstoke/New York, pp 134–154

Deiaco E et al (2009) From social institution to knowledge business. In: McKelvey M, Holmen M (eds) Learning to compete in European Universities. Edward Elgar, Cheltenham/Northampton, pp 329–356

Denninger E (2001) Art. 5 Abs. 3 I GG. In: Denninger E et al (eds) Kommentar zum Grundgesetz fuer die Bundesrepublik Deutschland (English translation: Commentary on the Basic Law of the Federal Republic of Germany), 3rd edn. Hermann Luchterhand Verlag, Neuwied/Kriftel

Diez T, Wiener A (2009) Introducing the mosaic of integration theory. In: Wiener A, Diez T (eds) European integration theory, 2nd edn. OUP, Oxford, pp 1–24

Dougan M (2008) Cross-border educational mobility and the exportation of student financial assistance. Eur Law Rev 5:723–738

Dougan M, Spaventa E (2005) Social welfare and EU law. Hart Publishing, Oxford/Portland/Oregon

Enders J, de Weert E (2009) The changing face of academic life. Palgrave Macmillan, Basingstoke/New York

Erbe M (2007) Die frühe Neuzeit (English translation: The early modern period). Kohlhammer, Stuttgardt

Esping-Andersen G (1990) The Three Worlds of Welfare Capitalism. Princeton University Press, Princeton

Esping-Andersen G (1999) Social Foundation of Postindustrial Economies. OUP, Oxford

Farrington DJ, Palfreyman D (2012) The Law of Higher Education. OUP, Oxford

Garben S (2008) The Belgian/Austrian Education Saga. Harvard European Law Working Paper

Garben S (2010) The Bologna Process: from a European Law Perspective. ELJ 16:186–210

Garben S (2011) EU Higher Education Law—The Bologna Process and Harmonization by Stealth. Kluwer, Alphen aan den Rijn

Geis M-E (2010) Universitäten im Wettbewerb, 1. Bericht. (English translation: Universities in competition, 1st report). VVDStRL 69:364–406

Gideon A (2012) Higher Education Institutions and EU Competition Law. Compet Law Rev 8:169–184

Gideon A (2015a) The Position of Higher Education Institutions in a Changing European Context: An EU Law Perspective. JCMS. J Common Market Stud 53:1045–1060

Gideon A (2015b) Blurring Boundaries between the Public and the Private in National Research Policies and Possible Consequences from EU Primary Law. J Contemp Eur Res 11:50–68

Greaves R, Scicluna A (2010) Commercialization and competition in the education services sector—challenges to the education service sector from the application of Articles 101 and 102 TFEU. IJELP 6:13–25

Hoeveler JD (1976) The university and the social gospel: the intellectual origins of the 'Wisconsin Idea'. Wisconsin Magazine of History 59:282–298

Hooghe L, Marks G (2006) The neo-functionalists were (almost) right: politization and European integration. In: Crouch C, Streeck W (eds) The Diversity of Democracy: Corporatism. Social Order and Political Conflict. Edward Elgar, Cheltenham, pp 205–222

Huber S, Prikozsovits J (2008) Universitäre Drittmittelforschung und EG-Beihilfenrecht (English translation: External funding for universities and EC state aid law). EuZW 19:171–174

Hubig L (2009) Die Universität - Leistungsbemessung und -bewertung in einer komplexen Organisation (English translation: The University - performance measurement and evaluation in a complex organization). JOSEF EUL, Lohmar/Cologne

Jaycox F (2005) The Progressive Era. Facts on File, New York

Jongbloed B, van der Meulen B (2006) Investeren in Dynamiek - Eindrapport Commissie Dynamisering Deel 1 (English translation: Investing in dynamic - Final Report Commission Dynamisation Part 1). http://www.utwente.nl/cheps/publications/Publications%202006/dynamiek1.pdf. Accessed 10 Dec 2015

Kempen B (2009) Universität - Zentrum der Forschung? Forschung & Lehre 5:334–335

Koch H-A (2008) Die Universität - Geschichte einer europäischen Institution (English translation: The University - History of a European institution). Wissenschaftliche Buchgemeinschaft, Darmstadt

Konsortium Bildungsberichterstattung (2006) Bildung in Deutschland (English translation: Education in Germany). Bertelsmann Verlag, Bielefeld

Lange B, Alexiadou N (2010) How to govern for solidarity? An introduction to policy learning in the context of open methods of coordinating education policies in the European Union. In: Ross M, Borgmann-Prebil Y (eds) Promoting solidarity in the European Union. OUP, Oxford, pp 235–261

Link AS (1959) What happened to the Progressive Movement in the 1920's? Am Hist Rev 64:833–851

Marginson S (2007) The public/private divide in higher education; a global revision. High Educ 53:307–333

McGowan L (2007) Theorizing European integration: revisiting neo-functionalism and testing its suitability for explaining the development of EC competition policy. EIoP 11

McKelvey M, Holem M (2009) Learning to compete in European Universities. Edward Elgar, Cheltenham/Northampton

Moravcsik A, Schimmelfennig F (2009) Liberal Intergovernmentalism. In: Wiener A, Diez T (eds) European integration Theory, 2nd edn. OUP, Oxford, pp 67–88

Mossialos E et al (2010) Health systems governance in Europe: the role of EU law and policy. CUP, Cambridge

Neave G (2009) The Academic Estate Revisited: Reflections on Academia's Rapid Progress from the Capitoline Hill to the Tarpeian Rock. In: Enders J, de Weert E (eds) The changing face of academic life. Palgrave Macmillan, Basingstoke/New York, pp 15–35

Neergaard U et al (2009) Integrating Welfare Functions into EU Law—from Rome to Lisbon. DJØF, Copenhagen

Neergaard U et al (2013) Social Services of General Interest in the EU. T.M.C. Asser Press, The Hague

Niemann A, Schmitter PC (2009) Neofunctionalism. In: Wiener A, Diez T (eds) European integration theory, 2nd edn. OUP, Oxford, pp 45–66

OECD (2002) Frascati Manual. OECD, Paris

Palfreyman D, Tapper T (2009a) Structuring Mass Higher Education. Routledge, New York/
    London
Palfreyman D, Tapper T (2009b) What is an 'Elite' or 'Leading Global' University? In:
    Palfreyman D, Tapper T (eds) Structuring Mass Higher Education. Routledge, New York/
    London, pp 203–218
Radder H (2010) The commodification of academic research: science and the modern university.
    University of Pittsburgh Press, Pittsburgh
Reich N (2009) Herkunftsprinzip oder Diskriminierung als Maßstab für Studentenfreizügigkeit?
    (English translation: Principle of origin or discrimination as a benchmark for free movement
    of students?) EuZW 18:637–638
Risse T (2009) Social constructivism and European integration. In: Wiener A, Diez T (eds)
    European integration theory, 2nd edn. OUP, Oxford, pp 144–160
Röhrs H (1995) Der Einfluss der klassischen Deutschen Universitätsidee auf die Higher
    Education in Amerika (English translation: The influence of the classic German idea of the
    University on Higher Education in America). Deutscher Studienverlag, Weinheim
Sandholtz W, Stone Sweet A (2012) Neo-functionalism and supranational governance. In: Jones
    E et al (eds) The Oxford handbook of the European Union. OUP, Oxford, pp 18–33
Schiek D (2011) Re-embedding economic and social constitutionalism: normative perspectives
    for the EU. In: Schiek D et al (eds) European economic and social constitutionalism after the
    Treaty of Lisbon. CUP, Cambridge, pp 17–46
Schiek D (2012) Economic and social integration—the challenge for EU Constitutional Law.
    Edward Elgar, Cheltenham
Schiek D (2013a) The EU economic and social model in the global crisis. Ashgate, Farnham
Schiek D (2013b) The EU's socio-economic model(s) and the crisi(e)s—any perspectives? In:
    Schiek D (ed) The EU economic and social model in the global crisis. Ashgate, Farnham/
    Burlington, pp 1–22
Schiek D et al (2011) European economic and social constitutionalism after the Treaty of Lisbon.
    CUP, Cambridge
Schmitter PC (2004) Neo-Neofunctionalisms. In: Wiener A, Diez T (eds) European integration
    theory, 1st edn. OUP, Oxford, pp 45–73
Scott JC (2006) The mission of the university: medieval to postmodern transformations. J Higher
    Educ 77:1–39
Shumar W (2013) (republication, originally 1997) College for sale: a critique of the
    commodification of higher education. Routledge, Milton Park/New York
Sklar MJ (1992) The United States as a developing country: studies in U.S. history in the
    progressive era and the 1920s. CUP, Cambridge/New York
Slaughter S, Leslie LL (1997) Academic Capitalism. The John Hopkins University Press,
    Baltimore/London
Smith J (2015) An academic in the Europe of knowledge. J Contemp Eur Res 11:135–143
Steinfeld T (2009) Unternehmen Universität (English translation: Undertaking University).
    Forschung & Lehre 5:346–347
Steyger E (2002) Competition and education. In: de Groof J et al (eds) Globalisation and
    competition in education. Wolf Legal Publishers, Nijmegen, pp 275–280
Stichweh R (2009) Universität in der Weltgesellschaft (English translation: Universities in the
    world society). Academic speech at the Dies Academicus der Universität Luzern, 1st October
    2009
Swennen H (2008/2009) Onderwijs en Mededingsrecht (English translation: Teaching and
    competition law). Tijdschrift voor Onderwijsrecht en Onderwijsbeleid 4:259–280
Teichler U (2007) Geschichte und Entwicklung der Bildungsprogramme der Europäischen
    Union (English translation: History and development of educational programs of the
    European Union). In: Teichler U (ed) Die Internationalisierung der Hochschulen - Neue
    Herausforderungen und Strategien (English translation: The internationalisation of higher
    education—new challenges and strategies). Campus Verlag, Frankfurt am Main, pp 105–114

Thornton M (2012) Privatising the public university. Routledge, Abingdon

Van der Mei AP (2005) EU Law and education: promotion of student mobility versus protection of the education systems. In: Dougan M, Spaventa E (eds) Social welfare and EU law. Hart Publishing, Oxford/Portland/Oregon, pp 219–240

Van der Ploeg F, Veugelers R (2007) Higher education reform and the renewed Lisbon strategy: role of member states and the European Commission. CESifo Working Paper 1901

Walkenhorst H (2008) Explaining change in EU education policy. J Eur Public Policy 15:567–587

Weber M (2005) Wirtschaft und Gesellschaft (English translation: Economy and society). Zweitausendundeins, Frankfurt am Main

Whyman P et al (2012) The political economy of the European social model. Routledge, Milton Park/New York

Wiener A, Diez T (2009) Taking stock of integration theory. In: Wiener A, Diez T (eds) European integration theory, 2nd edn. OUP, Oxford, pp 241–252

Wissema JG (2009) Towards the third generation university. Edward Elgar, Cheltenham/Northampton

Chapter 2
The Position of Higher Education Institutions in EU Policy and Law

Abstract The aim of this chapter is to provide an overview of the position of HEIs in European policy (the EU and beyond) and to discuss potential spill-over from directly applicable EU law. It will be shown that the EU hard law framework contains limited competences in devising policies regarding HEIs. Instead, policy is often made through soft law at the EU and European (beyond EU) level. Nevertheless, other provisions of EU law, such as Union citizenship, the free movement provisions and competition law, can, and already have, spilled over into the HEI sector influencing national policy concepts. Ongoing commodification could increase this effect, thereby endangering the traditional non-economic mission of European HEIs.

Keywords EU higher education policy · EU research policy · Diploma recognition · Bologna Process · Lisbon Strategy/Europe 2020 Strategy · Union citizenship · EU free movement law and higher education institutions · Public procurement law and higher education institutions · Spill-over

Contents

© T.M.C. ASSER PRESS and the author 2017

A. Gideon, *Higher Education Institutions in the EU: Between Competition and Public Service*, Legal Issues of Services of General Interest, DOI 10.1007/978-94-6265-168-5_2

2.1 Introduction

The aim of this chapter is to provide an overview of the position of higher education institutions (HEIs) in European policy (EU and beyond) and to discuss potential spill-over from directly applicable EU law.[1] It will be shown that the EU hard
law framework contains limited competences in devising policies regarding HEIs.
Instead, policy is often made through soft law at the EU and European (beyond
EU) level. Nevertheless, other provisions of EU law have already spilled over into
the area of HEIs influencing national policy concepts. Ongoing commodification
could increase this effect, thereby endangering the traditional non-economic mission of European HEIs as explored in Chap. 1 (Sect. 1.3.1).

The chapter is divided into two parts. The first part (Sect. 2.2) explores how
HEIs are positioned within EU policy and law and what reasons might be behind
this. The second part (Sect. 2.3) is dedicated to the examination of potential 'acci-
dental' effects EU law might have on HEIs in overview. The chapter ends in a
conclusion (Sect. 2.4) bringing together the results and leading to the next chapter
which provides a more in-depth appreciation of such effects of competition law on
HEIs.

2.2 Locating HEIs in European Policy

As has been discussed in Chap. 1 (Sect. 1.3.1), the two main activities of HEIs are
providing higher education and research. An exploration of the position of HEIs
in EU law and policy thus requires an examination of the policy areas of education and research and development (R&D). It will be shown that 'hard' EU competences are limited in both areas. The need for a certain degree of coordination
beyond the Member States, as already touched upon in Chap. 1 (Sects. 1.3.3 and
1.3.4), has instead led to policies outside of the supranational EU framework. In
the following, EU competences in education (Sect. 2.2.1.1), as well as the special
area of diploma recognition (Sect. 2.2.1.2), and R&D (Sect. 2.2.1.3) will first be
discussed. This will be followed by an analysis of EU and beyond-EU soft law
mechanisms.

---

[1] A condensed version of this chapter is contained in Gideon 2015.

2.2.1 Supranational EU Policy on Education and Research and Development

When the European Communities (European Coal and Steel Community, European Atomic Energy Community and European Economic Community (EEC)) were founded, the founding Treaties contained only a few isolated provisions on education and R&D.[2] This might have been the case because European integration started as an economic integration endeavour and the economic value of HEIs was not apparent at the time.[3] Applying a neo-functionalism analysis as conceived by Sandholtz and Stone Sweet, this might also be due to the fact that initially there were not sufficient 'transactors' desiring cross-border interaction.[4] With further development of the European Community, however, these areas became part of EU policy, potentially because the commodification of HEIs made their economic value more apparent, whilst simultaneously the EU expanded its mission and activities. This latter phenomenon can be equally explained both by neo-functionalism and social constructivism. Schmitter's version of (neo-)neo-functionalism[5] accounts for political spill-over through the shifting of expectations to the EU level and for cultivated spill-over through EU Institutions working towards integration in new areas. According to Sandholtz' and Stone Sweet's neo-functionalism, transactors, or 'agents' in social constructivist language, influence integration, if this seems desirable to them.[6] Nevertheless, Member States have been reluctant to give up their power in the area of HEIs. This is perhaps unsurprising considering the fact that HEIs are regarded, partly, as belonging to the welfare state (directly affecting national finances) and also as part of national culture and identity and as such educating future leaders and civil servants and stimulating national industry and development.[7] The competences of the EU thus remain limited.

---

[2] For more on the limited EU dimension of these policy areas in the beginning of the European integration project see Chou and Gornitzka 2014.

[3] Similar Walkenhorst 2008, p. 571 seq.

[4] Sandholtz and Stone Sweet 2012.

[5] Schmitter 2004; Niemann and Schmitter 2009.

[6] On active entrepreneurship towards policy integration with regards to the HEI sector see Corbett 2003.

[7] See Teichler 2007, p. 105; Walkenhorst 2008, p. 567 with further references, Chou and Gornitzka 2014; Chou and Ulnicane 2015; Hadfield and Summerby-Murray 2015. On the purpose of HEIs see also Sect. 1.3.1 above.

2.2.1.1 EU Education Policy

Article 128 EEC was most significant amongst the few provisions on education in the founding Treaties; it gave the Council the power to 'lay down general principles for implementing a common vocational training policy'.[8] The Treaty of Maastricht 1992[9] specified the provision on vocational training and renumbered the Article to Article 127 EC. Furthermore, general education, including higher education, became a policy area to be found in Article 126 EC. Yet, these provisions only provided supplementary competences and did not enable the Community to harmonise national education systems. The Treaty of Amsterdam 1997 merely renumbered the provisions to Articles 149–150 EC and neither the Treaty of Nice 2001 nor the draft European Constitution 2004 included any content changes. Since the Treaty of Lisbon 2007, education is to be found in Articles 165–166 TFEU and sport has been added to the title, but the competences remained unchanged. When it comes to the division of competence, the Union, therefore, still has very limited competences basically amounting to the possibility of adopting EU programmes in addition to national education policies such as the Erasmus programme.[10]

However, from the 1970s onwards the EU did begin to recognise the importance of education for the Council of Education Ministers started meeting in formal sessions, the European Parliament and Commission created education divisions, education received a budget and education policy could be reviewed by the Court of Justice of the European Union (CJEU). There have been successful EU programmes,[11] most significantly the Erasmus programme established in the late 1980s which aims to encourage the mobility of students and in the course of which the European Credit Transfer System (ECTS) was invented.[12] Therefore, despite its being limited to supporting and complementing national policies, there is an EU education policy at the supranational level which is driven by economic factors (to facilitate the internal market) and politically (to achieve European integration and identity).[13] It has been argued that, in line with the general trends discussed in Chap. 1 (Sect. 1.3.3), the former has recently been more pronounced than the latter.[14]

---

[8] For more on Article 128 EEC and problems resulting from this limited competence in the field of vocational education, see Hummer 2005, p. 56 seq.

[9] Dates used here are those of the publication in the Official Journal.

[10] On EU competences for education see further Hummer 2005, p. 33 seq, 57 seq, 71; Teichler 2007, p. 105 seq; Van der Ploeg and Veugelers 2007, p. 19; Walkenhorst 2008, p. 568; Garben 2010, p. 189 seq.

[11] See further Teichler 2007, p. 111 seq.

[12] On EU education policy see Teichler 2007, p. 105 seq, 109 seq; Van der Ploeg and Veugelers 2007, p. 22, 24 seq; Walkenhorst 2008, p. 568 seq; Garben 2010, p. 187 seq; Chou and Gornitzka 2014, p. 9 seq; Hadfield and Summerby-Murray 2015.

[13] On motives and developments see Walkenhorst 2008, p. 571 seq; Chou and Gornitzka 2014; Hadfield and Summerby-Murray 2015.

[14] Chou and Gornitzka 2014; Hadfield and Summerby-Murray 2015.

2.2.1.2 Diploma Recognition

Despite the limited competences for education at the EU level, functional spill-over from the free movement provisions occurred early on. To achieve free movement of persons in the internal market it was necessary to harmonise certain aspects of access to individual professions and therefore, inter alia, to harmonise professional recognition[15] of diplomas to guarantee access to regulated professions.[16] A regime of directives based on what is now Article 53 TFEU has been passed in this respect, which have later been consolidated into Directive 2005/36/EC.[17] Additionally, the Court has made it clear[18] that Member States should check the substantive comparability of qualifications received in another Member State in cases not covered by secondary law.[19]

It is generally assumed that academic diploma recognition cannot be harmonised on the basis of Article 53 TFEU since the internal market competences are regarded as having strict functionality and, therefore, not allowing abstract content or structural harmonisation, especially if the strict subsidiarity of Articles 165 and 166 TFEU is taken into account.[20] Academic recognition thus still takes place according to national law, potentially influenced by the Bologna Process, which will be discussed below (Sect. 2.2.3). The only other requirements arising from primary EU law concern cases where both academic and professional recognition are possible. Here, the migrant may not be forced to choose and if one form of recognition has been obtained, the other can still be sought at a later stage under certain circumstances. In particular, when academic recognition is requested for professional reasons in addition to professional recognition, it cannot be denied. Also, if academic recognition has been obtained, but does not in itself give access to the profession, professional recognition can be additionally demanded.[21]

---

[15] Professional recognition allows the migrant the right to carry the title of the profession, but not the host state's academic title, Hummer 2005, p. 67.

[16] Regulated professions can, according to national law, only be executed after the fulfilment of certain qualifications, Hummer 2005, p. 61.

[17] Directive 2005/36/EC on the recognition of professional qualifications OJ [2005] L 255/22. There have been additional amendments since. A consolidated version of Directive 2005/36/EC can be found on http://eur-lex.europa.eu/legal-content/EN/ALL/?uri=CELEX:02005L0036-20140117.

[18] See C-340/89 *Vlassopoulou* (Judgment of 7 May 1991, EU:C:1991:193). This has recently been reaffirmed in C-298/14 *Brouillard* (Judgment of 6 October 2015, EU:C:2015:652) and C-342/14 *X-Steuerberatungsgesellschaft* (Judgment of 17 December 2015, EU:C:2015:827). Further on the latter two cases and the inconsistency with the Court's own procurement and employment decisions see Gideon 2016.

[19] On diploma recognition see further Hummer 2005, p. 60 seq; Van der Ploeg and Veugelers 2007, p. 22 seq; Garben 2010, p. 191. For a more extensive discussion see Schneider 1995.

[20] Hummer 2005, p. 58 seq. See also Garben 2010, p. 191 seq; Garben 2011, p. 186 seq who thinks that a different interpretation would be possible and a CJEU judgement would be needed for clarification.

[21] Hummer 2005, p. 67 seq.

2.2.1.3 EU Research and Development Policy

Whilst the Founding Treaties contained no competences for R&D, a common R&D policy was starting to be adopted from the 1970s onwards. This was based on Article 235 EEC (now Article 352 TFEU) which gave the EEC the competence to 'take the appropriate measures' where action was deemed necessary to achieve the Community's objectives. This led to the adoption of the First Framework Programme[22] in 1983, which defined a budget and activities for a period of three years and focussed mainly on energy research. Efforts amplified from the late 1980s onwards, as R&D was considered increasingly important for the development and competitiveness of Europe.[23] With the Single European Act 1987 the policy area 'research and technological development' was incorporated into primary law as Articles 130f–130q EEC. These provisions officially foresaw the multi-annual Framework Programmes as a basis for more detailed initiatives. The competences given to the EEC were complementary in nature, intending to support actions of the Member States. However, unlike in education policy they did not stand under strict subsidiarity and an absolute prohibition of harmonisation. The policy aims were to increase collaborative research with businesses, support cooperation beyond the EU, the dissemination and transfer of knowledge, increase of competition and support of mobility in the Community. The Maastricht Treaty 1992 made 'research and technology' a Community objective (Article 3m EC), while the Treaty of Amsterdam 1997 only renumbered the provisions. Yet, the content was neither changed with that Treaty nor with Treaty of Nice 2001.[24]

The provisions on R&D have been located in Article 179–190 TFEU since the Treaty of Lisbon 2007 and they have been slightly strengthened. Under Article 4 TFEU research policy has become a shared competence and the Union can pass legislation in addition to Framework Programmes to attain the European Research Area following the ordinary legislative procedure (Article 182(5) TFEU). Paragraph 1 of Article 179 TFEU makes R&D a Union objective and explicitly mentions the establishment of the European Research Area in which 'researchers, scientific knowledge and technology circulate freely'. The latter is stressed again in para 2 which foresees that the Union shall aim at 'permitting researchers to cooperate freely across borders and at enabling undertakings to exploit the internal market potential to the full'. Furthermore, the title 'research and technological development' is complemented by the words 'and space' and a new Article 189 TEFU on a common space policy has been inserted.[25]

---

[22] Framework Programme for Research 1984–87 COM(83) 260 final.

[23] Jones 2001, p. 325 seq. This corresponds with the changing nature of HEIs as described in Chap. 1.

[24] On the development of supranational R&D policy and its objectives see Jones 2001, p. 325 seq; Hummer 2005, p. 33 seq, 70 seq; Lenaerts and Van Nuffel 2005 p. 318 seq, Chou and Ulnicane 2015; Ulnicane 2015.

[25] This would have been similar under the Constitution. See Lenaerts and Van Nuffel 2005, p. 319.

The broadening of the competences has not led to significant regulatory initiatives or harmonisation of R&D policy. Indeed, Article 4(3) TFEU contains the caveat that the exercise of the shared competence 'shall not result in Member States being prevented from exercising theirs'. The Member States thus remain the main actors responsible for designing research policy which is not to say that EU policy has had no influence. Indeed many have researched the effects of EU research policy, despite it being still mainly distributive in nature.[26]

Since 2014 the Framework Programmes have been replaced by Horizon 2020[27] aligning EU research funding with the Innovation Union Flagship of the Europe 2020 Strategy (which will be discussed further below in Sect. 2.2.2), the European Institute of Innovation and Technology, the Competitiveness and Innovation Framework Programme and the building of the European Research Area.[28] Overall, as research has shown, European R&D policy has become increasingly influenced by economic thinking over the last decades,[29] more recently supplemented by ideals of excellence and societal impact.[30]

2.2.1.4 Interim Conclusion on Supranational EU Policy

The value of education and research became more apparent towards the end of the 20th century with the shift from an industrial production-based society to a knowledge-based one.[31] Additionally, as discussed in Chap. 1, the nature of HEIs changed towards commodification and internationalisation. These developments made European coordination desirable. EU education and R&D policy began to develop, but the Member States seemed reluctant to provide the Union with extensive competences or indeed to utilise potential possibilities of existing competences. Garben, for example, argues conclusively that there might already be a basis in primary law for legislation on academic recognition of diplomas.[32] This might be explained with ongoing controversies in the public realm about

---

[26] For an in-depth analysis of the governance and functioning of EU research policy see Pilniok 2011; Chou and Gornitzka 2014; Chou and Ulnicane 2015; Ulnicane 2015; Young 2015.

[27] For more information see the European Commission's 'Horizon 2020—The EU Framework Programme for Research and Innovation' website on http://ec.europa.eu/research/horizon2020/index_en.cfm?pg=h2020.

[28] Young 2014, 2015; Chou and Ulnicane 2015.

[29] Young 2014, 2015; Chou and Ulnicane 2015.

[30] Young 2014, 2015; Ulnicane 2015. Young raises the question if the focus on excellence can lead to a two-speed Europe in R&D policy and whether increasingly competitive EU funding is truly efficient considering the significant investments into the preparation of applications with only small chances of success.

[31] Walkenhorst 2008, p. 574 seq.

[32] See Garben 2010, p. 189 seq; Garben 2011, p. 184 seq.

'competence creep', the legitimacy of the European Union project and the desire to keep these policy areas national and retain power. Nevertheless, further coordination appears to have been deemed necessary. Therefore, a significant part of European policies affecting HEIs started using soft law mechanisms to avoid the supranational policy mode.[33]

2.2.2 EU Soft Law: The Lisbon/Europe 2020 Strategy

As it was deemed that Europe was in need of reform to keep up with its competitors, the European Council in Lisbon in 2000 announced that its strategic goal for the next ten years would be for the EU 'to become the most competitive and dynamic knowledge-based economy in the world'.[34] As regards HEIs it was considered necessary that these face internationalisation. The European Research Area was announced, the concept of which encourages many of the commodification trends discussed in Chap. 1,[35] and the aims of the Bologna Process (discussed below in Sect. 2.2.3) were endorsed as part of the Lisbon Strategy.[36]

The Lisbon Strategy itself is only a declaration and not legally binding. Instead the OMC has been chosen as the appropriate instrument for achieving the aims of the Lisbon Strategy which have been further specified in numerical targets. The aim of the OMC is to allow for the formation of a 'common will' and enhance social learning by providing a network for EU organs, national authorities and social partners as well as the private and the third sector.[37] The EU Institutions (mainly the Commission and European Council/Council) evaluate and steer the process.[38] This allowed the EU organs to get involved in policy areas which are/ were the primary responsibility of the Member States. Inter alia the 'Commission now has an entry to Bologna coordination'[39] and it gave a new impetus to research

---

[33] See also Teichler 2007, p. 114; Walkenhorst 2008, p. 573 seq; Maassen and Musselin 2009; Garben 2010, p. 187 seq; Chou and Ulnicane 2015; Young 2015.

[34] Lisbon European Council 23 and 24 March 2000 Presidency Conclusion para 5.

[35] Presidency Conclusion (n 34) para 12 seq. The European Research Area is based on Commission Communication 'Towards a European Research Area' COM (2000) 6 final, 18.01.2000. See further on the European Research Area Ulnicane 2015.

[36] Presidency Conclusion (n 34) para 25 seq.

[37] On the OMC see Hummer 2005, p. 72 seq; Begg 2008; Cohen-Tanugi 2008, p. 23 seq, 47 seq. An in-depth account of the OMC can be found in, for example, Kröger 2009.

[38] European Commission (2014) European institutions and bodies. Europe2020, http://ec.europa.eu/europe2020/who-does-what/eu-institutions/index_en.htm. Accessed 4 March 2016.

[39] Chou and Ulnicane 2015, p. 8.

policy for which it is next to Horizon 2020 still an important governance mechanism.[40]

However, the progress towards the ambitious numerical targets has been slow[41] and the Lisbon Strategy was re-launched in 2005[42] and re-introduced after the financial crisis as the new Europe 2020 Strategy in 2010.[43] The most important numerical targets in higher education and research to be achieved by 2020 are: an increase in research spending to 3 % GDP, a decrease of school drop-out rates to less than 10 % and an increase to 40 % of all 30–34 year olds with tertiary education. None of these differ significantly from the original aims.[44] Young has described this as the Member States opting in as regards the targets, 'but opting out in practice by not meeting those'.[45]

2.2.3 The Bologna Process

Following the initiative of the education ministers of Italy, France, Germany and the UK to reform European higher education systems expressed in the 'Sorbonne-Declaration',[46] the education ministers of 29 European countries[47] officially launched the Bologna Process with the 'Bologna Declaration' in 1999.[48] The Bologna Declaration is not legally binding and, with 48 countries involved at present, the Bologna Process goes far beyond the EU.[49] The overall aim of the

---

[40] Chou and Gornitzka 2014; Chou and Ulnicane 2015; Young 2015.

[41] See further with regards to the latest mid-term review Vanhercke 2014 who describes a 'continuous and sharp deterioration' as regards meeting the targets and attributes the limited successes in education and energy at least partly to the financial crisis since high unemployment incentivises people to return to education and the worsened economic situation required savings which could lead to the reduction in emissions.

[42] Brussels European Council 22 and 23 March 2005 Presidency Conclusions.

[43] Brussels European Council 17 June 2010 Conclusions (EUCO13/10 CO EUR 9 CONCL 2).

[44] For an overview of targets and current achievements see Eurostat (2016) Europe 2020 Indicators. http://ec.europa.eu/eurostat/web/europe-2020-indicators. Accessed 4 March 2016.

[45] Young 2015, p. 24.

[46] Sorbonne Joint Declaration on harmonisation of the architecture of the European higher education system by the four Ministers in charge for France, Germany, Italy and the United Kingdom, Paris, the Sorbonne, 25 May 1998.

[47] The 15 EU Member States of the time, the countries which became Member States in 2004 and 2007 except Cyprus as well as Iceland, Norway and Switzerland. On the beginnings of the Bologna Process see Eurydice 2010, p. 9 seq.

[48] Joint declaration of the European Ministers of Education of 19 June 1999.

[49] For the latest up-dates of the Bologna Process see French Bologna Secretariat (2016) Bologna Process—European Higher Education Area http://www.ehea.info/article-details.aspx?ArticleId=5. Accessed 4 March 2016. For more detailed information and evaluations see European Commission/EACEA/Eurydice 2015.

Bologna Process was to establish an internationally competitive 'European Higher Education Area' (EHEA) by 2010 which was specified through long-term and intermediate targets in regular ministerial meetings. Additionally, a follow-up group tasked with facilitating the development of the process was set up. It contains, alongside representatives of the Bologna countries and the Commission (which joined as a member in 2001), representatives of the Council of Europe, the European University Association (EUA), the European Students Union and other organisations.[50] The main features include the achievement of a common three-cycle study structure (undergraduate, master and doctoral level), the standard issuing of diploma supplements, the implementation of a module system, the usage of the ECTS, the establishment of national qualification frameworks describing the qualifications available and the introduction of quality assurance.[51] At the 2009 Leuven conference it was agreed to proceed with the Bologna process until 2020, as it was generally regarded as successful by the participating countries.[52] Consequently, in 2010 the EHEA was officially launched at the meeting in Budapest-Vienna.[53] The last Bologna ministerial meeting was held in 2015 in Yerevan (Armenia) the commitments of which included a strong focus on mobility (including the promotion of portability of grants, professional recognition and staff mobility) and the next meeting is planned to take place in France in 2018.[54]

2.2.4 Interim Conclusion: The Location of HEIs in EU Policy

While originally not featuring in primary law, policies on education and research have developed at the supranational level. The main (regulatory) competences, however, still lie with the Member States. Yet, it has already been shown that functional spill-over from the free movement provisions can interfere with this division of competences as it has led to the need for secondary legislation on the professional recognition of diplomas. Furthermore, coordination beyond what has been achieved within these policy areas seemed necessary, but the Member States opted for the OMC and the beyond-EU Bologna Process rather than extending primary law competences or using existing competences to their full potential. Only with

---

[50] On the history and set up of the Bologna process see Hummer 2005, p. 49 seq; Eurydice 2010, p. 9 seq.

[51] See Hummer 2005, p. 47 seq; Van der Ploeg and Veugelers 2007, p. 21 seq; Eurydice 2012, p. 7 seq.

[52] Communiqué of the Conference of European Ministers Responsible for Higher Education, Leuven and Louvain-la-Neuve, 28–29 April 2009 para 1, 24.

[53] Budapest-Vienna Declaration on the European Higher Education Area 12 March 2010 para 1.

[54] Yerevan Communiqué of the EHEA Ministerial Conference of 14–15 May 2015.

the Treaty of Lisbon has the competence base for R&D been slightly strengthened. However, that does not appear to have led to extensive legislation realising significant regulatory changes so far.

The Lisbon/Europe 2020 Strategy and the Bologna Process are soft law and thus not legally binding. Their alleged bottom-up nature and involvement of various stakeholders, their flexibility and the possibility of avoiding the supranational frame and thereby potentially losing control are considered as advantages.[55] However, there are also negative sides to the chosen modes of cooperation. The non-binding nature enables Member States to 'opt-out' when it comes to actually achieving the targets, as can be seen especially with regard to the Lisbon/Europe 2020 Strategy. On the other hand, research shows that soft law can nevertheless create perceived binding effects.[56] Indeed, many have described the Bologna Process and the Lisbon/Europe 2020 Strategy as developing a certain inevitability and, in addition, as intertwined and as reinforcing commodification.[57] In particular, the Bologna Process has led to significant changes in European higher education. It has done so despite being unpopular with stakeholders such as students and academics who, inter alia, criticise the, in their eyes, too inflexible three cycle structure and the focus on employability. It has also been felt that the process would lead to fierce competition among students, be too paternalistic and would not fit with every subject.[58] In the face of this, and considering the soft law nature as well as the fact that the Bologna Process only provides guidelines (e.g. the length of three years of undergraduate study is a minimum requirement not a fixed term), the question arises why the national reforms are implemented in this way. Garben has argued in this respect that the Bologna Process serves as 'an efficient smokescreen for governments to agree on unpopular reforms'[59] while advertising them as binding and thus putting implementation pressure on national parliaments. Furthermore, despite these approaches being advertised as bottom-up alternatives to hard law, only certain actors participate. In particular, since the European

---

[55] See Begg 2008, p. 430 seq (especially 433), Ştefan 2012 p. 8.

[56] Ştefan 2012 p. 15 seq. She also explores how under specific circumstances soft law can create legal effects, but this is of less concern to the areas explored here.

[57] E.g. Nóvoa 2002; Neave and Maassen 2007; Ravinet 2008; Croché 2009; Gornitzka 2010; Corbett 2012.

[58] See, for example, Banscherus et al. 2009, p. 11 seq with further references on criticism in Germany, Cardoso et al. 2008 on criticism regarding the degree structure, Hummer 2005, p. 78 seq on problems in Austria, Cippitani and Gatt 2009, p. 391 on legal and practical problems with a focus on Italy, Garben 2012, p. 20 seq with further references on student and teacher protests.

[59] Garben 2010, p. 206.

Parliament, the CJEU and the general public are not involved, this could be regarded as causing democratic concerns.[60]

These democratic concerns, the commodification trends apparent in the European policies which endanger the traditional non-economic mission of HEIs (as discussed in Chap. 1, Sect. 1.3.1) as well as the confusing jungle of EU law, EU soft law and international instruments which appear as mainly fragmented sectoral policies lacking a clear mission or horizontal approach (though somewhat less so for R&D)[61] make one wonder whether a coherent supranational policy would not be the better choice for HEIs in Europe.[62] However, the negative perceptions of the soft law measures and the EU in general might, as explained above in Chap. 1 (Sect. 1.3.4), make further integration into the EU hard law frame momentarily unlikely. At the same time, HEIs are not immune to the forces of other area of (directly applicable) EU law which can lead to spill-over.

2.3   Spill-over from Directly Applicable EU Law

Spill over from EU law on HEIs can arise from different provisions. Firstly, the Union Citizenship provisions (Sect. 2.3.1) in their broad application by the Court potentially open higher education systems to more students than was originally anticipated. This could have an increasing impact on the organization of national higher education systems.[63] Secondly, HEIs might, as a result of the commodification tendencies analysed in Chap. 1 (Sect. 1.3.3), more regularly fall under the free movement provisions (Sect. 2.3.2). Thirdly, HEIs could (in part) be regarded as undertakings and thus fall under the competition rules (Sect. 2.3.3). Finally, if research and education are to be regarded as economic services, the state might be required to commission these in public procurement procedures (Sect. 2.3.4).

---

[60] See further Garben 2010, p. 205 seq; Garben 2011, p. 210 seq. See also Walkenhorst 2008, p. 579 seq, Maassen and Musselin 2009, p. 9 seq; Ştefan 2012 p. 8. Garben also explores the question of whether the Bologna Process could be seen as depriving the Union of its power and contradicting Article 4(3) TEU and Article 5 TEU and therefore it could be regarded as illegal for Member States to undertake action collectively instead of using the EU frame (Garben 2010, p. 198 seq; Garben 2011, p. 203). She concludes, though, that while the course taken was not exactly in the spirit of cooperation, it would probably not amount to a breach of EU law. Considering C-370/12 *Pringle* (Judgment of 27 November 2012, EU:C:2012:756) it also seems unlikely that the Court would follow such an argumentation, though the judgment was, of course, related to the specific circumstances of the case.

[61] Chou and Gornitzka 2014; Chou and Ulnicane 2015; Ulnicane 2015.

[62] As will be seen below in Chap. 6, such policy involving the European Parliament and consulting stakeholders and the general public could lead away from the tendency towards commodification and create exemptions from the more economic provisions of EU law.

[63] See Dougan 2009, p. 154 seq; Neergaard et al. 2009, p. 7. On the role of the Court in the sphere of citizenship see, Dougan 2012.

These provisions of EU economic law might then require further commodification creating additional constraints on the traditionally non-economic mission of European HEIs. In the following, a brief description of these areas of law will be undertaken.

2.3.1 Union Citizenship

Traditionally, national public services were based on nationality and territoriality. These traditional settings changed through European integration. According to the free movement provisions, economically active citizens of other Member States have to be treated as nationals, which, inter alia, allows them to take part in their host state's education system and makes them eligible for benefits (further below in Sect. 2.3.2). With the introduction of Union Citizenship, free movement and the prohibition of discrimination were then extended to all Union Citizens.[64]

2.3.1.1 Union Citizenship and HEIs

According to Article 21 TFEU every Union Citizen has the right to reside wherever he or she wishes within the EU and Article 18 TFEU provides that a Union Citizen legally residing in the territory of another Member State has the right to equal treatment. However, this is subject to Directive 2004/38/EC,[65] which gives Member States the right to deny residency if the Union Citizen does not have sufficient resources and health insurance (Article 7(b) and (c)) and would thus become 'an unreasonable burden' on the host state. A line of CJEU case law broadened the latter somewhat in that the financial independence of the economically inactive EU migrant does not have to cover absolutely every circumstance, as a certain amount of solidarity from the host state can be expected and such limited reliance on the host state's finances does not give the host state the right to deny residency.[66] When it comes to equal treatment, the lawfully residing EU migrant

---

[64] See Dougan and Spaventar 2003, p. 699 seq; Dougan 2008, p. 723; Kohler and Görlitz 2008, p. 93 seq; Dougan 2009, p. 154 seq; Schrauwen 2009, p. 4 seq.

[65] Directive 2004/38/EC on the right of citizens of the Union and their family members to move and reside freely within the territory of the Member States amending Regulation (EEC) No 1612/68 and repealing Directives 64/221/EEC, 68/360/EEC, 72/194/EEC, 73/148/EEC, 75/34/EEC, 75/35/EEC, 90/364/EEC, 90/365/EEC and 93/96/EEC OJ [2004] L 158/77.

[66] C-184/99 *Grzelczyk* (Judgment of 20 September 2001, EU:C:2001:458), C-413/99 *Baumbast* (Judgment of 17 September 2002, EU:C:2002:493).

(and his or her family members) can generally expect equal treatment, but this can be limited through secondary law (in particular Article 24 of Directive 2004/38).[67] Outside such limitations, unless there is a 'real link' to the host state's society,[68] Union Citizenship provides the right to equal treatment regarding access to social benefits without the security of residency rights.[69] Indeed, in *Dano* and *Alimanovic*[70] the Court allowed for Member States to combine the criteria for residency and access to social benefits (and to rely on general rules rather than individual assessment) to deny access to social benefits.[71]

In *Gravier*[72] the Court applied this general line that residency and equal treatment for EU migrants should be ensured without creating 'an unreasonable burden' on the host state in field of higher education. Here it developed the approach (now to be found in Article 24(2) Directive 2004/38) that no discrimination is allowed in any area connected to access to higher education (e.g. entry grades, fees), but the eligibility to additional support (e.g. maintenance grants) can be limited to permanent residents.[73]

A similar approach is taken towards the home state and the exportation of grants; generally no territoriality requirement can be imposed unless either the increased number of potential benefit recipients would provide an unreasonable

---

[67] In previous case law, it appeared that equal treatment can also be expected if the circumstances of the case warrant this (e.g. the reliance is only temporary) even if secondary measures normally exclude the reliance on benefits (C-184/99 *Grzelczyk*, C-140/12 *Brey* (Judgment of 19 September 2013, EU:C:2013:565)). However, more recent case law seems to move away from requiring to make individual assessments and instead allows Member States to set more general rules (in line with secondary EU law) on when such reliance is excluded (C-333/13 *Dano* (Judgment of 11 November 2014, EU:C:2014:2358), C-67/14 *Alimanovic* (Judgment of 15 September 2015, EU:C:2015:597)).

[68] C-85/96 *Martínez Sala* (Judgment of 12 May 1998, EU:C:1998:217), C-209/03 *Bidar* (Judgment of 15 March 2005, EU:C:2005:169). In C-158/07 *Förster* (Judgment of 18 November 2008, EU:C:2008:630) the Court up-held this line of reasoning. It did, however, allow a rather long residency requirement (five years) for the 'real link' to be established.

[69] C-456/02 *Trojani* (Judgment of 7 September 2004, EU:C:2004:488).

[70] C-333/13 *Dano*, C-67/14 *Alimanovic*.

[71] C-333/13 *Dano*, C-67/14 *Alimanovic*.

[72] 293/83 *Gravier* (Judgment of 13 February 1985, EU:C:1985:69), C-39/86 *Lair* (Judgment of 21 June 1988, EU:C:1988:322) para 16. These cases were decided before Union Citizenship had been established with the Treaty of Maastricht and the Court thus needed to go into some length to explain why students would fall under the Treaty provisions in the first place. They were, however, decided on the basis of what is now Article 18 TFEU. The latter has, with the Treaty of Lisbon, been incorporated into the citizenship provisions after it has been read together with what is now Article 21 TFEU for some time. Recently, this differentiation between access and maintenance has been discussed and reaffirmed in C-233/14 *Commission v Netherlands* (Judgment of 2 June 2016, EU:C:2016:396).

[73] See further Van der Mei 2005, p. 225 seq; Dougan 2005; Kohler and Görlitz 2008, p. 95 seq; De Groof 2009, p. 80, 92 seq.

burden or no 'real link' to the home state exists anymore.[74] The two approaches are regarded as cumulative and interactive in that the migrant's home state is supposed to support him or her until his or her ties to the host state are close enough to allow benefits to be granted there. The latter argument was posited as the way forward in the field of educational mobility.[75]

Overall, Member States have eagerly tried to retain control over more social policy areas. In health (Article 168 TFEU), education (Article 165 seq TFEU) and social security (Article 151 seq TFEU) the EU has only limited competences. In the field of education, the Member States avoided the supranational mode of harmonisation and during the negotiations for the Treaty of Lisbon[76] much emphasis was placed on the principle of conferral of competences and the principle of subsidiarity. The Court's (earlier) judgements on EU citizenship have thus been criticised for interfering with national welfare systems which are particularly sensitive areas closely related to national finances.[77] Additionally, the Court's case to case approach makes this area of law somewhat unpredictable. Even if one disagrees with this criticism and instead finds the Court's overall approach to be reasonable, appearing as it does, to strike a balance between upholding the free movement of citizens and the concerns of the Member States, the cases discussed in the following demonstrate that the citizenship provisions, under certain circumstances, can in fact lead to significant spill-over into national HEI policies.

2.3.1.2 The Infringement Procedures Against Austria and Belgium

The infringement procedures against Austria and Belgium[78] concerned the 'open-access to education' policies which both countries had implemented to increase

---

[74] C-499/06 *Nerkowska* (Judgment of 22 May 2008, EU:C:2008:300) and, in the field of education, C-11-12/06 *Morgan and Bucher* (Judgment of 23 October 2007, EU:C:2007:626), C-523-585/11 *Prinz and Seeberger* (Judgment of 18 July 2013, EU:C:2013:524), C-220/12 *Thiele* (Judgment of 24 October 2013, EU:C:2013:683) and C-275/12 *Elrick* (Judgment of 24 October 2013, EU:C:2013:684) (all on restrictions to the exportation of maintenance grants in Germany) and, recently, C-359/13 *Martens* (Judgment of 26 February 2015, EU:C:2015:118). On the exportation of grants and the earlier case law see further Dougan 2005, p. 980 seq; Shuibhne 2008; Dougan 2008, p. 727 seq; Schrauwen 2009, p. 4 seq, 9 seq.

[75] For an in-depth discussion see van der Mei 2005. See also Dougan 2008, p. 737.

[76] In this regard it is even been suggested that the problems during the constitutional reform process might partly have been caused by a negative opinion towards Union Citizenship and what it brings with it (Dougan 2009, p. 164 seq).

[77] On this point see Dougan 2008, p. 729, 738; Dougan 2009, especially p. 161 seq, 181 seq; Schrauwen 2009, p. 10 seq.

[78] Cases C-147/03 *Commission v Austria* (Judgment of 7 July 2005, EU:C:2005:427) and C-65/03 *Commission v Belgium* (Judgment of 1 July 2004, EU:C:2004:402) respectively. There had already been an infringement procedure against Belgium for quota legislation in the 1980s (case 42/87, Judgment of 27 September 1988, EU:C:1988:454) which had been found to infringe the Treaty. See further Kohler and Görlitz 2008, p. 97.

the percentage of their population in tertiary education.[79] Residents only had to have a secondary school certificate to be admitted to an HEI. For students from other Member States, however, additional requirements were imposed; they had to qualify for the same course of study in their home state. Austria and Belgium deemed this necessary to avoid an influx of German and French students respectively who, given the much stricter requirements for university access in their home states, would come to the neighbouring states where they could gain access more easily and also study in their native language. It was feared that a large influx of students would create a burden on state finances and could ultimately threaten the open access policy. The Court, however, decided that these rules constituted indirect discrimination and therefore infringed Article 18 TFEU. It did not accept the justification due to a lack of evidence and as it deemed the discriminatory system disproportionate.[80] The judgments received fierce academic criticism because the Court was regarded as having overstepped its competences in an area of primary responsibility of the Member States. While the Court, in fact, just followed its long established case law that access to higher education requires equal treatment, whilst additional benefits do not, these cases, indeed, had a significant impact on the policy choice of the open education system which either had to be surrendered or opened up to a large influx of non-residents. It was generally considered that the Court should at least have been more lenient at the justification stage rather than demanding hard proof and applying a strict proportionality test.[81]

After the judgments, Austria and Belgium abolished the discriminatory measures which led to disproportionately high numbers of German and French students respectively in certain subjects, especially in the field of medicine.[82] As these were considered to be mostly 'free-riders', it was feared that this would also result in a threat to the health care system. Both countries thus introduced quota systems reserving 75 % (Austria) and 70 % (Belgium) of the places for residents.[83] The Commission then, again, initiated infringement procedures against Austria and Belgium, but suspended them in order for the countries to gather evidence that the quota system might be necessary.[84]

---

[79] The fact that this is after all a goal of the Lisbon Strategy has, however, not been brought as a justification in the proceedings.

[80] For more on the cases see Damjanovic 2012, p. 157 seq; Reich 2009, p. 637; Kohler and Görlitz 2008, p. 95 seq; Garben 2008, para 6 seq, Rieder 2006.

[81] See Damjanovic 2012, p. 158 seq; Reich 2009, p. 637 seq.

[82] Up to 80 % of French students were, for example, enrolled in medical subjects in Belgium (Damjanovic 2012, p. 162 with further references).

[83] Damjanovic 2012, p. 163 with further references.

[84] It has been suggested that Austria's strong demand during the Lisbon Treaty negotiations to expressly declare public education as a non-economic service of general interest for which Article 2 Protocol 9 reassures the competence of the Member States might also have played a role in that respect (Damjanovic 2012, p. 163).

However, in line with both neo-functionalism and social constructivism, integration cannot necessarily be halted by such arrangements and in the meantime a preliminary reference from a Belgian court came before the CJEU.[85] Upon a claim for access by French students, the national court asked about the compatibility of the quota system with Article 18 TFEU and any potential justifications due to the threats to the national education and, potentially, health care system. In its questions, the national court also pointed to the fact that open access to education was equally an aim of Article 165 TFEU, which the Union shall support, as well as of Article 13(2) of the International Covenant on Economic, Social and Cultural Rights which contains a standstill obligation towards measures achieving that aim. The CJEU, confirming its earlier case law, decided that Articles 18 and 21 TFEU do prohibit such a quota system, but that 'the objective of protection of public health' could constitute a justification. It was left to the national court to determine the latter. A similar outcome had been suggested in the pre-ruling literature, since by doing this the Court could reach a political compromise by upholding its former case law and avoiding the more general questions of who pays for cross-border education and how an open access system can be upheld in net receiver states.[86] The issue, on a more general level, is thus unresolved and seems to remain a sore point, as can be seen by the Austrian attempt to reduce fares on public transport for permanent resident students only, something that has equally been found to infringe the citizenship provisions.[87]

2.3.1.3 Interim Conclusion on Union Citizenship and HEIs

Union Citizenship generally only provides students with the right to reside in the territory of another Member State and to access higher education in that Member State. Additional benefits are generally excluded for EU migrant students unless a 'real link' to the host state can be established. Instead these benefits can be exported from the home state. Whilst this system does not seem to cause too many concerns generally, the cases of Belgium and Austria have shown that the citizenship provisions can have significant spill-over effects threatening the whole concept of an open access to education policy in certain circumstances. Here, further regulation seems required.[88]

---

[85] Case C-73/08 *Bressol* (Judgment of 13 April 2010, EU:C:2010:181).

[86] See, Garben 2008, para 20 seq. Rieder 2006, p. 1725, by contrast, suggested that the quota system would infringe EU law.

[87] C-75/11 *Commission v Austria* (Judgment of 4 October 2012, EU:C:2012:605).

[88] Van der Mei 2005, p. 232 seq had suggested a justified quota system which, however, seems difficult as the Court only let the concerns about the health system count as a justification and not the threats to the education system itself. On the attempts to establish a reimbursement scheme between certain Member States see Damjanovic 2012, p. 162 seq with further references.

2.3.2 The Free Movement Provisions

The free movement provisions are the core of internal market law. They require that goods (Articles 34 TFEU seq), workers (Article 45 TFEU seq), self-employed persons and business (Article 49 TFEU seq), services (Article 56 TFEU seq) and capital (Article 63 TFEU seq) can move freely within the EU. They are therefore provisions of economic law, which on the surface do not have anything to do with HEIs.

Early on, however, the free movement of persons spilled over into the sphere of HEIs with regards to the professional recognition of diplomas as discussed above (Sect. 2.2.1.2). Furthermore, the free movement of economically active persons also requires that these are treated equally without the limitations applicable to mere citizens. Any limitations to receiving maintenance grants and other non-access-related support can thus not be applied to free moving economically active persons.[89] Economically active EU migrants can also extend rights to their family members including third country nationals. These can access education (Article 10 Regulation 492/2011/EU)[90] and, once in education, obtain an independent residency right which can be further extended to their family members.[91]

As regards the free movement of services or, if on a more permanent basis, establishment, the Court has initially not considered education (including higher education) to be a service in the meaning of Article 56 TFEU, since it is not 'normally provided for remuneration'.[92] Yet, if education is provided by institutions which are 'financed essentially out of private funds, in particular by students or their parents, and which seek to make an economic profit', it would, according to

---

[89] C-39/86 *Lair*. This has been reaffirmed in C-46/12 *N* (Judgment of 21 February 2013, EU:C:2013:97). In C-542/09 *Commission v the Netherlands* (Judgment of 14 June 2012, EU:C:2012:346) and C-20/12 *Giersch* (Judgment of 20 June 2013, EU:C:2013:411) the Court also declared the denial of the portability of a grant to the child of a migrant and frontier worker respectively, if they did not fulfil a certain length of residence, as incompatible with Article 45 TFEU. However, the aim of increasing the percentage of residents with tertiary education has been considered as a valid justification ground in *Giersch*, though the Court did not find the residency requirement to be proportionate in this case. The latter is interesting, since increasing the percentage of residents with tertiary education is after all an aim of the Lisbon/Europe 2020 Strategy, but this had not been brought as a justification in the citizenship cases of Austria and Belgium mentioned above (Sect. 2.3.1.2). It now seems that it can potentially be a valid justification for a limitation of the free movement of economically active persons.

[90] Regulation 492/2011/EU on freedom of movement for workers within the Union OJ [2011] L 141/1.

[91] C-529/11 *Alarape* (Judgment of 8 May 2013, EU:C:2013:290), C-115/15 *NA* (Judgment of 30 June 2016, EU:C:2016:487).

[92] Cases 263/86 *Humbel* (Judgment of 27 September 1988, EU:C:1988:451) and, for higher education, C-109/92 *Wirth* (Judgment of 7 December 1993, EU:C:1993:916).

the Court, amount to a service in the meaning of Article 56 TFEU.[93] One would assume that a similar distinction would need to be made for research with basic, curiosity driven research in public institutions without a recipient paying remuneration not constituting a service, while essentially privately financed research does.[94] For education as well as for research, the distinction would probably have to be made on a case to case basis. During the last decades of on-going commodification at the national level, there have already been a number of cases where the Court declared educational activities by (higher) education institutions to be services in the meaning of the Treaty and applied Article 56 and 49 TFEU respectively. In the cases *Schwarz*,[95] *Jundt*,[96] and *Zanotti*[97] the freedom to provide services required tax changes in national policy,[98] in *Neri*[99] the freedom of establishment required a change in diploma recognition policy and in *Dirextra*[100] the Court found an infringement of the free movement of services in requiring ten years of experience of private HEIs in order for its postgraduate students to be able to receive certain funding. While the infringement in *Dirextra* was found to be justified,[101] these cases illustrate that, especially with increasing commodification, the free movement of services and establishment respectively can have unforeseen consequences for HEIs. Exclusion of or stricter regulation with regards to private providers, as often requested to safeguard quality and equality in higher education,[102] could, for example, constitute a restriction of these provisions. Furthermore, as the cases mentioned above illustrate, tax advantages could no longer be granted exclusively to national (public) providers.

Finally, a case in the area of the free movement of capital touched upon HEI policy. In an infringement procedure against Austria,[103] the Court declared the

---

[93] Case C-109/92 *Wirth* para 13 seq.

[94] A similar differentiation is made by the Commission in its 'Framework for State aid for research and development and innovation' OJ [2014] C 198/01 Sect. 2.1 (Research Framework) for the field of state aid law (see further Chap. 3 Sect. 3.2.4.2 below).

[95] C-76/05 *Schwarz* (Judgment of 11 September 2007, EU:C:2007:492).

[96] C-281/06 *Jundt* (Judgment of 18 December 2007, EU:C:2007:816).

[97] C-56/09 *Zanotti* (Judgment of 20 May 2010, EU:C:2010:288).

[98] In *Zanotti* the Court, however, allowed a maximum limit for reimbursement set at the level of the costs of the same education in a national public HEI.

[99] C-153/02 *Neri* (Judgment of 13 November 2003, EU:C:2003:614).

[100] C-523/12 *Dirextra* (Judgment of 12 December 2013, EU:C:2013:831).

[101] C-523/12 *Dirextra* para 25. The Court found a justification ground in the desire of the local authorities to ensure that 'the post-graduate education to which access for young, unemployed graduates is made easier through the award of a study grant is of a high standard, in order to facilitate the access of such students to the labour market' and also declared the measure as proportionate.

[102] See on concerns regarding private providers in higher education UCU 2011.

[103] C-10/10 *Commission v Austria* (Judgment of 16 June 2011, EU:C:2011:399).

policy of allowing only gifts to HEIs established in Austria to be deducted from income tax as an infringement of the free movement of capital. With HEIs becoming increasingly reliant on external sources including private donation, this decision could potentially also become consequential in the future.

2.3.3 The Competition Rules

Competition and state aid law aims to avoid anti-competitive collusion, unilateral conduct by dominant undertakings, mergers and state interference. However, entities only fall under these provisions, if they are 'undertakings'. The CJEU has defined an undertaking as 'every entity engaged in an economic activity, regardless of the legal status of the entity and the way in which it is financed'.[104] An economic activity consists, according to the Court, of 'offering goods or services on the market'.[105] With ongoing commodification of HEIs, they might qualify as undertakings. How far this can be expected and what consequences this could have for them will be discussed in detail in Chap. 3.

2.3.4 Public Procurement Law

Though not directly applicable, as passed as a directive, the public procurement rules could equally affect HEIs and should thus be briefly discussed here.[106] Directive 2014/24/EU[107] lays down rules public authorities need to follow when purchasing goods, services and works. This could affect HEIs as buyers and providers of educational and research services.

As buyers they are bound if they have to be regarded as 'contracting authorities'. According to Article 2(1) of the Directive this is the case when they classify as state authorities per se which is of less relevance to HEIs[108] or if they need to be classified as a 'body governed by public law'. The latter question largely depends on the funding they receive, as, according to the Court in *University of Cambridge*,[109] over 50 % of public funding would be necessary for an HEI to be regarded as a body governed by public law. Funding will only be considered as

---

[104] C-41/90 *Höfner* (Judgment of 23 April 1991, EU:C:1991:161) para 21.

[105] 118/85 *Commission v Italy* (Judgment of 16 June 1987, EU:C:1987:283) para 7.

[106] For an extensive discussion see Gideon and Sanchez-Graells 2016.

[107] Directive 2014/24/EU on public procurement and repealing Directive 2004/18/EC OJ [2014] L 94/65.

[108] As regards central government authorities these are laid down in a closed list determined by the Member States in Annex I of the Directive which does not normally include HEIs.

[109] C-380/98 *University of Cambridge* (Judgment of 3 October 2000, EU:C:2000:529).

public in nature if it is provided 'without any specific consideration'. Thus contract research, for example, even if it is conducted for a public sector entity would not constitute public funding. With increasing income from fees and research contracts, HEIs might thus be able to free themselves from the public procurement rules, though this would have to be determined on a case by case basis. However, in a situation, where the public funding exceeds 50 %, yet HEIs are obliged to compete with private providers on a market, they might perceive the obligation to comply with the public procurement rules as a disadvantage.[110]

As providers HEIs could fall under the public procurement rules if the services they provide are classified as economic activities. As has been seen above (Sect. 2.3.3) this question is equally relevant for the application of the notion of undertaking in competition law and will thus be discussed in Chap. 3 (Sects. 3.2.1 and 3.2.4). Further the way through which HEIs receive public funding for teaching and research would need to be classified as a contractual relationship. Both would depend on the system a Member State adopts. Suffice to say here that this means that in cases where there indeed is an economic activity and a contractual relationship, HEIs could not necessarily be directly entrusted with a service anymore without going through a public procurement procedure.[111] For educational activities this would mean applying the Directive's light touch regime in Article 74 seq and for research applying the general regime of the Directive or the alternative arrangements under the Research Framework. In particular, this includes that in such situations it would be difficult to per se exclude foreign and/or private providers from public funding arrangements.[112] HEIs might also come in conflict with the procurement rules if they submit abnormally low tenders due to their public funding[113] or if HEI experts are involved in committees deciding about tenders and work for a participating HEI at the same time.[114]

There are exemptions for public-public and in-house cooperation in public procurement law (Article 12 Directive 2014/24/EU). Considering the recent case

---

[110] Gideon and Sanchez-Graells 2016 p. 7 seq. As analysed there, fees paid through a public student loan company directly to the HEIs thereby guaranteeing the receipt of the funds, as is the case in England, may qualify as public funding.

[111] See also C-159/11 *Ordine degli Ingegneri della Provincia di Lecce* (Judgment of 19 December 2012, EU:C:2012:817).

[112] Gideon and Sanchez-Graells 2016, p. 22 seq. In the case of England, for example, according to the analysis conducted there, it might mean that funding for educational activities from the Higher Education Funding Council should comply with the light touch regime of Directive 2014/24/EU or at least with the general principles of transparency and non-discrimination.

[113] See, on a public hospital, 568/13 *Data Medical Service* (Judgment of 18 December 2014, EU:C:2014:2466).

[114] C 538/13 *eVigilo* (Judgment of 12 March 2015, EU:C:2015:166).

Datenlotsen,[115] it seems unlikely, though, that HEIs could benefit from this as providers.[116] However, these exemptions might be beneficial if universities are buyers attempting to commission services from their own spin-offs. This could lead to increased use of these for commercialisation activities.[117]

2.4 Conclusion

This chapter has illuminated the rather complicated situation of HEIs in EU policy and law. Whilst HEIs did not originally play a role in EU policy and law, ongoing commodification and internationalisation seem to have required a certain amount of coordination. Nevertheless, the policy areas appear to be too treasured by Member States to provide the EU with far reaching competences. Rather than utilising the supranational framework, Member States have thus opted for EU and extra-EU soft law mechanisms. It has been suggested that these cause democratic concerns, as they are agreed upon by national governments without involvement of the European Parliament and without review by the Court. Furthermore, despite their soft law character, many have pointed to implementation pressures on national legislators, the intertwining of the two mechanisms and the emanating tendency towards commodification. It has thus been suggested that especially the Bologna 'rules' serve to justify unpopular, national policy choices.

Additionally, HEIs are not immune to other areas of EU law. Spill-over can result from the citizenship, free movement, competition and public procurement law provisions. That this can have severe effects on national policy choices has been shown by the cases of Austria and Belgium. Whilst the Court has suffered a great deal of criticism for ruling on matters affecting HEIs due to spill-over from directly applicable EU law, Member States remain reluctant to establish a coherent supranational strategy. Therefore the law in this area is made on a case to case basis without a coherent strategy, which creates fragmentation and can lead to legal uncertainty.[118] As regards the economic provisions of EU law, the likeliness that HEIs will fall into their ambit increases with ongoing commodification which, in turn, might require even further commodification potentially endangering the traditional non-economic mission of European HEIs as discussed in the Chap. 1. In the remainder of the book this will be studied more specifically on the example

---

[115] C-15/13 *Datenlotsen* (Judgment of 8 May 2014, EU:C:2014:303).

[116] However, the approach adopted by the Court does not seem to take into account the specific characteristics of HEIs. A more sensible approach has been advocated by AG Mengozzi in this case (Opinion of the AG para 73). If the latter were to be adopted in the future HEIs in some systems might be more likely to benefit from the in-house exemption. See further Gideon and Sanchez-Graells 2016 p. 48 seq.

[117] Gideon and Sanchez-Graells 2016, p. 47 seq.

[118] Similar Schrauwen 2009, p. 10 seq.

of EU competition law, a thus-far less explored area. The next chapter will begin this study with an in-depth legal doctrinal assessment of potential competition law constraints on HEIs.

References

Banscherus U et al (2009) Der Bologna-Prozess zwischen Anspruch und Wirklichkeit (English translation: The Bologna Process between pretension and reality). Leutheusser Druck, Coburg

Begg I (2008) Is there a convincing rationale for the Lisbon Strategy? JCMS. J Common Market Stud 46:427–435

Cardoso AR et al (2008) Demand for higher education programs: the impact of the Bologna Process. CESifo Econ Stud 54:229–247

Chou M-H, Gornitzka Å (2014) Building a European knowledge area: an introduction to the dynamics of policy domains on the rise. In: Chou M-H, Gornitzka Å (eds) Building the knowledge economy in Europe. Edward Elgar, Cheltenham/Northampton, pp 1–26

Chou M-H, Ulnicane I (2015) New Horizons in the Europe of Knowledge. J Contemp Eur Res 11:4–15

Cippitani R, Gatt S (2009) Legal developments and problems of the Bologna Process within the European higher education area and European integration. Higher Educ Eur 34:385–397

Cohen-Tanugi L (2008) Beyond Lisbon—a European Strategy for globalisation. PIE Peter Lang, Brussels

Corbett A (2003) Ideas, institutions and policy entrepreneurs: towards a new history of higher education in the European Community. Eur J Educ 38:315–330

Corbett A (2012) Education and the Lisbon Strategy. In: Copeland P, Papadimitriou D (eds) The EU's Lisbon Strategy: evaluating success, understanding failure. Palgrave MacMillan, Basingstoke, pp 149–167

Croché S (2009) Bologna Network: a new sociopolitical area in higher education. Glob Soc Educ 7:489–503

Damjanovic D (2012) "Reserved areas" of the Member States and the ECJ: the case of higher education. In: Micklitz H-W, De Witte B (eds) The European Court of Justice and the Autonomy of the Member States. Intersentia, Cambridge, pp 149–174

De Groof J (2009) European higher education in search of a new legal order. In: Kehm BM et al (eds) The European higher education area: perspectives on a moving target. Sense Publishers, Rotterdam, pp 79–106

Dougan M (2005) Fees, grants, loans and dole cheques: who covers the costs of migrant education within the EU? C.M.L. Rev 42:943–986

Dougan M (2008) Cross-border educational mobility and the exportation of student financial assistance. Eur Law Rev 5:723–738

Dougan M (2009) The spatial restructuring of national welfare states within the European Union: the contribution of Union Citizenship and the relevance of the Treaty of Lisbon. In: Neergaard U et al (eds) Integrating welfare functions into EU Law: from Rome to Lisbon. DJØF Forlag, Copenhagen, pp 147–190

Dougan M (2012) Judicial activism or constitutional interaction? Policymaking by the ECJ in the Field of Union Citizenship. In: Micklitz H-W, De Witte B (eds) The European Court of Justice and the Autonomy of the Member States. Intersentia, Cambridge/Antwerp/Portland, pp 113–147

Dougan M, Spaventar E (2003) Educating Rudy and the (non-)English patient: a double bill on residency rights under Article 18 EC. Eur Law Rev 28:699–712

European Commission/EACEA/Eurydice (2015) The European higher education area in 2015: Bologna Process implementation report. Publications Office of the European Union, Luxembourg

Eurydice (2010) Focus on higher education in Europe 2010: the impact of the Bologna Process. Eurydice, Brussels

Eurydice (2012) The European higher education area in 2012: Bologna Process implementation report. Education, Audiovisual and Culture Executive Agency, Brussels

Garben S (2008) The Belgian/Austrian Education Saga. Harvard European Law Working Paper

Garben S (2010) The Bologna Process: From a European Law Perspective. ELJ 16:186–210

Garben S (2011) EU Higher Education Law—the Bologna Process and harmonization by stealth. Kluwer, Alphen aan den Rijn

Garben S (2012) The future of higher education in Europe: the case for a stronger base in EU Law. LSE 'Europe in Question' Discussion Paper Series 50:1–44

Gideon A (2015) The position of higher education institutions in a changing European context: an EU Law Perspective. JCMS: J Common Market Stud 53:1045–1060

Gideon A (2016) The Saga of Mr Brouillard and the EU Courts (F-148/15, T-420/13, C-298/14 … and C-590/15 P). How to Crack a Nut, 29 February 2016. http://www.howtocrackanut.com/blog/2016/2/26/the-saga-of-mr-brouillard-and-the-eu-courts-f14815-t42013-c29814-and-c-59015-p. Accessed 29 Feb 2016

Gideon A, Sanchez-Graells A (2016) When are universities bound by EU public procurement rules as buyers and providers?—English universities as a case study. Ius Publicum 1–58

Gornitzka Å (2010) Bologna in context: a horizontal perspective on the dynamics of governance sites for a Europe of Knowledge. Eur J Educ 45:535–548

Hadfield A, Summerby-Murray R (2015) Vocation or vocational? Reviewing European Union education and mobility structures. Eur J Higher Educ (online first): 1–19

Hummer W (2005) Vom "Europäischen Hochschulraum" zum "Europäischen Forschungsraum". Ansätze und Perspektiven einer europäischen Bildungs- und Forschungspolitik (English translation: From "European Higher Education Area" to "European Research Area". Approaches and perspectives of a European education and research policy). In: Prisching M et al (eds) Bildung in Europa - Entwicklungsstand und Perspektiven (English translation: Education in Europe - Status and Prospects). Verlag Österreich, Wien, pp 33–84

Jones RA (2001) The Politics and Economics of the European Union, 2nd edn. Edward Elgar, Cheltenham/Northampton

Kohler C, Görlitz N (2008) Auswirkungen des europarechtlichen Diskriminierungsverbots auf den Bildungssektor - Grundlinien der Rechtsprechung des Europäischen Gerichtshofs (English translation: Impact of the EU law prohibition of discrimination on the education sector—fundamentals of the jurisprudence of the European Court of Justice). IJELP 4:92–100

Kröger S (2009) The Open Method of Coordination: Underconceptualisation, overdetermination, de-politicisation and beyond. EIoP Special Issue: What we have learnt: advances, pitfalls and remaining questions in OMC research 1:1–23

Lenaerts K, Van Nuffel P (2005) Constitutional Law of the European Union, 2nd edn. Sweet & Maxwell, London

Maassen P, Musselin C (2009) European Integration and the Europeanisation of Higher Education. In: Amaral A et al (eds) European Integration and the Governance of Higher Education and Research. Springer, Dordrecht/London, pp 3–14

Neave G, Maassen P (2007) The Bologna Process: an intergovernmental policy perspective. In: Maassen P, Olsen J (eds) University dynamics and European integration. Springer, Dordrecht, pp 135–154

Neergaard U et al (2009) Introduction. In: Neergaard U et al (eds) Integrating Welfare Functions into EU Law—From Rome to Lisbon. DJØF Forlag, Copenhagen, pp 7–28

Niemann A, Schmitter PC (2009) Neofunctionalism. In: Wiener A, Diez T (eds) European integration theory, 2nd edn. OUP, Oxford, pp 45–66

Nóvoa A (2002) Ways of thinking about education in Europe. In: Nóvoa A, Lawn M (eds) Fabricating Europe—the formation of an education space. Kluwer, Dordrecht, pp 131–155

Pilniok A (2011) Governance im europäischen Forschungsförderverbund (English translation: Governance in the European research funding network). Mohr Siebeck, Tübingen

Ravinet P (2008) From Voluntary Participation to Monitored Coordination: why European countries feel increasingly bound by their commitment to the Bologna Process. Eur J Educ 43:353–367

Reich N (2009) Herkunftsprinzip oder Diskriminierung als Maßstab für Studentenfreizügigkeit? (English translation: Principle of origin or discrimination as a benchmark for free movement of students?). EuZW 18:637–638

Rieder C (2006) Case C-147/03, Commission of the European Communities v. Republic of Austria. C.M.L. Rev 43:1711–1726

Sandholtz W, Stone Sweet A (2012) Neo-functionalism and Supranational Governance. In: Jones E et al (eds) The Oxford Handbook of the European Union. OUP, Oxford, pp 18–33

Schmitter PC (2004) Neo-Neofunctionalisms. In: Wiener A, Diez T (eds) European Integration Theory, 1st edn. OUP, Oxford, pp 45–73

Schneider H (1995) Die Anerkennung von Diplomen in der Europäischen Gemeinschaft (English translation: Diploma recognition in the European Community). Maklu, Antwerpen

Schrauwen AAM (2009) The Future of EU Citizenship: Corrosion of National Citizenship? SSRN eLibrary. http://papers.ssrn.com/sol3/papers.cfm?abstract_id=1375413

Shuibhne NN (2008) Case C–76/05 Schwarz and Gootjes-Schwarz v. Finanzamt Bergisch Gladbach, Judgment of the Grand Chamber of 11 September 2007, not yet reported; Case C–318/05, Commission v. Germany, Judgment of the Grand Chamber of 11 September 2007, not yet reported; Joined Cases C–11/06 & C–12/06 Morgan v. Bezirksregierung Köln; Bucher v. Landrat des Kreises Düren, Judgment of the Grand Chamber of 23 October 2007, not yet reported. C.M.L. Rev 45:771–786

Ştefan O (2012) Soft Law in Court: Competition Law, State Aid and the Court of Justice of the European Union. Kluwer, Alphen aan den Rijn

Teichler U (2007) Geschichte und Entwicklung der Bildungsprogramme der Europäischen Union (English translation: History and development of educational programmes of the European Union). In: Teichler U (ed) Die Internationalisierung der Hochschulen - Neue Herausforderungen und Strategien (English translation: The Internationalisation of Higher Education—New Challenges and Strategies). Campus Verlag, Frankfurt am Main, pp 105–114

UCU (2011) High cost, high debt, high risk: why for-profit universities are a poor deal for students and taxpayers. UCU, London

Ulnicane I (2015) Broadening Aims and Building Support in Science, Technology and Innovation Policy: The case of the European Research Area. J Contemp Eur Res 11:21–49

Van der Mei AP (2005) EU Law and Education: promotion of student mobility versus protection of the education systems. In: Dougan M, Spaventa E (eds) Social welfare and EU law. Hart Publishing, Oxford/Portland/Oregon, pp 219–240

Van der Ploeg F, Veugelers R (2007) Higher education reform and the renewed Lisbon Strategy: role of Member States and the European Commission. CESifo Working Paper 1901

Vanhercke B (2014) Commission takes stock of 'Europe 2020'—EU to miss its employment, research and poverty reduction targets. NEUJOBS Blog, 19 March 2014. http://blog-neujobs. eu/?p=619. Accessed 21 March 2014

Walkenhorst H (2008) Explaining change in EU education policy. J Eur Public Policy 15:567–587

Young M (2014) Where is Horizon 2020 leading us? Europe of Knowledge. http://era.ideasoneurope.eu/2014/01/17/where-is-horizon-2020-leading-us/. Accessed 5 February 2014

Young M (2015) Shifting Policy Narratives in Horizon 2010. J Contemp Eur Res 11:16–30

Chapter 3
Higher Education Institutions and EU Competition Law

Abstract This chapter conducts an in-depth legal doctrinal assessment of potential competition law constraints on HEIs. It thereby lays the ground for a detailed discussion of competition law effects on research in HEIs in three Member States in the subsequent chapters. First, the concept of 'undertaking' and services of general economic interest will be assessed to determine how far HEIs might fall under the competition law provisions in the first place. It will be shown that this becomes increasing likely the more commercial elements an HEI system adopts. Then, possible constraints arising from the application of Article 101 TFEU (prohibition of anti-competitive collusion), Article 102 TFEU (prohibition of abuse of dominance), Regulation 139/2004/EC (merger control) and Article 107 TFEU (prohibition of state aid) will be explored. We will see that, whilst the application of the competition rules might occasionally aid 'consumers' or HEIs themselves, they can also lead to detrimental effects in cases where the economic competition and state aid law provisions might clash with the public service nature of the teaching and research activities of HEIs.

Keywords Competition law and higher education institutions · Universities as undertakings · Higher education and research as economic activities · Services of general economic interest · Framework for state aid for research and development · Anti-competitive practices of higher education institutions · Price fixing of tuition fees · General Block Exemption Regulation · Full costing in universities

Contents

© T.M.C. ASSER PRESS and the author 2017

A. Gideon, *Higher Education Institutions in the EU: Between Competition and Public Service*, Legal Issues of Services of General Interest, DOI 10.1007/978-94-6265-168-5_3

3.1 Introduction

The aim of this chapter is to conduct an in-depth legal doctrinal assessment of potential competition law constraints on higher education institutions (HEIs).[1] As introduced in more detail in Chap. 1, this book uses the relatively unexplored relation between HEIs and EU competition law as an example of how applying the EU's economic constitution to former public sectors may increase tensions between economic integration and the EU's wider aims, including social integration. The general analysis of potential competition law constraints on HEIs in this chapter lays the ground for a detailed discussion of research in HEIs in three Member States in the following chapters.

Since there is only one EU level case so far,[2] the analysis has to be conducted theoretically by drawing on experiences in national case law as well as on experiences of the application of competition law to public services[3] in other areas, such as health care. The chapter will employ a contextual approach by, firstly, discussing the notions of 'undertaking' and 'SGEIs', as, in effect, they are both limits on the reach of competition law (Sect. 3.2). Section 3.3 then discusses possible constraints arising from the application of the competition rules on HEIs, namely from the prohibition

---

[1] A condensed and much earlier version of this chapter has been published as Gideon 2012.

[2] T-488/11 *Sarc* (state aid).

[3] Similar to Sauter 2015, p. 9 the term is used here widely comprising utilities and more social services such as health, education and social welfare services.

of anti-competitive collusions in Article 101 TFEU (Sect. 3.3.2), from the prohibition of the abuse of a dominant market position in Article 102 TFEU (Sect. 3.3.3), from the merger control regime in Regulation 139/2004/EC (Sect. 3.3.4) and from the prohibition of state aid in Article 107 TFEU (Sect. 3.3.5). This will be followed by a conclusion bringing together the results of this chapter (Sect. 3.4).

3.2 Application of EU Competition Law on HEIs?— The Notions of 'Undertaking' and 'SGEIs'

As we have seen in Chap. 2, competition law is only applicable to 'undertakings' which, as will be discussed further below, are defined as entities which are conducting an economic activity. Through competition law undertakings are supposed to be prevented from disrupting competition in the single market, while state aid law prohibits Member States to disrupt competition by selectively benefitting undertakings. Competition law is, in so far, the counterpart to the free movement provisions which prevent barriers by the Member States.[4] Originally public services, such as utilities and employment and health services were thus not the focus of the competition law regime. However, with increasing liberalisation of these services[5] they have, over time, been progressively regarded as economic activities.[6] Therefore, the entities which conduct them, as well as public market regulations regarding such service have been subjected to EU competition law.[7] The aim behind this development has been to achieve the single market in public service sectors by excluding national protectionism.[8] The problem is, however, that such services cannot always both be provided in a competitive market and, at the same time, retain their general interest character including such elements as universal provision, trust based relationships[9] or

---

[4] Schiek 2012, p. 25; Sauter p. 110 seq.

[5] For more on liberalisation tendencies in the Member States, see Vincent-Jones 2006, p. 358 seq.

[6] This is in line with critical political economist assumptions that the European integration project became more neo-liberal in the last quarter of the 20th century and can also be seen as a functional spill-over. For more on integration theory, see Chap. 1, Sect. 1.3.4 above.

[7] For more on the inclusion of public services into EU competition and internal market law see Steyger 2002, p. 275; Prosser 2005, 2010; Neergaard 2011, p. 174 seq; Chalmers et al. 2014, Chapter 25 (online resource), p. 1 seq; Sauter 2015, pp. 12, 18, 125, 222 seq, 228, 233, 238.

[8] In the sphere of the utilities this had led to EU level sectoral approaches. An extreme example of liberalisation in this respect is Directive 2008/6/EC amending Directive 97/67/EC with regard to the full accomplishment of the internal market of Community postal services OJ [2008] L 52/3, which, in Article 1(8) provides that all special and exclusive rights shall be abandoned in postal services. In rare cases, liberalisation has, instead of with national regulation, been met with regulatory failure and the EU legislator intervened due to the cross-border nature of the service as in the case of Regulation 531/2012 on roaming on public mobile communications networks within the Union OJ [2012] L 172/10. See further on the relation between liberalisation, regulation and application of competition law as well as on the sectoral approaches Sauter 2015 p. 12, 32 seq, 125, 133 seq, 222, 225 scq, 231 seq.

[9] On the latter, see Newdick 2007.

equality of access.[10] Therefore, Article 106(2) TFEU offers an exemption for SGEIs in cases where the application of the competition rules obstructs their provision. The importance of Article 106(2) TFEU has increased with more public services being regarded as economic in nature. Nevertheless, placing public services 'in the market' requires a more commercial mode of operation and the exemption is not necessarily always available because the Court sometimes conducts a very strict proportionality test.[11] The rest of this section (Sect. 3.2) is organised as follows: the notion of 'undertaking' (Sect. 3.2.1), the relationship between public regulation of markets and EU competition law (Sect. 3.2.2) and the concept of 'SGEIs' (Sect. 3.2.3) will be analysed before evaluating the position of HEIs in these regards (Sect. 3.2.4).

3.2.1 The Notion of 'Undertaking'

An entity is subject to the Treaty provisions on competition law, if it is an 'undertaking' in the meaning of these provisions. The concept of 'undertaking' is not defined in the Treaty. Instead the definition is to be derived from the Court's case law according to which 'the concept of undertaking encompasses every entity engaged in an economic activity, regardless of the legal status of the entity and the way in which it is financed'.[12] An activity is economic in nature if it consists of 'offering goods or services on a market'[13] which *can*, in principle, be done commercially. All entities engaged in such activities are thus undertakings, irrespective of whether or not the goods or services *have* actually been offered commercially. In particular, it does not matter if the entity is profit-making or not, nor whether or not it forms part of the state's administration. It also does not have to have legal personality, as the legal form is irrelevant for the definition. Therefore, third sector[14] and public sector organisations can be regarded as undertakings even if they do not make a profit and, in the case of public organisations, are financed from taxes or social insurance contributions. Obviously, this broad definition leaves very few activities outside the competition law regime, as it seems hard to imagine an activity that could not, at least in principle, be conducted commercially.[15]

---

[10] Additionally, the question has been raised by Chalmers et al. 2014, Chapter 25 (online resource), p. 36 seq with further references, if liberalisation has actually practically led to more competitive markets and, in effect, to greater consumer welfare or if any such results may have been due to other factors such as technical advances.

[11] Prosser 2005, pp. 544, 549, 560; Prosser 2010, p. 315 seq, 335 seq.

[12] C-41/90 *Höfner* (Judgment of 23 April 1991, EU:C:1991:161) para 21.

[13] 118/85 *Commission v Italy* (Judgment of 16 June 1987, EU:C:1987:283) para 7.

[14] Most commonly defined as neither the public nor the private sector, the third sector (also referred to as, for example, voluntary sector or community sector) is made up of organisations with specific charitable goals which operate on a not-for profit basis. See Wendt and Gideon 2011, p. 255.

[15] On the concept of 'undertaking' see Steyger 2002, p. 276; Sauter 2008, p. 181 seq; Swennen 2008/2009, p. 263 seq, 278 seq; Aicher et al. 2009, para 51, 56 seq, 67 seq; Sauter and Schepel 2009, p. 75 seq, 80 seq, 95, p. 124 seq; Chalmers et al. 2014, p. 999; Jones and Sufrin 2014, p. 127 seq; Sauter 2015, p. 117.

However, the Court has acknowledged two exceptions: the exercise of sovereign power and the offering of services governed by the principle of solidarity. The sovereignty exception applies when an entity acts in the service of the state's prerogatives to conduct acts of official authority, irrespective of whether this authority is executed by a public or private entity.[16] The principle of solidarity[17] exception has been found to apply to national schemes, such as health, pension and accident at work insurance schemes, if contributions were disproportionate to the risks and the benefits paid to the beneficiaries had no relation to the amount of the contribution. The schemes thus involved an element of cross-subsidy where insured persons with higher incomes or constituting lower risks supported those with lower incomes or those suffering from higher risks. Additionally, the Court took aspects such as the public nature and necessity of compulsory schemes to ensure their financial equilibrium into consideration when employing this exception.[18] Without the principle of solidarity, entities operating in such national schemes could be regarded as undertakings.[19] The concept of an undertaking is relative 'in the sense that a given entity might be regarded as an undertaking for one part of its activities while the rest fall outside the competition rules'.[20] Therefore, the CJEU does not consider a whole entity as an undertaking per se, but uses a functional approach to differentiate between its tasks. Only for the economic activities, does the undertaking (as it is then defined), have to comply with the competition rules, unless it is exempted by Article 106(2) TFEU. However, if activities are not severable from the main non-economic activity (such as purchasing inputs for that activity),[21] they might equally be regarded as non-economic.[22]

---

[16] C-364/92 *Eurocontrol* (Judgment of 19 January 1994, EU:C:1994:7) para 19 seq, in particular paras 30 and 31, C-343/95 *Diego Cali v SEPG* (Judgment of 18 March 1997, EU:C:1997:160) para 16 seq, C-113/07 P *SELEX* (Judgment of 26 March 2009, EU:C:2009:191) para 65 seq, C-138/11 *Compass* (Judgment of 12 July 2012, EU:C:2012:449), SA.34646 *The Netherlands E-procurement platform TenderNed* para 67 (the latter is currently being challenged in front of the General Court (T-138/15 *Aanbestedingskalender*)).

[17] For more on the principle of solidarity in competition law see Boeger 2007; Ross 2007, p. 1067 seq.

[18] C-159, 160/91 *Poucet et Pistre* (Judgment of 17 February 1993, EU:C:1993:63) para 18 seq, C-218/00 *Cisal* (Judgment of 22 January 2002, EU:C:2002:36) para 38 seq, C-264, 306, 354, 355/01 *AOK Bundesverband* (Judgment of 16 March 2004, EU:C:2004:150) para 45 seq, C-205/03 P *FENIN* (Judgment of 11 July 2006, EU:C:2006:453) para 25 seq, Commission Decision 2015/248/EU Measures implemented by Slovak Republic for Spoločná zdravotná poisťovňa, a. s. and Všeobecná zdravotná poisťovňa, a. s. OJ [2015] L 41/25.

[19] C-244/94 *FFSA and others* (Judgment of 16 November 1995, EU:C:1995:392) para 15 seq, in particular para 22, C-67/96 *Albany* (Judgment of 21 September 1999, EU:C:1999:430) para 77 seq.

[20] Opinion of the Advocate General in C-475/99 *Ambulanz Glöckner* (Judgment of 25 October 2001, EU:C:2001:577) para 72.

[21] C-205/03 P *FENIN*, Decision 2015/248/EU para 93.

[22] On the exceptions and the functional approach see Steyger 2002, p. 276; Baquero-Cruz 2005, p. 179 seq; Sauter 2008, p. 182 seq; Swennen 2008/2009, p. 263 seq, 278 seq; Aicher et al. 2009, paras 52, 61, 70 seq; Sauter and Schepel 2009, p. 79 seq, 83 seq, 95; Prosser 2010, p. 319 scq; Chalmers et al. 2014, Chapter 25 (online resource), p. 14 seq; Jones and Sufrin 2014, p. 129 seq; Sauter 2015, pp. 18, 111, 118 seq; Szyszczak 2015, p. 681 seq.

In addition to these two exceptions, it also worth mentioning that employees, are generally not considered undertakings.[23] However, it is debated if this applies to employees who do not act as such (i.e. have a certain amount of independence from their employer, bear financial risks and are subject to rivalry). Such employees may potentially be regarded more like the self-employed and thus in consequence as undertakings in some cases.[24]

In summary, for an entity (which is not merely an employee) not to fall under the competition rules, it has to conduct an activity that is, per se, not economic in nature, is part of the state's prerogatives or is organised on the basis of solidarity. Demonstrating the former seems nearly impossible, as it is difficult to imagine which activities might not theoretically be offered on a market. Regarding the exceptions, it appears from case law that the more commercial elements an entity or a system adopts, the more likely it becomes that it will be regarded as an undertaking.

3.2.2 Anti-competitive Regulation of Markets by Member States

It was not only entities providing public services that came under the scrutiny of EU competition law, however, but also public market regulation. Firstly, according to the case law, a general obligation regarding anti-competitive state regulation arises from Article 4(3) TEU which contains the 'principle of sincere cooperation' in achieving the aims of the Treaties. The *effet utile* of competition law would be undermined, according to the Court, if the Member States were allowed to keep in force legislation which allows or even requires undertakings to engage in anti-competitive conduct.[25] There seems to be no public interest exemption from this principle.[26] However, state legislation based on a recommendation by a committee of experts from industry will not be regarded as a decision by an association of undertakings if the experts come to their decision independently from any interested undertakings and if governmental review of the composition of the

---

[23] C-22/98 *Becu* (Judgment of 16 September 1999, EU:C:1999:419) para 26. That then also means that trade unions are not associations of undertakings and, more generally, competition law does not apply to collective agreements (C-67/96 *Albany* para 59).

[24] Lucey 2015.

[25] 13/77 *INNO v ATAB* (Judgment of 16 November 1977, EU:C:1977:185) para 30 seq.

[26] Chalmers et al. 2014, Chapter 25 (online resource), p. 6 suggest that this might change in the future after the Court considered 'ancillary constraints' in C-309/99 *Wouters* (Judgment of 19 February 2002, EU:C:2002:98) as part of Article 101 TFEU. The Court also followed this line of reasoning in C-519/04 P *Meca-Medina* (Judgment of 18 July 2006, EU:C:2006:492). Both cases, however, concerned very specific circumstances and it has to be seen how far this line of reasoning can actually be utilised beyond such cases.

committee and the decision is possible.[27] Such safeguards based on procedure can be used as a defence to show that national law is in the public interest rather than national governments giving into industrial lobbying.[28] The Court has applied Article 4(3) TEU in conjunction with Article 101(1) TFEU only in cases where an actual infringement of competition law by undertakings took place. Review purely of governmental regulation of the market without such an infringement does not seem possible under this provision.[29]

Secondly, Article 106(1) TFEU has led to the opening of markets because it prohibits national measures regarding 'public undertakings and undertakings to which Member States grant special or exclusive rights' to infringe the TFEU. In contrast to Article 4(3) TEU, which is not limited in its substantive scope, Article 106(1) TFEU is thus applicable only to such undertakings.[30] It does not, however, prohibit the existence of these,[31] but only those measures[32] regarding such undertakings which infringe the Treaty. Article 106(1) TFEU has been used to review legislation without an actual infringement by an undertaking having occurred.[33] Whilst Article 4(3) TEU has mostly been employed in cartel cases, the abuse of a dominant position has predominantly been dealt with under Article 106(1) TFEU.[34] In this respect it seems that any legislation containing the threat of putting an undertaking into a position where it is abusing, cannot help but or is likely to abuse its dominance, infringes Article 106(1) TFEU in conjunction with Article 102 TFEU.[35]

---

[27] C-185/91 *Reiff* (Judgment of 17 November 1993, EU:C:1993:886) para 14 seq, case C-35/99 *Arduino* (Judgment of 19 February 2002, EU:C:2002:97) paras 34–37.

[28] Chalmers et al. 2014, Chapter 25 (online resource), p. 5 seq; Sauter 2015, p. 127 seq.

[29] C-2/91 *Meng* (Judgment of 17 November 1993, EU:C:1993:885) para 14 seq. As there was no actual collusion between undertakings in this case, the Court did not find an infringement of Article 4(3) TEU in conjunction with Article 101 TFEU.

[30] On the definition of 'public undertakings and undertakings to which Member States grant special or exclusive rights' see Whish 2015, p. 235 seq.

[31] 155/73 *Sacchi* (Judgment of 30 April 1974, EU:C:1974:40) para 14.

[32] On the definition of 'measures' see Whish 2015, p. 238, who concludes that a wide approach, similar to the approach concerning the definition of the term in respect to the free movement provisions, is envisaged here.

[33] 18/88 *RTT* (Judgment of 13 December 1991, EU:C:1991:474) para 23 seq. In T-169/08 *Greek Lignite* (Judgment of 20 September 2012, EU:T:2012:448) the General Court initially annulled a Commission decision where there was no infringement by an undertaking. However, this was quashed on appeal (C-553/12 P *Greek Lignite* (Judgment of 17 July 2014, EU:C:2014:2083)). Thus it is still possible to act against anticompetitive market regulation by Member States even without an actual infringement by an undertaking. On the case see also Szyszczak 2015, p. 684 seq who argues that the language the Court uses in the appeal case may even present a modernisation and expansion in that it 'provides greater scope to examine the potential effects on competition by the creation and exercise of monopoly/quasi monopoly rights by the State' (quote on p. 686).

[34] See, for example, C-49/07 *MOTOE* (Judgment of 1 July 2008, EU:C:2008:376) para 50.

[35] On Article 106(1) TFEU see Sauter and Schepel 2009, p. 93 seq, 96; Neergaard 2011, p. 182; Chalmers et al. 2014, Chapter 25 (online resource), p. 8 seq; Whish 2015, p. 234 seq.

Article 4(3) TEU and Article 106(1) TFEU may thus render inapplicable such national measures which infringe competition law (or other Treaty provisions). Yet, these provisions have so far been used somewhat more sparingly. Buendia Sierra has in particular criticised a certain reluctance on the side of the Commission to utilise Article 106(1) TFEU to its full potential to review state action[36] and others have discussed that the Court has used these provisions more as a threat to encourage the 'voluntary' opening of markets.[37] In this respect, it has also been remarked that the Court seems less strict in its assessment the more 'public' or 'social' the service and that it sometimes does not seem to go through the effort of demonstrating an infringement with regards to public services at all, but goes straight to examining the exemption under Article 106(2) TFEU.[38]

3.2.3 SGEIs

If public services are regarded as economic, the competition rules have to be complied with unless they can be exempted as SGEIs by Article 106(2) TFEU. However, SGEIs are not a straightforward concept and confusion has arisen in many areas.[39]

3.2.3.1 Terminology

The term SGEIs is, itself, bewildering, since, despite the word 'economic' being part of the term, the interest behind those services[40] is public rather than economic. The criterion 'economic' refers to the fact that these are economic services to start with, as otherwise they would not fall under competition law and thus would not need to be exempted. The term 'services of general interest' (SGIs) is used as an umbrella category for SGEIs and non-economic services by the Commission.[41] According to Hatzopoulos the notion of SGIs seems to correspond with the French 'service public' and the 'overriding principles of general interest'

---

[36] Buendia Sierra 2016.

[37] Chalmers et al. 2014, Chapter 25 (online resource), p. 2, 14.

[38] See Neergaard 2011, p. 183 seq, Chalmers et al. 2014, Chapter 25 (online resource), p. 14 seq with further references, Whish 2015, p. 241 seq.

[39] Steyger 2002, p. 276; Mestmäcker and Schweitzer 2004, §34 para 17; Sauter 2008, pp. 167, 183; Aicher et al. 2009, para 69; Neergaard 2011, p. 183 seq; Whish 2015, pp. 234, 247 seq.

[40] The term 'services' under Article 106(2) TFEU is to be understood in a wider sense than 'services' under Article 57 TFEU to also include the production and distribution of goods. See Mestmäcker and Schweitzer 2004, §34, para 17.

[41] See Communication 'Services of general interest in Europe' OJ [2001] C 17/04 Annex II.

established as a justification in the field of the free movement provisions.[42] The terms 'public services' and 'public service obligations' are not used by the Commission, as it deems them 'ambiguous'.[43] Yet, 'public services' is used as a term by the Court and in literature in the same context as SGIs or SGEIs.[44] The main characteristics of SGIs are universality, equality of access, a certain level of quality, continuity and a public aim.[45]

Additionally, a new category, called 'social services of general interest' (SSGIs), was introduced by the Commission in the early 2000s.[46] The definition of SSGIs is still rather disputed. In its Communication from 2006, the Commission states that 'in addition to health services, which are not covered by this communication, we find two main categories of social services'. These categories are, according to the Commission, social security schemes and 'other essential services provided directly to the person'. In a footnote to the latter category the Commission explains that 'education and training, although they are services of general interest with a clear social function, are not covered by this Communication'.[47] This vague definition has led to different interpretations in the literature; whilst some believe health and education are included in the definition others argue in favour of separate categories, namely health services of general interest (HSGIs) and education and training services of general interest (ETSGIs).[48] Either way, it seems that SSGIs (and, if separate categories, also HSGIs and ETSGIs), comprise services which have a social aim in the broader sense. In them, Member States have primary competences and they are often traditionally regarded as non-economic, but have recently also sometimes been categorised as economic. These services thus seem to contain the unclear cases and seem to be situated somewhat in the middle of SGEIs and non-economic services with overlaps into both. The question of whether or not such services fall under the competition law regime, however, still depends on their classification as economic in nature.[49]

---

[42] Hatzopoulos 2009, p. 226. Regarding the correspondence of the term with the French 'service public' see Mestmäcker and Schweitzer 2004, §34, para 17. See Sauter and Schepel 2009, 89 seq, 95 regarding convergence with internal market reasoning.

[43] See SGEIs in Europe Communication (n 41) Annex II.

[44] Sauter 2015, p. 9.

[45] For more on terminology see Mestmäcker and Schweitzer 2004, § 34, para 17 seq, Sauter 2008, p. 181; Hatzopoulos 2009, p. 225 seq; Neergaard 2011, p. 175 seq; Jones and Sufrin 2014, p. 632 seq; Sauter 2015, p. 10 seq.

[46] See Neergaard 2013, p. 206 who spotted the first use of the term SSGIs in the Commission's Report to the Laeken European Council COM(2001) 598 final, where the term is, however, only mentioned and not further elaborated upon.

[47] Commission Communication 'Implementing the Community Lisbon Programme: Social Services of General Interest in the European Union' COM (2006) 177 final p. 4.

[48] See Neergaard 2013, p. 210 seq. A useful diagram is also provided in Neergaard 2009a, p. 20. Explanations of SGIs, SGEIs, non-economic services, market service and the disputed categories of SSGIs, HSGIs and ETSGIs are provided on the following pages.

[49] See further Neergaard 2009a, p. 19 seq; Neergaard 2013, p. 210 seq, 239 seq; Sauter 2015 p. 17 seq, 28.

3.2.3.2 The Development of SGEIs

Whilst Article 106(2) TFEU has been part of EU law from the very beginning, (then Article 90 EEC), it gained in importance when public services were increasingly subjected to the competition law regime as mentioned above.[50] Neergaard thus describes the provision as being directly in the middle of the diverging interest of market rules and social objectives.[51] With the introduction of what is now Article 14 TFEU (then Article 16 EC) by the Treaty of Amsterdam 1997, the requirement that Member States and the Union ensure that SGEIs are enabled to 'fulfil their missions' has been inserted into the Treaty principles even though the scope seems to have been limited.[52] The Treaty of Lisbon broadened Article 14 TFEU by the insertion that the 'economic and financial conditions' for the provision of such services need to be ensured and a legislative competence in this respect was given to the EU legislator[53] in addition to the competence of the Commission to issue directives and decisions according to Article 106(3) TFEU.[54] Unlike the latter, which has been used for sectoral regulation and the *Altmark* package (discussed in Sect. 3.3.5 below), there seems to be a certain reluctance to use the new competence.[55] It is also stressed in Article 14 TFEU that the legislative competence is to be used 'without prejudice to the competence of the Member States' and Protocol 26 reiterates the wide discretion of the Member States regarding SGEIs (Article 1) and the exclusive competence regarding non-economic services (Article 2). In addition to the Treaties, SGEIs are also mentioned in Article 36 of the Charter of Fundamental Rights of the European Union (Charter), which became legally binding with the Treaty of Lisbon 2007.[56] Aside from the developments in primary law, there have been harmonisation efforts for certain fields of SGEIs in secondary law.[57]

3.2.3.3 The Application of Article 106(2) TFEU

In order for a measure to be exempted by Article 106(2) TFEU, three conditions have to be fulfilled. Firstly, the undertaking in question must have been entrusted

---

[50] Neergaard 2011, p. 176.

[51] Neergaard 2009a, p. 17; Neergaard 2009b; p. 195, Neergaard 2011, p. 175. Similarly Sauter 2008, p. 167.

[52] See Sauter 2008, p. 168 seq, 171 seq; Neergaard 2009b, p. 196 seq; Neergaard 2011, p. 177 seq; Sauter 2015, p. 21.

[53] This competence is, however, limited to passing regulations, in contrast to the proposed provision in the Constitution, which, in Article III-122, referred to 'European laws' in general.

[54] See Sauter 2008, p. 169 seq, 172; Neergaard 2011, p. 179.

[55] See further Sauter 2015 pp. 23, 27, 222, 241.

[56] See Sauter 2008, p. 171 seq; Neergaard 2009b, p. 196 seq; Neergaard 2011, p. 178 seq; Chalmers et al. 2014, Chapter 25 (online resource), p. 26 seq.

[57] For more see Chalmers et al. 2014, Chapter 25 (online resource), p. 28 seq, 36 seq.

with an SGEI by the Member State. The Member States have a wide margin of discretion regarding what they consider to be an SGEI, but, as it is an EU concept, the Commission and the Court can review their decisions for manifest errors[58] and Member States may not abuse the concept of SGEIs to avoid the competition rules.[59] Generally it seems that the service needs to be associated with a public duty and be provided in the general, rather than satisfying only particular, interests. Additionally, a 'uniform' and 'binding nature' of the service seems to be required.[60] These criteria are, however, not interpreted strictly. The 'uniform nature', does not mean that the service has to be supplied in the whole territory of the Member State or be applicable to the whole of the population and the 'binding nature' does not require prescribing the details of the service to the provider.[61] In particular, utilities, telecommunications and transport services are considered to be SGEIs.[62] If they are seen as economic services in the first place, services such as health insurance,[63] pension schemes or services including elements of environmental protection have also been regarded as SGEIs.[64] The undertaking has to be entrusted with the SGEI by the Member State in an official act (for example, by legislation)[65] which also should include a description of the SGEI.[66] The classification of an undertaking as being entrusted with an SGEI is, as when deciding if an entity is an undertaking in the first place, relative.[67] It might therefore be that

---

[58] 10/71 *Muller* (Judgment of 14 July 1971, EU:C:1971:85) para 13 seq, C-67/96 *Albany* para 103 seq and T-17/02 *Olsen* (Judgment of 15 June 2005, EU:T:2005:218) para 216.

[59] T-309/12 *Zweckverband Tierkörperbeseitigung* (Judgment of 16 July 2014 EU:T:2014:676) para 106, T-295/12 *Germany v Commission* (Judgment of 16 July 2014, EU:T:2014:675) para 46.

[60] T-289/03 *BUPA* (Judgment of 12 February 2008, EU:T:2008:29) para 172 seq.

[61] Ibid para 186 seq.

[62] SGEIs in Europe Communication (n 41) Annex II.

[63] On the problematic classification of health care see van de Gronden 2004; Prosser 2010.

[64] See, for example, case T-289/03 *BUPA*.

[65] 10/71 *Muller* (n 58) para 10 seq.

[66] Commission Decision 2012/21/EU on the application of Article 106(2) of the Treaty on the Functioning of the European Union to State aid in the form of public service compensation granted to certain undertakings entrusted with the operation of services of general economic interest OJ [2012] L 7/3 Article 4. In recital 4 of the preamble the Commission refers to the *Altmark* judgment (C-280/00, Judgment of 24 July 2003, EU:C:2003:415) in which the Court required, inter alia, that a public service obligation must be clearly defined for the compensation of such a service not to constitute state aid. The General Court in T-461/13 *Spain v Commission* (Judgment of 26 November 2015, EU:T:2015:891) para 63 seq equally made clear that there needs to be a clearly defined public service obligations that has been entrusted to certain undertakings. The case is currently being appealed (C-81/16 P *Spain v Commission*). See further on relevant case law Szyszczak 2016 (forthcoming).

[67] See, for example, 18/88 *RTT* para 22.

an undertaking provides an SGEI in one market, but is not exempted from the application of competition law in another.[68]

Secondly, according to Article 106(2), the application of the competition rules would have to 'obstruct the performance, in law or fact, of the particular tasks assigned' to the undertaking and the setting aside of the competition rules would have to be proportional to the aim pursued. Concerning the criterion of 'obstruction' it appears that the Court has become much more lenient. Whilst in the initial judgments on the issue the viability of the undertaking had to be threatened in order for its performance to be 'obstructed',[69] the Court, in more recent judgments, deems an 'obstruction' to be present if it would not be possible for the undertaking to perform the particular tasks entrusted to it under 'economically acceptable conditions'.[70] Whilst the Court occasionally conducts a strict proportionality test focussing on necessity,[71] such a strict test is not undertaken in every case. Sometimes the Court does not explicitly conduct a proportionality test at all and sometimes it seems to focus rather on overall proportionality than on strict necessity.[72] Neergaard[73] assumes this might be the case because of the controversial nature of such a strict test and Sauter[74] concludes that the question of EU 'pre-emption' in the field might play a role here.[75]

Finally, the development of trade must not be affected in such a way that it would be contrary to the EU's interests. Obviously, this condition requires more than an 'effect on trade between Member States' since the cross border element is generally necessary for there to be an infringement of the Treaty provisions in the first place as will be discussed below. Thus, if any effect on trade between

---

[68] On the first criterion see further Prosser 2005, p. 550; Sauter 2008 (in particular p. 178 seq on the universal service obligation as part of SGEIs), Neergaard 2009b, p. 211 seq, 219 seq; Neergaard 2011, pp. 185, 191 seq; Chalmers et al. 2014, Chapter 25 (online resource), p. 18 seq; Sauter 2015, p. 10, 13 seq, 27. For a different take on the first criterion see Mestmäcker and Schweitzer 2004, § 34, para 17 seq who argue in favour of a strict European definition and a tight margin of discretion for the Member States.

[69] See, for example, 155/77 *Sacchi* para 15 and C-41/90 *Höfner* para 24 both referring to the 'incompatibility' of the undertaking to comply with competition rules and to fulfil its tasks.

[70] See, for example, C-475/99 *Ambulanz Glöckner* para 57.

[71] See, for example, C-203/96 *Dusseldorp* (Judgment of 25 June 1998, EU:C:1998:316) para 67 where the Court held that the national government had to show that the SGEI mission, if given at all, 'cannot be achieved equally well by other means' for the measure to be proportional.

[72] See, for example, C-475/99 *Ambulanz Glöckner* para 62 seq. Whilst the Court does not explicitly conduct a proportionality test, and, even if it does, it is not a very strict one focussing on necessity, it seems to come to the conclusion that the extension of a right into a connected market would be disproportionate if demand in the connecting market could not be satisfied.

[73] Neergaard 2011, p. 190 seq.

[74] Sauter 2008, p. 186; Sauter 2015, p. 227.

[75] See, for a more detailed analysis of the second criterion, Mestmäcker and Schweitzer 2004, § 34, para 19, Prosser 2005, p. 550; Sauter 2008; Neergaard 2009b, p. 211 seq; Prosser 2010, p. 325; Neergaard 2011, p. 185 seq, 190 seq; Chalmers et al. 2014, Chapter 25 (online resource), pp. 18, 21 seq; Sauter 2015, pp. 27, 227.

Member States meant that the exemption could not be applied, this would render the exemption useless.[76] Yet, what *exactly* this condition pertains to, is, thus far, not entirely clear.[77]

3.2.3.4 Interim Conclusion on SGEIs

Generally it appears that the Court's approach to SGEIs has become less stringent in recent years. This might be connected to the fact that the Court seems to have been stricter regarding the question whether a situation falls under a certain EU law provision (i.e. whether an entity is an undertaking) in the first place. If EU law is more frequently held to be applicable, the exemption becomes more relevant and needs to be interpreted less strictly to allow, at least, a certain balance between economic and public interests. However, this field of law is still developing, so changes in this respect might occur.[78] In addition, despite this potential leniency (at least in areas of primary responsibility), the fact that a particular SGEI needs to be entrusted to an undertaking makes this exemption much more limited than the broad possibility of exemption on public interest considerations in the area of free movement law[79] and, as will be seen below (Sects. 3.3.2–3.3.5), the individual provisions mainly contain efficiency based exemptions. Therefore, there is a real potential for public services to fall under the competition provision if they are regarded as economic activity.

3.2.4 HEIs

Traditionally public HEIs have not been regarded as undertakings. Instead they were seen as state institutions administering a scheme funded by general taxation

---

[76] See C-157/94 *Commission v Netherlands* (Judgment of 23 October 1997,EU:C:1997:499) para 67. In this case a Dutch company's exclusive right of electricity imports had been challenged by the Commission. A potential effect on trade between Member States was given, as it would have been theoretically possible that the exclusive right led to reduced imports compared to a situation where every potential customer could have imported electricity directly. As the Commission had not shown, however, that 'the development of intra-Community trade in electricity had been and continued to be affected to an extent contrary to the interests of the Community' the Court dismissed the case.

[77] For more on the final criterion see Neergaard 2009b, p. 211 seq; Neergaard 2011, p. 185; Chalmers et al. 2014, Chapter 25 (online resource), p. 18 seq.

[78] See Neergaard 2009b, p. 223 seq; Neergaard 2011, pp. 184, 194 seq; Sauter 2015, p. 155.

[79] Szyszczak 2016 (forthcoming).

to provide education and research in the public interest.[80] The students were not deemed to be consumers, they did not pay fees (or at least not significant ones) and research was not conducted for a customer but was, as the Research Framework phrases it, 'independent R&D for more knowledge and better understanding'.[81] However recent developments suggest that not necessarily all activities of HEIs fall under these definitions of non-economic teaching and research activities any longer.[82]

Universities would be conducting an economic activity if they provided research or education (or additional activities, such as offering accommodation or selling certain products) on a market. The mere aim of increasing student numbers as such is not significant to show that there is an economic activity occurring. Instead a service would have to be provided on a market in the interest of the consumer by a potentially profit-oriented entity.[83] Whilst the absence of profit could be an indicator that a given entity does not operate on a market, it is insufficient in itself. Similarly, cross-subsidy of possible profits into other charitable parts of its activities would not hinder the classification as an undertaking generally. Thus non-profit and not-for-profit entities can be included in the definition if the services they provide could theoretically be conducted in a market setting. Likewise,

---

[80] As regards education see Commission Communication on the application of the European Union State aid rules to compensation granted for the provision of services of general economic interest OJ [2012] C 8/02 para 26 seq and Commission Decision 2006/225/EC on the aid scheme implemented by Italy for the reform of the training institutions OJ [2006] L 81/13 para 41 seq. In both these, the Commission explicitly imported the reasoning from internal market law in the field of education into competition and state aid law. In internal market law the Court had established in C-263/86 *Humbel* (Judgment of 27 September 1988, EU:C:1988:451) and C-109/92 *Wirth* (Judgment of 7 December 1993, EU:C:1993:916) that public education is generally not a service in the meaning of the Treaty (see further Chap. 2, Sect. 2.3.2 above). Similarly, in two cases of notified state aid concerning the Czech Republic (State aid NN54/2006-*Czech Republic Přerov Logistics College*) and Hungary (State aid NN343/2008-*Hungary College of Nyíregyháza Partium Knowledge Centre*) the Commission found the activities of colleges to be of a non-economic nature. As regards research see the Communication on state aid and SGEIs mentioned earlier in this note in para 29 as well as Commission Communication 'Framework for State aid for research and development and innovation' OJ [2014] C 198/01 (hereinafter Research Framework) para 19 where the principle that research in the public interest in public HEIs is usually not an economic activity is established.

[81] Research Framework para 19(a).

[82] For more on recent developments in the HEIs sector see Chap. 1 (Sect. 1.3.3). On the classification of HEIs, see also Steyger 2002, p. 275 seq, 277 seq; Swennen 2008/2009, pp. 265, 268, 279; Gideon 2012, p. 173 seq.

[83] In the field of the free movement provisions, the emphasis is more on the aspect of remuneration while in competition law the existence of a market and the potential profit-making ability are the key factors (see similar Odudu 2011, p. 235). However, the changing definition in the field of the free movement provisions (Chap. 2, Sect. 2.3.2 above) and the fact that remuneration was found there can be an indicator that a market is developing, that there is the potential to make a profit and that the service is thus of an economic nature. For example, in C-153/02 *Neri* (Judgment of 13 November 2003, EU:C:2003:614) the Court in para 39 explicitly stated that the 'organisation for remuneration of university courses is an economic activity'.

as has been seen above, the public character of an entity does not hinder the categorisation as an undertaking. Instead, the classification solely depends on the activities' (potentially) economic character. Whether or not that is the case has to be evaluated on a case by case basis.[84]

3.2.4.1 Higher Education

As regards higher education activities, their classification as economic activities very much depends on the way a system is constructed and the likeliness increases with further commodification. The Commission, for example, stated in Decision 2006/225/EC that

> [...] the concept of economic activity is an evolving concept linked in part to the political choices of each Member State. Member States may decide to transfer to undertakings certain tasks traditionally regarded as falling within the sovereign powers of States. Member States may also create the conditions necessary to ensure the existence of a market for a product or service that would otherwise not exist. The result of such state intervention is that the activities in question become economic and fall within the scope of the competition rules.[85]

Similarly, in its Communication on state aid and SGEIs, the Commission stated that 'in certain Member States public institutions can also offer educational services which, due to their nature, financing structure and the existence of competing private organisations, are to be regarded as economic'.[86] Somewhat confusingly in para 31 of its Notice on the Notion of State Aid,[87] the Commission after reiterating this distinction,[88] continues that 'education for more and better skilled human resources' by 'universities and research organisations' would 'in the light of the principles set out in [the previous paragraphs] [...] fall outside the scope of the State aid rules'. On the one hand, this may appear as if all 'education for more and better skilled human resources' by universities falls outside the state aid rules. On the other hand, this paragraph refers to the previous ones where the distinction made by the Court and the Commission in previous judgments and secondary law has been set out. One may thus conclude that only the non-economic activities educational activities are meant. Otherwise, that would be a new and significant exemption from the state aid rules which would seem somewhat at odds

---

[84] See also Steyger 2002, p. 277 seq; Swennen 2008/2009, p. 265 seq, 268 seq, 275, 279 seq; Gideon 2012, p. 173 seq, Gideon 2015a, p. 1053 seq; Gideon 2015b 29, p. 59 seq, Gideon and Sanchez-Graells 2016, p. 30 seq. For an analysis of the question as to whether an entity is an undertaking in the field of health care (as a similar field of public service provisions), see Prosser 2010; p. 335, Odudu 2011.

[85] See Decision 2006/225/EC para 50.

[86] Communication on state aid and SGEIs (n 80) para 28.

[87] Commission Notice on the notion of State aid as referred to in Article 107(1) of the Treaty on the Functioning of the European Union OJ [2016] C 262/1.

[88] Ibid para 30.

with previous developments, though it may have been purposely created when it became apparent that the previously made distinction in combination with ongoing commodification could lead to significant spill-over. In any case, this only concerns the scope of the state aid rules and does not affect the categorisation as economic and non-economic per se for which the principle still applies that the more market-like structures a system adopts, the more likely it becomes that the teaching activities will be regarded as economic in nature.

Changes in the way in which a Member State organises its HEI system (namely by integrating more market like structures) can thus lead to a more general classification of HEIs as undertakings. For example, in the UK students are paying around £9000 a year in public universities and the very aim of the policy changes since Browne report[89] is to make them customers and to create a marketplace for higher education.[90] Taking this into consideration, it seems conceivable that HEIs of such systems will be regarded as undertakings for their educational activities.[91] Indeed, the former national competition authority of the UK, the Office of Fair Trading (OFT), has conducted a Call for Information on the English higher education sector to evaluate the competition situation after the reforms of the last few years. As it was phrased by Carmen Suarez from the OFT 'clearly the Government reforms put an emphasis on choice and competition so there should be no surprise that the competition and consumer body looks at the sector'.[92]

Whilst the classification of teaching activities as economic in many other HEI settings might presently still not generally be given, there might, due to the relative concept of undertaking, nevertheless be individual teaching activities that do classify as economic in nature and the number of such activities may increase with further commodification. An indicator that an economic activity is being conducted could be seen in the fact that private for-profit providers are operating on a specific market. Public HEIs providing services on such a market could then be considered as undertakings for those activities. For example, a business school in a university could be seen as competing with private business schools even if the rest of the teaching activities of the public university are to be regarded as non-economic, since in such cases there exists a profitable market for this particular service.[93]

---

[89] Browne et al. 2010.

[90] These policy changes are supposed to be taken even further into the direction of a market place with the new Higher Education and Research Bill currently debated in the UK parliament as outlined in the UK government's Green and White Papers (see BIS 2015, 2016).

[91] See also Gideon and Sanchez-Graells 2016, p. 30 seq.

[92] Suarez 2014, p. 8 of the conference proceedings.

[93] See also Swennen 2008/2009, pp. 266, 268, 275 seq with examples of national cases, 279 seq. Steyger 2002, p. 278 seq also discusses in how far HEIs might be undertakings, but differs on the point that the concept of undertaking is relative. On p. 278 she states: 'Under community law, the entity as a whole will be seen as such undertaking. Contrary to national law, there is no separation of the commercial activity from the government activity'.

3.2.4.2 Research

Already in the previous version of the Research Framework,[94] the Commission acknowledged in Section 3.1.2 that research organisations such as HEIs might be conducting economic activities if they are 'renting out infrastructure, supplying services to business undertakings or performing contract research' which has later been reinforced in the Communication on state aid and SGEIs.[95] During the revision process of the Research Framework, the Commission in its 2011 Staff Working Paper[96] as well as in the 2012 Issue Paper on the revision of the Research Framework[97] acknowledged that this separation had become more important and needed clarification. The new Research Framework now defines non-economic research as 'independent R&D for more knowledge and better understanding' including such research as part of an effective collaboration.[98] The Research Framework provides further that 'dissemination of research results on a non-exclusive and non-discriminatory basis, for example through teaching' and publication are non-economic activities. Also generally of a non-economic character are 'knowledge transfer activities' by, jointly with or on behalf of (if contracted out by open tender) the research organisation (here HEI)[99] if all profits are re-invested into the primary activities.[100]

In the revision process certain areas had particularly been considered as needing clarification. The Issue Paper, for example, pointed out that the simple 'labelling' of an activity as 'collaborative research' does not make it non-economic, but that it depends on the actual activity conducted.[101] In the new Research Framework the clarification on collaborations can now be found in para 15(h) and para 27 saying that effective collaboration involves that parties 'jointly define the scope of the project, contribute to its implementation and share its risks,[[102]] as

---

[94] Community framework for state aid for research and development and innovation OJ [2006] C 323/01 (previous Research Framework).

[95] Communication on state aid and SGEIs (n 80) para 30.

[96] European Commission 2011, p. 8.

[97] European Commission 2012, p. 7 seq.

[98] Research Framework para 19(a).

[99] A research organization under the Research Framework is 'an entity (such as universities, [...]), irrespective of its legal status (organised under public or private law) or way of financing, whose primary goal is to independently conduct [...] research [...] or to widely disseminate the results of such activities by way of teaching, publication or knowledge transfer' which must not give 'undertakings that can exert a decisive influence [...] [on the research organisation] preferential access to the results generated' (Research Framework para 15(ee)).

[100] Research Framework para 19(b).

[101] European Commission 2012, p. 8.

[102] However, one party can bear the financial risk by itself, an addition which had not been contained in the first draft of the new Research Framework (Paper of the services of DG Competition containing a draft Framework for state aid for research and development and innovation of 19 December 2013).

well as its results', while 'contract research and provision of research services are not considered forms of collaboration' no matter what the parties might label them.[103]

As regards knowledge transfer, the Issue Paper had stated that this can amount to an economic activity if exclusive or if arising from work outside the 'primary non-economic activities'.[104] However, the classification of knowledge transfer activities has become somewhat confusing in the actual new Research Framework. While the description of non-economic activities as regards knowledge transfer in para 19(b) (stated above) as such is similar to the old version, a new, very broad, definition of 'knowledge transfer' has been added in para 15(v). Accordingly, 'knowledge transfer' is 'any process which has the aim of acquiring, collecting and sharing explicit and tacit knowledge, including skills and competence in both economic and non-economic activities such as research collaborations, consultancy, licensing, spin-off creation, publication and mobility of researchers and other personnel involved in those activities [emphasis added]'. The combined reading of paras 19(b) and 15(v) seems to suggest that, while knowledge transfer can generally be of an economic nature, it is always going to be regarded as non-economic if conducted by a research organisation and if the profits are re-invested. Yet, this appears strange, as it would then per se exclude consultancy, licensing, spin-off creation and staff exchanges from economic activities. Consultancy, for example, has previously widely been regarded as an economic activity, as it is a service provided for a recipient who usually pays for it and which could be (and sometimes is) conducted on a market in competition with private sector competitors.[105] Indeed, the Court in *University of Cambridge*,[106] a public procurement case, considers income from research services, consultancy and public conference organisation, etc. as contractual income for the purposes of public procurement law. One may draw the analogy here that this would also have to be regarded as an economic activity then. If the combined reading of paras 19(b) and 15(v) would render all such activities as per se non-economic if profits are reinvested this also seems to contradict the differentiation made in the Issue Paper. It would appear that either the Commission purposely substantially broadened the scope of what is to be regarded as non-economic in nature here (perhaps to accommodate European research policy which encourages such activities)[107] or this in fact rather refers to particular areas of knowledge transfer (e.g. intellectual property right (IPR)

---

[103] This distinction has been made even clearer since the draft Research Framework (n 102) where it had just mentioned subcontracting not being collaboration.

[104] European Commission 2012, p. 7 seq.

[105] Section 3.1.1 of the previous version of the Research Framework did also not mention consultancy as a technology transfer activity.

[106] C-380/98 *University of Cambridge* (Judgment of 3 October 2000, EU:C:2000:529) paras 24–26.

[107] See Chap. 2, Sects. 2.2.1.3 and 2.2.2 above.

exploitation)[108] which are based on non-economic research activities and are non-exclusive (thus generally excluding consultancy work, for example). In the latter case, which seems to fit better with the overall conception of competition law and the declared intention of the Commission in the Issue Paper, the revision of the Research Framework does not seem to have achieved its goal to clarify the distinction between economic and non-economic knowledge transfer 'in a clearer and more comprehensive way, in order to provide a maximum of legal certainty'.[109] One thing that does, in any case, seem clear is that, if the exploitation is not handled by, with or on behalf of the HEI and/or all profits are not reinvested (e.g. when venture capital firms are brought on-board), this would need to be regarded as economic in nature.

Finally, an entirely new addition to the section on non-economic activities is para 20 of the new Research Framework on purely ancillary activities. Accordingly, if a non-economic activity by a research organisation requires a merely ancillary economic activity, this may be regarded as a whole and as such fall outside the state aid rules if the economic activity is limited in scope (less than 20 %).[110] This section is equally a bit unclear. It can be assumed, however, that this does not take all research organisations which conduct less than 20 % of non-economic activities automatically out of the state aid frame. Firstly, para 20 talks about an organisation which conducts 'a non-economic activity' which seems to point to either a specific activity or an organisation that just conducts one activity which is not the case for most research organisations and, especially, not for HEIs, though it may well be for research infrastructures. Indeed, the example given in the competition policy brief on the new state aid rules for research and development[111] is that of a large research infrastructure mainly used for non-economic research which conducts certain economic activities 'that are inseparable from its predominant area of activity'. This focus on the research infrastructure may suggest that para 20 has been inserted mainly with research infrastructures in mind. This would be supported by the Issue Paper where the concept of ancillary activities first appeared in context with revisions of the rules on research infrastructures.[112] Accordingly, it was planned to widen the application of the framework to research infrastructures generally (previously it had been limited to situations where the infrastructure construction was in itself research or part of an innovation cluster) and then to differentiate between economic and non-economic activities.[113] More specifically, research infrastructures owned by a research organisa-

---

[108] Licensing and spin-offs creation were the examples named for potentially non-economic knowledge transfer in Section 3.1.1.1 of the previous Research Framework.

[109] European Commission 2012, p. 8.

[110] Interestingly, in the first draft of the new Research Framework, the threshold was only 15 %. See draft Framework (n 102) para 20.

[111] European Commission 2014, p. 3.

[112] European Commission 2012, p. 2, 10 seq.

[113] The differentiation between economic and non-economic research infrastructure as such can now also be found in the new Notice on the Notion of State Aid (n 87) in para 218.

tion should be presumed as non-economic if they are in the relevant field of activity of a research organisation, are primarily used for non-economic purposes and any potential access for other parties is non-exclusive. Here, the concept of the ancillary activities first appeared (in nearly the same terms as in para 20 of the new Research Framework). One may thus assume that this concept was envisioned for research infrastructures, where it seems to fit in more clearly, and was then broadened to also include research organisations where these conduct a single activity. Such an interpretation would thus mean that not all research organisations and certainly not HEIs could per se be taken out of the state aid frame if they conduct less than 20 % of economic activities.

Secondly, para 20 provides that the activity must be purely ancillary ('correspond to an activity that is directly related to and necessary for the operation of the research organisation or research infrastructure or intrinsically linked to its main non-economic use') which is hardly the case for all economic activities (e.g. contract research). In the new Notice on the Notion of State Aid[114] an example given is the renting out of laboratories or equipment to industrial 'partners'. In the footnote of that paragraph the difference is made between strictly ancillary and secondary economic activities and it is made clear that the latter are economic. This and the use of the term 'partners' would imply a strong link to the non-economic activity such as a situation where a collaborative non-economic project is being conducted and the partner rents the equipment/ laboratory to conduct its part of the project rather than general renting out of infrastructure to undertakings.[115] Thirdly, it says further that 'the Commission will consider that to be the case where the economic activity consumes exactly the same inputs (such as materials, equipment, labour and fixed capital) as the non-economic activities'. This seems equally not the case for all economic activities as for certain projects additional staff will be hired and the whole point of contract research is that it is funded from external capital. This might rather point to a case where, for example, a product is created through a teaching measure (e.g. an art student creates a piece of art as part of their coursework) and this is then sold. Fourthly, it would seem at odds with the whole logic of competition law and the market liberalisation agenda if whole organisations were taken out of the state aid frame despite conducting 20 % of economic activities unless very specific circumstances were applicable. If that would have been the intention, the Commission could have just stated clearly in the Research Framework that, if in a public research organisation the economic

---

[114] Notice on the Notion of State Aid (n 87) para 207.

[115] Similarly, in T-347/09 *Germany v Commission* (Judgment of 12 September 2013, EU:T:2013:418) the General Court states in para 34 that the link between activities is to be examined in each individual case to establish if they can be regarded as activities ancillary to the non-economic activities or have to be considered economic in nature ('Daher ist zu prüfen, ob die [...] Tätigkeiten mit den Hauptaufgaben der Naturschutzorganisationen, die ausschließlich sozialer Natur sind, zusammenhängen oder ob sie diesen Rahmen sprengen und Tätigkeiten wirtschaftlicher Natur darstellen. Entgegen dem Vorbringen der Bundesrepublik Deutschland ist es in jedem Einzelfall erforderlich').

activities took up less than 20 %, the whole organisation was to be regarded as only conducting non-economic activities. It would not have to go through the length of elaborating about the ancillary nature of specific economic activities. It thus seems to follow that this provision does not take HEIs per se out of the state aid frame if they conduct less than 20 % of economic activities. Instead this only seems to concern certain activities related to the main activity, while other economic activities will still fall within the state aid rules. In any case, the Research Framework does not actually provide that such ancillary activities would be non-economic, but merely that they 'may fall outside State aid rules'. Therefore, the other competition provisions would still apply regardless.

Overall, as regards research in HEIs, it seems clear that contract research and research services are economic activities (for example, a research institute in a university providing research for a private business or research commissioned from a university by the state). Whether or not a research activity qualifies as a research service, depends on the facts (does the receiving undertaking specify the terms, own the results, carry the risk, etc.) and not on how it is labelled by the providing HEI. Thus, the more externally pre-defined the research and the expected results and the more of the results are to be received by the other party, the likelier it is that a research project qualifies as an economic activity.[116] Equally renting out infrastructure would be an economic activity[117] and, arguably, and in light of the Court's elaborations in *University of Cambridge*, so would consultancy services, despite the ambiguity in the new Research Framework. Furthermore, other areas of knowledge transfer are economic in nature if the exploitation is not handled by, with or on behalf of the research organisation and/or not all profits are reinvested (e.g. when a venture capital firm is involved). Research that could be classified as economic under these definitions has increasingly been encouraged by EU and national research policies and has become more common in European HEIs.[118] For all such economic research activities the HEI in question would be an undertaking and fall under the competition rules.

3.2.4.3 Interim Conclusion on HEIs

Increasing commodification of HEIs in Europe makes it more likely that competition law becomes applicable to their teaching and research activities. In such cases, it would normally be the HEI which would be the undertaking. University associations (e.g. the Russell Group in the UK) do not usually have sufficient ties as regards ownership and control with the HEIs they represent to be regarded as a

---

[116] Research Framework paras 21, 25, 27 (and 15).

[117] Ibid para 21.

[118] On commodification in HEIs in general see Chap. 1 (Sect. 1.3.3) and on further developments in the Member States under scrutiny see Chap. 4. See also Swennen 2008/2009, pp. 271, 275 with further references, Gideon 2012, p. 173; Gideon 2015a, p. 1046 seq; Gideon 2015b.

single economic unit,[119] though they could be an association of undertakings inducing collusion under Article 101 TFEU (e.g. by information exchange about prices or other confidential information) which will be implemented at the individual HEI level as will be discussed below (Sect. 3.3.2). While individual institutes are likely to mostly not be independent enough to be regarded as an undertaking separately from the HEI, individual academics may potentially be under specific circumstances (i.e. if they conduct services for a fee, bear the risk of the transactions and compete excessively for the contracts).[120] However, in most circumstances, one would have to assume that it is the HEI which would be the undertaking for the purposes of competition law.

If HEIs are regarded as undertakings and are in danger of infringing competition law, one would have to raise the question of whether they could be exempted under Article 106(2) TFEU. That would mean that the specific task would still fall under their general interest obligation (research in the public interest and teaching) and could not be achieved under economically acceptable conditions if the competition rules were to be enforced. This would, however, depend on the individual case. It would not be possible for a Member State to simply declare all tasks undertaken by HEIs as SGEIs, but a specific SGEI would have to be entrusted to them. Additionally, the proportionality requirement might necessitate questioning whether less severe measures could have been used and the demand also has to be met in markets for which exclusive rights are granted. Finally, intra-Union trade must not be affected to an extent contrary to the Union's interest. It is, however, thus far not quite clear what the latter criterion entails.[121]

3.2.5 Interim Conclusion

With the liberalisation of ever more public services, an increasing number of activities have been classified as economic activities and competition law has therefore been applied to them. This led to the exemption in Article 106(2) TFEU playing a more significant role and the Court seemingly becoming slightly more relaxed in the application of the exemption (e.g. it only requires that a measure allows an undertaking to conduct its task under 'economically acceptable conditions' rather than requiring the viability of the undertaking to be threatened). Nevertheless, 'by applying exceptions instead of ruling activities out of bonds, the authorities involved evidently gain leverage over the undertakings/entities involved'.[122]

---

[119] On the concept of a single economic unit under EU competition law see further Jones and Sufrin 2014, p. 137 seq.

[120] See Lucey 2015 on the possibility of employees being regarded as undertakings.

[121] Also on SGEIs and HEIs Steyger 2002, p. 278 seq; Swennen 2008/2009, p. 266; Gideon 2012, pp. 175, 183 seq; Gideon 2015b, 62.

[122] Sauter 2015, p. 122. See also ibid pp. 118, 227.

Neither research in the public interest in public HEIs nor education has traditionally been regarded as an economic service. However, the Court has, in more recent judgments regarding the free movement provisions, declared primarily privately financed education to be a service. The Commission has, over the last decade, stated in a couple of documents that it intends to import the reasoning developed in internal market law into competition law and that the classification of an educational activity as economic or not is not a fixed definition. Instead it is linked to the way in which the Member States organise their systems. If market mechanisms are introduced, the activities can become economic activities. A very similar distinction is made for research in the new Research Framework (though the new version of the framework has also created some confusion as to some of the details). If, therefore, HEIs can be regarded as undertakings for certain activities, they have to comply with the competition rules unless they can be exempted by Article 106(2) TFEU. The ongoing commodification of higher education and research in many Member States makes it seem likely that certain activities in public HEIs, and, in some Member States, potentially the whole higher education system, could already be regarded as economic. This tendency may increase in the future. HEIs would thus have to be prepared to take competition law into account.

3.3 Consequences Resulting from the Application of EU Competition Law on HEIs

The goals of competition law are a controversial field and depend, inter alia, on the school of thought one is following. While economic efficiency and consumer welfare (in the more general sense rather than actual consumer protection) are more widely acknowledged goals, some schools of thought follow broader notions and aim at more generally protecting the competitive process which sometimes may include protecting competitors.[123] In the EU context, market integration has equally always been an, albeit controversial, aim.[124] Despite the differences, it seems clear that the original focus of competition law were rather private companies than public services. Due to the general interest objectives that public services pursue, application of competition law to the latter may lead to tensions. The aim of the following sections is to explore possible consequences of EU competition law for HEIs.

EU competition and state aid law are located in Title VII, Chap. 1, Articles 101–109 TFEU. The substantive provisions are Article 101 TFEU (prohibiting any collusion between undertakings which negatively impacts on competition),

---

[123] Monti 2007, p. 53 seq; Greaves and Scicluna 2010, p. 15; Chalmers et al. 2014, p. 944 seq; Jones and Sufrin 2014, p. 21 seq.

[124] Odudu 2010; Chirita 2014; Sauter 2015, p. 113.

Article 102 TFEU (forbidding the abuse of a dominant market position) and Article 107 TFEU (disallowing state aid). Furthermore, mergers between undertakings are subject to EU merger control if they have a Union dimension. In the following, after some initial deliberations on market definition (Sect. 3.3.1), these provisions will be explored further with regards to potential constraints for HEIs (Sects. 3.3.2–3.3.5). This does not entail that the application of competition law could not also have positive effects in some cases, for example, when HEIs fix prices at an unreasonably high level. However, these are consequences envisaged by competition law, while this subchapter is aiming at illuminating potential unforeseen (negative) consequences.

3.3.1 Market Definition

As will be seen below, the application of both the competition rules and certain exemptions often depends on the undertakings holding a certain market share. Therefore, before moving on to the competition law provisions, it is necessary to briefly sketch the subject of market definition in this respect.[125]

To determine the relevant market, one has to evaluate both the product and the geographical market.[126] The product market is defined by examining product interchangeability and the concept of the geographical market is based on homogeneity of the conditions of competition.[127] When evaluating the relevant market the Commission mainly examines 'demand substitution'.[128] 'Supply substitution' might be considered only in specific cases where an undertaking can easily produce a variety of products which from a demand perspective are not interchangeable.[129] The third competitive constraint, 'potential competition', will only be evaluated at a later stage if necessary.[130] In order to assess demand substitution, the SNIP (small but significant and non-transitory increase in price) test is used. This test asks whether the consumers would switch to a different product or receive the same product from a different region if the price of the original product is increased.[131] All products which would be bought as an alternative and all regions, from which the products would be received, would be part of the same market.[132]

---

[125] See also Amato and Farbmann 2010, p. 8 seq; Greaves and Scicluna 2010, p. 16.

[126] Commission Notice 'on the definition of the relevant market for the purposes of Community Competition law' OJ [1997] C 372/5 para 9.

[127] Ibid para 7 seq.

[128] Ibid para 13 seq. If the concentration is on the side of the buyer the same test is used to find out alternative supply routes (para 17).

[129] Ibid para 20 seq.

[130] Ibid para 24 seq.

[131] Ibid para 15 seq.

[132] On market definition see also Amato and Farbmann 2010, p. 9 seq.

Regarding the product market from a demand perspective this would mean for HEIs that the market for research would have to be separated from the higher education market. Furthermore, undergraduate education, taught postgraduate and postgraduate research education would all constitute separate markets. One would also generally assume that education taking place in different languages is not interchangeable and thus that every language forms an independent market (with perhaps the exception of English). Additionally, every subject will constitute a separate market since a course or research in electrical engineering, for example, is hardly interchangeable with those activities in philosophy. However, aside from these obvious considerations, it is difficult to determine the product market. The question could, for example, be if courses in electrical engineering would be regarded as interchangeable with other engineering courses and thus be part of the market for higher education in engineering in general or form an individual product market. The type of institution might also play a role. In Germany, for example, the *Fachhochschulen* (a more vocational type of HEI) might not be considered to be in the same market as universities, inter alia, as their degrees do not necessarily allow postgraduate studies.[133] This might be similar in other Member States where a binary system exists. Even in England, where the distinction has been abandoned[134] and the market opened to a variety of alternative providers, HEIs[135] might nevertheless not necessarily be regarded as interchangeable by consumers due to questions of prestige. On the other hand, as regards such detailed questions it has to be born in mind that not the average consumer's perspective is decisive, but that a significant number of the marginal consumers considering a course or an institution as an alternative is sufficient to broaden a market. For research market definition is complicated even more by increasing specialisation and specification, since every level of specification could potentially be regarded as a separate market for a consumer requiring a very specific piece of research.[136]

Market definition becomes even more complex when defining the relevant geographical market. In particular regarding the education of undergraduates, who might prefer to stay close to their parents' homes, one might wonder if the geographical market might be limited to one city, one area or at least one Member State. The cases of Belgium and Austria[137] have, however, shown that at least in the markets for medical education in the German and French languages, the

---

[133] In the German federalist system this is a matter of the federal German states and thus provisions concerning this will be found in state laws. See, for example, § 65 *Bremisches Hochschulgesetz* (Bremen HEIs Act).

[134] See Chap. 4 (Sect. 4.2) below.

[135] The market is to be opened further to alternative providers in the future (see BIS 2016, p. 21 seq).

[136] See also on the product market in respect to HEIs Amato and Farbmann 2010, p. 9 seq; Gideon 2012, p. 176 seq.

[137] See Chap. 2 (Sect. 2.3.1.2) above.

geographical market went beyond the borders of the Member States. With the encouragement of educational mobility, the harmonisation of degree structures and a growing number of courses being offered in English, it is likely that markets will increasingly exists across borders. On the other hand, views (whether founded or not) on quality of higher education systems in some Member States might play a limiting role in defining the geographical market. Regarding research, markets are even more likely to exist across borders, as only feasibility of transport, as well as the price and quality of the services play a role rather than emotional considerations.[138]

If one considers supply substitution (the question of how easily an HEI could switch between different 'products' even if they are not interchangeable from a demand side perspective), this might lead to undergraduate and postgraduate taught education being considered as one market, as it might be easily possible for HEIs to switch between them. Postgraduate research studies, on the other hand, may have to be regarded separately due to the special position between student and researcher inherent in PhD students.[139] Additionally, postgraduate research education requires a higher staff-student ratio and in some Member States only specific members of academic staff are allowed to supervise such students at all. Finally, in certain subjects, more laboratories could be required. Therefore it would be more difficult to switch 'production' in this respect. It might also be possible that from a supply substitution perspective, sub-subjects which are not interchangeable for the 'consumer' (student or research client), are easily interchangeable for the 'producer' and could thus be regarded as one market. Finally, the geographical extent of supply might be easily broadened, for example, through distance learning options which could lead to a bigger market.[140]

To make this more accessible, an attempt should be made to illustrate this with a few hypothetic scenarios from the HEI sector. Very specialised research in the medical field might, for example, be regarded as a market independent from general medical research. This market might thus just consist of a very limited number of HEIs and/or research institutes which then would each have a very large market share. To illustrate the point further, postgraduate research degree studies in 'oriental philology' in the Dutch/Flemish language shall be considered as another example of a small market. Higher education in the Dutch/Flemish language is only provided by HEIs in the Netherlands and Flemish HEIs in Belgium, not all of which are necessarily able to provide doctorates. This would reduce the

---

[138] See also Amato and Farbmann 2010, p. 9 seq; Greaves and Scicluna 2010, p. 20 seq.

[139] In some Member States, such as the Netherlands, PhD researchers are traditionally regarded and treated as staff and earn a salary (though the Netherlands also offer other 'pathways' by now). See VSNU (vereniging van universiteiten—association of universities in the Netherlands), (2016) Education at Dutch universities. http://www.vsnu.nl/nl_NL/education-at-dutch-universities-en.html. Accessed 11 March 2016. In other Member States, such as England, they are regarded as more akin to students.

[140] See also Amato and Farbmann 2010, p. 10.

number of potential providers to a small number of universities, not all of which necessarily teach 'oriental philology'. These universities are, therefore, also likely to have big market shares. On the other hand, subjects such as business administration at taught postgraduate level are widely taught and often in English. Educational mobility at the master's level is considered to be generally higher than at the undergraduate level and there are a variety of distance learning options. Such a market is, therefore, expected to be rather big and the market shares of individual HEIs relatively small. As these examples show, what exactly the market is depends very much on the individual case.

3.3.2 Article 101 TFEU

Under Article 101(1) TFEU undertakings[141] are prohibited to engage in any collusion (enter into an agreement, make a decision to coordinate behaviour in an association or conduct tacit collusion)[142] which has as its 'object or effect[[143]] the prevention, restriction or distortion of competition'. The list of examples of anticompetitive behaviour in Article 101(1) TFEU is not exhaustive, instead a broad range of behaviour can fall under the provision.[144] Whilst collusion with an anticompetitive *object* is always illegal the Courts seem to be slightly more flexible when it comes to the *effects* of a collusion. The General Court, however, rejected the thought that this establishes a rule of reason in EU competition law. Instead it stated that the actual weighing of pro-and anti-competitive aspects should only take place under Article 101(3) TFEU.[145] Finally, such a collusion has to 'affect trade between Member States' in order to fall under Article 101(1) TFEU which

---

[141] See above (Sect. 3.2.1 and 3.2.2) on the notion of 'undertaking' and on the fact that in conjunction with other Treaty provisions, Article 101 TFEU can also apply to state action.

[142] Tacit collusion takes place if there is some indication that there is an understanding between the undertakings involved concerning their market conduct without them having formed an agreement. Whilst parallel behaviour is an indicator for a concerted practise it does not in itself establish it (48/69 *Imperial Chemical Industries* (Judgment of 14 July 1972, EU:C:1972:70) para 8). See further Bishop and Walker 2010, p. 164 seq; Horspool and Humphreys 2014, p. 398 seq.

[143] As the provision states, the collusion must have as its object *or* effect the negative impact on competition. It is not necessary that both can be established. This was reinforced by the Court in C-501, 513, 515 and 519/06 P *GlaxoSmithKline* (Judgment of 6 October 2009, EU:C:2009:610) para 55.

[144] See further Lübbig 2008, para 20 seq.

[145] T-112/99 *Métropole* (Judgment of 18 September 2001, EU:T:2001:215) para 72 seq. In this respect it is also worth mentioning that certain potentially anti-competitive clauses which are essential for the main agreement (ancillary restraints), are to be considered together with the latter under Article 101(1) and, if necessary, (3) TFEU rather than individually (ibid para 104 seq, in particular 104, 115 seq).

has been widely interpreted; the closing of a national market[146] and even potential effects[147] on intra-EU trade are sufficient under this criterion.[148] In addition to the elements inherent in the provision itself, any effect on competition must be appreciable.[149] In this respect object restrictions are always deemed appreciable,[150] while, according to the Commission's *De Minimis* Notice,[151] effect restrictions below an aggregated market share of 10 % in horizontal[152] and a market share below 15 %[153] for each party in vertical cases is not deemed appreciable.[154]

A collusion prohibited by Article 101(1) TFEU is, according to Article 101(2) TFEU, automatically void,[155] unless it falls under the exemption of Article 101(3) TFEU.[156] Accordingly, a collusion can be exempted if it involves efficiency gains ('improving the production or distribution of goods' or 'technical or economic progress') of which the consumer receives 'a fair share' (they at least must not be worse off), is necessary for these gains to be achieved and does not completely prevent competition. According to Regulation 1/2003,[157] Article 101(3) TFEU has become directly applicable overcoming the necessity of prior notification. It also decentralised competition law giving more investigative and decisive powers to national competition authorities (NCAs). Nevertheless, the Commission's

---

[146] 8/72 *Vereeniging van Cementhandelaren* (Judgment of 17 October 1972, EU:C:1972:84) para 29.

[147] 56/65 *Maschinenbau Ulm* (Judgment of 30 June 1966, EU:C:1966:38) p. 249.

[148] On the criterion of effect on intra-Union trade see Commission Notice 'Guidelines on the effect on trade concept contained in Articles 81 and 82 of the Treaty' OJ [2004] C 101/81. In particular the effect on trade must be appreciable (para 44 seq of the Notice). This is, however, not to be confused with the concept of appreciability regarding the impact on competition mentioned below (n 149 seq). See further on the effect of trade concept Chalmers et al. 2014, p. 1001; Horspool and Humphreys 2014, p. 411.

[149] First established by the Court in 5/69 *Völk* (Judgment of 9 July 1969, EU:C:1969:35) para 7.

[150] C-226/11 *Expedia* (Judgment of 13 December 2012, EU:C:2012:795) para 37.

[151] Commission Notice on agreements of minor importance which do not appreciably restrict competition under Article 101(1) of the Treaty on the Functioning of the European Union (*De Minimis* Notice) OJ [2014] C 291/1 Section II 8 seq.

[152] Horizontal collusion is collusion between competitors, while vertical collusion is collusion between undertakings operating on different levels of production. In the latter, the concern is rather the portioning of the internal market than consumer welfare which is why the threshold regarding such collusion is higher. See Horspool and Humphreys 2014, p. 404 seq.

[153] See the *De Minimis* Notice for further details as regards markets share thresholds in specific circumstances such as cumulative foreclosure effects.

[154] On Article 101(1) TFEU see further Bishop and Walker 2010, pp. 158, 160 seq, 163 seq; Horspool and Humphreys 2014, p. 395 seq. With a focus on HEIs see Amato and Farbmann 2010, p. 8; Greaves and Scicluna 2010, pp. 15, 20; Gideon 2012, p. 175.

[155] This applies only to the anti-competitive parts of the collusion, other parts might retain validity. See Horspool and Humphreys 2014, p. 395.

[156] As regards public undertakings or undertakings with special or exclusive rights there is, of course, also the exemption provided in Article 106(2) TFEU as discussed above (Sect. 3.2.3).

[157] Regulation 1/2003/EC on the implementation of the rules on competition laid down in Articles 81 and 82 of the Treaty OJ [2003] L 1/1 Article 1(2).

approach still is the major guideline for the application of Article 101(3) TFEU. In its approach the Commission seems to strictly interpret the above mentioned criteria, focussing mainly on economic considerations.[158] There thus seems to be little chance[159] of exempting collusions in the HEI sector on grounds of public policy considerations under Article 101(3) TFEU.[160]

Exemptions are often provided for a specific kind of coordination in block exemptions regulations (BERs).[161] Regarding HEIs, three BERs in particular, could be useful. The Specialisation BER exempts specialisation agreements with a combined market share of below 20 %, unless they contain the hardcore restrictions price fixing, limitation of outputs or market division.[162] HEIs might utilise this BER for joint course agreements or joint research programmes. The Research and Development BER exempts vertical research cooperation agreements as well as horizontal ones with a combined market share which does not exceed 25 %, unless they contain certain hardcore restrictions and only if 'the parties have full access to the final results'.[163] Finally, the Technology Transfer BER exempts bilat-

---

[158] See, for example, Commission White Paper on the modernisation of the rules implementing Articles 85 and 86 of the EC Treaty Programme No 99/027 OJ [1999] C 132/01 para 57 describing the purpose of Article 101(3) TFEU (then Article 85(3) EC) as 'to provide a legal framework for the economic assessment of restrictive practices and not to allow application of the competition rules to be set aside because of political considerations'. Also, see Commission Communication 'Guidelines on the application of Article 81(3) of the Treaty' OJ [2004] C 101/08 para 42 stating that 'the four conditions of Article 81(3) [now Article 101(3) TFEU] are also exhaustive. When they are met, the exception is applicable and may not be made dependent upon any other condition. Goals pursued by other Treaty provisions can be taken into account to the extent that they can be subsumed under the four conditions of Article 81(3) [now Article 101(3) TFEU]'. See also Monti 2007, Chap. 4; in particular p. 89 seq, 102 seq and 122 seq and Jones and Sufrin 2014, p. 254 seq. Especially on HEIs in this respect see Greaves and Scicluna 2010, p. 20.

[159] Townley has argued that, despite the Commission's emphasis on economic efficiency in these documents, a different reading may be possible in the light of former Commission decisions and judgments by the Court and thus broader considerations could potentially be taken into account under Article 101(3) TFEU (Townley 2009).

[160] On Article 101(2) and (3) TFEU see Bishop and Walker 2010, p. 158 seq; Horspool and Humphreys 2014, p. 412 seq, 414 seq; Sauter 2015, p. 115 seq and, specifically on HEIs, Greaves and Scicluna 2010, pp. 16, 19 seq and Gideon 2012, p. 179.

[161] For a critical analysis of BERs in the system of competition law after Regulation 1/2003 see Marcos and Sanchez-Graells 2010.

[162] Commission Regulation 1218/2010/EU on the application of Article 101(3) of the Treaty on the Functioning of the European Union to certain categories of specialisation agreements OJ [2010] L 335/43. A specialisation agreement requires that one or more competing undertakings specialise in one area and therefore receive goods or services from competing undertakings in this area which they would have normally provided themselves (Article 2(1)). The BER also covers certain aspects of IPR related to specialisation (Article 2(2)).

[163] Commission Regulation 1217/2010/EU on the application of Article 101(3) of the Treaty on the Functioning of the European Union to categories of research and development agreements OJ [2010] L 335/36.

eral technology transfer agreements related to the production of contractual goods and services, unless they contain certain hardcore restrictions or other excluded restrictions, if the aggregated market share does not exceed 20 % in horizontal cases and the market share of each party does not exceed 30 % in vertical cases.[164] Additionally, the vertical agreement BER[165] exempts all vertical collusions below a market share of 30 % of the buyer and the seller respectively, except for certain hardcore restrictions.[166]

In the following a few scenarios will be discussed in which HEIs might come into conflict with Article 101 TFEU. These are by no means exclusive; there may well be other scenarios where constraints arise from this provision aside from the ones discussed here. In individual cases there might, of course, always be the possibility of exemption.

3.3.2.1 Price Fixing

Any kind of cooperation between HEIs regarding prices for higher education or research[167] could be regarded as price fixing. This seems less problematic when it comes to research. As has been said above, HEIs only fall under the competition provision if they conduct research of an economic nature. In that case they must not fix prices. This fact does not generally seem to result in any unforeseen detrimental consequences for HEIs. On the other hand, the prohibition of price fixing might indeed cause problems for HEIs regarding tuition fees. If governmental regulations set, or put a cap on, tuition fees, this could still constitute price fixing, in cases where government rules allow scope for price competition and HEIs collaborate within this margin, for example by exchanging information in university associations. Additionally, governmental measures demanding or encouraging price fixing could equally be anti-competitive according to Article 4(3) TEU in conjunction with Article 101 TFEU.

Whilst there is no case law by the Court yet, the OFT has already investigated a group of private schools and found them to have been engaged in anti-competitive

---

[164] Commission Regulation 316/2014/EUC on the application of Article 101(3) of the Treaty on the Functioning of the European Union to categories of technology transfer agreements OJ [2014] L 93/17.

[165] Commission Regulation 330/2010/EU on the application of Article 101(3) of the Treaty on the Functioning of the European Union to categories of vertical agreements and concerted practices OJ [2010] L 102/1.

[166] On BERs regarding HEIs see also Amato and Farbmann 2010, p. 8 seq; Greaves and Scicluna 2010, pp. 16, 19 seq; Gideon 2012, p. 180. On BERs generally see Bishop and Walker 2010, p. 158 seq; Horspool and Humphreys 2014, p. 414 seq.

[167] Any additional potentially economic activities conducted by HEIs (e.g. housing for students, university branded merchandise etc.) shall be left aside in the following, as they are not the main purpose of an HEI as explored in Chap. 1 (Sect. 1.3.1) above.

collusion.[168] The schools had conducted a 'survey' each year from 2001 to 2003 regarding each other's future pricing. The sharing of confidential information, such as the prices for the coming academic year, is regarded as an infringement of competition by object, if it is conducted on a regular basis, relates to future conduct and the information is not available to the public. The OFT, therefore, did not evaluate the question whether this actually had any effect on the price levels. Instead it found the schools guilty of 'participating in an agreement and/or concerted practice having as its object the prevention, restriction or distortion of competition in the relevant markets for the provision of educational services'. The schools each had to pay a fine of £10,000.[169]

The OFT in its 'call for information' on the English higher education sector had also taken an interest in the fact that, after the fee cap was set to £9000 in England for most HEIs, a move which had initially expected fee competition below this threshold, a majority of providers had charged the maximum possible with very little competition as regards fees. While it stated that any collusion in this regard would clearly be anti-competitive, it did not take any immediate steps as it had found no clear evidence for collusion and other explanations to justify the parallel behaviour were possible.[170] Yet, it has to be born in mind that the absence of evidence, does not necessarily indicate the absence of collusion and it can certainly be said that fierce price competition did not materialise. Indeed, the OFT did advise its successor, the Competition and Markets Authority (CMA), to investigate in the future should any further information submerge.[171]

Another possible price fixing incident occurred in the Netherlands. Due to newer legislation (Wet Versterking Besturing, Strengthening Administration Act 2010), Dutch universities could set tuition fees independently. It appears from media coverage that, after the government discontinued funding for second degrees and the universities had therefore introduced higher fees for such degrees, a student organisation (Stichting Collectieve Actie Universiteiten, Foundation Collective Action Universities) initiated legal proceedings against eight Dutch

---

[168] OFT Decision CA98/05/2006 from 20 November 2006 available on http://webarchive.nationalarchives.gov.uk/20140402142426/http://www.oft.gov.uk/OFTwork/competition-act-and-cartels/ca98/decisions/schools. The OFT applied the prohibition in s 2(1) Competition Act 1998, the equivalent to Article 101(1) TFEU. For more on the case see Swennen 2008/2009, p. 277; Amato and Farbmann 2010, p. 10 seq; Greaves and Scicluna 2010, pp. 13, 21 seq; Gideon 2012, p. 175.

[169] Certain exception where applicable, for example, because of Crown immunity. The schools had also agreed to pay into an 'educational trust fund for the benefit of pupils who attended the Participant schools during the academic years' which was taken into consideration by the OFT when calculating the fine (ibid). Interestingly and somewhat strangely, the latter was (unsuccessfully) attempted to be used as precedent in T-486/11 *Orange Polska* (Judgment of 17 December 2015, EU:T:2015:1002) (an abuse of a dominance case in front of the General Court in which a former public monopolist in the telecommunications sector abused its dominance in providing the network in order to enhance its position in the neighbouring broadband market) to offset part of the fine by subsequent investments into the network.

[170] OFT 2014, para 6.5 seq.

[171] Ibid.

universities for charging excessive prices.[172] The writ for these proceedings apparently also included minutes of common discussions between the Universiteit Amsterdam and the Vrije Universiteit Amsterdam agreeing on prices for second masters degrees. This has then led to investigations by the Dutch competition authority (Nederlandse Mededingsautoriteit, NMa) into a possible cartel between these universities fixing prices for second bachelor and/or masters degrees except for medical subjects.[173] The investigation was closed when the universities offered to discontinue fixing prices with each other or other universities.[174]

These examples illustrate that educational institutions are not beyond the reach of the competition provisions. The prohibition of price fixing is, inter alia, intended to protect the consumer. In the cases reported above, the application of competition law would presumably achieve that aim. However, currently, with governmental funding still prevailing and higher education still considered as being in the general interest, one could imagine cases where such a collusion would be to the advantage of the students, encouraging fair pricing and equal access. Challenging this could thus be harmful to the general interest involved. This can be illustrated in a German case regarding public music schools.[175] The music schools entered into contracts with self-employed teachers, requiring them not to charge prices higher than 85 German Marks per hour of tuition. In return, the teachers were allowed to use the facilities of the music schools for their lessons and the school would arrange their contracts. The school fixed the price with the teachers in order to allow equal and low pricing, so that everybody could have access to music education. The arrangement was challenged by a music teacher, who wanted to charge higher prices for her lessons. The German court regarded

---

[172] de Pous I (2011) Amsterdamse universiteiten gedaagd om prijsafspraken (English translation: Amsterdam universities sued for price-fixing). de Volkskrant, 1 September 2011 http://www.volkskrant.nl/vk/nl/4884/Bezuinigingen-in-het-hoger-onderwijs/article/detail/2880822/2011/09/01/Amsterdamse-universiteiten-gedaagd-om-prijsafspraken.dhtml. Accessed 14 October 2011, Myklebust JP and O'Malley B (2011) NETHERLANDS: Dawn raids over 'illegal' tuition fees. University World News, 7 September 2011 http://www.universityworldnews.com/article.php?story=20110907191951868. Accessed 23 September 2011, Dijkstra PT (2011) Amsterdam Universities fix prices: how to prevent this from happening? knowledge debate, 5 September 2011 http://www.rug.nl/kennisdebat/onderwerpen/actueel/universitiesFixPrices. Accessed 14 October 2011.

[173] NMa (2011) Bedrifsbezoeken NMa bij Amsterdamse universiteiten (English translation: Company inspection by NMa in Amsterdam universities). http://www.nma.nl/documenten_en_publicaties/archiefpagina_nieuwsberichten/webberichten/2011/20_11_bedrijfsbezoeken_nma_bij_amsterdamse_universiteiten.aspx. Accessed 12 October 2011. For more on the case see Gideon 2012, p. 175.

[174] NMa (2012) NMa accepteert maatregelen van UvA en VU (English translation: NMa accepts commitments by UvA and VU). https://www.acm.nl/nl/publicaties/publicatie/10780/NMa-accepteert-maatregelen-van-UvA-en-VU/. Accessed 16 October 2012.

[175] BGH Judgement 23.10.1979 in (1980) 82 GRUR 249. For more on the case see Kroitzsch 1980, p. 251 seq; Swennen 2008/2009, p. 277; Gideon 2012, p. 178.

the music school, as well as the self-employed teachers, as undertakings[176] and the contract terms of the music school as price fixing. This case nicely illustrates how in such cases the prohibition of price fixing could be to the detriment of the students. Additionally, the constellation of the case makes one wonder whether, in the final consequence of the thought, even governmental regulation regarding tuition fees could be challenged under Article 4(3) TEU in conjunction with Article 101(1) TFEU. While not actually challenging the fee cap in England, the OFT and CMA in their evaluations[177] have in fact pointed to competitive issues in this regards. In particular it was pointed out that the fee cap would hinder innovation as regards course structures. Since it is set per year, accelerated courses would, for example, be made less attractive to providers.[178]

Another example where price fixing could have positive effects for students can be derived from a case in the US. The Department of Justice has investigated HEIs for price fixing violating the Sherman Act (US American Competition Law Act) in the early 1990s.[179] HEIs had agreed on a policy according to which they would discuss what they believed an applicant who had applied to a variety of HEIs could pay. They would then offer financial aid to this applicant accordingly, so that the student's financial burden would remain unchanged, regardless of which offer he or she accepted, although the level of tuition fees differed between universities. The aim of the scheme was to ensure that students would pay a price they could afford and that financial help would only be given as to the shortfall. In this way, HEIs would not compete on the basis of financial aid, thereby allowing more

---

[176] In C-413/13 *FNV Kunsten Informatie en Media* (Judgment of 4 December 2014, EU:C:2014:2411) the Court declared that self-employed musicians may under certain circumstances (i.e. work under direction, no sharing of commercial risks, economic unit with the employer's undertaking) be regarded as 'false-self-employed'. It was left open to the national court to determine that. In any case, however, the situation was different from that in the German Music School Case, as it did not concern music teachers, but replacement musicians for orchestras who conducted exactly the same tasks as employed replacements. Furthermore, the agreement had been made in the context of collective bargaining between a union representing employed and certain self-employed musicians and the employers. Thus it seems doubtful in how far this could be applicable in a scenario such as the one in the German Music School Case. Indeed, the Court stated that in general the self-employed musicians were to be regarded as undertakings (para 27).

[177] Being a national competition authority examining the sector under national law, they did not challenge the national legislation, but evaluated it as an advisory body for policy changes (OFT 2014, para 7.3), as a variety of issues with competitive neutrality had been identified following the Call for Information. On these issues see OFT 2014, Chap. 7 and CMA 2015.

[178] OFT 2014 para 7.17, CMA 2015 para 5.45 seq. It would appear that the envisaged changes in the English higher education sector still foresee the cap for the future. However, it is intended to be adjusted with inflation which only certain HEIs which perform well in the planned Teaching Quality Framework can charge. See BIS 2015, p. 57 seq, BIS 2016, p. 40 seq.

[179] Complaint, *United States v. Brown Univ.*, No. 91-CV-3274 (E.D. Pa., filed May 22, 1991). For more on the case see Salop and White 1991; Carlson and Shepherd 1992; Stachtiaris 1993/1994; Petronio 1994–1995.

students to profit. Instead, HEIs would compete on the quality of their services.[180] Whilst some HEIs ended the dispute in a settlement agreeing to discontinue the allegedly anti-competitive behaviour,[181] the Massachusetts Institute of Technology continued the trial and was found guilty of price fixing in the first instance.[182] In the appeal decision, the Third Circuit decided that the rule of reason in US American Antitrust law requires a more thorough weighing of pro- and anti-competitive effects and referred the case back.[183] Before a final decision could be reached, a compromise was found and the dispute ended in a settlement the terms of which were then to be applicable to all HEIs.[184] This settlement, inter alia, provides that HEIs are allowed to give financial aid according to need, to agree on methods to determine need and to involve a third party to gather financial background information on applicants which will then be provided to all HEIs involved. It prohibits, however, agreement on common fees.

Whilst, thus, in the end, a compromise was reached which was actually very close to the original scheme, the case nevertheless shows the possible threats arising from competition law for the public service character of HEIs.[185] At the same time, it also shows the possibility of compromise in this regard and could serve as an example for European HEIs should competition law become more generally applicable to them. A problematic aspect in this regard is the fact that there is no rule of reason in EU competition. Thus it would have to be seen in how far the case law on ancillary restraints[186] or Article 101(3) or 106(2) TFEU could be utilised. As regards the ancillary restraints case law, the price fixing in this case was not just a side effect of an otherwise unproblematic main agreement. The more economic approach towards Article 101(3) TFEU and the fact that price fixing is a hardcore restrictions makes such an agreement neither an obvious fit under this provision. Article 106(2) TFEU seems to be the most likely avenue. However, that would require an entrustment act.

---

[180] See Salop and White 1991, p. 198 seq who, however, doubt that such arguments would stand up in Court under antitrust law (the article was written before the actual proceedings had been started), Carlson and Shepherd 1992 who, however, oppose the scheme, as they believe it was economically inefficient and Stachtiaris 1993/1994, p. 746 seq.

[181] Stipulation, *United States v. Brown Univ.*, No. 91-CV-3274 (E.D. Pa., filed May 22, 1991).

[182] Decision and Order, *United States v. Brown Univ.*, No. 91-CV-3274 (E.D. Pa., filed Sept. 2, 1992).

[183] Opinion of the Court, *United States v. Brown Univ.*, No. 92-1911 (3d Cir. Sept. 17, 1993).

[184] Letter of 22 December 1993 by the US Department of Justice—Antitrust Division, available on http://www.appliedantitrust.com/06_reasonableness/brown/litan_thane_settlement12_22_1993.pdf.

[185] Similar Stachtiaris 1993/1994, who argues that therefore HEIs should not fall under antitrust law in the first place.

[186] See n 145 above.

3.3.2.2 Market Foreclosure or Disturbance

Another example where HEIs might infringe Article 101(1) TFEU is if they cooperate in bodies which essentially define who can enter (a significant part of) the market such as accreditation or quality assurance agencies for teaching and research or bodies distributing study places. These could, if consisting mainly of experts from within HEIs, be regarded as making a decision by an association of undertakings foreclosing (parts of) the market and preventing access to newcomers. If such bodies themselves conducted an economic activity and are thus undertakings, this could be regarded as a vertical cartel.[187] Even if such bodies are foreseen in national law, this could still fall under the prohibition of Article 101(1) TFEU if read in conjunction with Article 4(3) TEU.

A body distributing university places could, for example, be regarded as an association of undertakings. If this association only allows certain HEIs to be registered within it (for example, only national ones) and thus only allocates places to them, this forecloses the market to newcomers. The case of Maastricht University applying for registration in the British Universities and Colleges Admission Service (UCAS) has, for example, been discussed in the press.[188] The request was, according to the *Sunday Times*, turned down because Maastricht University is not British. The article further reported that Maastricht University planned to challenge the decision under EU law, as it constitutes discrimination.[189] It might also be conceivable, though it is difficult to specify without knowing the details of this case, that such arrangements could be challenged under Article 101(1) TFEU or Article 4(3) TEU in conjunction with Article 101(1) TFEU, if bodies such as UCAS are required by a state measure.[190] Indeed, the OFT has, inter alia, raised concerns about 'UCAS' corporate governance and the extent to which all institutions have access to its services'.[191] It is now apparently planned that HEIs from

---

[187] For example, see 107/82 *AEG* (Judgment of 25 October 1983, EU:C:1983:293) para 35 seq. The case concerned a distribution network which is, as such, not incompatible with Article 101(1) TFEU, if any undertaking, which wishes to do so and which fulfils objective qualitative criteria, can enter the network. However, if undertakings which meet the qualitative criteria are prevented from entering, this does constitute an infringement. It is regarded as collusion, as the acceptance of the conditions by the participating undertakings is seen as approval. See also Horspool and Humphreys 2014, p. 398 seq.

[188] See Grimston J and Winch J (2010) Maastricht University is fighting for a listing in order to attract British students. The Sunday Times, 24 October 2010 News: 4. There does not seem to be anything available on the case since initial press coverage.

[189] This might probably have referred to the free movement of services, but the article is not very precise here and also talks about effects on competition. A challenge under the free movement provisions would imply that UCAS would be regarded as part of the Member State (the UK) which discriminates against foreign service providers. Higher education would thus have to be regarded as a service in the meaning of the free movement provisions (see Chap. 2, Sect. 2.3.2 above).

[190] On the market foreclosure scenario see Gideon 2012, p. 179.

[191] OFT 2014, para 1.10. See also ibid para 7.28 seq.

other EU Member States can become part of UCAS,[192] though currently this still appears to be under the section 'alternatives to higher education' rather than in the normal system.[193]

In the USA the accreditation of, in particular legal, education has been discussed widely in the context of its compatibility with the Sherman Act.[194] Indeed, there have been some privately initiated cases against legal and other educational accreditation agencies, which have, however, not been successful.[195] A case by the US Department of Justice against the American Bar Association (ABA),[196] however, ended in a consent decree in which the ABA consented to refrain from specific accreditation practices. In particular, they consented to accredit for-profit institutions on equal terms. Therefore, while there is some support for applying stricter rules to for-profit HEIs in the sector in order to 'mitigate the extra risk posed by for-profit corporate forms',[197] the US case implies that accreditation practices are not beyond the reach of competition law and may require equal treatment. Again, even if accreditation is foreseen by national law, this might, in EU law, be challengeable under Article 4(3) TEU in conjunction with Article 101(1) TFEU.

However, such bodies might disturb the market beyond preventing access completely. UCAS has made it into the press again when it decided not to publish university application figures believing this to be anti-competitive.[198] It was alleged that publishing the figures would lead to a competitive disadvantage for some HEIs since the figures 'could be overinterpreted by both institutions and applicants, and give rise to unintended markets effects'.[199] Whilst publishing such

---

[192] Ward L (2015) European universities to be part of Ucas admissions. The Guardian, 17 February 2015 https://www.theguardian.com/education/2015/feb/17/european-universities-to-be-part-of-ucas-admissions. Accessed 8 April 2016.

[193] See the subsection 'studying overseas' in the section 'alternatives to higher education' on the UCAS website: https://www.ucas.com/ucas/undergraduate/getting-started/alternatives-higher-education/studying-overseas.

[194] For an evaluation of accreditation agencies under US American antitrust law see Havighurst and Brody 1994. For an evaluation of legal education accreditation under the Sherman Act see First 1979; Lao 2001; Areen 2011.

[195] See those discussed in First 1979, p. 1062, p. 1080, Havighurst and Brody 1994, pp. 201, 203 and Lao 2001, p. 1037.

[196] Competitive Impact Statement, *United States v American Bar Association*, No. 95-1211(CR) (D. D. C. 1996). In this case the fixing of salaries and working conditions had also been challenged and was amongst the conduct the ABA had to agree to stop in the consent decree (Sect. I A). In Europe such problems seem less likely due to different labour law traditions and a cautious approach by the European judiciary in this respect (see Monti 2007, p. 96 seq). For more on *United States v American Bar Association* see Lao 2001, p. 1037 seq; Areen 2011, p. 1487 seq.

[197] UCU (2012) UCU politics monthly—June 2012—Response to HE consultation. http://www.ucu.org.uk/index.cfm?articleid=6194#wmin. Accessed 29 June 2012.

[198] Morgan J (2013) Ucas withholds 2013–14 application data. THE, 14 February 2013 http://www.timeshighereducation.co.uk/news/ucas-withholds-2013-14-application-data/2001543.article. Accessed 17 April 2013.

[199] Ibid.

information might indeed have a negative effect on certain institutions, it might also, as a student organisation has argued, enhance consumer protection to have the relevant information available. Furthermore, while it may be anti-competitive to exchange and make publicly available certain kinds of sensitive information such as future pricing intentions, an unequal provision of information may also raise anti-competitive concerns. The OFT in this regard pointed to 'the way in which UCAS information is integrated with other sources of information available to students, and the extent to which applications data is available to others (including alternative choice tool providers)'.[200] The CMA in its evaluation also acknowledged that differences in information offered makes it more difficult to compete for providers.[201] In addition to UCAS, the OFT more widely mentions issues with (self-)regulatory bodies in England (e.g. the Higher Education Funding Council for England (HEFCE) or the Quality Assurance Agency (QAA)), since they partly offer certain service only to certain providers or charge different fees[202] and the CMA equally points to various issues in regards to market access arising from regulation (access to generic funding, degree awarding powers, course designation, ability to sponsor visas, scrutiny by the QAA and different sanctions).[203]

Overall the above shows that competition law can have potential effects on the bodies regulating teaching or research activities. Yet, the opening of such institutions to every interested HEI from every Member State could put a significant strain on the national systems. This would particularly cause problems if such institutions are publicly funded. Additionally, potential judicial reviews of accreditation standards under competition law might lead to lower quality and a further opening of education systems to private providers. In some cases, of course, an exemption might apply, but the English example shows that, inter alia, the competition law assessment by OFT and CMA have already led to the suggestion of far more commodification in the planned reforms.[204]

3.3.2.3 Market Division

It might be conceivable that HEIs, whether by agreement, through information exchange or even decisions in university associations or by tacitly coordinating their behaviour, divide the subject market. This would be the case if they decide to offer a certain variety of subjects in coordination with what other HEIs in the area

---

[200] OFT 2014 para 1.10. See also ibid para 7.28 seq.

[201] CMA 2015, para 6.9.

[202] OFT 2014, para 7.26 seq, 7.36 seq.

[203] CMA 2015, para 5.2 seq.

[204] Some of the issues mentioned in this section have been addresses in the UK government's recent Green and White Paper where plans are expressed to level the playing field. Yet, there still appcar to be certain differences remaining. See further BIS 2015, 2016.

are offering. Whilst orienting their behaviour around others in an economically reasonable way would not amount to collusion, actual coordination on the matter could.[205] HEIs could then be regarded as dividing the market into segments of subjects which are only offered by few HEIs which are geographically distant and thus not in direct competition. This might create local monopolies regarding teaching and research at the same time, if one considers the history of the university which traditionally aimed at teaching and research going hand in hand.[206] Considering the fact that most students still study in their home state[207] and that small and medium size undertakings often also seek partners locally, this would limit their choices and they might be encouraged to challenge such coordination. With decreasing public funding, however, it might no longer be possible for every HEI to offer every subject[208] and (local) collaboration dividing the subjects (joint course agreements) between them might be the only solution for HEIs. If, at the same time, they cooperate by consulting primarily with each other in areas in which they do not themselves conduct research and teaching, this might be regarded as a cartel with the aim of driving a competitor out of the market. Of course, HEIs might be able to utilise the previously mentioned BER on specialisation agreements in this respect[209] or utilise the Article 101(3) TFEU exemption more generally.[210]

Another example of potential market division might be seen in practices such as UCAS' practice of allowing applications to only five courses at a time and usually to only one of either Oxford or Cambridge.[211] Through such practices HEIs could ensure that the education market is divided (more or less equally) between them as regards student numbers. In its assessment the OFT did not see any issues here,[212] since there would still be competition at the pre-application stage and post-application there would still be competition between five HEIs (even if these could only contain either Oxford or Cambridge). The OFT thus seemed to find the

---

[205] If the collaboration goes as far as creating a new organisation this might have to be considered as a merger, which is discussed below (Sect. 3.3.4).

[206] See Chap. 1 (Sect. 1.3.1) above.

[207] For more on student mobility see Lanzendorf 2006, p. 8 seq. According to the data given there, an average of only 3 % of students in the Eurodata countries study abroad. The Eurodata countries comprised the EU-27 as well as Turkey, Switzerland, Iceland, Liechtenstein and Norway (see Kelo et al. 2006, p. 5).

[208] As will be seen in Chaps. 4 and 5 as regards research, this is in fact encouraged in some national policies.

[209] See n 162 above.

[210] In its assessment the OFT had not been able to generally find evidence regarding any anti-competitive collaborations in the English higher education market and considered that, if there were any anti-competitive collaborations, such agreements may often give rise to efficiency gains. It only saw information sharing for benchmarking as potentially problematic, but since this was a government policy it did not address this directly, but instead pledged to work with the government to attempt to create pro-competitive policies. See OFT 2014 para 6.15 seq.

[211] On UCAS' practise and its potential anti-competitiveness see Morgan (n 198).

[212] OFT 2014, para 6.24 seq.

anti-competitive effects of this rule not significant. However, it has to be born in mind that market division is a restriction by object and that therefore, if there is effect on trade between Member States, it is not necessary to assess the anti-competitive effects, nor does the *de minimis* rule apply.[213] At the same time, however, it might be unfeasible to allow unlimited applications, since the relevant bodies might not be able to process them. Such collaboration may therefore be exempted as providing efficiency gains under Article 101(3) TFEU, as has equally been suggested by the OFT. However, this argument seems stronger when it comes to limiting the overall number of applicants. The prohibition of applying to both Oxford and Cambridge, where the alleged efficiency gains are the fact that more applicants could be interviewed by those universities seem weaker considering that all other HEIs would still have to manage without such an additional restriction, which would question the necessity of this rule, and it eliminates competition between them completely at the post-application stage.

If market division is required or encouraged by public regulation in these (or other) scenarios this would not lead to non-application of EU law. Instead it could potentially be challenged according to Article 4(3) TEU in conjunction with Article 101 TFEU.

3.3.2.4   Research Co-operation

Research cooperation between two or more HEIs or HEIs and other research undertakings with a view to exploiting the results may conflict with Article 101(1) TFEU if it restricts competition. This could, for example, be the case if the cooperation limits the activities of the parties beyond the research, if the parties were not far from achieving the research result individually and thus competition is limited or if the collusion comprises constraints on the parties regarding exploitation of the research.[214] Further, sharing facilities and excluding other undertakings, unless on the basis of objective criteria, could be anti-competitive. It might also be conceivable that vertical cooperation between HEIs and research users, could be regarded as a vertical cartel when the research users do not pay a representative price and/or different prices are charged to different users. This might cause problems for HEIs in the future (given that cooperation with non-academic partners is increasingly encouraged), if, for example, a vertical cooperation is limited to a certain region or favourable prices are charged regarding undertakings from that region. However, HEIs might in some cases, be able to utilise the previously mentioned Research and Development BER,[215] if the relevant conditions are fulfilled.[216]

---

[213] C-226/11 *Expedia*.

[214] For more on research and development agreements see Lübbig and Schroeder 2008, para 120 seq.

[215] See above n 163.

[216] See also on anti-competitive behaviour as regards research Gideon 2015b, p. 60 seq.

3.3.2.5 Limiting Markets

Article 101(1) TFEU also prohibits the limitation of markets. In this respect one might wonder whether restrictions on education places through a collusion of HEIs could be regarded as such. With regards to higher education places, demand is, in general, higher than supply, particularly in certain subjects.[217] If HEIs were to be considered as undertakings it is imaginable that students, who have been turned away, challenge such limitations. This would also be the case if HEIs decide collusively to limit their private research output to a certain number of contracts or if governmental regulations require it. A limit on student numbers, might, however, be necessary to retain the public (or, in some Member States, even free of charge) character of higher education and limitations to research contracts might be necessary to ensure enough capacity for public interest research. Therefore, such limitations, depending on the individual case, might be able to benefit from Article 106(2) TFEU.

3.3.3 Article 102 TFEU

Article 102 TFEU prohibits the abuse of a dominant market position. According to the Court an undertaking holds a dominant position if it enjoys 'a position of economic strength […] which enables it to prevent competition being maintained on the relevant market by giving it the power to behave to an appreciable extent independently of its competitors, customers and ultimately its consumers'.[218] Usually, the dominance of an undertaking is established according to its market share and barriers to entry. Whilst a market share of more than 50 % in the relevant market normally leads to the presumption of dominance, the undertaking is, nevertheless, not considered dominant if market entry is easy.[219] At the same time, depending on the market, undertakings with lower market shares could also be regarded as dominant. The dominant undertaking is abusing its dominance if its actions are

---

[217] See, for example, Chap. 2 (Sect. 2.3.1.2) above on the high number of students in the medical field who cannot gain a study place in their home state and therefore emigrate to other Member States, thus meaning demand can also not be met in those states anymore. On the re-occurring problem that demand for study places could not be met in England see, for example, Richardson H (2010) Thousands "to miss out on university degree". BBC News, 1 February 2010 http://news.bbc.co.uk/1/hi/education/8487354.stm. Accessed 9 February 2010. However, caps on study places have since been lifted for some and completely abolished for certain other providers (see CMA 2015, para 3.3).

[218] 27/76 *United Brands* (Judgment of 14 February 1978, EU:C:1978:22) para 65.

[219] 62/86 *Akzo* (Judgment of 3 July 1991, EU:C:1991:286) para 60.

regarded as having an anti-competitive effect[220] which goes beyond the non-exhaustive list of examples in Article 102 TFEU. Whilst dominance as such is not prohibited, the concept of abuse is influenced by the established dominance; a behaviour which is regarded as competitive if conducted by a non-dominant undertaking, can be classified as an abuse if conducted by a dominant one. Unlike under Article 101 TFEU, there are no exemptions for the abuse of a dominant position foreseen in the Treaty.[221] However, as part of the concept of abuse, the Court sometimes assesses inherent objective justifications.[222] The Commission, similarly to its approach under Article 101(1), also recently developed a more economic approach towards Article 102 TFEU which would lead to those exclusionary practices which can be proven to be economically efficient, not being considered as abuse.[223] As under Article 101(1) TFEU, the abuse must have an effect on intra-Union trade.[224]

In the following some examples will be explored. Obviously, these require an HEI to be an undertaking and to be in a dominant position or for a few HEIs to be in a position of collective dominance, which depends on market definition. It is not unimaginable, however, that for subjects which are less common, HEIs do hold a dominant position or that they do so in an area of specialised research.[225] Generally, the strong position of public HEIs, due to their long-term (near) monopoly status in many Member States, makes them susceptible to challenge by private providers entering the market and this might not always be to the advantage of students or in the interest of public research.[226] As will be seen, some

---

[220] This question is closely linked to the aims of competition law, a detailed discussion of which would go beyond the scope of this book (on the aims of competition law see briefly above text accompanying n 123 and 124). For more on the concept of abuse see Monti 2007, p. 160 seq; Jung 2009, para 101 seq.

[221] Except for SGEIs under Article 106(2) TFEU (see above Sect. 3.2.3).

[222] C-95/04 P *British Airways* (Judgment of 15 March 2007, EU:C:2007:166) para 86. For more see Monti 2007, p. 162 seq, in particular p. 171 on the *British Airways* case and p. 203 seq on justifications. Rousseva and Marquis separate the unwritten justification into objective necessity justification and an efficiency defence. For the latter they advertise using the same four conditions as under Article 101(3) TFEU (see Sect. 3.3.2 above) and see evidence of the Court following such an approach in C-209/10 *Post Danmark* (Judgment of 27 March 2012, EU:C:2012:172). See further Rousseva and Marquis 2013, p. 48 seq.

[223] See Commission Communication 'Guidance on the Commission's enforcement priorities in applying Article 82 of the EC Treaty to abusive exclusionary conduct by dominant undertakings' OJ [2009] C 45/02 para 19.

[224] See further on Article 102 TFEU Monti 2007, p. 160 seq; Jung 2009; Chalmers et al. 2014, p. 1031 seq. With a focus on HEIs see Amato and Farbmann 2010, p. 9; Greaves and Scicluna 2010, p. 15. With a focus on health care provision as a similar area see Wendt and Gideon 2011, p. 270 seq.

[225] See Sect. 3.3.1 above.

[226] For this argument in a reversed fashion, namely regarding the use of Article 102 TFEU to the advantage of third sector providers in their relationship towards established NHS (UK National Health Service) providers in health care 'markets' see Wendt and Gideon 2011, p. 271.

behaviour discussed above for Article 101 TFEU, could also fall under Article 102 TFEU if conducted by a dominant undertaking unilaterally rather than by a collusion of undertakings. This might be more detrimental to HEIs, because, as has been mentioned above, there are no exemptions to Article 102 TFEU.

3.3.3.1 Exploitative Abuses

Article 102 TFEU is, inter alia, intended to restrict exploitative unilateral conduct by dominant undertakings. This includes abuses such as setting excessive prices if the undertaking in question is the provider and requiring abusively low prices if it is the buyer. Furthermore, the dictation of unreasonable contract conditions, artificially limited out-puts, the refusal to enter into contractual relations, the refusal to provide licenses or the requirement of unreasonably long license duration, would fall under this kind of abuse. The abuses could take place indirectly if the dominant undertaking is not dealing directly with the consumer, but requires the passing-on of the abuse.[227]

Whilst the elimination of exploitative abuses is obviously intended to protect the consumer, the application of this to public HEIs might cause problems with their public service character. Similarly to what is mentioned above regarding collusion, one might, for example, wonder if the limitation of study places could be regarded as limiting outputs under Article 102(b) TFEU. In England, for example, plans were, first, aired that additional places for students willing and able to pay higher fees could be created[228] and eventually student number controls were abolished entirely for certain providers,[229] which seems to suggest that the limitation of study places is not a business necessity from the point of view of the HEIs. If places are limited artificially, this could enable students to challenge such behaviour under Article 102 TFEU if conducted by a dominant HEI. Article 106(1) TFEU in conjunction with Article 102 TFEU would also allow challenges to government regulations which enable dominant undertakings to abuse their position this way. As the citizenship cases of Belgium and Austria discussed in Chap. 2 have shown, the equilibrium of public finances might, however, not necessarily allow the offering of publicly financed places for everybody, particularly if one considers that all EU students have to be granted equal access.[230] Additionally, in the field of research, there could equally not be artificial limits placed on output,

---

[227] See Jung 2009, para 143 seq.

[228] See Vasagar J (2009) Richest students to pay for extra places at Britain's best universities. The Guardian, 9 May 2011 http://www.guardian.co.uk/education/2011/may/09/universities-extra-places-richest-students. Accessed 11 July 2011. The plans were not taken over into the 2011 government White Paper as such, but the White Paper still included the possibility of such extra places being funded by business and charities (see BIS 2011, p. 51 para 4.22 seq).

[229] CMA 2015 para 3.3. Further lifting of student number controls is envisaged (BIS 2016, p. 27).

[230] See Chap. 2 (Sect. 2.3.1) above.

which could possibly lead to an increase in commercial research in comparison to public service research.

With regards to education, a student in Ireland has, indeed, already attempted to challenge the limitation of study places for medicine for European students in that country inter alia under Article 102 TFEU.[231] Whilst publicly subsidised European students had to fulfil very high entrance criteria, international students who paid full cost prices did not. The student in question had offered to match the full cost price, if he would then be admitted with his lower grades, which was denied. The national court dealt at length with the issues of national law, but only discussed EU competition law in two short paragraphs which are not overly clear. It appears that the national court assumed that because medical schools could, in theory, opt out of government subsidies and offer private education at full cost rates and because medical education is expensive for the government to subsidise 'that there is nothing wrong in competition terms'. However, the medical schools offered medical education as a market service at least for international students, it appears from this case that there are only five medical schools in Ireland which therefore all hold positions of economic strength and it might also be assumed that barriers to entry are rather high in the medical education market. It, thus, seems possible to regard the individual medical schools as undertakings in a dominant position which abuse that position by limiting outputs for certain consumers. A reference for a preliminary ruling might have been indicated in this case.

Furthermore, if governments were to adopt a strategy of different prices for different students based on their financial background, as had been explored by the British Government,[232] this could be regarded as price discrimination and could therefore also be an abuse of a dominant market position. Similarly, excessive prices for research, favourable purchase prices or contract conditions regarding supplies for research or discounts for certain undertakings (for example for local undertakings) could be challenged. It might, in particular, cause problems to charge undertakings from other Member States more than national ones because this would cause partitions in the internal market. Whilst price discrimination, particularly the originally envisaged price strategy for tuition fees in England, is generally debatable, it could theoretically also be used to enhance equality (for example, higher prices for better-off students could cross-subsidise places for less well-off students). Price reductions for local undertakings regarding research could help to promote a certain region. Furthermore, high priced private research could be utilised to cross-subsidise teaching and research in the public interest. The application of Article 102 TFEU would also take away the opportunity to attach additional contract conditions which are not economically justified to the contracts. The behaviour of some HEIs in demanding that students not only prove that they can pay the fee, but also prove in advance that they can cover their living

---

[231] *Prendergast v Higher Education Authority & Ors* [2008] IEHC 257.

[232] See n 228 above.

costs for the time of the study[233] might potentially be regarded as such. Whilst, as mentioned above, there are no exemptions for Article 102 TFEU, an exemption under Article 106(2) TFEU might be possible if the application of competition law would obstruct the public service obligation entrusted to an HEI.

3.3.3.2 Exclusionary Abuses

Exclusionary abuses are aimed at driving competitors out of the market and retaining or strengthening the dominant position. Such abuses could lie in technical restrictions, predatory pricing, refusal to issue licenses to competitors, refusal to supply competitors and abusing a monopoly (for example, excluding competitors despite not being able to fulfil demand).[234]

With regards to HEIs it would be possible that problems arise concerning low tuition fees or low prices for research contracts. Such low prices could be regarded as predatory pricing which is aimed at driving (or keeping) competitors out of the market. Due to their financial support from the state, public HEIs are in a position to provide research for lower prices than their competitors and to hold tuition fees at a low level. Disregarding for now what that could entail in state aid terms,[235] this might cause a problem with Article 102 TFEU.[236] The Dutch NMa had already had to deal with a case in this respect involving music schools.[237] In contrast to the German music school case, wherein a vertical cartel between the self-employed teachers and the music school was in question, this case involved a collective dominant position of public music schools. The schools were accused of predatory pricing by a competitor. As the schools were bound to certain prices by law and had no free choice the NMa could not find an abuse on the side of the schools. Furthermore, it was not in the authority of the NMa to review national legislation. This would sit differently with regards to EU law, since such national legislation could potentially be challenged under Article 102 in conjunction with 106(1) TFEU.

Furthermore, as in the scenario under Article 101 TFEU, any agencies, such as UCAS, which have a significant influence on market access for study places, could get into conflict with Article 102 TFEU. It would depend on whether the collusion aspect is more pronounced or whether the case concerns unilateral conduct to determine which provision would be applicable. Under Article 102 TFEU such

---

[233] Such a policy at the University of Oxford has been challenged by a student under the British Human Rights Act 1998. See BBC News (2013) Judgement reserved over Oxford University student discrimination row. BBC News, 15 February 2013 http://www.bbc.co.uk/news/uk-england-21465879. Accessed 17 February 2013.

[234] See Jung 2009, para 186 seq.

[235] On state aid see below Sect. 3.3.5.

[236] Similar Greaves and Scicluna 2010, p. 18.

[237] Besluit bk005-9801 available on www.nmanet.nl/Images/0005BEMP_tcm16-97472.pdf. On the case see also Swennen 2008/2009, p. 275, Gideon 2012, p. 177.

agencies could potentially abuse their dominant position as such, if they are regarded as undertakings themselves, while a group of HEIs acting together in such a body might be seen as abusing collective dominance. The abuse could lie in not allowing newcomers any access to the distribution network, as this could be regarded as controlling market access. If the entry criteria to the distribution network are based on the HEI's home Member State this seems particularly problematic given that it contributes to the partitioning of the internal market. If the HEIs in question cannot fulfil demand, this would be especially abusive conduct. Similarly any specific information which such bodies may hold could be an essential facility and it may be problematic to limit access to certain providers.[238] Again, under EU law, it does not play a role if national law prescribes such practices as the national law can also be challenged according to Article 106(1) TFEU in conjunction with Article 102 TFEU. Such challenges might be more severe under Article 102 TFEU, as it contains no express exemptions and exemptions are thus mainly possible under Article 106(2) TFEU.

Finally, abuse of dominance may be present in the relationship between HEIs which are not in a position to issue their own degrees and those HEIs validating their degrees if the latter are in a dominant position. In its report on the situation in England the OFT states that it has received a variety of concerns in this regard including that the degree awarding bodies dictate fee levels, refuse validation for competing courses, withdraw validation on short notice, take unreasonably long to validate or impose overly stringent conditions. Yet, the OFT did not find any evidence for such practises and also pointed out that as regards some of these examples the conduct would only be anti-competitive if there was no option to switch the validator which is why this would not be an immediate area of action.[239] This is, however, not to say that no such situations are present in this or other Member States' HEI systems. The CMA later also considered this issue and pointed especially to the fact that the more competitive, market based system, which the English HEI sector has become, may encourage refusal to validate competing courses and that stringent quality assurance might equally make validators reluctant.[240] There is thus not only some indication that competition law can become applicable to such situations, but, indeed, also that it can create further commodification, as envisaged policy changes aim at making it easier for new (commercial) providers to get degree awarding powers and for validation to potentially be conducted by a new sector regulator rather than by HEIs in the future.[241]

---

[238] The OFT in its report expressed some concern regarding UCAS data sets in the context of consumer choice and envisaged that the CMA conducts further work on the matter (OFT 2014 para 4.39 seq.).

[239] OFT 2014 para 1.16, 6.8 seq.

[240] CMA para 5.30 seq.

[241] BIS 2016, p. 29 seq.

3.3.4 Mergers

Merger control is not regulated in the Treaty itself, but in the Merger Regulation.[242] The regulation subjects concentrations[243] of undertakings[244] to merger control by the Commission if these have a Union-dimension.[245] Undertakings planning to conduct a merger need to notify this (Article 4(1)). The merger can be prohibited[246] if it would appreciably[247] impede competition

---

[242] Council Regulation 139/2004/EC on the control of concentrations between undertakings (the EC Merger Regulation) OJ [2004] L 24/1. Before the first Merger Regulation (Council Regulation 4064/89/EEC on the control of concentrations between undertakings OJ [1989] L 395/01) was passed, the Court had assessed mergers through Article 102 TFEU (e.g. in 6/72 *Continental Can* (Judgment of 21 February 1973, EU:C:1973:22)). See further Marco Colino 2011, p. 357 seq. The Commission has started a review procedure of Regulation 139/2004/EC the latest document of which is the 'White Paper "Towards more effective EU merger control"' of 9 July 2014. Updates on the review process can be found on http://ec.europa.eu/competition/mergers/legislation/regulations.html.

[243] These can be mergers of undertakings, the acquisition of undertakings and permanent joint ventures (Article 3 Merger Regulation). The term acquisition is broadly defined to include all means by which 'decisive influence' over an undertaking can be obtained. For more see Marco Colino 2011, p. 360 seq.

[244] The Merger Regulation also applies to 'persons' holding interests in undertakings and thus executing the relevant control. 'Persons' in this respect can be individuals and even Member States if they are acting in a commercial manner. See Marco Colino 2011, p. 361.

[245] According to Article 1(2) Merger Regulation, a merger has a Union dimension if it either has at least a combined world turnover of €5000 M and an individual Union turnover of at least €250 M in at least two involved undertakings unless the undertakings involved achieve two-thirds of their Union turnover in only one Member State or if it has at least a combined world turnover of €2500 M, a combined turnover of at least €100 M in at least three Member States, in at least three of these Member States the individual turnover of at least two undertakings is at least €25 M and the individual Union turnover of at least two undertakings is at least €100 M unless the undertakings involved achieve two-thirds of their Union turnover in only one Member State. The actual seat of an undertaking or the question of where their main activities take place is irrelevant. In addition, mergers of undertakings which do not have a Union dimension, but would need to be reviewed under the national competition law of at least three Member States, can be reviewed by the Commission if the undertakings in question apply for the Commission to do so and the Member States do not object (Article 4(5) Merger Regulation). Member States may also request the Commission to investigate a merger if they feel it has an effect on competition and trade between Member States (Article 22 Merger Regulation). On the other hand, mergers which do have a Union dimension can also be referred back to the Member States, if appropriate (Articles 9, 4(4) Merger Regulation) and Member States can take necessary actions if legitimate national interest are at stake (Article 21(4) Merger Regulation and Article 346 TFEU).

[246] The Commission can also ask for modifications or impose conditions (Article 8(2) Merger Regulation).

[247] This is not deemed to be the case if the undertakings concerned have a market share below 25 % (recital 32 Merger Regulation).

(Article 2), particularly by acquiring (collective) dominance[248] in respect of the merging undertakings. Executed mergers might have to be disentangled or restorative measures can be imposed.[249] Whilst there are no justifications for mergers that are found to impede on competition, the Commission can take inherent justifications[250] into consideration when making its decisions on whether or not a merger impedes competition (Article 2(1)) which may include that one of the parties might otherwise be failing.[251] Differing from the regime under Articles 101 and 102 TFEU, merger control does not fall under Regulation 1/2003 (Article 1(2)), but the Merger Regulation sets out its own procedural rules.[252]

Due to the requirement of a high common world turnover in EU merger control, HEI mergers will probably only exceptionally fall under the EU merger control regime.[253] However, HEIs might more frequently be evaluated under national competition law. Indeed, the OFT has already twice checked educational institutions in England, both times in Manchester. The merger between the City College Manchester and the Manchester College of Arts and Technology has not been further investigated as the relevant market shares were not met.[254] The merger of the University of Manchester, the Victoria University of Manchester and the University of Manchester Institute of Science and Technology, however, was investigated further by the OFT.[255] The OFT came to the conclusion that these

---

[248] Article 2(3) Merger Regulation. A merger can lead to an undertaking achieving individual dominance, undertakings achieving collective dominance (this would be given if the actors would not be able to execute independent market strategies without the other market players copying such strategies) or a merger can cause an oligopoly in a market in which unilateral effects of the merger can restrict competition. See further Marco Colino 2011, p. 367 seq; Simon 2009, para 53 seq.

[249] See Marco Colino 2011, p. 375 seq.

[250] See recital 29 Merger Regulation. See also Guidelines on the assessment of horizontal mergers under the Council Regulation on the control of concentrations between undertakings OJ [2004] C 31/05 (Horizontal Merger Guidelines) para 76 seq, Guidelines on the assessment of non-horizontal mergers under the Council Regulation on the control of concentrations between undertakings OJ [2008] C 265/07 para 53 referring to the relevant section in the Horizontal Merger Guidelines. For more on the weighing of pro- and anti-competitive effects see Marco Colino 2011, p. 373 seq.

[251] Horizontal Mergers Guidelines para 89 seq. See further on the failing firm defence European Commission 2009.

[252] For more on merger control see Marco Colino 2008, p. 357 seq; Amato and Farbmann 2010, p. 9; Horspool and Humphreys 2014, p. 440.

[253] The annual turnover of UK HEIs, for example, varies between less than £9 M and over £600 M (Kelly et al. 2009, p. 7). Taking this as indicative for HEIs' annual turnovers, there would need to be at least five HEIs with a relatively high annual turnover each in a merger to meet the world turnover requirement.

[254] Case ME/3080/07 available on https://www.gov.uk/cma-cases/city-college-manchester-manchester-college-of-arts-and-technology. On the case also see Swennen 2008/2009, p. 277.

[255] Case ME/1613/04 available on https://assets.publishing.service.gov.uk/media/555de401ed 915 d7ae20000df/uompublish.pdf. On the case also see Swennen 2008/2009, p. 277; Gideon 2012, p. 181.

institutions were, for the most part not competitors and, for those parts in which they were, there was still enough competition available and market entry would still remain possible. It therefore allowed the merger. More generally one might assume, however, that an oligopolistic nature of the market might easily be given in certain scenarios depending on how the market is defined and that, in other cases, mergers could be prohibited (for example, ancient languages might be provided by only few universities, a merger of which then could be stopped). With the further commodification of HEIs, the desire to join forces might increase[256] and the application of EU or (more likely) national merger regulation might then hinder such endeavours. Of course, if one of the merging undertakings would otherwise actually fail and competition would thus not be reduced more than in the absence of the concentration, it may be possible to employ the failing firm defence.

3.3.5 State Aid Law

Article 107(1) TFEU prohibits Member States from granting any aid involving state resources selectively to undertakings if this distorts competition and affects trade between Member States. In addition to these elements of Article 107(1) TFEU, the Commission requires a certain amount of appreciability thereby excluding *de minimis* aid of less than €200,000 over any period of three fiscal years from the scope of Article 107(1) TFEU.[257] The concept of 'aid' is much broader than direct subsidies involving a wide spectrum of benefits for undertakings. The Court has taken an 'effects based approach' which focuses solely on the effects on competition rather than analysing aims or causes of a certain measure.[258] The criterion 'transfer of public resources' is, according to the Court, necessary to distinguish state aid from a mere advantage that an undertaking might have.[259] Regarding the criterion of 'selectivity' the aim of a measure, different from when determining whether or not a measure constitutes 'aid', can be taken into consideration; if different treatments of undertakings are justified by the general nature of a scheme, the measure is not regarded as selective.[260] The criterion

---

[256] Fazackerley A (2013) Students not told which universities are struggling. The Guardian, 11 March 2013 https://www.theguardian.com/education/2013/mar/11/universities-falling-applications-ucas-protecting. Accessed 13 March 2014.

[257] Commission Regulation 1407/2013/EU on the application of Articles 107 and 108 of the Treaty on the Functioning of the European Union to de minimis aid' OJ [2013] L 352/1.

[258] 173/73 *Italy v Commission* (Judgment of 2 July 1974, EU:C:1974:71) para 13.

[259] See, for example, C-189/91 *Kirsammer-Hack* (Judgment of 30 November 1993, EU:C:1993:907) para 17 seq. The Commission also emphasises this in Communication on state aid and SGEIs (n 80) para 31.

[260] 173/73 *Italy v Commission* para 15.

of 'effects on intra-Union trade' is, as under the competition law provisions discussed above, a broad concept.[261] The Commission issued a draft communication in this respect,[262] providing for a simplified assessment procedure for certain activities including education, which, however, has never been followed up by a final document. Instead, the Commission now refers to some of its recent decisions[263] for guidance and provides some more detail including examples of typically 'purely local' situations in its new Notice on the Notion of State Aid[264] neither of which makes specific provisions for education and research in this respect.[265]

As long as this is not disguised state aid, Member States are allowed to invest their money as well as to 'buy' public services for their citizens. According to the 'private investor principle' the former is not state aid, if the state acts as a private investor would have done. After some contradictory earlier judgements,[266] the approach towards public service compensation was clarified in the Court's *Altmark*[267] decision. Four conditions need to be fulfilled for public service compensations not to be regarded as state aid: The public service obligations must be clearly defined, the parameters on which the compensation is calculated must be transparent and must have been established in advance, the compensation must not be excessive and the costs included in the calculation of the compensation must themselves be reasonable. In order to establish the latter a public procurement

---

[261] See, for example, T-55/99 *CETM* (Judgment of 29 September 2000, EU:T:2000:223) para 86.

[262] Draft Commission Communication (2004) 'A new framework for the assessment of State aid which has limited effects on intra-Community trade' available on http://ec.europa.eu/competition/state_aid/reform/sit_let_en.pdf.

[263] European Commission (2015) State Aid: Commission gives guidance on local public support measures that can be granted without prior Commission approval. http://europa.eu/rapid/press-release_IP-15-4889_en.htm. Accessed 14 July 2016.

[264] Notice on the Notion of State Aid (n 87) para 190 seq, in particular para 196/197. In para 207 it is stated that amenities such as parking and canteens of research infrastructures are equally unlikely to have an effect on trade.

[265] On the state aid criteria see also Biondi and Rubini 2005, p. 80 seq, 102 seq; Sauter 2015, p. 138; Szyszczak (2016 (forthcoming)).

[266] The Court initially did not regard public service compensation as state aid (240/83 *ADBHU* (Judgment of 7 February 1985, EU:C:1985:59)). The General Court then took a different approach and did consider such compensation as state aid, but then exempting it under Article 106(2) TFEU (T-106/95 *FFSA* (Judgment of 27 February 1997, EU:T:1997:23) and T-46/97 *SIC* (Judgment of 10 May 2000, EU:T:2000:123)). The Court in C-53/00 *Ferring* (Judgment of 22 November 2001, EU:C:2001:627) upheld its original approach deeming public service compensation not as state aid unless exceeding the actual costs borne by the public service provision in which case the aid could then also not be exempted under Article 106(2) TFEU, as it would not meet the proportionality requirement. This judgement received fierce criticism because it was felt, inter alia, that Article 106(2) TFEU would lose its meaning, that the discretionary powers of the Commission to exempt aid would be severely limited and that there was no necessity for the undertakings to keep the costs low. See further Biondi and Rubini 2005, p. 93 seq; Prosser 2005, p. 554 seq.

[267] C-280/00 *Altmark*.

procedure or an analysis of the normal price of such a service in this particular sector would have to be undertaken. Whilst the *Altmark* conditions have been applied strictly in fields such as transportation, energy or waste management,[268] the General Court in *BUPA*[269] followed a more indulgent approach regarding the establishment of a 'public service obligation' which may suggest that the Union's judicial bodies are prepared to follow a more lenient approach in areas of primary responsibility of the Member States.[270] Further, *Spezzino*[271] suggests that under certain circumstances social services can be directly awarded to third sector organisations, thereby avoiding public procurement and state aid law, if these are single objective and exclusively non-profit organisations. Strictly interpreted this case law thus seems of a narrow scope, as it would not cover third sector organisations if they pursue multiple objects and/or are not-for-profit rather than strictly non-profit. It would thus mostly not apply to HEIs, as these are usually not single objective institutions and neither are they necessarily third sector institutions, nor, if they are, are they usually strictly non-profit, but rather not-for-profit organisations. Therefore, under a strict interpretation, the *Spezzino* requirements would not be fulfilled. However, the case nevertheless also suggest some leniency in social areas and it may thus not be impossible that this case law could be widened or interpreted less strictly in the future. On the other hand, the reasoning of the Court seems to partly derive from the particular treatment of ambulance services under the procurement rules which might stand against extendibility to other types of social services.[272] In any case, there still appears to be some development in case law in the area of SGEIs and state aid law[273] even after *Altmark*.[274]

---

[268] On the latter see, for example, the recent cases T-309/12 *Zweckverband Tierkörperbeseitigung* and T-295/12 *Germany v Commission* on management of animal carcasses.

[269] T-289/03 *BUPA*.

[270] Similar Hatzopolous 2009, p. 236 seq; Sauter 2015, p. 142 seq; Gideon and Sanchez Graells 2016, p. 42 seq, 53. Szyszczak similarly highlights that healthcare is a unique area under EU economic law which poses interesting questions as regards economic activities and SGEIs were the European institutions are more willing to protect national schemes (Szyszczak 2015, p. 681 seq, 686 seq; Szyszczak 2016 (forthcoming)).

[271] C-113/13 *Spezzino* (Judgment of 11 December 2014, EU:C:2014:2440).

[272] For a more in-depth analysis of the *Spezzino* decision see Gideon and Sanchez Graells 2016, p. 41 seq.

[273] See, for example, also Sauter 2015, p. 153 suggesting the General Court in T-79/10 *Colt* (Judgment of 16 September 2013, EU:T:2013:463) recently set a different emphasis when relying strongly on market failure.

[274] On the 'private investor principle' and public service compensation generally see Biondi and Rubini 2005, p. 80 seq, 89 seq; Huber and Prikoszovits 2008, p. 171; Hatzopoulos 2009, p. 228 seq; Wendt and Gideon 2011, p. 272; Gideon 2012, p. 182 seq; Sauter 2015, p. 139 seq; Gideon and Sanchez Graells 2016, p. 39 seq.

The Commission followed up on the *Altmark* judgment by issuing clarifying legislation and communications many of which have since been up-dated. Directive 2006/111/EC[275] requires separate accounting for the public service obligations and Decision 2012/21/EU provides a block exemption for compensation below €15 M per annum for SGEIs generally (except in the field of transport) as well as for smaller air and sea ports, for hospitals and for SGEIs 'meeting social needs as regards health and long term care, childcare, access to and reintegration into the labour market, social housing and the care and social inclusion of vulnerable groups'.[276] A Union Framework[277] sets out guidelines of the Commission's position regarding exemptions under Article 106(2) TFEU for state aid which is not covered by Decision 2012/21/EU and a Communication[278] sets out the 'key concepts underlying the application of the state aid rules to public service compensation'. Additionally, the Commission issued a *de minimis* Regulation for SGEIs which takes aid below €500,000 'over any period of three fiscal years' out of the scope of Article 107(1) TFEU.[279] In particular the latter as well as the exemption for aid below €15 M per annum for SGEIs in Decision 2012/21/EU may be utilised by HEIs if all relevant conditions are fulfilled.

Any, illegally granted state aid has to be paid back unless it can be exempted by Article 107(2) and (3) TFEU. The Commission has the power to decide upon this. The approach towards these paragraphs is different from that taken towards Article 107(1) TFEU, which solely relies on economic analysis, since it involves broader assessments of diverging factors.[280] Article 107(2) TFEU exempts aid with a social character for individual consumers, aid for recovery after natural catastrophes and aid for the German states affected by the division of Germany. Generally, only the former may, in particular circumstances, apply to HEIs. Article 107(3) provides for exemptions for aid for (a) economically deprived regions, (b) 'an important project of common European interest' or economic disturbances, (c) the

---

[275] Commission Directive 2006/111/EC on the transparency of financial relations between Member States and public undertakings as well as on financial transparency within certain undertakings OJ [2006] L 318/17.

[276] Decision 2012/21/EU Article 2(1). Sauter describes this as 'an unlimited block exemption [...] for welfare services' (Sauter 2015, p. 145 and, similar, 225). However, while the exemption for SGEIs below €15 M is indeed for all SGEIs, the exemption for SGEIs 'meeting social needs' is only for the services specified which notably does not include education. Further, it only applies to public service compensation if the undertaking has been entrusted with the public service for a maximum period of 10 years.

[277] Commission Communication 'European Union framework for State aid in the form of public service compensation' OJ [2012] C 8/03.

[278] Communication on state aid and SGEIs (n 80) para 3.

[279] Regulation 360/2012/EU on the application of Articles 107 and 108 of the Treaty on the Functioning of the European Union to de minimis aid granted to undertakings providing services of general economic interest OJ [2012] L 114/12.

[280] On Articles 107(2) and (3) see Biondi and Rubini 2005, p. 79 seq; Sauter 2015, p. 116.

facilitation in the development of 'certain economic activities' or 'certain economic areas', (d) 'culture and heritage conservation' and (e) 'other categories of aid as may be specified by decision of the Council'. Of these (b)–(d), might in particular be helpful in exempting state aid for HEIs.[281]

The Commission has also issued secondary legislation providing for exemptions. For research in HEIs, the General Block Exemption Regulation (GBER)[282] might be particularly helpful. It contains an exemption for mainly basic research[283] of up to €40 M per project with 100 % aid intensity,[284] for mainly applied research of up to €20 M per project with 50 % aid intensity and for mainly experimental development of up to €15 M with 25 % aid intensity.[285] Feasibility studies can receive a maximum of €7.5 M with 50 % aid intensity,[286] research infrastructures of €20 M per infrastructure with 50 % aid intensity,[287] innovation clusters of €7.5 M per cluster with 50 % aid intensity,[288] innovation aid for small and medium sized enterprises (SME) of €5 M per undertaking and project with 50 % aid intensity[289] and process and organisational innovation of €7.5 M per undertaking and project with 15 % (30 % for SME) aid intensity.[290] There are

---

[281] See Gideon 2012, p. 183 seq.

[282] Commission Regulation 651/2014/EU declaring certain categories of aid compatible with the internal market in application of Articles 107 and 108 of the Treaty (General Block Exemption Regulation) OJ [2014] L 187/1.

[283] The Commission uses the terms 'fundamental research', 'industrial research' and 'experimental development'. The definitions provided (GBER Article 2(84) seq, Research Framework (para 15 (j), (m), (q)) for these terms lead to the conclusion that they are used in a similar way as the terms 'basic research', 'applied research' and 'experimental development' as defined by the Frascati Manual (see OECD 2002), though somewhat confusingly the new version of the Research Framework uses 'applied research' as an umbrella term for 'industrial research' and 'experimental development'. As laid out in Chap. 1 (Sect. 1.3.3, n 35) the Frascati Manual definitions are used in this book.

[284] Aid intensity describes the aid amount as percentage of the total eligible costs (Article 2(26) GBER).

[285] GBER Articles 3, 4(1) (i), 25(5) seq. The amounts double if the project in question is a EUREKA project or a joint undertaking according to Article 185 and 187 TFEU (public-private partnerships of strategic importance) and the amount can be increased by 50 % if the aid is provided as a repayable advance. The aid intensity of both applied research and experimental development can be increased up to 80 % in total if bonuses for small and medium sized enterprises and effective collaboration or wide dissemination can be applied.

[286] Article 4(1) (i), 25(5). The bonuses for SME (mentioned in n 285) are also available for feasibility studies.

[287] Article 4(1) (j), 26(6). Research infrastructures can also receive regional investment aid under chapter III, Sect. 1 of the GBER which may increase the aid ceiling.

[288] Article 4(1) (k), 27. The intensity can be increased in 'assisted areas' as regards investment aid. Operating aid for innovation clusters may not exceed 10 years.

[289] Article 4(1) (l), 28. Only eligible costs (IPR, secondment of personnel, advisory and support services (e.g. consultancy, access to libraries)) can be covered.

[290] Article 4(1) (m), 29. An SME has to be involved in process and organisational innovation measures which must incur at least 30 % of the eligible costs.

special provisions for agricultural research and research in the fisheries sector (Article 30). However, there are certain rules to be complied with. According to Article 5 only transparent aid is exempted[291] and projects may not be split artificially (Article 4(2)). Further, aid must have an incentive effect and thus only aid to projects which would not have been undertaken otherwise falls under the regulation.[292] As regards aid for research, there may be no restrictions on exploitation in other Member States (Article 1(5) (c)), the aided part of a project must fall entirely within one or more of the above named categories and can only be provided for eligible costs (personnel, equipment, building use, contract research, IPR or overheads directly related to the project).[293] Aid schemes of over €150 M annually in the research sector can only be exempted under the GBER for six months which can be extended by the Commission (Article 1(2) (a)). The exemptions provided for training activities in the GBER are not generally applicable to HEIs because they concern training for employees rather than the higher education of students.[294] Most HEIs will also not be able to utilise the exemption for SME, since SME are undertakings with 250 or less employees and an annual turnover of less than €50 M.[295] In particular the former will be too low a threshold for most HEIs.[296] Aid which does not fall under these (or potentially any other) exemptions would have to be notified.

With regards to exemptions after notification, the Research Framework provides guidance on how the Commission will proceed in the application of Article 107(3) (c) TFEU to research and development activities. In Sect. 3 (paras 35–39) of the Research Framework the Commission lays out general principles for exemption and in Sect. 4 (paras 40–119) it provides details on the conditions which, if all are fulfilled, would mean that aid without a maximum ceiling may be exempted. These conditions are:

1. Contribution to a well-defined objective of common interest (paras 42–47),
2. Need for state intervention (paras 48–55),
3. Appropriateness of the aid measure (paras 56–61),
4. Incentive effect (paras 62–71),

---

[291] That means the aid must be able to be calculated in advance and there are (presumably exhaustive) examples of transparent aid. See also para 17 of the preamble. Member States must publish information about aid measures (Article 9(1)).

[292] Article 6 and para 18 of the preamble. This means in particular that aid is not exempted if work has commenced before the application for aid was made to the Member State in question.

[293] Article 25(2).

[294] Preamble para 53.

[295] Article 2(2) in conjunction with Annex I.

[296] However, university spin-offs may benefit from these exemptions, even if the university holds more than 25 % of the spin-off's shares (Article 3(2)), unless they are linked with the university in the sense of Article 3(3) (i.e. majority of voting rights, right to appoint management, etc.). Further, more generally, aid provided through the HEI to SME (e.g. consultancy aid (Article 18) or start-up aid (Article 22)) may be exempted if it is transparent aid.

5. Proportionality of aid (paras 72–93); the aid may only cover eligible costs (Annex 1) up to a certain intensity (Annex 2),[297] including where aid is cumulating, and only the minimum needed and there should usually be an open procedure if there is more than one candidate,
6. Avoidance of undue negative effects on competition and trade (paras 94–118),[298]
7. Transparency (para 119).

HEIs and Member States might in particular have to pay attention to cumulative aid, as it may be conceivable that aid does not create concerns on an individual level, but on a cumulative basis the aid schemes lead to distortions. Section 5 (paras 120–123) lays down principles for evaluation of the implementation of exempted schemes. Aid which would fall under a BER except for its large budget, can undergo a simplified exemption procedure where the Commission will only assess its evaluation plan (para 122). Unlike the previous version, the new Research Framework is not concerned with exemption according to Article 107(3) (b) which are now dealt with in a separate Communication[299] for all sectors. Accordingly, inter alia, an important project of common European interest is a project that is 'of major importance for the Europe 2020 strategy [or/and] the European Research Area' (para 15). It must involve 'more than one Member State', have clearly defined benefits (para 16) and, as regards research, must be truly innovative (paras 21 and 22). Further, the importance of exploitation and dissemination of results is stressed (paras 10(c) and 43).

3.3.5.1 Hidden Aid

HEIs could get into conflict with Article 107(1) TFEU if they conduct research or teaching services on a market and do not charge the full price for these services. The same would be true for the use of facilities such as research infrastructures. This would thus require HEIs to generally use full costing for all such activities since all unaccounted use of state facilities would constitute state aid either to the

---

[297] Generally the aid intensities for R&D projects are 100 % for basic research, 50–70 % for applied research (depending on size of enterprise) and 25–45 % for experimental development with higher intensity (65–80 and 40–60 % respectively) for effective collaborations and/or wide dissemination. Aid intensities may be even higher (up to 90 % for both applied research and experimental development) where strict necessity can be shown (to paras 87–89). Other intensities apply to activities other than projects (e.g. feasibility studies or innovation aid for SME). Overall the aid intensities are now higher than in the previous Research Framework.

[298] This includes, in particular, discriminatory schemes (para 104, 116 seq), schemes maintaining or creating market power (para 113 seq) or schemes which are not exemptible due to accumulation (para 106 seq).

[299] Commission Communication Criteria for the analysis of the compatibility with the internal market of State aid to promote the execution of import projects of common European interest OJ [2014] C 188/44.

HEI itself or to the undertaking the HEI is providing the services for.[300] Whilst there have been no cases regarding HEIs yet, the General Court had to deal with an action to annul a Commission decision regarding aid from a public research organisation.[301] Here

> the aid had come about as a result of the existence of commercial subsidiaries and the concurrent conclusion of exclusive agreements between those subsidiaries and the parent company, in so far as those subsidiaries did not guarantee total coverage of the costs of work carried out by [...] [the public research organisation] on behalf of [...] [the commercial subsidiaries].[302]

The Commission had, however, exempted the measure, as it fulfilled the criteria for exemption under Article 107(3) (c) TFEU as set out in an earlier version of the Research Framework.[303] In this case a competitor had challenged the decision which had been dismissed because the competitor was found not to have standing. The case shows, however, that public research organisations such as HEIs can come into the ambit of state aid law if they do not apply full costing to economic activities. To avoid this, a more economic mode of operation with separate accounting of economic and non-economic activities and a full cost methodology would be necessary and the previous Research Framework indeed required implementation of such measures until January 2009 for research organisation. Yet, as will be seen in the next chapters, this had still not entirely happened in the Member States under scrutiny at the time the empirical study has been conducted[304] and may have not happened yet in some Member States.

The Commission also specifically stressed in the Issue Paper that Member States seem to have assumed that all support to research infrastructures is inherently not state aid which is incorrect since the same differentiation between economic and non-economic activities need to be made as with research organisations.[305] The new Research Framework continues to stress that economic and non-economic activities must be accounted for separately (paras 15(ee), 18) so that there can be no cross-subsidisation of economic activities and that public funding for economic activities will be regarded as state aid (para 21). If these benefits are passed on, a research organisation is providing state aid (para 22 seq). Thus if HEIs wish to conduct an economic activity, they have to receive adequate

---

[300] See Huber and Prikoszovits 2008, p. 171 seq; European Commission 2012, p. 11 seq; Gideon 2012, p. 183 seq; Gideon 2015b, p. 61 seq. In respect to hospitals see Hatzopoulos 2009, p. 244 seq; Wendt and Gideon 2011, p. 271 seq.

[301] T-198/09 *UOP* (Order of 7 March 2013, EU:T:2013:105).

[302] Ibid para 8.

[303] Community framework for State aid for research and development OJ [1996] C 45/5.

[304] See Chaps. 4 and 5 below.

[305] European Commission 2012, pp. 2, 10 seq.

compensation for this activity (para 25) either by charging the market price,[306] full-costs plus a typical profit margin[307] or by charging the, at arm length negotiated, maximum economic benefit if it at least covers the marginal costs. The latter was not included in the previous Research Framework and seems to make the rules somewhat more lenient by leaving a lot of room for interpretation rather than insisting on a strict full cost plus approach. Again, this may be attributed to the EU itself promoting cooperation with the private (or third) sector and having considered that enforcing the state aid rules strictly might hamper this.[308] However, the definition of 'arm-length in para 15(f) provides that there should be no element of collusion and ideally an open procedure. Thus, if the market price or full cost plus cannot be achieved, transparency and non-discrimination would still have to be shown as well as that the HEI tried to achieve maximum benefit. Random reductions, conventional pricing below full cost plus or pricing based on costing methodologies which do not capture the full costs would still be state aid.

It seems questionable in how far any exemptions can be applied to hidden aid. For the SGEI exemptions, the service would need to qualify as an SGEI and would have to have been entrusted to the entity which seems doubtful at least in cases of contract research for the private sector. As regards the Research Framework and the GBER, these at various places, make clear that aid can only be exempted if there had been separate accounting for economic and non-economic activities, clear identification into aid categories, appropriate pricing, access on transparent and non-discriminatory basis and that the aid intensities may not be exceeded if the amount of economic activities increase.[309] Further, Article 5 of the GBER provides that only transparent aid can be exempted which means it has to be possible to calculate the aid in advance and the (presumably exhaustive) examples of transparent aid do not include hidden aid which one would thus assume does not constitute transparent aid. Member States must also publish information about aid measures (Article 9(1)) which is doubtful they do for hidden aid. Thus, it would appear that mainly the general *de minimis* Regulation may be applicable and thus only aid below €200,000 over any period of three fiscal years could be exempted.

Of course, exemptions could still be granted generally on the basis of Article 107(2) and (3) TFEU. A recent case in this regard concerned subsidies by the Czech Republic to third sector organisations to build sporting facilities.[310] A competitor had complained to the Commission alleging this to be state aid, inter alia, raising the point that the beneficiaries were in an advantageous position as they did

---

[306] If the research organisation gets to keep IPR, these can be deducted from the price (para 26).

[307] Compared to the draft the Framework (n 102) the final version now talks about 'generally' including a margin thus making it potentially wider.

[308] See also Sect. 3.2.4.2 above in regards to the potentially broad scope of non-economic knowledge transfer.

[309] For example, para 15(f) Research Framework, para 47 seq preamble of the GEBR, Article 2(83), Article 26 GBER on research infrastructures, Article 27 GBER on innovation clusters.

[310] T-693/14 *Hamr* (Judgment of 12 May 2016, EU:T:2016:292).

not have to offer their services at full cost plus levels.[311] Here, the Commission decided that the exemption for aid to facilitate the development of certain economic activities of Article 107(3) (c) TFEU would apply, as the promotion of sport was a common objective (envisaged in Article 165 TFEU), the measures were appropriate and necessary and it was unlikely that there was an effect on interstate trade. It did admit that there may be losses to commercial operators of such facilities, but, since leaving the promotion of sport entirely to the market would not satisfy the common interest by providing sporting facilities at affordable prices for a great number or people, this would have to be tolerated.[312] The General Court supported the Commissions assessment and dismissed the case. It may be possible that HEIs could utilise this case law in some cases where they are offering services benefitting the general public. In cases of hidden aid for clearly commercial activities for individual companies such as contract research, on the other hand, this avenue seems less likely to lead to success.

3.3.5.2 Public Funding of Higher Education and Research

If a market system is introduced in a Member State and therefore most of the services an HEI conducts need to be regarded as economic in nature, the Member State would also have to follow the *Altmark*[313] criteria for these services. This would mean that if the Member State aims to pay certain providers to conduct these services for the public, the Member State would normally need to commission these services in a public procurement procedure. If the Member State aims at having a system where it leaves the choice to the consumer and just pays the bill or gives out vouchers or other financial help to consumers to buy these services themselves, the consumer must also be able to choose the provider freely or choose from a range of providers which have been established according to objective criteria, normally in a public procurement procedure.[314]

If a system has progressed far on the path towards commodification, like in the English case, arguably teaching services[315] should thus generally be procured[316] or public financial support should travel with the student who can choose freely between providers (including foreign and private providers) for this not to constitute state aid. Indeed, Hogenboom has conducted an in-depth analysis of the

---

[311] Ibid para 80.

[312] Ibid para 66.

[313] See text surrounding n 267 above.

[314] Gideon 2012, p. 181 seq; Gideon 2015a, p. 1056; Gideon 2015b, p. 61.

[315] Provided they do fall under the state aid rules and are not meant to be entirely exempted as the Notice on the Notion of State (n 87) could potentially suggest as was discussed above (Sect. 3.2.4.1).

[316] See further Gideon and Sanchez Graells 2016, p. 22 seq. See also Chap. 2, Sect. 2.3.4 above and Gideon and Sanchez Graells 2016 on public procurement and the in-house and public-public exemptions.

conformity with state aid rules of the difference made in the English higher education system for loans that can be accessed by students in publicly financed HEIs
(£9000) and students in privately financed HEIs (£6000) and concluded that this
might likely constitute state aid.[317] Furthermore, there are student number controls
for private providers whose students access public loans which do not apply to
publicly funded providers.[318] There are also other advantages for certain providers
in the English system as regards, for example, VAT exemptions,[319] access to wid-
ening participation funding, access to generic teaching funding grants from
HEFCE and differences in sustainability requirements. Arguably, the differences
convey a selective advantage on certain providers.[320] Such difference in the funding of providers is not unique to England, though. In the Italian free movement
law case *Dirextra*[321] there was a requirement of 10 years of experience before students of HEIs could access certain funding. The case had only been assessed under
free movement law, but arguably the HEIs also received a financial advantage
which could be regarded as state aid. However, in this case this may be inherently
justified by the general nature of the scheme, since all HEIs had to fulfil the age
requirement. In so far it might not be selective. Overall, the more commodified a
system becomes, the more difficult it may be to exclude private providers from
public funding arrangements. Yet, the dangers of funding private providers have
been widely discussed and appear to be highlighted by the financial difficulties
which have occurred in England in this respect a few years ago.[322]

As regards research, unlike the previous version, the new Research Framework
now actually specifies the *Altmark* criteria for research services in para 31 seq and
lays out the rules that need to be adhered to when the state is paying for economic
research. Accordingly, if a public authority purchases such research, it has to follow the public procurement rules (para 32). Otherwise the price has at least to
reflect the market value which is, in particular, the case if the selection procedure is
open, all rights and obligations are made available to everyone interested, there is
no preferential treatment and either the results may be widely disseminated and the

---

[317] Hoogenboom 2015.

[318] CMA 2015, para 3.3. See also Malik S et al. (2013) Poorest students face £350 m cut in
grants. The Guardian, 22 November 2013 http://www.theguardian.com/education/2013/nov/22/
poorest-students-face-350m-cuts. Accessed 29 November 2013.

[319] UCU (2016) Fighting privatisation in tertiary education. https://www.ucu.org.uk/stopprivati-
sation. Accessed 11 March 2016.

[320] Similarly, while assessing regulation in its advocacy role rather than looking at issues of state
aid, the OFT and CMA in their reports pointed out that there should be a more level playing field
as currently it seems nearly impossible for certain providers to achieve certain statuses (e.g. there
are differences as regards student visa, degree awarding powers, etc.) or obtain certain funding
(OFT 2014, para 7.20 seq, CMA 2015, para 5.2 seq). Again, the reforms outlined in the White
Paper (BIS 2016) aim at introducing changes here which may resolve some of the issues by making the system more permeable, but, at same time, more commercial.

[321] C-523/12 *Dirextra* (Judgment of 12 December 2013, EU:C:2013:831). This has been discussed in Chap. 2, Sect. 2.3.2 above.

[322] Malik et al. (n 318), UCU (n 319).

public purchaser gets the IPR or the public purchases gets free access of all IPR and other parties can get non-exclusive licenses for the market price (para 33). Where this is not the case, 'Member States may rely on an individual assessment of the terms of the contract between the public purchaser and the undertaking, without prejudice to the general obligation to notify R&D&I aid pursuant to Article 108(3) of the Treaty' (para 34). The Research Framework thus offers alternatives to a procurement procedure which, if followed, would mean that the purchasing of the research service does not constitute state aid. This seems to provide slightly more leeway which may be due to research, despite being a shared competence now, being an area in which the Member States still hold major responsibilities due to the caveat in Article 4(3) TFEU[323] as well as due to EU research policy having encouraged investment into research and collaboration with the private sector.[324] Nevertheless, as we have seen, the emphasis in these more relaxed approaches is on non-discrimination and open dissemination which can potentially be assumed as minimum standards. Thus directly awarding economic research would generally still have to be regarded as state aid. Instead, such services should be commissioned according to objective criteria and it must be possible for public, private, third sector and foreign providers to apply. As we will explore further in the following chapters, one might wonder if certain governmental funding programmes could be regarded as purchasing economic research and whether they thus should be open for all undertakings to apply for them. This could then create a very different, more commercial character as regards certain publicly funded research.

Economic research services which would infringe the state aid rules might benefit from the *de minimis* rule. If they qualify as SGEI they may equally benefit from the special SGEI *de minimis* rule and the exemption for state aid for SGEIs below €15 M. Further, research services that fulfil the conditions of the GBER could be exempted that way. Should none of these exemptions be applicable the aid would need to be notified and could potentially be exempted according to Article 107(3) or 106(2) TFEU. As regards the former, the details in the Research Framework need to be taken into consideration. If, in a rather market based system, teaching services would generally have to be regarded as economic in nature, the overall value is likely to go far beyond the €15 M threshold. Therefore, an infringement of the state aid rules as regards higher education, can only potentially be justified under Article 107(2), (3) or 106(2) TFEU rather than secondary legislation if notified. How successful such an avenue would be, would depend on the particular case.[325]

---

[323] See Chap. 2, Sect. 2.2.1.3 above.

[324] See Research Framework para 3, European Commission 2012, pp. 2, 6 seq. Contrary to the seeming relaxation of the rules in the new Research Framework, Nicolaides in his evaluation of EU state aid rules for research and development, concludes that subsidies should be limited and provided competitively (Nicolaides 2013).

[325] In his analysis of the difference in the English loan system, Hoogenboom conclusively submits that it seems unlikely that these exemption are applicable (Hoogenboom 2015).

3.3.5.3 Aid Through Knowledge Transfer

If we are assuming that para 19b of the Research Framework means that all knowledge transfer in the broad definition given to it para 15(v) including 'research collaborations, consultancy, licensing, spin-off creation, publication and mobility of researchers and other personnel' is entirely non-economic in nature if profits are re-invested, there will be little tension with the state aid rules as long as indeed all profits are reinvested. Yet, as discussed in Sect. 3.2.4.2 above, there seem some inconsistencies with this interpretation. It has thus been suggested above that this may only refer to particular areas of knowledge transfer (e.g. IPR exploitation) which are based on non-economic research activities and are non-exclusive as has been initially advised by the Commission in the Issue Paper.[326]

Furthermore, the new Research Framework contains detailed rules on when state aid might be present in collaboration. Nowhere in these section is there a reference to para 19(b) or any other indication that it is intended that these rules are not applicable if profits are reinvested. It therefore seems possible that HEIs provide state aid to companies they collaborate with, even if any potential profits are reinvested. As we have seen above (Sect. 3.2.4.2) collaboration has to be effective and the research has to be 'independent R&D for more knowledge and better understanding' otherwise the activity may have to be regarded as a research service no matter as what it labelled as. Effective collaboration is usually longer term and more open-ended, following a common objective the scope of which has been jointly defined, risks and labour are shared and terms and conditions should be clearly set out in advance, so that industry does not receive advantage.[327] In an effective collaboration with an HEI no state aid is present, according to para 28, if either (1) the other undertakings carry all costs, (2) the results maybe widely disseminated and the HEI gets to keep its IPRs, (3) IPRs are allocated reflecting work packages or (4) the HEI receives compensation at market price levels for IPRs. The other undertakings must at least bear their own costs. Only if other undertakings contribute beyond that, can such contributions be deducted from the market price it has to pay to keep IPRs. The latter has particularly been emphasised by the Commission as an area that has not been clearly understood in the past.[328] Para 29 provides when the compensation is equivalent to market price:[329] either the price has been established through an open sales procedure or through expert evaluation or through arm length negotiation or, if right of first refusal exists, the possibility to get other offers which have to be matched is existent. Para 30 of the Research Framework makes very clear that if these conditions are not fulfilled 'the full value

---

[326] European Commission 2012 para 7 seq.

[327] Research Framework para 27, European Commission 2012, p. 7 seq.

[328] European Commission 2011, p. 8 seq.

[329] In the draft (n 102) para 29 it said that 'particularly' if the four conditions are fulfilled the price would be equivalent to market price, now the four options seem exhaustive.

of the contribution of the research organisation [...] will be considered as an advantage for the collaborating undertakings, to which State aid rules apply'.

Licensing seems to be a clear example of a non-economic activity given that profits are reinvested. However, one may still wonder if the condition of non-exclusivity suggested by the Commission in the Issue Paper[330] as well as, as is the case for collaboration, a requirement to achieve a reasonable price does or should apply, as otherwise situations may arise where an undertaking can legitimately receive a significant advantage. The thus far only EU level competition law case on research in HEIs, *Sarc*,[331] has indeed concerned such a case. Here Sarc, a Netherlands company for ship design software, complained to the Commission alleging that its competitor Delftship had received state aid through 'advantageous conditions' in a software licence agreement with the Technische Universiteit Delft (TUD) of whom Delftship was a spin-off. Sarc essentially saw the state aid in the low royalty that Delftship had to pay TUD which allowed it to offer its software at a low rate on the market. The Commission indeed looked into the case, thus seemingly indicating that it did not consider this a non-economic activity under the previous version of the Research Framework,[332] but decided that Delftship did not receive an advantage and that there was thus no state aid present in this case. Sarc then brought the case before the General Court which, due to Sarc's limited standing in this case,[333] only checked for manifest errors in the Commission decision and decided against Sarc. However, the arguments brought (e.g. that royalties paid to universities in the UK are around ten times as high, that TUD had exclusively negotiated with Delftship and that independent assessments had come to the result that Delftship had received an advantage) were rather strong and it seems possible that had the Court applied Article 107 TFEU itself rather than checking for obvious errors that the result might have been different. On the other hand, the fact that the Commission and the Court found the practice by TUD acceptable might once again point to a more considered approach in an area were not only significant responsibility remains with the Member State, but also a research policy is being followed which is encouraged at the EU level (namely the interplay between the public and the private as regards research policy and encouragement of exploitation). In any case, *Sarc* also shows that the more the activities of HEIs intertwine with the market place, the more competitors might feel their rights to be infringed which can open the practises of HEIs to EU level scrutiny and thereby potentially to spill-over from competition law.

---

[330] European Commission 2012, p. 7 seq.

[331] Case T-488/11 *Sarc*.

[332] The previous Research Framework in its Section 3.1.1 also provided that licensing would be non-economic if handled by, with or on behalf of the research organisation and all income was reinvested.

[333] Sanchez Graells argues that in 'adopting such a strict approach and imposing such a high [...] burden of proof of significant alteration of its competitive position, the GC only recognises the applicant's standing to protect its procedural rights, which fundamentally limits the possibility for competitors to challenge State aid decisions' (Sanchez Graells 2014).

Since the two previously discussed examples of knowledge exchange (collaboration and licensing) may indicate that knowledge exchange activities might not as easily be regarded as non-economic activities as the combined reading of paras 15(v) and 19(b) of the Research Framework might initially suggest, one might also wonder if there are other areas of knowledge exchange where HEIs could get into conflict with state aid law. One such example may be students writing their Masters or PhD theses with a private firm. In such cases a student writes his or her dissertation on a subject that interests the company and normally has a supervisor in the company as well as in the HEI.[334] If such an activity has to be considered a research service for the company and the student is not or only marginally paid by the firm or even receives state funding (e.g. from a research council), this could possibly be regarded as state aid.

Of course, if in any of these examples state aid is deemed present it may be *de minimis* or exempted according to the rules set out above. It would depend on the individual case in how far this would be possible. In any case the rules for such exemptions (e.g. on transparency) would have to be adhered to.

3.3.6 Interim Conclusion

It has been shown that many activities conducted by HEIs could potentially be in conflict with EU competition and state aid law. The result would not only be that the actions would have to be discontinued, but, according to Articles 23 and 24 of Regulation 1/2003, fines and periodic penalty payments until the infringement is stopped can be imposed. Additionally, the infringement of competition law could constitute a tort under national law and give rise to actions for damages.[335] Thus, aside from the question of whether the application of EU competition law leads to tensions with national policy concepts, it might also lead to financial problems. Facing an imposed fine the HEIs would have to cut back on their resources or increase prices (tuition fees, research costs and prices of other activities such as student accommodation or meals) which would, either way, endanger their mission of providing high quality and equally accessible teaching and research in the public interest.[336]

---

[334] This is, for example, increasingly popular in Germany. See Zander H (2009) Starthilfe. Der Tagesspiegel, 26 April 2009 http://www.tagesspiegel.de/studium-starthilfe/1797792.html. Accessed 28 February 2012, Studieren.net (2012) Abschlussarbeit Teil 4. http://www.studieren.net/studienphase/studienabschluss/abschlussarbeit-teil-4.html. Accessed 28 February 2012.

[335] Directive 2014/104/EU on certain rules governing actions for damages under national law for infringements of the competition law provisions of the Member States and of the European Union OJ [2014] L 349/1. See also C-295-298/04 *Manfredi* (Judgment of 13 July 2006, EU:C:2006:461) and C-453/99 *Courage* (Judgment of 20 September 2001, EU:C:2001:465).

[336] Similar Greaves and Scicluna 2010, pp. 21, 24.

There are, of course, still exemption possibilities for infringements of competition law under Articles 101(3), 107(2) and (3) and 106(2) TFEU and secondary legislation. This might, however, make the conduct of HEIs increasingly complicated from a legal/administrative perspective and the exemptions might not capture every situation. As regards the SGEI exemption, for example, the performance of the SGEI might not be seen as obstructed by the competition rules, especially if a strict necessity test is applied.[337] Especially in systems such as the English one (which is consciously being turned into a market system) it might be difficult to then rely on Article 106(2) TFEU.[338] Even if the EU institutions might adopt a more careful approach regarding higher education, since this area is mainly the responsibility of the Member States and potentially even regarding research despite it having become a shared responsibility due to the caveat in Article 4(3) TFEU and potentially also due to EU research policy encouraging commodification of research, they might not apply the law themselves. Since Regulation 1/2003 the enforcement of competition law is decentralised and therefore much depends on the NCAs. As the national case law examined in this chapter has shown NCAs were less reluctant to apply competition law to educational institutions.[339]

3.4 Conclusion

The aim of this chapter was to conduct an in-depth legal doctrinal assessment of potential competition law constraints on HEIs. It has been shown that the main activities of HEIs, teaching and research, could, especially with increasing commodification, be regarded as economic in nature. This would then mean that HEIs would have to be regarded as undertakings and would have to comply with EU competition and state aid rules. Whilst this can potentially lead to positive results, especially in cases where a high degree of commodification is already achieved and HEIs are actually acting in commercial way (as demonstrated in the price fixing case of the two Amsterdam universities), the application of competition law can also lead to detrimental effects in cases where the public service character of the services performed by HEIs still prevails. The analysis of individual competition provisions has shown that this can cause potential tensions because the economic competition and state aid law provisions might clash with the public service nature of the teaching and research activities of HEIs. To avoid conflict HEIs would have to operate even more commercially by separating accounts for

---

[337] See Sect. 3.2.3.3 above on the test.

[338] Similar regarding health care markets see Wendt and Gideon 2011, p. 274.

[339] Similar Greaves and Scicluna 2010, p. 24.

economic and non-economic activities, adhering to full costing for teaching and research, refraining from price fixing even if it is to the advantage of the consumer and private providers would have to be treated equally.

Additionally, fines for competition law infringements could be imposed and the question would arise how or by whom these would be paid. With the decentralisation of competition law, NCAs would have to investigate cases regarding HEIs and they might be less reluctant to apply competition rules to them than EU institutions which occasionally seem to have shown a certain reluctance to get involved in these policy areas in some newer cases. While there are exemptions for competition law infringements, these might not always apply. Even if they are applicable, they might require a more commercial way of operation for a measure to be proportionate. Aside from Article 106(2) TFEU, exemptions from the competition provisions are mainly efficiency based[340] and as regards the case law on SGEIs the Court has also sometimes applied a strict necessity test as we have seen above (Sect. 3.2.3.3) and a service would have to be clearly entrusted to HEIs. The assumption that commodification of HEIs may lead to the application of competition law which, in turn, may require an even more commercial system seems already be proven true by the assessment of the OFT and CMA and the CMAs suggested changes to regulation of higher education in England[341] which widely have been taken up in the recent Green and White Papers.[342] Other Member States following the path towards commodification may equally come to face consequences from competition law application.

The legal doctrinal analysis of potential competition law constraints on HEIs in general provided in this chapter will serve as the basis for examining competition law constraints on research in HEIs in three Member States in more detail by employing socio-legal methods in the subsequent chapters. Chapter 4 will prepare this examination by exploring the research systems of the three countries under scrutiny.

References

Aicher J et al (2009) EGV Art. 81 Verbot wettbewerbsbeschränkender Vereinbarungen und Verhaltensweisen (Nizza-Fassung) (English translation: Article 81 EC prohibition of anti-competitive agreements and practices (Nice Version)). In: Grabitz E et al (eds) Das Recht der Europäischen Union (English translation: Law of the European Union), 40th edn. Beck, Munich
Amato F, Farbmann K (2010) Applying EU competition law in the education sector. IJELP 6:7–13

---

[340] Sauter 2015, p. 126 seq, 224.

[341] In essence the CMA suggests to establish a baseline quality which should be kept to the minimum to allow an equal playing field of all providers while other public policy goals should not be reflected in regulation of providers above baseline, but through other, competitively neutral measures. See CMA para 1.10 seq.

[342] BIS 2015, 2016. The envisaged system is to create a single entry route where providers can more easily access the market and achieve certain statuses, while it is also foreseen that they can exit the market.

Areen J (2011) Accreditation reconsidered. Iowa Law Rev 96:1471–1494

Baquero Cruz J (2005) Beyond competition: services of general interest and European Community Law. In: De Burca G (ed) EU law and the welfare state. OUP, Oxford, pp 169–212

Biondi A, Rubini L (2005) Aims, effects and justifications: EC state aid law and its impact on national social policy. In: Dougan M, Spaventar E (eds) Social welfare and EU law. Hart, Oxford/Portland, pp 79–104

BIS (2011) Higher education—students at the heart of the system. The Stationery Office, Norwich

BIS (2015) Fulfilling our potential—teaching excellence, social mobility and student choice. Williams Lea Group on behalf of the Controller of Her Majesty's Stationery Office, London

BIS (2016) Success as a knowledge economy. Williams Lea Group, London

Bishop S, Walker M (2010) The economics of EC competition law. Sweet & Maxwell, London

Boeger N (2007) Solidarity and EC competition law. Eur Law Rev 32:319–340

Browne J et al (2010) Securing a sustainable future for higher education. http://webarchive.nationalarchives.gov.uk/+/hereview.independent.gov.uk/hereview/report/

Buendia Sierra JL (2016) Enforcement of Article 106(1) TFEU by the European Commission and the EU Courts. In: Lowe P et al (eds) European competition law annual 2013. Hart, Oxford/Portland, pp 279–306

Carlson DR, Shepherd GB (1992) Cartel on campus: the economics and law of academic institutions' financial aid price fixing. Oregon Law Rev 71:563–629

Chalmers D et al (2014) European Union law, 3rd edn. CUP, Cambridge

Chirita AD (2014) A legal-historical review of the EU competition rules. Int Comp Law Q 63:281–316

CMA (2015) An effective regulatory framework for higher education: A policy paper. Crown Copyright, London

European Commission (2009) Roundtable on failing firm defence—note by the delegation of the European Commission. OECD. http://ec.europa.eu/competition/international/multilateral/failingfirmdefence.pdf

European Commission (2011) Commission Staff Working Paper: mid-term review of the R&D&I Framework. European Commission, Brussels

European Commission (2012) Revision of the state aid rules for research and development and innovation. European Commission, Brussels

European Commission (2014) Supporting R&D and innovation in Europe: new State aid rules. Competition policy brief 1–4

First H (1979) Competition in the legal education industry (II): an antitrust analysis. New York Univ Law Rev 54:1049–1130

Gideon A (2012) Higher education institutions and EU competition law. Compet Law Rev 8:169–184

Gideon A (2015a) The position of higher education institutions in a changing European context: an EU law perspective. JCMS: J Common Market Stud 53:1045–1060

Gideon A (2015b) Blurring boundaries between the public and the private in national research policies and possible consequences from EU primary law. J Contemp Eur Res 11:50–68

Gideon A, Sanchez-Graells A (2016) When are universities bound by EU public procurement rules as buyers and providers?—English universities as a case study. Ius Publicum 2016(1):1–58

Greaves R, Scicluna A (2010) Commercialization and competition in the education services sector—challenges to the education service sector from the application of Articles 101 and 102 TFEU. IJELP 6:13–25

Hatzopoulos V (2009) Services of general interest in healthcare: an exercise in deconstruction? In: Neergaard U et al (eds) Integrating welfare functions into EU law—from Rome to Lisbon. DJØF Forlag, Copenhagen, pp 225–252

Havighurst CC, Brody PM (1994) Accrediting and the Sherman Act. Law Contemp Probl 57:199–242

Hoogenboom A (2015) Commodification of higher education: students, study loan systems and state aid. EStAL 4:492–502

Horspool M, Humphreys M (2014) European Union law, 8th edn. OUP, Oxford

Huber S, Prikoszovits J (2008) Universitäre Drittmittelforschung und EG-Beihilfenrecht (English translation: external funding for universities and EC state aid law). EuZW 19:171–174

Jones A, Suffrin BE (2014) EU competition law, 5th edn. OUP, Oxford

Jung C (2009) EGV Art. 82 Missbrauch einer marktbeherrschenden Stellung (Nizza Fassung) (English translation: Article 82 EC Abuse of a dominant market position (Nice Version)). In: Grabitz E et al (eds) Das Recht der Europäischen Union (English translation: Law of the European Union). 40th edn. Beck, Munich

Kelly U et al (2009) The impact of universities on the UK economy. Universities UK, London

Kelo M et al (2006) Introduction. In: Kelo M et al (eds) Eurodata—student mobility in European higher education. Lemmens, Bonn, pp 1–6

Kroitzsch H (1980) Anmerkungen BGH 23.10.1979 KZR 22/78 "Berliner Musikschule" (English translation: case note BGH 23 October 1979 KZR 22.78 "Berlin Music School"). GRUR 82:249

Lanzendorf U (2006) Foreign students and study abroad students. In: Kelo M et al (eds) Eurodata—student mobility in European higher education. Lemmens, Bonn, pp 7–53

Lao M (2001) Discrediting accreditation?: Antitrust and legal education. Washington Univ Law Q 79:1035–1102

Lübbig T (2008) § 7 Rechtsgrundlagen (English translation: § 7 Legal Bases). In: Wiedemann G (ed) Handbuch des Kartellrechts (English translation: Handbook of antitrust law), 2nd edn. Beck, Munich, pp 131–197

Lübbig T, Schroeder D (2008) § 8 Einzelfragen (English translation: § 8 Selected Issues). In: Wiedemann G (ed) Handbuch des Kartellrechts (English translation: Handbook of antitrust law), 2nd edn. Beck, Munich, pp 197–292

Lucey MC (2015) Should professionals in employment constitute 'undertakings'? Identifying 'false-employed'. J Eur Compet Law Pract 6:702

Marco Colino S (2011) Competition law, 7th edn. OUP, Oxford

Marcos F, Sánchez Graells A (2010) A missing step in the modernisation stairway of EU competition law—any role for block exemption regulations in the realm of Regulation 1/2003? Compet Law Rev 6:183–201

Mestmäcker E-J, Schweitzer H (2004) Europäisches Wettbewerbsrecht (English translation: European competition law), 2nd edn. Beck, Munich

Monti G (2007) EC competition law. CUP, Cambridge

Neergaard U (2009a) Services of general economic interest: the nature of the beast. In: Krajewski M et al (eds) The changing legal framework for services of general economic interest. T.M.C. Asser Press, The Hague, pp 17–50

Neergaard U (2009b) Services of general (economic) interest: what aims and values count? In: Neergaard U et al (eds) Integrating welfare functions into EU Law—from Rome to Lisbon. DJØF Forlag, Copenhagen, pp 191–224

Neergaard U (2011) Services of general economic interest under EU law constraints. In: Schiek D et al (eds) European economic and social constitutionalism after the Treaty of Lisbon. CUP, Cambridge, pp 174–196

Neergaard U (2013) The concept of SSGIs and the asymmetries between free movement and competition law. In: Neergaard U et al (eds) Social services of general interest in the EU. T.M.C. Asser Press, The Hague, pp 205–244

Newdick C (2007) Charities in the health care market: can trust survive NHS competition? King's College Law J 18:415–425

Nicolaides P (2013) The economics of subsidies for R&D: implications for reform of EU state aid rules. Intereconomics 48:99–105

Odudu O (2010) The last vestiges of overambitious EU competition law. Camb Law J 69:248–250

Odudu O (2011) Are state-owned health-care providers undertakings subject to competition law? Eur Compet Law Rev 32:231–241

OECD (2002) Frascati manual. OECD, Paris

Office of Fair Trading (2014) Higher education in England. Crown copyright, London

Petronio MC (1994/1995) Eliminating the social cost of higher education: the Third Circuit allows social welfare benefits to justify horizontal restraints of trade in United States v. Brown University. Georgetown Law J 83:189–216

Prosser T (2005) Competition law and public services: from single market to citizenship rights? Eur Public Law 11:543–563

Prosser T (2010) EU competition law and public services. In: Mossialos E et al (eds) Health systems governance in Europe. Cambridge University Press, Cambridge, pp 315–336

Ross M (2007) Promoting solidarity: from public services to a European model of competition? Common Market Law Rev 44:1057–1080

Rousseva E, Marquis M (2013) Hell freezes over: a climate change for assessing exclusionary conduct under Article 102 TFEU. J Eur Compet Law Pract 4:32–50

Salop SC, White LJ (1991) Antitrust goes to college. J Econ Perspect 5:193–202

Sanchez Graells A (2014) State aid and (university) software licensing: who's interested? (T-488/11). How to crack a nut, 12 June 2014 http://www.howtocrackanut.com/blog/2014/06/state-aid-and-university-software.html?rq=sarc. Accessed 15 Sept 2014

Sauter W (2008) Services of general economic interest and universal service in EU law. Eur Law Rev 33:167–192

Sauter W (2015) Public services in EU law. CUP, Cambridge

Sauter W, Schepel H (2009) State and market in European Union law. CUP, Cambridge

Schiek D (2012) Economic and social integration—the challenge for EU constitutional law. Edward Elgar, Cheltenham

Simon S (2009) 9. Teil. Fusionskontrollverordnung (English translation: Part 9 Merger Control Regulation). In: Loewenheim U et al (eds) Kartellrecht (English translation: Antitrust Law). Beck, Munich, pp 1249–1536

Stachtiaris TJ (1993/1994) Antitrust in need: undergraduate financial aid and United States v. Brown University. Fordham Law Rev 62:1745–1768

Steyger E (2002) Competition and education. In: de Groof J et al (eds) Globalisation and competition in education. Wolf Legal Publishers, Nijmegen, pp 275–280

Suarez C (2014) Competition in the HE sector. Competition in the higher education market

Swennen H (2008/2009) Onderwijs en Mededingsrecht (English translation: Teaching and Competition Law). Tijdschrift voor Onderwijsrecht en Onderwijsbeleid 4:259–280

Szyszczak E (2015) Services of general economic interest and state measures affecting competition. J Eur Compet Law Pract 6:681–688

Szyszczak E (2016 (forthcoming)) Services of general economic interest and state measures affecting competition. J Eur Compet Law Pract 7

Townley C (2009) Article 81 EC and public policy. Hart, Oxford

van de Gronden J (2004) Purchasing care: economic activity or service of general (economic) interest? Eur Compet Law Rev 25:87–94

Vincent-Jones P (2006) The new public contracting. OUP, Oxford

Wendt I, Gideon A (2011) Services of general interest provision through the third sector under EU competition law constraints: the example of organising healthcare in England, Wales and the Netherlands. In: Schiek D et al (eds) European economic and social constitutionalism after the Treaty of Lisbon. CUP, Cambridge, pp 251–276

Whish R (2015) Competition law, 8th edn. OUP, Oxford

Chapter 4
The Structure of Research Funding in Germany, the Netherlands and England (UK)

Abstract This chapter examines the research systems of England (UK), the Netherlands and Germany from a competition law perspective; thereby conducting the groundwork for the empirical study in Chap. 5. Each country is explored in a separate subchapter discussing the general funding streams and research conducting entities before focussing more specifically on research in HEIs. The systems investigated differ in a variety of ways from the general national expenditure on research and the overall character of the systems to the importance of individual sectors and the extent to which the recent trend of commodification has influenced the research systems. As regards research in HEIs, the importance of competitive factors in funding allocation has increased in all three systems, but it plays by far the most significant role in England where competitive factors even play a major role in generic research funding allocation. The growing importance in non-generic funding is associated with a variety of concerns, most significantly with threats to academic freedom and budget constraints due to matching requirements as non-generic funding is not always provided at full cost levels. The country specific subchapters will be followed by a tentative competition law analysis. It will be shown that differentiation between non-economic research, which does not fall under competition law, and research services, which do, is more difficult than it may appear, since this line can be fluid. However, the more economically oriented the system, the more frequently this may happen. If an activity does fall under competition law, potential tensions in all three systems could arise from this with national research policies on HEIs.

Keywords Research policy in the UK, the Netherlands and Germany · Universities in the UK, the Netherlands and Germany · Research funding · Research as a statutory task · Full costing of research · Research and EU competition law · Research and state aid · Academic freedom

© T.M.C. ASSER PRESS and the author 2017
A. Gideon, *Higher Education Institutions in the EU: Between Competition and Public Service*, Legal Issues of Services of General Interest, DOI 10.1007/978-94-6265-168-5_4

Contents

4.1 Introduction

Chapter 3 concluded that HEIs may be classified as 'undertakings' under EU competition law if they offer services on a market. It has also been shown that requiring compliance from HEIs with the EU competition law regime may create tensions with their traditional mission of providing research and teaching freely and equally accessible in the public interest.[1] The following chapters are dedicated to empirically examining university practices as well as the perceptions of key

---

[1] On the mission of public HEIs see Chap. 1 Sect. 1.3.1 above.

officers. By this research design the book aims to answer the questions of whether there is indeed increased exposure to EU competition law in countries where commodification of HEIs[2] is further developed, what consequences such exposure might have and also whether professional actors in the field are aware of the risks.

Obviously, it is only possible to empirically analyse a small sample within the limited scope of a book. The sample chosen here is research in (public) HEIs in Germany, England and the Netherlands. Research has been chosen as the area of analysis, because it is a particularly competitive field;[3] not only do private and/or public HEIs compete with each other, but also other private and public research organisations conduct research. It is, therefore, to be expected that some research is conducted in a market setting, meaning that competition law may be applied. Furthermore, as mentioned in Chap. 1 (Sect. 1.1) it is a field which has thus far hardly been explored from a competition law perspective. The three national systems chosen for comparison differ in terms of their welfare state models, which makes it likely that the degree to which university research has been commodified also differs. These differences will be relevant to the analysis of how EU competition law, which is analysed as an important element of EU economic law, impacts on the systems.

In Esping-Andersen's categorisation of welfare states, which is based on the questions of how far they de-commodify, socially stratify and rely on the market and the family,[4] Germany is categorised as conservative, the Netherlands as social democratic and the UK as liberal.[5] A liberal system relies highly on the market with a low-degree of de-commodification and enables social stratification. A conservative system has a higher degree of de-commodification, but due to its conservative values it relies more on the family and retains social stratification. Finally, a social democratic system has a high degree of de-commodification, decreases social stratification and has no particular reliance on either the market or the family.[6] Whilst in further research these categorisations have been confirmed, overwhelmingly for Germany and to a large extent for the UK, the Netherlands has been categorised in many different ways within and beyond Esping-Andersen's original categories.[7] It has even been suggested that the Netherlands are incapable of categorisation.[8]

If one turns towards the commodification of HEI systems, one can observe that all of these countries' HEIs have been increasingly developed to react to market pressures and compete with commercial sector entities. Yet, the degree to which this commodification has progressed differs; England has progressed furthest along the path to commercialisation of the activities of its HEIs[9] (though without

---

[2] On commodification of HEIs see Chap. 1 Sect. 1.3.3. above.

[3] See Enders 2007, p. 19; Candemir and Meyer 2010, p. 511.

[4] Esping-Andersen 1990, p. 26 seq.

[5] Ibid p. 52.

[6] Ibid p. 26 seq.

[7] For an overview see Ferragina and Seeleib-Kaiser 2011.

[8] Ibid p. 591 with further references.

[9] Candemir and Meyer 2010, p. 511.

much litigation or clear policies on the legal implications),[10] whilst in Germany only the first steps have been taken in this direction.[11] This positioning is also mirrored in the reactions of these Member States to the financial crisis. While Germany is amongst those states which have, inflation considered, increased spending on HEIs by 20 % or more since 2008, the Netherlands are located amongst those having retained a similar level of spending and the UK is amongst the states which decreased spending by 20 % or more and is relying on high tuition fees for funding the HEI sector instead.[12] The different degrees of commodification might have different consequences as to the assessment of HEIs as 'undertakings' and thus on the pressures that might arise from competition law.

At the same time, these Member States also represent very different governance structures. Germany is a federal republic and for this reason the organisation of research funding can vary between the federal states. Specific attention will be paid to the states of Bremen, Berlin, Bavaria and Baden-Württemberg, as these are the states in which the universities selected for the empirical study are located.[13] The Netherlands, on the other hand, is governed in a centralised manner. Finally, the UK is a devolved state with four separate countries each with largely independent structures.[14] As it would not be possible to analyse all four devolved countries here and since England has the highest degree of commodification regarding HEIs, only England, which itself has a rather centralised system of governance, will be analysed.

In order to assess the relevance of competition law for HEI research in the three countries, it is necessary to provide an overview of their research systems which is the aim of this chapter.[15] The subchapters (Sect. 4.2 on England, Sect. 4.3 on the Netherlands and Sect. 4.4 on Germany respectively) will start with a general overview of the systems; the general funding streams and which entities conduct research will be introduced. They will proceed to a more in-depth examination of research in HEIs. Firstly, how far research in HEIs is an official public task and if there are any limitations as to privately funded research in HEIs will be assessed. Secondly, public funding of HEI research will be evaluated and the extent to which it is provided generically or on a project related basis will be identified. Thirdly, an overview of funding from non-public sources will be provided. Finally, how far full costing for research is applied will be examined. The subchapters will end with an interim conclusion integrating the results. The country specific subchapters will be followed by a tentative competition law analysis (Sect. 4.5) which will focus on research funded by national public, private and third sector sources (rather than by EU or international funding), as this book investigates EU

---

[10] Aside perhaps from the OFT/CMA reports discussed in Chap. 3 (OFT 2014; CMA 2015).

[11] See Enders 2007, p. 19; Jansen 2010, p. 43.

[12] EUA 2015, p. 9, 11.

[13] On the selection of the universities see below Chap. 5.

[14] It would go beyond the scope of this book to discuss differences and similarities between devolution and federalism. See further Horowitz 2006–2007.

[15] A very condensed and earlier version of this chapter has been published as Gideon 2015.

competition law constraints on research in public HEIs as an example of tension between EU law and national public service concepts more generally. The chapter conclusion (Sect. 4.6) will then bring together the results for all three countries.

4.2 England (UK)

Among the three countries compared in this study, the UK[16] is the one with the lowest expenditure on R&D as a percentage of gross domestic product (GDP); in 2014 UK expenditure amounted to only 1.7 % of its GDP. This expenditure has been relatively stable over the previous ten years with the lowest (1.62 % GDP) in 2012 and the highest (1.74 % GDP) in 2009.[17] The system has been in state of reformation since the early 2000s.[18] The relatively low spending (compared to the 3 % target of the Europe 2020 Strategy)[19] has been identified as a problematic area in the UK research system, as have an insufficient capacity for attracting researchers and generating knowledge transfer between academic and commercial sectors, particularly with an eye on innovation.[20] However, as a result of devolution, the governments of the devolved countries have some freedom in devising their policies and budgets in devolved policy areas.[21] As mentioned above, the focus here will be on England where the trend has been towards less public funding and more commodification, especially after the change in government in 2010 as regards HEIs.[22]

---

[16] In certain areas statistics/information were only available for the UK as a whole and have been used. However, were possible figures/information for England only have been utilised. It has always been made clear in the text if the UK as a whole or England is being referred to.

[17] EUROSTAT, 'Gross domestic expenditure on R&D (GERD)' (2016) http://ec.europa.eu/euro-stat/web/products-datasets/-/t2020_20. Accessed 2 August 2016. GERD is defined as the 'total intramural expenditure on R&D performed within a country [from all sectors], funded nationally and from abroad but excludes payments for R&D performed abroad' (accompanying notes on http://ec.europa.eu/eurostat/cache/metadata/EN/t2020_20_esmsip.htm). Eurostat is, according to these notes, following the OECD guidelines laid down in the Frascati Manual (OECD 2002). The latter defines R&D as comprising basic and applied research as well as experimental develop-ment (on these terms see Chap. 1 Sect. 1.3.3 and Chap. 3 Sect. 3.3.5 above) conducted formally in R&D units and informally or occasionally in other units (ibid p. 30).

[18] Candemir and Meyer 2010, p. 496.

[19] See Chap. 2 Sect. 2.2.2 above.

[20] Candemir and Meyer 2010, p. 496; Elsevier 2011, p. 5.

[21] Directgov, 'Devolved government in the UK' http://webarchive.nationalarchives.gov.uk/20121015000000/http://www.direct.gov.uk/en/governmentcitizensandrights/ukgovernment/devolvedgovernment/dg_073306. Accessed 2 August 2016. See also UCU 2014, p. 1 according to whom the freedom is limited through the UK wide REF (on the REF see Sect. 4.2.2.2 "Public Generic Funding" below).

[22] UCU 2014, p. 3 seq; 10, EUA 2015, pp. 9, 11.

4.2.1 General Overview

The private sector is the most important research funder in the UK and its funding input increased steadily in real terms from 2000 with only slightly lower spending in 2009 and 2012. The public sector (government, research councils, the higher education funding council and HEIs) is the second most important funder (29.6 %), but foreign funding also plays a significant role (17.5 %). The third sector contributes about 5 %. The private sector is also the most important research provider conducting an even higher share of the research than it finances (almost two thirds of all research) as the private sector receives significant foreign contributions and some public funding. HEIs are the second most important research provider, whilst less than 7.5 % of all research is conducted by government institutions and research councils and only 1.8 % by the third sector.[23] Traditionally, military research has been very strong in the UK. While this has dropped considerably from 52 % in 1960[24] to 5.7 % in 2014[25] the proportion of all research spending used on defence is still significant.

4.2.1.1 Public Research

The UK has a relatively long tradition of close links between public and private sector research and commercial use of publicly funded research.[26] With lower public research funding since 2010,[27] public research organisations are increasingly encouraged to attract external funding and to cooperate with industry. Furthermore, research policy planning considers the needs of industry and the commercial sector also receives public support for research.[28]

The Governmental Structure

Since July 2016 the main accountability for research policy lies with the Department for Business, Energy and Industrial Strategy (BEIS) which replaced

---

[23] Office for National Statistics 2016, Tables 1, 2. The Office for National Statistics is following the guidelines of the Frascati Manual (ibid p. 2 seq).

[24] Candemir and Meyer 2010, p. 496.

[25] Office for National Statistics 2016, Table 1. For an overview of the decrease in defence spending since 1990 see ibid p. 7.

[26] Candemir and Meyer 2010, pp. 505, 511.

[27] Research Information Network 2010, p. 4; UCU 2014, p. 4; Office for National Statistics 2016, Table 4. According to the latter, the total public funding (research councils, funding councils, government and HEIs combined) was £9445 M (inflation adjusted) in 2009, but only £9058 M in 2014 with the lowest level (£8425) in 2012.

[28] See Candemir and Meyer 2010, p. 505 seq.

the Department for Business, Innovation and Skills (BIS) and within which the Minister of State for Universities, Science, Research and Innovation (a joint appointment with Department for Education) is responsible for UK research and English HEIs.[29] Alongside the BEIS, other departments might issue research policies concerning their remit. Advice for the government is provided by the Government Office for Science through the Government Chief Scientific Advisor and independent advice can be obtained from the Council for Science and Technology.[30]

Public sector funding is provided directly by the government, through research councils, through higher education funding councils and HEIs themselves contribute their own resources for research activities. The majority of direct governmental funding goes to the private sector and governmental research institutions. The research councils mainly fund HEIs and research in own institutes. The higher education funding councils only fund research in HEIs. HEIs use their own resources to support the research they conduct, but they also, to a limited extent, contribute to research by the third sector, research councils and governmental institutions.[31] Whilst direct governmental funding and research council funding has fluctuated since 2003, funding provided by higher education funding councils has risen till 2010 and then decreased while HEI funding has increased.[32]

Most public funding in England is administered by the Higher Education Funding Council for England (HEFCE) and the seven research councils. HEFCE provides generic funding and the research councils competitive public funding. Innovate UK (formerly the Technology Strategy Board) is responsible for technology and innovation with a business focus.[33] With the planned Higher Education and Research Bill (s 83 seq) it is envisaged to merge these bodies into a new overarching, arm-length body to be called United Kingdom Research and Innovation (UKRI).[34] Finally, academies and learned societies such as the British Academy and the Royal Society also play roles in the research system. Despite being partly publicly funded, they are independent scholarly institutions which offer advice to government and provide funding for research.[35]

---

[29] Gov.uk (2016) New ministerial portfolios confirmed at Department for Business, Energy and Industrial Strategy. https://www.gov.uk/government/news/new-ministerial-portfolios-confirmed-at-department-for-business-energy-and-industrial-strategy. Accessed 3 August 2016. On the previous situation see also Research Information Network 2010; Candemir and Meyer 2010, p. 500 seq.

[30] Research Information Network 2010, p. 6 seq, 14 seq.

[31] Office for National Statistics 2016, Table 1.

[32] Office for National Statistics 2016, Table 4 (inflation adjusted numbers).

[33] Research Information Network 2010, p. 10 seq, Gov.uk (2016) Innovate UK—About us. https://www.gov.uk/government/organisations/innovate-uk/about#our-work-so-far. Accessed 3 August 2016.

[34] See further BIS 2015, p. 69 seq; BIS 2016, p. 67 seq.

[35] Research Information Network 2010, p. 13.

Public Research Organisations

The 162 UK HEIs, 80 % of which are located in England,[36] are the most important
public research providers and the amount of research conducted by them has
increased more or less steadily since 2003.[37] Whilst there are a number of
specialised HEIs, England, unlike the other two countries under scrutiny, no
longer maintains a binary HEI system. The separation between vocational HEIs
and universities was abolished in the Further and Higher Education Act 1992
(FHEA). The HEI sector is rather heterogeneous with regards to student numbers,
income and research-teaching focus.[38] Unlike many continental HEIs, English
public HEIs 'are legally independent entities and are classified [traditionally] as
non-profit institutions'.[39] However, Privy-Council involvement is required for their
creation[40] and government influence is asserted to a large extent through the
public funding they receive. Despite officially being completely independent,
English HEIs therefore, as Palfreyman puts it, 'are in practice [...] closely
Government-regulated via its Higher Education Funding Council "quango" and
are depressingly weak in terms of asserting their potential independence'.[41]

Before the move towards privatisation during the Thatcher government, there
were a variety of other public research organisations, especially in the field of
military research.[42] Today there are only a limited number of other public
institutions conducting research. Among them are research institutes in research
councils which carry out 2.7 % of all research in the UK. All the remaining public
research institutions together conduct just 4.6 % of all UK research.[43]

4.2.1.2 Non-public Research

The private sector is the largest funding contributor and conducts the most research.
For its research, the sector receives significant overseas funding. The funding
provided by the private sector goes to (in order of relevance) research in the private
sector itself, HEI research, governmental research, research in research councils and
research in the third sector.[44] Despite it being the largest research funder in the UK,

---

[36] Kelly et al. 2014, p. 7.

[37] Office for National Statistics 2016, Table 2.

[38] On HEIs in the UK see Scott 2009, p. 42 seq; Candemir and Meyer 2010, pp. 500, 505, 509
seq; Zoontjes 2010, p. 123; Farrington and Palfreyman 2012, para 1.22; Universities UK 2012,
p. 16; Kelly et al. 2014, p. 7 seq.

[39] Kelly et al. 2014, p. 8.

[40] This is supposed to change under the envisaged new legislation (BIS 2015, p. 66 seq; BIS
2016 p. 29 seq, 38 seq).

[41] Palfreyman 2003.

[42] Candemir and Meyer 2010, p. 506.

[43] Office for National Statistics 2016, Table 1, p. 4 seq, 6.

[44] Office for National Statistics 2016, Table 1.

compared to other countries, private sector investments on research are low and the government has implemented a variety of initiatives to encourage more private sector investment such as the 'catapult' scheme for translational research.[45]

International and third sector funding contributions together amount to nearly a quarter of all research funding in the UK. International funding has been fluctuating since 2003, while third sector funding has increased steadily. By far most third sector funding is used for research in HEIs. The third sector plays a less significant role as a provider of research services with just 1.8 % of all research in the UK being conducted by the sector. International funding is mainly received by the private sector, followed by HEIs.[46] The utilisation of international funding has been identified as a government priority.[47] In particular the importance of EU funding and the damaging consequences for the UK's research base of the potential loss of this funding with the withdrawal of the UK from the EU have been highlighted by various actors.[48]

4.2.2   Research in Public HEIs

As has been mentioned above, English HEIs are not public institutions in the same way as many of their continental counterparts. The complicated relationship between the public and the private in English HEIs has become even more difficult with English policy on HEIs increasingly leaning towards commercialisation, internationalisation, business style administration in governance and the encouragement of financial independence in recent years.[49]

4.2.2.1   Research as a Statutory Task of HEIs

The law governing HEIs in England is to be found within a vast variety of sources,[50] though it is planned to partly consolidate this with Higher Education and Research Act 2016 currently debated in parliament. Most important among the present legislation are the Education Reform Act 1988 (ERA), the FHEA, the

---

[45] UCU 2014, p. 4 seq.

[46] Office for National Statistics 2016, Tables 1, 4.

[47] Candemir and Meyer 2010, p. 507; Research Information Network 2010, p. 6; Nurse 2015, p. 25.

[48] See for example, British Academy, 'British Academy raises concerns over the future of EU research funding' (2013) http://www.britac.ac.uk/news/news.cfm/newsid/860. Accessed 8 February 2013, Ferguson D (2016) Academics feel blight of Brexit—from cancer research to peat projects. The Guardian, 2 August 2016 https://www.theguardian.com/education/2016/aug/02/academics-brexit-research-peat-fears-eu-funds. Accessed 3 August 2016.

[49] Zoontjes 2010, p. 123 seq; Farrington and Palfreyman 2012, para 1.01 seq, 3.01, 4.01 seq; Kelly et al. 2014, pp. 3, 7 seq, 11.

[50] For an overview see Farrington and Palfreyman 2012, para 1.04.

Teaching and Higher Education Act 1998, the Higher Education Act 2004 and the Education Act 2011 which changed/amended some of the earlier Acts.[51] ERA states in s 124 that 'a higher education corporation shall have the power [...] to carry out research and to publish the results of the research'. FHEA states in s 65 that

> activities eligible for funding [...] [by HEFCE] are (a) the provision of education and the undertaking of research by higher education institutions in the council's area, (b) the provision of any facilities, and the carrying on of any other activities [...] for the purpose of or in connection with education or research, [...] (d) the provision by any person of services for the purposes of, or in connection with, the provision of education or the undertaking of research.

Research thus appears to be an activity which HEIs may carry out and receive funding for, but not a statutorily required task. Indeed, conducting of research does not appear to be part of the definition of a public HEI or even of a university.[52]

According to s 68(1) FHEA the 'Secretary of State may make grants to [...] [HEFCE] of such amounts and subject to such terms and conditions as he may determine'. HEFCE then, if applicable, passes the latter on to HEIs and can attach its own terms and conditions (s 65(3) FHEA).[53] However, s 68(3) provides that the terms and conditions imposed upon HEFCE by the Secretary of State 'may not be framed by reference to particular courses of study or programmes of research (including the contents of such courses or programmes and the manner in which they are taught, supervised or assessed)'. Furthermore, s 202(2) ERA requires University Commissioners 'to ensure that academic staff have freedom within the law to question and test received wisdom, and to put forward new ideas and controversial or unpopular opinions, without placing themselves in jeopardy of losing their jobs or privileges'. These provisions seem to limit external steering of research in favour of academic freedom. In the planned legislation the government intends to establish UKRI 'in a way which [...][the government] consider[s] offers the best balance between scientific and academic independence and accountability to Parliament'.[54] This seems to refer mainly to s 93(2)(a) where it is established that directions 'may not be framed by reference to [...] programmes of research (including the contents [these] [...] programmes and the manner in which they are [...] supervised or assessed)'. Quantitative restrictions of research do not seem to exist by statute.

---

[51] The policy changes prior to the planned Higher Education and Research Act, have not been introduced by a comprehensive act, but by executive measures only (OFT 2014, p. 61 seq).

[52] See on these definitions Farrington and Palfreyman 2012, para 3.01 seq, 3.05 seq.

[53] On the powers of the government and HEFCE see further Farrington and Palfreyman 2012, para 4.16 seq.

[54] BIS 2016, p. 17. However, it has been questioned if the new Anti-Lobbying Rule prohibiting the use of public money for lobbying the government may provide a threat for academic freedom (Scott 2016 Academics' ability to lobby government under threat from new funding clause. The Conversation, 25 February 2016 http://theconversation.com/academics-ability-to-lobby-government-under-threat-from-new-funding-clause-55333. Accessed 11 March 2016).

4.2.2.2 Public Research Funding

There are three main research funding streams for English HEIs; they receive generic funding from HEFCE, project/programme related funding from research councils and funding from other sources. The first two are public funding streams and known as the 'dual support system'.[55] They comprise the majority of research funding for HEIs.[56] Funding allocation through the dual support system contains competitive elements tending to concentrate funding in a small number of institutions. While this seems to have improved the competitiveness of UK HEIs, it has also been criticised for potentially overlooking high quality research in those HEIs which are not generally regarded as research intensive institutions.[57] Funding from outside the dual support system is also increasingly gaining in importance. It comprises additional competitive public as well as private, third sector and international (currently still especially EU) funding.[58]

Public Generic Funding

Funding received through higher education funding councils amounts to less than a third of all research funding for HEIs in the UK.[59] This has been criticised for limiting academic freedom and threatening the research base, especially as part of the generic funding is needed to match not fully funded projects based on other funding streams.[60] As mentioned above (section "The Governmental Structure"), HEFCE is responsible in England for generic funding allocation. HEFCE receives its budget and directions on how to distribute it directly from the government.[61] HEIs funded by HEFCE need to comply with the requirements set out in HEFCE's memorandum of assurance and accountability[62] which inter alia set out rules on transparency, efficiency and accountability (including the use of full costing for all

---

[55] Even with the merging of the research councils and HEFCE in the planned Higher Education and Research Bill it is envisioned to keep the dual support system (BIS 2016, 67).

[56] Higher education funding council funding and research council funding amount to 56.9 % of all research funding for HEIs in the UK. Office for National Statistics 2016, Table 1.

[57] Adams and Gurney 2010, p. 1 seq; UCU 2014, p. 8; Stern 2016, p. 25.

[58] See on the funding streams Adams and Gurney 2010, p. 1; Candemir and Meyer 2010, p. 509; Farrington and Palfreyman 2012, para 1.01; Kelly et al. 2014, p. 8 seq; UCU 2014, p. 6; Nurse 2015, p. 3.

[59] Office for National Statistics 2016, Table 1.

[60] UCU 2014, p. 2; Stern 2016, pp. 33, 35. The recent Stern Review also suggests that publications stay with the university at which they have been researched. While this would limit last minute poaching of well performing academics which has been perceived as a problem around the submission period of the last REF (Stern 2016, p. 34), it might also put constraints on academic mobility.

[61] Thus far the relevant department was BIS. Presumably in the future HEFCE (or UKRI) will receive the research budget from BEIS. The planned Higher Education and Research Act in s 93 only refers to 'the Secretary of State' without further specification.

[62] HEFCE 2016b.

activities) as well as requiring the institutions to follow statutes and comply with quality assurance standards.[63]

Even the generic funding HEFCE distributes (also referred to as 'recurrent funding') is calculated using partly competitive parameters. In the 'main research funding method' (or 'mainstream quality-related research funding', for short 'mainstream QR') it is first determined how much money will be spent on a certain subject in general. The amount to be given to an individual HEI is then calculated on the basis of research volume, costs and quality. The latter is estimated on the basis of a peer review mechanism called the Research Excellence Framework (REF) which measures the strength of outputs, environment (measured in vitality and sustainability) and impact (measured in reach and significance).[64] The latter, which had been newly introduced for the allocation period starting in 2015/16, has been criticised as threatening academic freedom and undermining scholarship.[65] More generally, the REF has been seen critically as creating employment issues (demotivation and stress with selectivity of staff submitted) as well as general concerns about its suitability (potential subject bias in the use of metrics or personal bias in the peer review process).[66] Even the government itself acknowledged in the 2015 Green Paper that the REF had become too costly and burdensome, that there are negative views in the sector and that it had created '"industries" [...] around the REF' including practices such as 'multiple "mock REFs", bringing in external consultants and taking academics away from teaching and research'. Yet, the government intends to keep the REF, as it believes it to create accountability and it is encouraging further focus on impact and exploitation of results. However, it is planned to reform the REF to a more efficient and effective processes which may involve the use of more metrics.[67] To this end a review had been commissioned which suggests in its final report certain avenues for reform including submission of all staff, a broader notion of impact and generally more investment into generic funding.[68]

In addition to 'mainstream QR', HEFCE allocates recurrent funding for PhD supervision based on numbers and quality, supports charity funded research by paying overhead costs, rewards private sector research and supports national research libraries. Finally, HEFCE runs additional programmes such as the Higher Education Innovation Fund (HEIF, also referred to as Third Stream Funding or knowledge exchange funding), which aims at encouraging knowledge transfer, and non-recurrent funding such as capital grants and support for national facilities

---

[63] See Farrington and Palfreyman 2012, para 4.22 seq, 4.30 seq; HEFCE 2016a, p. 32 seq.

[64] REF (2014) Assessment criteria and level definitions. http://www.ref.ac.uk/panels/assessment-criteriaandleveldefinitions/. Accessed 4 August 2016, HEFCE 2016a, p. 6 seq, 23.

[65] BBC News, 'Top scientists attack funding plan' *BBC News* (4 December 2009) http://news.bbc.co.uk/1/hi/education/8392817.stm. Accessed 4 December 2009, Stern 2016, p. 16 seq.

[66] UCU 2013, 2014, p. 6 seq, 9; Stern 2016, p. 33 seq.

[67] BIS 2015, pp. 70, 72 seq.

[68] Stern 2016, p. 33 seq.

which are 'designed to provide incentives for institutions' to follow strategic aims. HEIs can freely administer HEFCE funding they receive unless it is earmarked for a specific purpose.[69]

Public Competitive Funding

27.2 % of funding of research carried out in HEIs in the UK is contributed by the research councils.[70] They are increasingly under pressure to justify the research they fund with public money. Therefore, national priorities determined by government play a role in research councils establishing their funding priorities and a tendency towards larger grants in strategic areas rather than smaller grants has been observed.[71] In the recent Nurse Review it has been encouraged that they focus even more on business engagement and strategic investment into government priorities.[72] Research councils funding is project/programme specific and distributed on a competitive basis. The assessment of which projects will receive funding is undertaken by peer review. Funding through research councils has gained in importance in the last couple of decades in comparison to HEFCE funding.[73]

As mentioned above (Sect. 4.2.2.2), HEIs also receive limited governmental funding from other institutions including ministries, local authorities and the National Health Service (NHS). Funding from these bodies is often more similar to research contracts.[74]

---

[69] See on HEFCE funding PACEC and the Centre for Business Research (University of Cambridge) 2009; Farrington and Palfreyman 2012, para 4.22 seq, 4.30 seq; HEFCE 2016a, p. 3 seq, 6 seq, 23 seq, 33.

[70] Office for National Statistics 2016, Table 1.

[71] UCU 2014, pp. 1, 10. In this respect the academic furore following the 'order' that the Arts and Humanities Research Council study the government's 'big society' policy made the news (Boffey D, 'Academic fury over order to study the big society' guardian.co.uk (27 March 2011) http://www.guardian.co.uk/education/2011/mar/27/academic-study-big-society.   Accessed   29 March 2011).

[72] Nurse 2015, p. 5 seq, 25, 32 seq. In this connection the merging of the research councils and better links between different strands of funding has equally been submitted (ibid p. 33).

[73] On the research councils see Berry 2010, pp. 5, 27, 31; Candemir and Meyer 2010, p. 510; UCU 2014, pp. 1, 10 seq; RCUK (2016) RCUK Funding. http://www.rcuk.ac.uk/funding/. Accessed 4 August 2016.

[74] Kelly et al. 2014, p. 9; University of Sheffield (2016) Funding of Research in UK Higher Education.   http://www.shef.ac.uk/finance/staff-information/howfinanceworks/higher_education/ funding_of_research. Accessed 4 August 2016.

4.2.2.3 Non-state Funding

Funding from outside the dual support system is gaining in importance and comprises of mainly foreign (especially EU) and third sector funding, but also of funding from the additional specific public competitive funding streams mentioned and private sector funding.[75] Third sector funding in particular has increased in recent years, but also private sector funding has gained in importance, though it currently makes up a smaller share.[76] Thus private sector funding 'looks to be permanently embedded within many HEIs'.[77] Strategic aims such as local partnerships and supporting small and medium sized enterprises (SME) are partly supported by government or EU funding. HEIs sometimes also form associations in order to encourage and facilitate private sector interaction.[78]

Private sector funding reaches HEIs in a variety of ways. In research co-operations, the partners commonly explore a topic on a long term basis. This form of collaboration in particular has gained in importance and is popular, since it can lead to the generation of new ideas and directions of research for both sides. Contract research and consultancy services have also gained in importance. Here, the work is commissioned by the external partners who specify the aim to be achieved. It is therefore a plain business transaction rather than a mutual relationship. HEIs also rent out infrastructure such as specialised laboratories, equipment or prototypes to the private sector. Whilst this form of collaboration is less common, it is an economically efficient way to use infrastructure and it is claimed that such transactions can also help with 'relationship building'.[79]

Another form of private sector collaboration is the commercial use of intellectual property rights (IPRs). Income from this source has risen significantly in recent years, even though it is not as high as that from research in the previously mentioned forms of collaboration.[80] The details of who owns rights depend on the contractual relations between, for example, the HEI and its staff or between the HEI and an external collaborator. Regarding the former, if no terms in the employment contract explicitly specify the question, it is usually assumed that implied contract terms grant the IPR to the employer.[81] For patentable inventions the same is specified in the Patents Act (s 39(1)), but it seems that staff are

---

[75] Office for National Statistics 2016, Table 1.

[76] HEFCE 2015, p. 5; Office for National Statistics 2016, Table 1.

[77] PACEC 2012, p. 2.

[78] Howells et al. 1998, pp. 92, 96; HEFCE 2015, pp. 11, 26.

[79] On these collaborative forms see Howells et al. 1998; Abreu et al. 2008; Kelly et al. 2014, p. 4, 8 seq; HEFCE 2015, p. 4 seq, 17 seq.

[80] HEFCE 2015, p. 4 seq.

[81] Farrington and Palfreyman 2012, para 14.31 seq; Clare et al. 2014, p. 17 seq; UCU (2016) Intellectual property rights. https://www.ucu.org.uk/article/2386/Intellectual-property-rights. Accessed 5 August 2016.

commonly rewarded for patentable inventions.[82] Regarding copyright, it is general practice that HEIs leave these to the academics.[83] When it comes to students, the general assumption is that they retain the IPR, though many universities have rules to the contrary in place.[84] In collaborations, the assumption was traditionally that the external party retains the rights, but with the establishment of the Lambert Tool-Kit there are now more sophisticated agreement options HEIs are advised to use. HEIs usually do not exploit the IPRs themselves, but sell them or a license for them to external parties. Some HEIs involve private parties to assist them in this process, set up exploitation companies, cooperate with other HEIs for this purpose or involve external investors. It has also become increasingly popular to exploit IPRs through spin-offs which may later be sold.[85]

HEIs might also set up new companies beyond spin-offs. Such companies are usually external to the HEI, but, depending on the individual case, they might be more or less controlled by it. Sometimes these companies can also be joint ventures with other partners. Income generated through such companies has increased in recent years. Though less common, HEIs also collaborate with the private sector through staff exchanges. The partner in such an exchange might also be a start-up grown out of the university, particularly if it was the entrepreneurial activity of a member of research staff which led to setting up the company in the first place. Another form of interaction is taking place through private sector funding for chairs or fellowships/lectureships.[86]

Finally, science parks are spaces dedicated to certain research fields in which relevant institutions can establish themselves, allowing easier access between institutions. Synergies are facilitated in such parks and they might function as incubators for new companies. Science parks are most often owned by HEIs or local authorities and only occasionally by private sector companies. Another form of interaction is through research clubs or networks. These can merely be dissemination and exchange platforms, clubs which are free for academic members who can bring proposals to the attention of the private sector and for which private sector companies have to pay, or clubs which uphold a limited number of research facilities for specific projects.[87]

---

[82] According to HEFCE 2012, p. 11 this was true for 84 % of HEIs at the time. The new report does not contain data on this issue.

[83] Farrington and Palfreyman 2012, para 14.36, UCU (n 81).

[84] Farrington and Palfreyman 2012, para 14.31 seq; Clare et al. 2014, p. 17; Else H (2015) "Huge amounts of confusion" over IP rights. THE, 16 April 2015 https://www.timeshighereducation.com/news/huge-amounts-of-confusion-over-ip-rights/2019696.article. Accessed 4 August 2016.

[85] Howells et al. 1998, p. 12, 35 seq, 79; Abreu et al. 2008; Elsevier 2011, p. 72 seq; Farrington and Palfreyman 2012, para 14.31 seq; Clare et al. 2014, p. 17 seq; HEFCE 2015, p. 4 seq, 15 seq, 20 seq.

[86] See on these interaction forms Howells et al. 1998, p. 35 seq, 52 seq, 79; Abreu et al. 2008, pp. 12, 15, 57; Elsevier 2011, p. 72, 76 seq; PACEC 2012, p. 5; HEFCE 2015, pp. 17, 25.

[87] On these interaction forms see Howells et al. 1998; Abreu et al. 2008, pp. 15, 54, 57; HEFCE 2009, p. 30.

4.2.2.4 Full Costing

Due to rising non-generic funding, sustainable costing of research became important in the 1990s and the Transparent Approach to Costing (TRAC) was established centrally in England.[88] It includes an annual reporting process (annual TRAC) on the basis of which indirect costs can be calculated as well as a full costing approach (TRAC fEC, introduced in 2004) in which these indirect costs are then added to direct and directly allocated costs in order to arrive at the full costs of a project.[89]

Research councils fund at a rate of 80 %, while other public non-generic funding is provided at 100 % of full cost. With regards to non-public funding, prices are negotiated individually or the funders have their own funding rules. However, TRAC fEC provides HEIs with knowledge about the full costs which they can take into consideration.[90] TRAC is said to have led to more sustainable financial arrangements and is being extended beyond research and the data collected is to be utilised for cost cutting.[91] However, there has also been criticism from research councils pointing out that projects have become much more expensive than predicted and academics complaining that their projects themselves do not seem to be better supported, but that the additional funding is 'disappearing into the university'.[92] Third sector organisations simply refer to their mission statements in denying paying full costs and private sector companies try to use their negotiating power to cut prices.[93] There is thus a real, if residual, danger that private research is not funded at least at full cost levels and that public resources are, therefore, used to make up the difference.

---

[88] J M Consulting Ltd 2005 (last updated 2012), executive summary para 2 seq, Part I, section A para 1 seq, Estermann and Claeys-Kulik 2013, p. 51 seq; HEFCE (2015) History of TRAC. http://www.hefce.ac.uk/funding/finsustain/trac/history/. Accessed 5 August 2016.

[89] J M Consulting Ltd 2005 (last updated 2012), executive summary para 4 seq, 10 seq, 19 seq, Part I, section A para 1, 3 seq, 15 seq, 26, Part V, HEFCE (n 88). HEFCE has recently up-dated its TRAC Guidance which is available on: http://www.hefce.ac.uk/funding/finsustain/trac/.

[90] See J M Consulting Ltd 2005 (last updated 2012), executive summary paras 5, 8, 10 seq, Part I, section A para 21 seq, 38, HEFCE (n 88), University of Sheffield (n 74).

[91] RCUK/UUK 2010, in particular, p. 4 seq and annex C; J M Consulting Ltd 2005 (last updated 2012), executive summary para 8 seq, Part I, section A para 5 seq, Estermann and Claeys-Kulik 2013, p. 52; HEFCE (2016) Current developments. http://www.hefce.ac.uk/funding/finsustain/current/. Accessed 5 August 2016.

[92] Corbyn Z, 'Cheques and balances' *THE* (19 June 2008). http://www.timeshighereducation.co.uk/story.asp?storycode=402420. Accessed 2 May 2009.

[93] Ibid. Some of these problems had already been foreseen shortly before the introduction of fEC. See, for example, Williams 2004.

4.2.3 Interim Conclusion on England

Neither the Lisbon/Europe 2020 target of 3 % GDP nor the economic crisis appear to have had a significant influence on overall research spending in the UK which has neither significantly increased nor decreased over the last ten years.[94] The private sector is providing most of the funding for research in the UK and its share in comparison to other funders has increased over the last few years to nearly half of all research funding. Government is the second largest funder, followed by overseas sources, while the third sector plays a smaller role. The private sector also conducts most of the research for which it receives significant foreign funding. Public research is mainly taking place in HEIs with only a limited amount of research being conducted by other public research organisations. The third sector equally only performs a small percentage of the overall research in the UK. The lack of knowledge transfer and innovation has been identified as a cause for concern and the system is constantly being reformed to address such perceived shortcomings and implement government policy objectives.

The English system of funding HEI research is very competitive. Even the generic funding provided through HEFCE is based on competitive assessment.[95] HEFCE also rewards HEIs who attract external funding. Furthermore, generic funding constitutes less than a third of all research funding for HEIs in the UK. The research councils equally provide less than 30 % and involve governmental steering.[96] Other public research funding is received from government institutions, often taking the form of research contracts. Therefore, unless they have own resources,[97] HEIs need to seek the rest of their research funding from private, third sector and foreign sources. It might be assumed that such funds focus on the particular interests of these funders. The academic freedom of the researcher to research into any area of his or her choice thus seems to be somewhat limited and a fierce competition for limited resources takes place.[98] Due to this competitive approach TRAC fEC has been introduced early and created clarity as regards costing, but there nevertheless still seems to be some ambiguity when it comes to pricing.

---

[94] However, as we have seen above (Sect. 4.1) funding for HEIs in England has significantly decreased with the onset of the Financial Crisis.

[95] For an analysis of the 'relationship between the state, the funding councils and the universities' in the current system see Filippakou et al. 2010.

[96] According to PACEC 2012, 80 % of HEIs stated they are 'taking steps to align with key national priorities of research councils'. In government policy there appears to be a strong preference for the so-called STEM (science, technology, engineering and mathematics) subjects (UCU 2014, p. 9).

[97] HEIs own contributions amount to about 4 % (Office for National Statistics 2016, Table 1) and are assumably mainly making up for funders not providing full costs.

[98] For an early critical voice on this see Willmoth 1995, more recently see UCU 2014, pp. 2, 7, 11.

4.3 The Netherlands

Overall research spending in the Netherlands is, with 1.97 % of its GDP in 2014, slightly higher than in England. Spending has gone down from 2004 to 2008, but steadily increased since.[99] The Netherlands' research system is a consociational system (i.e. a system that relies on consultation of a variety of different stakeholders) and as such characterised by involvement of a wide variety of actors in research policy setting processes. On the one hand, this allows using synergies. On the other hand, it can result in slow decision making processes.[100] Despite the fact that research in the Netherlands has done well when it comes to performance indicators such as the number of publications and citations and general attractiveness of the system, a number of challenges including a perceived need to establish elite institutions, strengthen private sector research, set research priorities with practical relevance, coordinate policies, increase innovation and utilise European funding streams have been identified.[101] The Dutch research system has, therefore, recently undergone some changes towards creating excellence, impact agendas, commercialisation and strengthening of institutional autonomy combined with external steering.[102]

4.3.1 General Overview

Just over 50 % of research conducted in the Netherlands is financed by the private sector, 33.2 % by the public sector, 12.7 % from abroad and almost 3 % from the third sector.[103] Whilst there was a dip in private sector funding in 2009, attributed to the financial crisis,[104] private sector funding has been on the highest level since 1999 in 2014. Public funding has equally increased more or less steadily.[105] Measured in funding received, the private sector also conducts most of the

---

[99] EUROSTAT (n 17).

[100] Braun 2006, p. 5 seq; Jongbloed 2010; van der Meulen 2010, p. 516 seq, 526; Leisyte 2011, pp. 441, 446.

[101] Braun 2006, p. 5; Jongbloed 2010, pp. 293, 312 seq, 318 seq; van der Meulen 2010, pp. 515, 518, 525; Mostert 2012, p. 1 seq; European Commission 2015, p. 464 seq, 480; Euraxess (2016) Research Landscape. http://www.euraxess.nl/incoming-researchers/research-landscape. Accessed 5 August 2016.

[102] Leisyte et al. 2008, p. 377; Jongbloed 2010, p. 318 seq; Mostert 2012, p. 4 seq. European Commission 2015.

[103] Centraal Bureau voor de Statistiek 2016. According to the *Centraal Bureau voor de Statistiek* R&D includes basic and applied research as well as development defined similar to the definitions in the Frascati Manual (explanatory note belonging to the table Sect. 2).

[104] Mostert 2012, p. 3.

[105] Centraal Bureau voor de Statistiek 2011, 2016.

research (56 %), followed by HEIs (32.1 %). All other institutions (public and third sector) put together conduct 11 % of all research in the Netherlands.[106]

4.3.1.1 Public Research

In line with the nature of a consociational system, public research in the Netherlands is characterised by a multiplicity of actors involved in both policy setting and conducting research. Nearly two thirds of governmental research funding goes to research in HEIs, but the public sector also contributes to research in other institutions.[107] Whilst the public sector still provides most funding generically, there is also a large variety of competitive project funding streams. Furthermore, there have been quite a few competitive institutional funding schemes which have led to the creation of new research performing entities.[108]

The Governmental Structure

Research policy is mainly coordinated by the Ministry for Education, Culture and Sciences (*Ministerie van Onderwijs, Cultuur en Wetenschap*, OCW) and the Ministry of Economic Affairs (*Ministerie van Economische Zaken*, EZ). The former is focussed on basic research and is responsible for the research system in general and for funding universities and various other research organisations. The EZ's involvement, which has increased over recent years, lies mainly in the areas of technology, innovation and agricultural research where it follows a more 'hands-on' approach. Other ministries might be involved as concerns their remit.[109] Advice on research policies is provided by a number of advisory bodies, particularly by the Advisory Council for Science, Technology and Innovation (*Adviesraad voor wetenschap, technologie en innovatie*) and the Royal Netherlands Academy of Arts and Sciences (*Koninklijke Nederlandse Akademie van Wetenschappen*, KNAW).[110]

---

[106] Centraal Bureau voor de Statistiek 2016.

[107] Centraal Bureau voor de Statistiek 2016.

[108] Jongbloed 2010, p. 321; van der Meulen 2010, p. 524 seq; den Hertog et al. 2012, p. 14 seq; Mostert 2012, p. 3 seq, 9, 13; Euraxess (n 101), Matthijs et al. 2016, pp. 38, 40 seq, 46 seq; Rathenau Instituut (2016) Science in figures. https://www.rathenau.nl/en/science-in-figures. Accessed 6 August 2016 section 'Investments—Funding and performance of R&D in the Netherlands'.

[109] Braun 2006, pp. 1, 5 seq; Jongbloed 2010, p. 287 seq; van der Meulen 2010, p. 516 seq, 523 seq; Leisyte 2011, p. 439; Mostert 2012, p. 2 seq, 8 seq, 11, Euraxess (n 101), Rathenau Instituut (n 108) section 'Policy and structure—Governance of Science'.

[110] Braun 2006, p. 2 seq; Jongbloed 2010, p. 290; van der Meulen 2010, p. 516; Mostert 2012, p. 3 seq, 9, Rathenau Instituut (n 108) section 'Policy and structure—Governance of Science'.

Several intermediate organisations, most significantly the Netherlands Research Council (*Nederlandse Organisatie voor Wetenschappelijk Onderzoek*, NWO), the Netherlands Enterprise Agency (*Rijksdienst voor Ondernemend Nederland*, RVO) and the Technology Foundation (*Stichting voor de Technische Wetenschappen*, STW), are responsible for implementing government policy and for acting as funding bodies for competitive public funding programmes.[111] The NWO focuses on basic research in all fields of enquiry in universities, their own institutes and other organisations. It funds researchers, research infrastructure and whole research institutes and receives its budget mainly from the OCW.[112] RVO falls under EZ and is responsible for supporting the private sector and research institutes in the area of technological innovation, sustainable development and international aspects.[113] The STW is mainly funding applied research and knowledge transfer in technical sciences. It receives its budget largely from the NWO, EZ and OCW.[114] In addition to intermediate organisations, there are a few important research facilitating organisations providing access to scientific materials such as the Royal Library (*Koninklijke Bibliotheek*).[115]

Public Research Organisations

Most public research is conducted by the 14 research-intensive universities which cooperate in the VSNU. The universities include three universities of technology, one agricultural university and the Open University. The Netherlands maintain a binary system with nearly 40 more vocational HEIs called *Hogescholen* (in English usually referred to as universities of applied sciences) next to the universities. Finally, there are other, more specific (e.g. belief focussed) public and private HEIs.[116]

In addition to their other tasks, the NWO and KNAW also maintain institutes in which research is being conducted and there are a (decreasing) number of research

---

[111] Jongbloed 2010, p. 289; van der Meulen 2010, p. 524 seq, 527; Mostert 2012, p. 2 seq, 10, Euraxess (n 101).

[112] Arnold et al. 2006, p. 30; Braun 2006, p. 3; De Weert and Boezerooy 2007, p. 45; Jongbloed 2010, p. 288; Leisyte 2011, p. 440; Mostert 2012, pp. 3, 10, 18 seq, Euraxess (n 101), Matthijs et al. 2016, pp. 49, 64, Rathenau Instituut (n 108) section 'Investments—Government funding of R&D'.

[113] Mostert 2012, pp. 3, 10, Euraxess (n 101), Matthijs et al. 2016, p. 43.

[114] Braun 2006, p. 3; Mostert 2012, pp. 4, 10, Euraxess (n 101).

[115] Directie Kennis 2012, p. 114.

[116] See on HEI research Arnold et al. 2006, p. 30; Braun 2006, p. 3; De Weert and Boezerooy 2007, p. 37; Jongbloed 2010, pp. 287, 290, 293; van der Meulen 2010, p. 515 seq; Leisyte 2011, p. 440; Chiong Meza 2012, p. 2 seq; Mostert 2012, pp. 7, 15, Euraxess (2016) Where does Dutch research take place? http://www.euraxess.nl/incoming-researchers/research-landscape/where-does-dutch-research-take-place. Accessed 10 August 2016, Matthijs et al. 2016, p. 18.

institutes affiliated with ministries.[117] Furthermore, there are also research organisations which receive public funding and focus on more applied research such as the Netherlands Organisation for Applied Scientific Research (*Nederlandse Organisatie voor Toegepast Natuurwetenschappelijk Onderzoek*), agricultural research institutes and large technology institutes.[118] In addition to these physical institutions, the Dutch government has, since the 1990s, begun initiatives for collaborative research organisations. These include the 'Top Technological Institutes' focusing on industrially relevant research[119] and the Top Consortia for Knowledge and Innovation (*Topconsortia voor Kennis en Innovatie*, TKI) focussing on research in nine sectors (horticulture and propagating stock, agriculture and food, water, life sciences and health, chemistry, high tech, energy, logistics and creative industries) which have been identified as the particular strengths of the Netherlands (*topsectoren*).[120] Research organisations are regularly evaluated on the basis of the Standard Evaluation Protocol[121] which has been established by VSNU, NWO and KNAW.[122]

4.3.1.2 Non-public Research

Most research in the Netherlands is conducted by the private sector, mainly in large enterprises which focus on product development. Private sector entities are organised in a variety of industry organisations which partly have separate research and technology commissions.[123] Research conducted by the private sector is financed, for the vast majority, by the private sector itself, but the sector also receives significant funding from abroad (14.4 %) and some public (1.9 %) and third sector (0.4 %) funding. Aside from funding its own research, the private sector invests in research abroad and, to a lesser extent, in research in HEIs and other institutions.[124] The government, in order to encourage private sector investment into R&D, initiated a number of general (tax incentives) and specific

---

[117] Arnold et al. 2006, pp. 30, 42; Braun 2006, p. 3; Jongbloed 2010, p. 282 seq, 288, 290; van der Meulen 2010, p. 516; Mostert 2012, p. 16 seq, Euraxess (n 116), Matthijs et al. 2016, p. 18.

[118] Jongbloed 2010, p. 290; Mostert 2012, pp. 12, 16, Euraxess (n 116).

[119] Arnold et al. 2006, p. 30; Braun 2006, pp. 4, 8; Jongbloed 2010, p. 292 seq, 307 seq; van der Meulen 2010, p. 520 seq; Mostert 2012, p. 16, Euraxess (n 116), Matthijs et al. 2016, p. 50.

[120] Mostert 2012, p. 5 seq, 20, Euraxess (n 101), Rathenau Instituut (n 108) section 'Policy and structure—Governance of Science', Topsectoren (2016) Innovatie (English translation: Innovation). https://www.topsectoren.nl/innovatie. Accessed 11 August 2016.

[121] KNAW et al. (2014 (up-dated 2015)).

[122] Becker 2009, p. 162; Jongbloed 2010, p. 301 seq; van der Meulen 2010, p. 518; Chiong Meza 2012, p. 21 seq; Mostert 2012, pp. 7, 9, 19; European Commission 2015, p. 468; Matthijs et al. 2016, pp. 17, 29, 90.

[123] Braun 2006, pp. 4, 7; Leisyte 2011, p. 440; Mostert 2012, p. 13 seq, Euraxess (n 116), Matthijs et al. 2016, p. 18.

[124] Centraal Bureau voor de Statistiek 2016.

funding programmes. The latter includes the Regional Attention and Action for Knowledge Circulation (*Regionale actie en aandacht voor kennisinnovatie*) focussing on cooperation between regional SMEs and *hogescholen*.[125]

At together less than 16 % of overall funding for research in the Netherlands international and third contributions play a smaller role in the Netherlands than in England. However, foreign funding has steadily increased. It is mainly received by the private sector and to a lesser extent by HEIs and other organisations.[126] The main sources of foreign funding are foreign companies and the EU. The latter was originally somewhat disregarded, but has increasingly gained in importance; today the Dutch research sector receives significantly more than the Netherlands contributes. The government currently tries to further encourage international cooperation, particularly to attract more foreign firms to invest into research in the Netherlands.[127] Whilst the third sector plays a small role as a funder, it is hardly distinguishable as a research provider.[128] The funding provided by the third sector mainly comes from charities engaged in the medical field[129] and is, for the vast majority, received by HEIs.[130]

4.3.2 Research in Public HEIs

Most of the 14 research-intensive universities are public organisations. Only the Vrije Universiteit Amsterdam, Radbound Universiteit Nijmegen and Tilburg University were, despite now being publicly funded, originally not set up by the government. Universities in the Netherlands focus especially on research in health, natural sciences and engineering.[131]

---

[125] Mostert 2012, pp. 3, 6 seq, 13; Subsidie.nl (2016) Regionale actie en aandacht voor kennisinnovatie (English translation: Attention and Action for Knowledge Circulation). http://www.123subsidie.nl/regelingen/94-regionale-actie-en-aandacht-voor-kennisinnovatie/. Accessed 11 August 2016.

[126] Centraal Bureau voor de Statistiek 2011, 2016.

[127] van der Meulen 2010, p. 522 seq; Directie Kennis 2012, p. 122; Mostert 2012, pp. 6, 14, 21 seq; Matthijs et al. 2016, pp. 56, 65, Rathenau Instituut (n 108) section 'Investments—Government funding of R&D'.

[128] Centraal Bureau voor de Statistiek 2011 explanatory note section 'Door instellingen', Centraal Bureau voor de Statistiek 2016.

[129] Mostert 2012, p. 15; Matthijs et al. 2016, p. 43, Rathenau Instituut (n 108) section 'Investments—Funding and performance of R&D in the Netherlands'.

[130] Centraal Bureau voor de Statistiek 2016.

[131] Chiong Meza 2012, p. 2 seq, 15.

4.3.2.1 Research as a Statutory Task of HEIs

In the Netherlands, HEIs are regulated in the Higher Education and Research Act (*Wet op het hoger onderwijs en wetenschappelijk onderzoek, WHW*). The WHW provides a task description for four different kinds of HEIs in Article 1.3; the 13 universities, the Open University, additional universities dedicated to certain religions or beliefs (*levensbeschouwelijke universiteiten*) and *hogescholen*. Accordingly, the universities have as their task the provision of higher education, the execution of scientific research, the education of researchers and innovators and the transfer of knowledge for the benefit of society (Article 1.3(1) WHW). The Open University's task is to provide higher education and higher vocational education via distance learning methods, to conduct scientific and practical research in accordance with its profile and to contribute to the renewal of higher education (Article 1.3(4) WHW). The *levensbeschouwelijke universiteiten* aim to provide higher education for an office or profession within a certain belief system, conduct research in the area of a belief system, educate researchers and transfer knowledge for the benefit of society (Article 1.3(2) WHW). Finally, *Hogescholen* are focussed on providing higher professional education, conducting professionally oriented design, development and research activities, transferring knowledge for the benefit of society and contributing to the development of the occupations in which they provide education (Article 1.3(3) WHW). Research is thus a statutory task of all four kinds of HEIs.

Article 1.9(1) WHW prescribes that universities receive public funding for research. With regards to *Hogescholen*, research is considered as part of education provision and is funded as such. According to para (3) the condition for HEIs to receive funding is that they take into account the provisions in the WHW. Articles 2.5(2) and 2.6(4) WHW specify this by allowing the relevant minister to attach conditions to research funding relating to quality assurance and making the criteria for determining research funding at universities conditional upon the social and scientific need for the research taking into account the profile of the institutions and the research quality.[132] However, Article 1.6 WHW declares that the academic freedom shall be observed in HEIs. These provisions thus seem to constitute some weighing of external factors in determining the lump sums for research funding awarded to HEIs and academic freedom. Quantitative restrictions of research do not seem to exist by statute. However, according to Article 2.7a rules regarding the use of public funding for private activities can be made.

4.3.2.2 Public Research Funding

In the following the focus will be on universities as the most research intensive HEIs. Government provides most funding generically to universities which is

---

[132] Further on the funding of universities (including teaching) according to Articles 1.9, 2.5 and 2.6 WHW see Schneider et al. 2009 Part IV p. 1 seq.

referred to as the first funding stream (*eerste geldstroom*). Other public funding is provided through intermediate organisations, in particular the NWO, known as the second funding stream (*tweede geldstroom*). The third stream (*derde geldstroom*) contains research income from industry, contract research for the government, third sector and foreign contributions (in particular from European funds). The fourth stream (*vierde geldstroom*) comes from philanthropic donations.[133] Despite generic governmental funding still being the most important funding stream, a shift towards a more competitive, impact and priority oriented research system can be observed. This includes some involvement of performance indicators in the determination of generic funding and the growing importance of competitive public funding as well as of commercialisation and industry cooperation.[134]

Public Generic Funding

Universities still receive the largest part of their research funding as generic funding (about 43 %),[135] even though there are differences between universities.[136] HEIs receive a lump sum for research which is calculated on the basis of a formula set out in a governmental decree.[137] The formula is mainly based on the number of degrees conferred and so-called strategic considerations which are mainly based on historical allocation.[138] Only a small part within the allocation of the research component can be set directly by the government on the basis of competitive/performance factors.[139] Resistance from the universities prevented attempts by consecutive governments since the early 1980s to give such competitive factors in the research allocation more weight and there have equally been protests about the performance based allocation of 7 % of the annual

---

[133] De Weert and Boezerooy 2007, p. 37 seq; Schneider et al. 2009, Part IV p. 12; Jongbloed 2010, p. 294 seq; Chiong Meza 2012, p. 8; Mostert 2012, p. 11 seq, 16; OCW (2016) Onderzoekscapaciteit universiteiten (English translation: Research capacity of universities). http://www.ocwincijfers.nl/wetenschap/inhoud/universitair-onderzoek/onderzoekscapaciteit-universiteiten. Accessed 11 August 2016, Rathenau Instituut (n 108) section 'Policy and structure—The Dutch knowledge infrastructure'.

[134] Leisyte et al. 2008, p. 378 seq; van der Meulen 2010, p. 516; Mostert 2012, p. 19; Matthijs et al. 2016, p. 47 seq, OCW (n 133).

[135] OCW (n 133).

[136] Chiong Meza 2012, p. 14 seq, Rathenau Instituut (n 108) section 'Investments—Income of universities in the Netherlands by source of funds'.

[137] Article 2.6(1) WHW. This has been specified in the WHW Executing Act 2008 (*Uitvoeringsbesluit WHW 2008*) Chap. 4. See also Schneider et al. 2009, Part IV p. 2 seq.

[138] For the research formula see *Uitvoeringsbesluit WHW 2008* Articles 4.20–4.23. For more details see Schneider et al. 2009, Part IV p. 5 seq; Jongbloed 2010, p. 294 seq; Chiong Meza 2012, p. 8; Matthijs et al. 2016, p. 47.

[139] *Uitvoeringsbesluit WHW 2008* Article 4.23. See also Schneider et al. 2009, Part IV p. 7; Chiong Meza 2012, p. 8; Mostert 2012, p. 19; Matthijs et al. 2016, p. 47.

teaching grant.[140] By providing the lump sum, the Netherlands follow a more indirect concept of research financing with institutional autonomy and (some) external steering policies. Within HEIs a more managerial style of university governance is envisaged giving HEIs the freedom to administer the lump sum as they see fit. In internal funding allocation, quality and impact can play a role.[141]

Public Competitive Funding

Competitive public funding from intermediary organisations (*tweede geldstroom*) has gained in importance over recent years.[142] How much of its research funding a university receives this way varies significantly.[143] NWO is the most important funder in this respect and covers all academic subjects. One of the most prestigious project funding programmes is the talent funding scheme *Vernieuwingsimpuls* (official English title: Innovational Research Incentive Scheme). This scheme contains special grants for early career (VENI), mid career (VIDI) and senior (VICI) researchers. NWO also offers open competitions where researchers can apply freely with their proposals, infrastructure funding, funding for international collaboration and thematic calls targeted to achieve certain government policy aims. Finally, it provides support for the publication of research results with a recent focus on open access publication.[144]

In recent years, there have also been attempts at targeted institutional funding. In 1998, the Dutch government had already introduced a programme for funding excellent research schools (*Dieptestrategie,* Depth Strategy) through which six top research schools have received additional institutional funding.[145] In 2010

---

[140] On the performance based allocation of the annual teaching grant see de Boer et al. 2015, p. 29 seq; European Commission 2015, p. 469; Matthijs et al. 2016, p. 47 seq and on criticism thereof see Matthijs et al. 2016, p. 48.

[141] On public generic funding for research in the Netherlands see De Weert and Boezerooy 2007, p. 46 seq; Leisyte et al. 2008, p. 378 seq; Becker 2009, p. 160; Jongbloed 2010, pp. 287, 294 seq, 300 seq, 323, 326 seq; van der Meulen 2010, p. 516; Mostert 2012, p. 19 seq; de Boer et al. 2015, p. 29 seq; European Commission 2015, p. 469; Matthijs et al. 2016, p. 47 seq. For an example of internal steering policies based on excellence and impact see the case study on the University of Twente in Arnold et al. 2006, p. 42.

[142] Chiong Meza 2012, p. 8; Mostert 2012, p. 16, OCW (n 133).

[143] Chiong Meza 2012, p. 14 seq and, in relation to the *Vernieuwingsimpuls* scheme, Rathenau Instituut (n 108) section 'Process—NWO "Vernieuwingsimpuls" research grants by university and type of grant'.

[144] NWO (2016) Financieringsvormen (English translation: Forms of funding). http://www. nwo.nl/financiering/financieringsvormen. Accessed 11 August 2016. On the *tweede geldstroom* generally see De Weert and Boezerooy 2007, p. 47; Jongbloed 2010, p. 294 seq; van der Meulen 2010, p. 520; Chiong Meza 2012, p. 23 seq; Directie Kennis 2012, p. 124; Mostert 2012, p. 10 seq, 20 seq.

[145] For more information see Umbrella Committee for the Evaluation of the Bonus Incentive Scheme 2009–2010.

Dieptestrategie was replaced by a new institutional funding programme entitled '*Zwaartekracht*' (Gravitation). The third round of *Zwaartekracht,* where consortia can apply for funding, is taking place in 2016.[146] Furthermore, many of the (semi-)public collaborative research organisations described above, in which HEIs are often involved, have been set up as a result of specific institutional research funding schemes.[147] Finally, public institutions might also commission research from HEIs (*derde geldstroom*).[148]

4.3.2.3 Non-state Funding

Non-state funding (*derde* or, if purely charitable, *vierde geldstroom*) amounts to a little less than a quarter of all research funding for HEIs provided almost equally by the third sector, the private sector and international sources.[149] The importance of such funding has grown over the last decades and government policy encourages the utilisation of these sources and steers collaborations towards government priorities.[150]

With regards to the third sector, it is mainly medical charities that cooperate with HEIs. Many of them have joint forces in the *Samenwerkende GezondheidsFondsen* (Cooperative Health Funds) which is 'selecting thematic areas (based on societal needs) and aligning her funding programs with NWO and the Top Sector Life Sciences & Health'.[151] In international funding the EU plays an especially important role, but Dutch researchers are also active in a variety of bilateral collaborations within and beyond the EU. To encourage cross-border collaboration, the NWO has specific funding options.[152]

As in England, collaboration with the private sector can take a variety of forms such as research co-operations between HEIs and the private sector, often taking the institutionalised public-private partnership (PPP) form of one of the

---

[146] NWO (2016) Graviation—Background. http://www.nwo.nl/en/research-and-results/programmes/gravitation/background. Accessed 11 August 2016.

[147] On competitive institutional funding see De Weert and Boezerooy 2007, p. 47; Jongbloed 2010, p. 297 seq, 305; van der Meulen 2010, p. 519 seq; Matthijs et al. 2016, p. 50 seq.

[148] Jongbloed 2010, p. 294 seq; Matthijs et al. 2016, p. 50.

[149] Centraal Bureau voor de Statistiek 2016. For on overview of the significance of this funding source in the different universities see Chiong Meza 2012, p. 14 seq.

[150] Braun 2006, p. 6 seq; Becker 2009, p. 159; Jongbloed 2010, pp. 294, 306; Leisyte 2011, pp. 439, 441; Chiong Meza 2012, pp. 8, 27; den Hertog et al. 2012, p. 16; Mostert 2012, pp. 12, 19 seq; VSNU 2012, p. 24 seq, 89 seq, Rathenau Instituut (n 108) section 'Policy and structure—Science policy and innovation policy'.

[151] Matthijs et al. 2016, p. 43.

[152] Chiong Meza 2012, pp. 19, 23, 26 seq; den Hertog et al. 2012, p. 30 seq, 99 seq; Mostert 2012, p. 21 seq; Matthijs et al. 2016, p. 50, Rathenau Instituut (n 108) section 'Investments—Funding and performance of R&D in the Netherlands', 'Investments—Government funding of R&D'.

collaborative research organisations mentioned above.[153] HEIs also undertake contract research and consultancy work which is sometimes internally rewarded.[154] Exploitation of IPRs has increased in recent years. Whilst HEIs usually own IPRs developed by their employees, in co-operations, it is often the private sector partner who receives IPRs, or they are jointly owned. However, there is no general policy on this and HEIs sometimes let the researcher receive some of the income generated. Some HEIs have recently introduced special 'valorisation centres' or technology transfer offices for the exploitation of IPRs and exchange of best practices. Occasionally, IPR valorisation is conducted by private holding companies established by the HEI or an HEI might create spin-offs for the purpose of exploiting IPRs.[155]

Start-ups, whether as IPR related spin-offs or beyond, are usually partly owned by the HEI and often managed through the mentioned technology-transfer units or through holding companies which themselves might also collaborate further with the private sector. To encourage entrepreneurship HEIs increasingly offer courses for staff and students in this respect. HEIs might equally collaborate with the private sector in science parks (also referred to as innovation campuses (*innovatiecampussen*)). Here, as in England, HEIs, private sector partners and, potentially, other research institutions all work in one geographical location, which is often at least partly owned by the HEI, in order to create synergies and encourage collaboration and entrepreneurship.[156] Finally, there are staff exchanges and more informal ways to collaborate, such as research networks or private sector representatives sitting on supervisory or executive boards of HEIs.[157]

4.3.2.4 Full Costing

Since 2006, universities in the Netherlands have implemented full costing methodologies on their own initiative[158] but following common standards agreed by the VSNU and in continuous exchange. The reasons were EU Framework

---

[153] Braun 2006, pp. 6, 10; Jongbloed 2010, p. 307 seq, 323, 327 seq; Leisyte 2011, p. 445; Directie Kennis 2012, p. 106; Mostert 2012, p. 19 seq; VSNU 2012, pp. 25, 91, Rathenau Instituut (n 108) section 'Process—Collaboration in R&D'.

[154] Jongbloed 2010, pp. 294, 309, 323 seq; Leisyte 2011, p. 446; Matthijs et al. 2016, p. 18.

[155] Jongbloed 2010, pp. 294, 307, 318; Leisyte 2011, p. 442 seq; Mostert 2012, p. 1, 15 seq, 20; VSNU 2012, p. 89; Matthijs et al. 2016, pp. 82, 88 seq. For an example of a university policy on IPR exploitation and spin-offs see the case study of the University of Twente in Arnold et al. 2006, p. 44 seq.

[156] On start-ups and science parks see Jongbloed 2010, p. 323; VSNU 2012, p. 24 seq, 90. See for an example of a university policy on science parks and entrepreneurship the case study of the University of Twente in Arnold et al. 2006, p. 44 seq; Leisyte 2011, p. 443.

[157] Braun 2006, p. 4 seq, 7, 10; Jongbloed 2010, p. 323 seq; Leisyte 2011, pp. 444, 447; den Hertog et al. 2012, p. 30 seq, 53; Directie Kennis 2012, p. 111; Mostert 2012, p. 20.

[158] For examples of methodologies in different universities see EUA 2008, pp. 27, 31, 61, 65; Estermann and Claeys-Kulik 2013, p. 23 seq, 29 seq.

Programme 7[159] requirements as well as the desire to attain financial sustainability unthreatened by matching requirements for non-generic funding (which was often not provided at full cost basis).[160] The latter is also problematic since matching limits the funds available for direction-free research. However, being able to analyse the full costs, universities still negotiate the prices individually with funders or funders determine which costs they cover.[161] In this context, the government in a number of regulations and guidelines reinforces EU state aid law for private sector collaboration especially in the context of receiving additional EZ subsidies.[162] Yet, aside from very clearly restating EU rules on collaborative research the regulations and guidelines seem general and vague. In particular, there seems to be little concrete guidance on pricing levels when it comes to public or third sector partners which also do not fund at full cost level.[163]   To simplify the calculation of direct costs of the various funding schemes the NWO, VSNU, KNAW and others have passed an agreement on common guidelines for direct costs in funding provision (*Akkord bekostiging wetenschappelijk onderzoek 2008*).

4.3.3 Interim Conclusion on the Netherlands

Overall R&D spending in the Netherlands as decreased between 2004–2008, but steadily increased since. Public sector spending has steadily increased and private sector spending, despite a dip in 2009, is now on the highest level of the last 15 years. The private sector provides most research funding and conducts

---

[159] Decision 1982/2006/EC concerning the Seventh Framework Programme of the European Community for research, technological development and demonstration activities (2007–2013) OJ [2006] L 412/01.

[160] EUA 2008, pp. 7, 28, 40, 65; Herlitschka 2009, pp. 41, 49; Estermann and Claeys-Kulik 2013, pp. 19, 23, 30, 47 seq; Neth-ER (2013) EUA toont Europese voortgang full cost (English translation: EU shows European progress in full costing). http://www.neth-er.eu/nl/nieuws/eua-toont-europese-voortgang-full-cost. Accessed 1 May 2013.

[161] Tweede Kamer der Staten-Generaal 2000, pp. 97, 108; De Weert and Boezerooy 2007, p. 37; Jongbloed 2010, p. 309; Smeets (2016) Matchingsdruk (English translation: Matching Pressure). http://www.vsnu.nl/matchingsdruk.html. Accessed 12 August 2016.

[162] For example, the *Kaderbesluit EZ-subsidies* (Framework decision EZ subsidies) essentially reinforces European state aid rules. The *Regeling nationale EZ-subsidies* (National EZ Subsidies Regulation) in Article 1.9 more specifically reinforces the rules of the Research Framework (Commission Communication 'Framework for State aid for research and development and innovation' OJ [2014] C 198/01) for collaborative research and otherwise requires approval by the minister which will only be granted if threshold of European state aid law are not exceeded. Section 4.5 *Kader Financieel Beheer rijkssubsidies* (Uniform Subsidy Framework) explicitly relates to the state aid rules and requires institutions not to breach these. The OCW requires and provides guidance for separation of public and private reserves/capital (Pirovano 2015, pp. 18, 45).

[163] Funding from the *tweede* and *derde geldstroom* on average requires matching of about €0.7 (Koier et al. 2016. p. 57).

most of the research. HEIs are the most important public research organisations. As well as research in the NWO, KNAW, institutes affiliated with ministries and more applied research organisations, there are a variety of collaborative research organisations which are publicly funded.

As a consociational system there are many actors involved in policy setting and implementation. Recent policy aims included mobilisation of the private sector, creating excellence, setting priorities and coordinating policies. This has led to a variety of policy programmes aimed at establishing elite institutions, supporting priority areas and increasing performance. The programmes have, due to the consociational character of the system, however, rather increased cooperation (e.g. in consortia) than competition and to some extent have led to a very confusing system with a large variety of actors and collaborations.[164]

HEIs still receive most of their research funding from public sources. About 43 % of their funding is provided generically in the *eerste geldstroom* which only involves limited recourse to competitive factors. However, the importance of the *tweede* and *derde geldstroom* (respectively *vierde geldstroom* if purely philanthropic) is growing. This has been regarded as problematic inasmuch as it might cause constraints for the academic freedom. Additionally, with the increase in the *tweede* and *derde geldstroom* 'matching' became a problem which, combined with the requirements of EU Framework Programme 7, led to the introduction of full costing systems and legislation reinforcing EU state aid rules at least for collaboration with the private sector.

4.4 Germany

Germany is the EU Member State with the fifth highest spending on R&D. In 2014 Germany spent 2.87 % of its GDP on R&D having increased spending more or less steadily over the previous ten years. Germany thus nearly met the 3 % goal of the Europe 2020 Strategy which has so far only been achieved by Finland, Sweden and Denmark.[165] Whilst the high spending is a strength of the German research system, weaknesses have been identified in regard to the lack of utilisation of synergies between actors, transparency, exploitation and efficiency of funding utilisation. Additionally, Germany decided to increase research funding in response to the economic crisis. Measures to overhaul the system in order to address its weaknesses and to distribute additional funding efficiently have thus been initiated in recent years and the system has, accordingly, been in a stage of reformation which also includes steps towards competition and commodification.[166]

---

[164] Jongbloed 2010, pp. 308, 329 seq; van der Meulen 2010, pp. 522, 526.

[165] EUROSTAT (n 17). Austria is, with 2.99 % in 2012, still slightly below the target.

[166] Enders 2007, p. 19 seq, 23 seq, 26 seq; Wissenschaftsrat 2007, p. 7 seq; Edler and Kuhlmann 2008, p. 265 seq, 268 seq; Hinze 2010, p. 171 seq; Schubert and Schmoch 2010, p. 244; Schreiterer 2015; BMBF 2016, p. 10 seq.

4.4.1 General Overview

About two thirds of Germany's overall R&D spending comes from the private sector, the importance of which has increased significantly since the early 1980s. This is followed by nearly 30 % from the public sector and about 5 % from foreign sources. Third sector spending plays an insignificant role in overall research spending in Germany amounting to less than 1 %.[167] The private sector mainly funds its own research, but increasingly is also providing funding for research in HEIs as well as in other public and third sector organisations. Public funding is provided at the federal as well state levels mainly for research in HEIs, followed by research in other public research organisations and the third sector,[168] and, to a lesser extent, for research in the private sector. The majority of international funding goes to the private sector.[169]

4.4.1.1 Public Research

Germany has in recent years begun to introduce measures towards commodification; non-generic public as well as non-public funding (*Drittmittel*) for research in public institutions have gained in importance and are increasingly provided competitively. Generic funding has begun to be allocated partly on the on the basis of competitive, performance based elements (*leistungsorientierte Mittelverteilung*). *Drittmittel* accumulation also became an important indicator of the accomplishments and quality of research organisations, especially HEIs, and thus started to play a role in the performance based elements of generic funding allocation.[170]

The Governmental Structure

As, according to Article 20(1) of the German constitution (*Grundgesetz*, GG), Germany is a federal republic with 16 federal states (*Länder*), competences are divided between the different levels of government. As regards research, a concurrent legislative competence[171] exists regarding 'the regulation of educational and training grants and the promotion of research' (Article 74(1) no.

---

[167] BMBF 2016, Table 1 and 2 (p. 55 seq of supplement 1).

[168] These are combined when it comes to research conducting sectors.

[169] See BMBF 2016, Table 1 (p. 55 seq of supplement 1).

[170] See Edler and Kuhlmann 2008, p. 265 seq; Hinze 2010, pp. 162, 167, 171. See also Albrecht 2009, p. 9 seq who provides a critical perspective of the recent developments. For an overview of policies in various federal states see BMBF 2016 supplement 3.

[171] Article 74 GG enumerates areas of concurrent competence. In these areas the *Länder* have competence as long and far as the federal level has not enacted any legislation.

13 GG) 'if and to the extent that the establishment of equivalent living conditions throughout the federal territory or the maintenance of legal or economic unity renders federal regulation necessary in the national interest' (Article 72(2) GG). All remaining research competences, in particular competences for HEIs, lie with the *Länder*. According to Article 91b(1) GG the federal level (*Bund*) and the *Länder* can, however, cooperate in cases of 'supraregional importance' on the basis of agreements in respect of financing science, research and education. Agreements which mainly concern HEIs need to be agreed to by all *Länder*, unless they are agreements on the construction of research facilities, including large scientific installations.

At the federal level, the Federal Ministry of Education and Research (*Bundesministerium für Bildung und Forschung*, BMBF) is mainly responsible for research, contributing the vast majority of the federal research budget. Aside from BMBF, mainly the Federal Ministry of Economics and Technology (*Bundesministerium für Wirtschaft und Technology*) and the Federal Ministry of Defence (*Bundesministerium für Verteidigung*) play a role in research policy, but other ministries also may be involved and provide some funding.[172] Overall the *Bund* contributes about 60 % of all public funding with the *Länder* contributing the remainder. *Bund* and *Länder* are coordinating their activities in the Joint Science Conference (*Gemeinsame Wissenschaftskonferenz*) and are advised by the Council of Science and Humanities (*Wissenschaftsrat*). Additionally, there have been a number of ad hoc advisory bodies. Common endeavours of the *Bund* and the *Länder* include, in particular, the financing of the German research foundation (*Deutsche Forschungsgemeinschaft*, DFG) and of the four major non-HEI public research organisations; Helmholts-Gemeinschaft, Leibniz-Gemeinschaft, Frauenhofer-Gesellschaft and Max-Planck-Gesellschaft. Except for the possibility of cooperation as provided for in Article 91b GG, the *Länder* are responsible for HEI finances and governance. They voluntarily coordinate their activities in the education minister conference (*Kultusministerkonferenz*) which the federal government may attend as a guest. According to the HEI Pact (*Hochschulpakt*) the *Länder* are to receive federal contributions to their HEI expenditure and the federal government will increase its own competitive funding for HEIs.[173]

The DFG is an intermediary body whose main task is the promotion of research in HEIs and other public research organisations in all areas of 'knowledge-oriented' (*erkenntnisorientiert*) research. It, however, also promotes the inter-play between research and users (e.g. industry) and conducts related activities. The DFG provides competitive project-related and institutional research funding. The latter has gained in importance over recent years. Furthermore, the DFG advises

---

[172] On the federal level see Wissenschaftsrat 2007, p. 62 seq; Edler and Kuhlmann 2008, p. 265 seq; Hinze 2010, p. 162 seq, 171; BMBF 2016, p. 60 seq.

[173] On the interplay between *Bund* and the *Länder* see Edler and Kuhlmann 2008, pp. 267, 269, 271 seq; Hinze 2010, p. 163 seq; BMBF 2016, p, 61 seq, 249 seq as well as p. 15 of supplement 1.

parliaments, governments and public bodies on academic questions. It is financed by the *Bund* and the *Länder* at rate of about 60–40 %.[174]

Public Research Organisations

There are 459 HEIs in Germany, 105 of which are universities. As with the Netherlands, Germany entertains a binary system with 209 vocational HEIs called *Fachhochschulen* (in English usually referred to as universities of applied sciences) existing alongside the universities. Additionally, there are 51 art academies, 37 academies for administration, 35 teaching hospitals, 16 academies for theology and 6 academies for educational science. 294 of all 459 HEIs are (mainly) financed by the *Länder,* 12 by the *Bund* and 153 by non-public sources including 36 HEIs which are financed by religious organisations.[175]

Non-HEI public research also has an important role in Germany. The most important players are the Max-Planck-Gesellschaft focussing on basic research, the Frauenhofer-Gesellschaft focussing on applied R&D, the Helmholtz-Gemeinschaft focussing on long term studies which require large scientific installations and the Leibniz-Gemeinschaft focussing on strategic, theme-related research. All these organisations consist of a variety of institutes. Their funding streams are dependent on their tasks; while the Max-Planck-Gesellschaft, for example, is financed for the most part by generic public funding, the Frauenhofer-Gesellschaft received 85 % of its funding through contract research in 2015. Generally, however, competitive funding has increasingly gained in importance and the non-HEI research organisations have been subject to reform. The Pact for Research and Innovation (*Pakt für Forschung und Innovation*) aims at a yearly funding increase for non-HEI research organisations as well as increasing synergies and international and private sector cooperation. The Freedom of Research Act (*Gesetz zur Flexibilisierung von haushaltsrechtlichen Rahmenbedingungen außeruniversitärer Wissenschaftseinrichtungen*)[176] is creating more organiational independence for the non-HEI research organisations. In addition to the four major non-HEI research organisation, some ministries also have their own research institutes.[177]

---

[174] See Wissenschaftsrat 2007, p. 65 seq; Edler and Kuhlmann 2008, p. 267; Hinze 2010, p. 168 seq, 172; BMBF 2016, p. 54 seq, 76, DFG (2016) DFG im Profil—Aufgaben (English translation: DFG profile—Tasks). http://www.dfg.de/dfg_profil/aufgaben/index.html. Accessed 13 August 2016.

[175] See Statistisches Bundesamt 2016, p. 160.

[176] On the Freedom of Research Act see BMBF (2016) Das Wissenschaftsfreiheitsgesetz (English translation: the Freedom of Research Act). http://www.bmbf.de/de/12268.php. Accessed 13 August 2016.

[177] On public research outside HEIs see Enders 2007, p. 23; Edler and Kuhlmann 2008, pp. 267, 270; Hinze 2010, p. 170 seq; Schubert and Schmoch 2010, p. 255 seq; BMBF 2016, p. 67 seq, 73 seq, 257.

4.4.1.2 Non-public Research

Most of Germany's R&D is financed by the private sector which also conducts more than two thirds of the research. The latter is almost entirely funded by the private sector with only limited contributions (less than 9 % together) from (in order of relevance) foreign, public and third sector sources.[178] Only since the late 1990s/early 2000s has cooperation with external partners such as HEIs, public research organisations and other private sector organisations become a major factor in private sector company strategies inter alia due to the increasing complexity of research.[179] The private sector has thus begun to invest into research in HEIs and public non-HEI research organisations.[180] Additionally, there are institutionalised co-operations between private sector entities such as the Federation of Industrial Research Associations (*Arbeitsgemeinschaft industrieller Forschungsgemeinschaften,* AiF) focussing on the interests of SME.[181] Government policy supports private sector R&D in particular through the 'High-Tech Strategy' which has recently been re-launched and the aim of which is to translate ideas quickly into products. It focuses on the areas digital economy, sustainability and energy, the 'innovative workplace', healthy living, mobility and security.[182]

As we have seen (Sect. 4.4.2.3 above), international funding plays only a minor role in the German research system, whilst third sector funding hardly has any part to play. 65.7 % of the international funding goes to the private sector and the rest is relatively equally divided between HEIs on the one hand and non-HEI public research organisations and third sector organisation combined on the other. Third sector funding goes to the majority to third sector and public non-HEI institutions.[183] However, the importance of, especially international funding, is increasing; in particular for HEIs. Government is encouraging this development and its policy is aiming at better coordination in this respect.[184]

---

[178] BMBF 2016, Table 1 (p. 55 seq of supplement 1).

[179] Rohrbeck 2010, p. 427 seq, 431 seq.

[180] For an overview of such investments in recent years see BMBF 2016, Table 1 (p. 55 seq of supplement 1).

[181] Wissenschaftsrat 2007, p. 66 seq; Hinze 2010, p. 169; AiF (2016) AiF im Profil (English translation: AiF in Profile). https://www.aif.de/aif/aif-im-profil.html. Accessed 13 August 2016.

[182] See Wissenschaftsrat 2007, p. 63 seq; Edler and Kuhlmann 2008, p. 271; Rohrbeck 2010, p. 429 seq; BMBF 2014.

[183] BMBF 2016, Table 1 (p. 55 seq of supplement 1).

[184] See Edler and Kuhlmann 2008, pp. 268, 270; BMBF 2016 p. 45 seq, Table 1 (p. 55 seq of supplement 1).

4.4.2 Research in Public HEIs

As mentioned above (section "Public Research Organisations" above) there are a vast variety of HEIs in Germany. The following will focus on public universities as research intensive public HEIs.

4.4.2.1 Research as a Statutory Task of HEIs

The division of competences between *Bund* and *Länder* regarding HEIs has long been a controversial subject. Before the federalism reform (a general re-structuring of competences in the federal system begun in 2006) the *Bund* had the competence to pass framework legislation (former Article 75 GG) and *Bund* and *Länder* had to cooperate regarding research funding. The removal of federal competences regarding HEIs during the federalism reform had been triggered by a decision of the German constitutional Court (*Bundesverfassungsgericht*) in which the court declared that the *Bund* had overstepped its competences.[185] However, Article 125a GG ensures that framework legislation already enacted remains valid, unless the *Länder* deviate from it. In the field of HEIs, the relevant framework legislation is the Framework Act for Higher Education (*Hochschulrahmengesetz*, HRG). The annulment of this act has since been discussed[186] but never realised. The HRG thus remains the relevant federal legislation.

Public HEIs are, according to § 58 HRG, bodies governed by public law as well as institutions of the state. According to § 2(1) HRG, HEIs 'shall contribute to the fostering and development of the arts and sciences through research, teaching, studies and continuing education'. Regarding research in HEIs § 22 HRG provides that

> the purpose of research at institutions of higher education shall be the acquisition of scientific knowledge and the scientific underpinning and development of teaching and study. Research at institutions of higher education may, subject to the specific role of the institution concerned, relate to any academic discipline and to the practical application of scientific findings, including the potential impact of such application.

---

[185] BVerfGE 111, 226, decision of 27 July 2004 (*Junior Professor*). Leaving the majority of the funding competences to the *Länder* then caused financial difficulties (Tagesschau. de (2014) Finanzierung der Hochschulen—Für Unis mehr Förderung vom Bund (English translation: Funding of higher education institutions—More funding from the federal government for universities). tagesschau.de, 16 July 2014 http://www.tagesschau.de/inland/hochschulbildung-100.html. Accessed 16 July 2014) which in turn led to a change of Article 91b GG in December 2014 which now provides for more options of the *Bund* to fund HEIs (including institutional funding) on the basis of agreements as elaborated upon above (section "The Governmental Structure").

[186] Seckelmann 2010, pp. 227, 229 seq, 232 seq.

There are no quantitative restrictions in the HRG as to the amount of externally funded research that can be carried out by an HEI as long as 'the fulfilment of the institution's other functions and the rights and obligations of other persons are not impaired and [...] adequate consideration is given to commitments that might result from the project' (§ 25(2) HRG). The results of such research should generally be made publicly available 'within a reasonable period of time'.

At state level the provisions are similar.[187] The Bremen HEI Act (*Bremisches Hochschulgesetz*), for example, contains almost identical provisions to § 2(1), § 22 and § 25(2) HRG in § 4(1), § 70(1) and § 74(2) respectively. The Berlin HEI Act (*Berliner Hochschulgesetz*) contains very similar provisions to § 2(1) and § 22 HRG in § 4(1) and § 37(1) respectively. With regards to externally funded research, it simply refers to § 25 HRG in its § 40. The Bavarian Higher Education Act (*Bayerisches Hochschulgesetz*) contains similar provisions to § 2(1), § 22 and § 25(2) HRG in Articles 2(1), 6(1) and 8(1–2) respectively. The Act on HEIs in Baden-Württemberg (*Gesetz über die Hochschulen in Baden-Württemberg*) contains similar provisions to § 2(1), § 22 HRG in § 2(1), § 40(1) respectively. Regarding § 25(2) HRG the corresponding provision is contained in § 41(1). In contrast to the federal provision, which only entitles staff to conduct externally funded research, this provision declares the active search for external funds as one of the official duties of research staff. Apart from this, the provision is similar to the relevant provision in the HRG. There is an additional provision on transparency as regards *Drittmittel* in § 41a.

It can thus be established that research, including applied research is a statutory task of public HEIs and that there do not seem to be any specific restrictions as to the amount of commercial research undertaken, so long as HEIs can still fulfil the tasks assigned to them and, in the case of Baden-Württemberg follow the requirements on transparency. There also cannot (theoretically) be too much external or internal steering, as Article 5(3) GG provides that the 'arts and sciences, research and teaching shall be free'. This provision essentially makes academic freedom a human right and thus gives it a very strong protection in Germany.

4.4.2.2 Public Research Funding

HEIs receive generic funding and *Drittmittel*. The latter includes public competitive and other funding. The aims behind the introduction of public competitive funding were to reward well-performing HEIs and create transparency after the introduction of lump sums in HEI funding.[188]

---

[187] The provisions of the federal states in which the universities chosen for the empirical study are located shall be looked at here as examples. On the choice of universities see Chap. 5 below.

[188] See Enders 2007, pp. 22, 28; Hinze 2010, p. 169 seq; Jaeger and In der Smitten 2010, p. 64; Schubert and Schmoch 2010, p. 248 seq, 251, 253.

Public Generic Funding

Whilst HEIs still receive the majority of their funding generically from the *Länder*, the importance of *Drittmittel* has grown.[189] Traditionally, generic funding was allocated on the basis of detailed criteria. However, emphasis on new public management structures and less public regulation, led to generic funding being increasingly provided as lump sums allowing more independence for the HEIs.[190] At the same time a criticism that has been made is that the new managerial structures decrease the potential for academic self-regulation[191] and create competition between teaching and research.[192] In how far generic funding allocation includes performance indicators and agreements towards achieving certain aims (*Zielvereinbarungen*) depends on the *Länder* and is subject to change.[193] A rare comprehensive overview of percentages of performance factors in generic funding allocation from 2010 suggest the weighting of such factors can differ between 0 % and over 35 %.[194]

Public Competitive Funding

Declining generic funding increased the importance of competitive public funding. The DFG is the most important public *Drittmittel* provider, followed by the *Bund*.[195] The DFG funds research in all disciplines and interdisciplinary research on the basis of applications by German research organisations or individual researchers within these. Purely commercial research organisations are generally not eligible. Next to non-specific funding on the basis of applications, the DFG also maintains more specific funding programmes as well as programmes for international collaborations. A board of volunteer experts assesses the proposals on the basis of scientific criteria. The DFG encourages collaborations with users of research and funded projects can apply for additional 'transfer' funding. However,

---

[189] BMBF 2016, Table 27 (p. 121 supplement 1).

[190] See Enders 2007, p. 20 seq; Edler and Kuhlmann 2008, p. 271; Albrecht 2009, p. 9 seq; Jaeger and In der Smitten 2010, p. 6; Jansen 2010, p. 42 seq; Schubert and Schmoch 2010, p. 245 seq; Seckelmann 2010, p. 233 seq.

[191] See Seckelmann 2010, p. 235 seq with further references, who also raises the question of whether this might infringe the democracy principle and academic freedom in the German constitution according to Articles 20 and 5(3) GG respectively.

[192] Enders 2007, p. 22 seq.

[193] On current policies in the *Länder* generally see BMBF 2016 p. 333 seq and supplement 3.

[194] See Jaeger and In der Smitten 2010, p. 6, Fig. 1.

[195] See Statistisches Bundesamt 2015, Table 2.6 (p. 240 seq) and 2.7 (p. 261 seq).

the research has to stay at the 'pre-competitive' stage and thus may not go beyond the development of a prototype.[196]

One of the most important programmes by the *Bund* is the 'Excellence Initiative' (*Exzellenzinitiative*), an institutional funding programme aimed at strengthening HEI research, changing the German HEI landscape and creating synergies between HEIs and other actors by financing graduate schools, excellence clusters and so-called 'future concepts' (*Zukunftskonzepte*) which aim to create elite universities. Decisions regarding which HEIs will be funded are taken by a common commission of the DFG and *Wissenschaftsrat*.[197] Reactions to the *Exzellenzinitiative* have been mixed. Seckelmann[198] expresses the thought that it has a reparatory purpose (because *Länder* have come into financial difficulties since the federalism reform), while at the same time encouraging inter-HEI competition. Others[199] believe that the 'Excellence Initiative' might have actually infringed the constitution in its form after the federalism reform and before the recent revision of Article 91b GG. The Bund asked an expert commission to evaluate the *Exzellenzinitiative* who presented their findings in early 2016.[200] Following the recommendations, the programme will be continued beyond 2017 under the name *Exzellenzstrategie* (Excellence Strategy), but without the graduate school funding stream, as these has been considered as 'ambivalent at best'.[201]

In addition to the *Exzellenzinitiative,* the *Bund* provides project funding in those areas it deems relevant for future development and economic growth. The *Bund* also encourages contract research by HEIs. The High-Tech Strategy, for example, from 2006 to 2009 included a measure (*Forschungsprämie*) which allowed HEIs and other public research organisations to apply for a 25 % premium on certain kinds of contract research for SME from the public purse. This money was then supposed to be used to establish further competences regarding

---

[196] Wissenschaftsrat 2007, p. 65 seq, DFG (n 174), DFG (2016) Erkenntnistransfer (English translation: Knowledge Transfer). http://www.dfg.de/foerderung/grundlagen_rahmenbedingungen/erkenntnistransfer/index.html. Accessed 14 August 2016.

[197] On the excellence initiative see Enders 2007, p. 23; Edler and Kuhlmann 2008, p. 270; Kehm and Pasternack 2009; Hinze 2010, p. 172; Schubert and Schmoch 2010, p. 250; Seckelmann 2010, p. 228 seq, 239; BMBF (2016) Die Exzellenzinitiative stärkt die universitäre Spitzenforschung (English translation: The Excellence Initiative strengthens leading university research). http://www.bmbf.de/de/1321.php. Accessed 14 August 2016.

[198] Seckelmann 2010, p. 228 seq, 239.

[199] For a short summary see Kühne (2010) Zweifelhafter Wettbewerb (English translation: Questionable competition). Zeit Online (14 January 2010) http://www.zeit.de/studium/hochschule/2010-01/exzellenzinitiative-verfassungswidrig. Accessed 9 November 2011 with references to the work of S. Sieweke.

[200] Internationale Expertenkommission Exzellenzinitiative 2016.

[201] Ibid p. 6. On the *Exzellenzstrategie* see BMBF (2016) Die Exzellenzstrategie (English translation: The Excellence Strategy). https://www.bmbf.de/de/die-exzellenzstrategie-3021.html. Accessed 14 August 2016.

knowledge transfer.[202] The *Länder* also started to introduce additional competitive funding programmes including for the interplay of research organisations and the private sector, though the share of such programmes in all *Drittmittel* is rather small. Finally, other public sector entities may provide some *Drittmittel* for HEIs.[203]

4.4.2.3 Non-state Funding

The main sources of non-state *Drittmittel* are (in order of significance) funding from the private sector, international (especially EU) funding and third sector funding.[204] As mentioned above (Sect. 4.4.2.2), the attraction of non-public *Drittmittel* is encouraged by government policy.

Whilst third sector funding hardly constitutes a factor in overall research spending in Germany (Sect. 4.4.1 above), it does have some significance for funding HEIs. Third sector organisations provide project and institutional funding including establishing their own HEIs, research institutes or chairs. Some charitable foundations of private sector organisations also have a for-profit section offering advisory services to research organisations such as 'CHE consult' of the Centre for HEI development (*Centrum für Hochschulentwicklung*).[205]

Funding from the private sector takes similar forms as in the other two countries. Research co-operations are conducted, especially in the natural sciences, which sometimes take the form of long term PPPs.[206] Another common form of collaboration between industry and HEIs in Germany is contract research. In this regard, the increasing integration of contract research into university structures and budgets posed new challenges to the traditional public non-profit character of universities.[207]

Universities might also receive private funding through the commercial use of IPRs. Whilst, according to the Copyright Act, the copyright always remains with the author rather than with the employer (§ 7, 11 *Gesetz über Urheberrecht und verwandte Schutzrechte*), universities became responsible for patenting

---

[202] BMBF (2016) Bekanntmachung des Bundesministeriums für Bildung und Forschung zur Förderrichtlinie "Forschungsprämie" (English translation: Announcement of the Federal Ministry for Education and Research regarding the funding guideline "Research Premium") https://www.bmbf.de/foerderungen/bekanntmachung-217.html. Accessed 14 August 2016.

[203] On competitive public funding see Enders 2007, pp. 22, 28; Wissenschaftsrat 2007, p. 64, p. 248 seq, 251, 253; Hinze 2010, p. 169 seq; Jaeger and In der Smitten 2010, p. 6; Schubert and Schmoch 2010; Statistisches Bundesamt 2015, Table 2.7 (p. 261 seq).

[204] Statistisches Bundesamt 2015, Table 2.7 (p. 261 seq).

[205] On third sector funding see Enders 2007, p. 26; Wissenschaftsrat 2007, p. 67 seq; Hinze 2010, p. 168 seq; Speth 2010, p. 392 seq; BMBF 2016, p. 76.

[206] Wissenschaftsrat 2007, p. 34 seq; Rohrbeck 2010, p. 435 seq; BMBF 2016, pp. 78, 208 seq.

[207] Enders 2007, p. 22 seq; Wissenschaftsrat 2007, p. 37 seq; Andersen 2010, p. 1235; Seckelmann 2010, p. 228; Statistisches Bundesamt 2015, p. 165.

innovations made by their employees through a change in the Employee Invention Act (*Deutsches Gesetz über Arbeitnehmererfindungen*) in 2002. Before 2002 there used to be an exemption for HEI personnel. This opened up another source of income from the private sector through licensing or spin-off creation. Patenting as a source of income is especially relevant for the natural and formal sciences. A negative consequence of patenting could, however, be that enjoyment of the publicly generated knowledge is forestalled if a patent is not actually exploited. Furthermore, agreeing on IPR ownership has occasionally been an issue in research co-operations.[208]

Staff exchanges are equally encouraged by the DFG, at the federal level and by the EU.[209] The private sector and, to a lesser extent, the third sector and philanthropists also fund chairs (*Stiftungsprofessuren*) in HEIs which are usually taken over by the HEI after a few years. Whilst the funder is not supervising or directing the research undertaken by the chair holder, the funder has previously defined the speciality in which the chair will be established. This form of collaboration has become increasingly popular in recent years.[210] 'Clusters' are what is being referred to as science parks in the other two systems; a regional agglomeration of organisations which are working on related topics. The organisations remain independent and compete with each other.[211]

Unique features of the German system are the so-called '*An-Institute*'. These institutes formally exist outside university structures but are affiliated with them through a cooperation agreement. They are often managed by a university professor, conduct mainly applied research and are usually incorporated as not-for-profit limited liability companies (*gemeinnützige Gesellschaften mit beschränkter Haftung*).[212] The Wissenschaftsrat describes them as being problematic in respect of their not-for-profit character, since they do conduct mainly market research.[213] Finally, university-industry research centres (*Universitäts-Industrie-Forschungs-Zentren, UIFZ*) are a currently less common form of collaboration between the private sector and HEIs in Germany. They are used for long-term collaboration on a topic without a specific aim and might just receive monetary contributions or involve more practical collaboration. An example for this kind of collaboration is the German Research Center for Artificial Intelligence (*Deutsches Forschungszentrum für Künstliche Intelligenz*),[214]

[208] On IPR exploitation see Enders 2007, p. 24; Wissenschaftsrat 2007, p. 34 seq, p. 41 seq; Seckelmann 2010, p. 228; BMBF 2016, p. 83 seq, 212 seq.

[209] Wissenschaftsrat 2007, p. 50 seq; BMBF 2016, p. 56.

[210] Wissenschaftsrat 2007, p. 36 seq; Claßen et al. 2009. According to the latter there were about 660 of such chairs in Germany in 2009 (p. 5). See also BMBF 2016, p. 232 on *Stiftungsprofessuren* as part of an initiative called InnoProfile-Transfer.

[211] Wissenschaftsrat 2007, p. 39 seq; BMBF 2016, p. 208 seq, 215 seq.

[212] On *An-Institute* see Enders 2007, p. 24; Wissenschaftsrat 2007, p. 36; BMBF 2016, p. 66.

[213] Wissenschaftsrat 2007, p. 36.

[214] For further information see their website on http://www.dfki.de/web.

a collaboration between three universities, the Frauenhofer Gesellschaft and a variety of private companies including John Deere and Microsoft.[215]

4.4.2.4 Full Costing

Full costing is relatively new in German HEIs. It became relevant because the funding provided by EU Framework Programme 7 was given out on a full cost basis and the previous Research Framework[216] required implementation of full costing in HEIs by 1 January 2009 (Section 10.2) for economic research.[217] While implementation has begun in the last years,[218] publications on different full costing models for HEIs,[219] workshops and conferences on the subject[220] and consultancies offering assistance and advice to HEIs[221] seem to indicate that HEIs still struggle with the details of full costing. Indeed a recent study commissioned by BMBF suggests that only few universities have managed to introduce a comprehensive full cost model.[222] Coordination at state level only takes place in a limited number of states.[223] The implementation of full costing thus differs from HEI to HEI in Germany. Further, it appears that HEIs partly simply accept the prices offered by external funders, as they do not consider external funding as 'negotiable'.[224] Therefore, *Drittmittel* have to be matched with generic funding to a significant extent (by about 41 %) which becomes increasingly difficult with reductions in generic funding and might bring some HEIs to the limit of their

---

[215] On UIFZs see Wissenschaftsrat 2007, p. 37 seq; Rohrbeck 2010, p. 435. See also, for another example, BMBF 2016, p. 96 (big data centre).

[216] Community framework for state aid for research and development and innovation OJ [2006] C 323/01.

[217] On the beginnings of full costing in Germany see also Enders 2007, p. 21; Wissenschaftsrat 2007, p. 86 seq; Andersen 2010, p. 1236 seq.

[218] See, for example, the resolution of the conference of German Vice Chancellors (Entschließung der 2. Mitgliederversammlung am 27.11.2007, p. 8 Sect. 4d) recommending the introduction of full costing following the Anglo-Saxon model or the Wissenschaftsrat's recommendation to this effect (Wissenschaftsrat 2007, p. 87).

[219] See, for example, Friedl 2008; Andersen 2010, p. 1240 seq.

[220] For example, Freie Universität Berlin and Syncwork, UniFinanz 2012: Vollkosten- und Trennungsrechnung—Chances und Risiken für die Steuerung von Hochschulen (English translation: Full costing and separate accounting—Chances and risks for the governance of higher education institutions) (Berlin 14 June 2012).

[221] See, for example, the specific service offer for HEIs as regards full costing by the company Syncwork on http://www.syncwork.de/leistungsangebote/vollkostenrechnung-in-hochschulen/vollkostenrechnung-in-hochschulen-zur-erfuellung-der-eu-anforderungen.html. Accessed 1 July 2012.

[222] Astor et al. 2014, p. 130 seq.

[223] Estermann and Claeys-Kulik 2013, p. 19 seq.

[224] Astor et al. 2014, p. 133. See also Hetze and Mostovova 2013 p. 31 seq.

capacity as regards acceptance of *Drittmittel* projects.[225] The *Bund* is trying to compensate for this with overhead allowances for DFG and BMBF funded projects which, however, cover only around half of the matching costs.[226]

4.4.3 Interim Conclusion on Germany

Germany has a strong research system with comparably high spending. The private sector finances and conducts most of all research in Germany by far. This is followed by funding from the public sector and, to a much lesser extent, international funding. Whilst third sector funding is negligible in the overall picture, it does have a small role to play when it comes to research funding in HEIs. Being a federal republic, responsibilities for research are divided between the *Bund* and the *Länder.* However, during the federalism reform, the *Bund* lost some of its former competences, in particular regarding HEIs. Next to HEIs, there are four major public non-HEI research organisations which each have a specific profile.

HEIs receive the majority of their funding as generic public funding from the *Länder* which has, however, declined in recent years. Instead public funding is increasingly given on a competitive basis and external funders have become more significant. Partly, this is due to an intentional turn towards competitiveness and cooperation between the private and public sector after a lack of transparency in funding and a lack of utilising synergies had been identified as some of the weaknesses of the system. However, it might also partly have been due to funding problems created by the federalism reform reducing the power of the *Bund* to fund HEIs. Therefore, a recent change of the Article 91b GG provided for more opportunities for collaboration as regards research funding. German law provides for constitutional protection of academic freedom. Should future developments involve too much steering and conditions/aims for research funding and thereby influencing the direction of research, it may be conceivable that this could be challenged under Article 5(2) GG.

---

[225] Astor et al. 2014, p. 1 seq.

[226] Astor et al. 2014, p. 5 seq; BMBF (2016) DFG-Programmpauschale (English translation: DFG Programme allowance). https://www.bmbf.de/de/dfg-programmpauschale-513.html. Accessed 14 August 2016. The *DFG Programmpauschale* has been lifted from 20 to 22 % of overheads in 2016 for which the *Länder* now contribute some funding. This issue had previously caused some controversy after the Federal Financial Court (*Bundesfinanzhof*) declared that the *Länder* ought to contribute to the overhead costs (see further Stalinski (2014) Wissenschaftskonferenz berät Hochschulpakt: Für die Forschung wird es eng (English translation: Science Conference advises on HEI Pact: It gets tight for research). http://www.tagesschau.de/inland/wissenschaftskonferenz-101.html. Accessed 30 October 2014).

4.5 HEI Research in the Three Countries and EU Competition Law

The analysis of the different systems has been offered in order to better assess the relevance of EU competition law for research in HEIs in the three countries under investigation. The interim conclusions allow the following provisional assessment, which will form the starting point for the qualitative empirical study conducted in Chap. 5. As stated in more detail in Chap. 3, EU competition law only applies to 'undertakings' a notion that has been defined as 'every entity engaged in an economic activity, regardless of the legal status of the entity and the way in which it is financed'.[227] To examine whether or not the research activities of HEIs are within the scope of application of EU competition law, an assessment of whether HEIs qualify as undertakings for (parts of) their activities thus needs to be made. This seems unlikely when it comes to research financed through public generic funding. According to the Research Framework,[228] 'independent R&D for more knowledge and better understanding' is a non-economic activity. Under generically funded research, the researchers are free to decide what they research and there is not generally any requirement that it has any practical uses or immediate impacts. Even in England where generic funding does dependent on, amongst other factors, impact, the researcher is still free to decide the directions of research and the impact does not have to be immediate or economically relevant.[229] A service is not defined, but instead it is generally assessed if the HEI in question generates impact at all. It is, therefore, hard to imagine how to conduct such research under market conditions. Instead it can be assumed that the non-economic research definition of the Research Framework is being fulfilled here.

Research financed through competitive public, international and third sector funding, on the other hand, may have to be regarded in a differentiated way. If such funding is provided merely on academic merit and researchers can decide freely about the directions of research as in German DFG funding and under the Dutch *Vernieuwingsimpuls* scheme, the assessment would probably have to be the same as with public generic funding. Even if the calls broadly pre-define a topic area, this is still unlikely to amount to an activity that could be conducted under market conditions. However, the more pre-set the conditions, the more practical the research and the more identifiable potential users become, the more it is possible to argue that this could be conducted by commercial entities in a market. Actual contract research for these funders, in particular, would clearly be an economic activity.

As regards collaboration with the private sector, this can more easily come into the ambit of competition law. The fact that the private sector is interested in the

---

[227] C-41/90 *Höfner* (Judgment of 23 April 1991, EU:C:1991:161) para 21. On the notion see Chap. 3 Sect. 3.2.1 above.

[228] Research Framework (n 162) Sect. 3.1.1.

[229] Indeed, the recent Stern Review suggested broadening the notion of impact under the REF (Stern 2016, p. 34).

research area in the first place already indicates a certain economic relevance. Nevertheless, collaborative forms differ. Contract research, consultancy[230] and the renting out of infrastructure are activities that could and partly are taking place on a market where competitors operate. IPR exploitation is, according to the Research Framework, a non-economic activity if the exploitation takes place internally and all income is reinvested into the non-economic research areas. It has been argued above[231] that, in addition, the Commission's assessment in the Issue Paper[232] that to be non-economic knowledge transfer should also be non-exclusive and have arisen in an area of non-economic research should be the guiding principle for assessing the economic nature of IPR exploitation. In any case, if external investors are brought on-board as happens in England, IPR exploitation is to be considered as an economic activity. In clusters/science parks, the individual undertakings remain separated and this collaborative form would, therefore, probably not constitute an economic activity as such, rather it provides a geographical location for undertakings. Start-ups, spin-offs and German *An-Institute* are separate entities despite HEIs holding shares in them or being affiliated with them. The determination of whether any interaction is an economic activity for the HEI would probably depend on the activities these entities conduct, perhaps together with the HEI and the exact ties of ownership.

   The determination might be more complicated when it comes to the more blurred forms of collaboration such as research co-operations, longer term PPPs, common centres, staff exchanges or research clubs/networks. It would also here depend on the question whether, in the individual case, the research is independent and 'for more knowledge and better understanding' or if particular pieces of research are in fact a research service conducted for another party. Private funding for a chair, lectureship or PhD which, aside from a pre-set subject area, does not have any conditions attached to it as well as purely charitable private sector donations are likely to be considered as non-economic activities. If the conditions are too defined and the funded researcher is essentially conducting a research service for another party which could take place on a market, the activity might well be economic in nature. These cases, therefore, often need to be assessed on an activity by activity basis.

4.5.1 Potential Tensions with Competition Law

If competition law is applicable, HEIs must not, according to Article 101(1) TFEU, enter into any form of anti-competitive collusion nor must national law bring them into a position where they would do so (Article 101(1) TFEU in

---

[230] On a discussion of the ambivalence of certain forms of knowledge exchange including consultancy in the new Research Framework see Chap. 3 Sects. 3.2.4.2 and 3.3.5.3 above.

[231] Ibid.

[232] European Commission 2012.

conjunction with Article 4(3) TEU).[233] An especially severe form of anti-competitive collusion is price fixing. HEIs in England and the Netherlands have real full cost methodologies that relate actual costs to a research project and which do not seem to pose a problem under EU competition law. In Germany, however, there still seems to be some confusion and occasionally overheads are being used instead of real full cost methodologies. If these are fixed between HEIs, by statute or information on them is exchanged, this could potentially be classified as price fixing. After having arrived at the costs, HEIs in all three systems negotiate prices or follow the rules set by the funders. In the area of economic research, this could lead to potential problems, as, for example, pre-set funding rules could be regarded as price fixing. Furthermore, common guidelines between funders such as the *Akkoord* by NWO, VSNU and KNAW might potentially be seen as anti-competitive if the research would have to be classified as economic in nature.

Aside from price fixing, Article 101(1) TFEU also prohibits undertakings agreeing on any other special conditions or limitations within the collusion without there being an economically justified reason. This could cause problems if government policies are in place that require or encourage HEIs to prefer SMEs or local companies such as in innovation voucher initiatives. If HEIs in an area of economic activity agree on a collaboration which is not open to all interested parties without an economically justified reason, this could equally be seen as anti-competitive. One might, for example, wonder, if plans for sharing facilities, as envisaged between certain research intensive universities in the North of England,[234] could fall under Article 101(1) TFEU, if other willing HEIs were not allowed to participate or preferential conditions were given to the partners. Furthermore, the provision prohibits market division. This could cause issues, if HEIs agree (or are forced by government policy), to focus on local economies, share the market according to subject areas or enter into specialisation agreements. Research co-operations as such could be anti-competitive if entered into shortly before an individual discovery would have been made anyway or if there are any limitations beyond the research including limitations on parties exploiting the results. Finally, Article 101(1) TFEU could be infringed if quantitative limits on research of an economic nature are agreed upon or prescribed by national legislation. The latter does not seem to be the case, however, in England and the Netherlands. In Germany § 25(2) HRG only limits economic research at a level where it would collide with the statutory tasks of the HEIs.

Article 102 TFEU makes the abuse of a dominant position illegal. As discussed in Chap. 3 (Sect. 3.3.3), HEIs could come into conflict with this provision if they conduct an economic activity and are considered dominant in a specific market. In such cases it might, for example, cause problems, if HEIs do not charge full costs

---

[233]13 /77 *INNO v ATAB* (Judgment of 16 November 1977, EU:C:1977:185) para 30 seq. See further on the state action doctrine Chap. 3 Sect. 3.2.2 above.

[234] See N8 Research Partnership (2016) N8 Efficiency. http://www.n8research.org.uk/asset-collaboration/. Accessed 14 August 2016.

and reasonable profit, since this could be regarded as predatory pricing by their competitors. Furthermore, if HEIs operate unilaterally as dominant undertakings and offer special conditions, impose special duties, cooperate only with specific partners or limit outputs, they could potentially come into conflict with Article 102 TFEU rather than with Article 101(1) TFEU as in the cases outlined above. Finally, according to Article 102, dominant undertakings might be prevented from refusing access to essential facilities or refusing licenses for IPRs, dividing the market through licenses or attaching specific conditions. Private sector partners might, however, desire special conditions or exclusivity. HEIs would thus need to be aware of these potential issues and avoid them in contracts if operating as an undertaking.

If an economic activity is conducted, the state may also not give particular undertakings advantages through state resources exclusively since this could constitute state aid according to Article 107 TFEU. HEIs could get into conflict with this provision specifically, if they do not charge full costs and reasonable profit for research because the receiver of the research (be it their own company)[235] could then be regarded as being subsidised. The Netherlands and England have set up full costing systems, while there is some doubt whether every HEI in Germany has yet done so and whether the systems are correctly measuring full costs. Aside from this, universities still negotiate prices individually or follow funder rules which might not always cover full costs. In the Netherlands, a variety of national legislation and guidelines specifically point out that EU state aid rules have to followed, though they do not always give very precise guidance to HEIs. Generally, even if full costs are charged in private sector collaboration, this could still fall under Article 107(1) TFEU. Firstly, in the area of economic research, generically requesting full costs is usually insufficient, but market prices or full costs and reasonable profit have to be charged or the price has, at least, to be the, at arm length negotiated, maximum economic benefit that can be achieved.[236] This appears to be especially questionable in Germany. Secondly, the concept of undertaking goes beyond private sector companies. Third and public sector organisations can also be classified as undertakings and if HEIs cooperate with them in what constitutes an economic activity, they also need to charge market prices or prices reflecting the mentioned alternatives from them.

Additionally, public funding (contracts or calls) which could be classified as an economic activity might potentially not be given directly to one undertaking or calls not be limited to certain types of undertakings respectively. Instead, such activities might have to be commissioned according to the rules set out by the

---

[235] If the companies do not belong to a single economic entity. Further, in some cases there may be a case of in-house provision under procurement law (see Chap. 2 Sect. 2.3.4 above).

[236] C-280/00 *Altmark* (Judgment of 24 July 2003, EU:C:2003:415), Research Framework para 25. See also Chap.3 Sect. 3.3.5.1 above.

Court or in the Research Framework[237] which usually requires a public
procurement procedure also allowing private and foreign providers to tender.[238]
Furthermore, Article 107(1) TFEU may be infringed if additional subsidies are
provided to HEIs and other partners in collaborations for research which could be
classified as economic in nature or innovation vouchers are given out by the state
or HEIs, as this way public funding would exclusively reach specific undertakings.
If HEIs reinvest commercially gained money in further commercial activities and
offer discounts in an economically reasonable way, this might, however, not pose a
problem in terms of state aid law. To an extent this is therefore a question of how
separate accounts are. Finally, if IPRs, created in the publicly funded area of
research, are given out exclusively or for preferential conditions or if staff use their
knowledge generated in the area of publicly funded research during an exchange
exclusively for the benefit of one other company, this could equally be regarded as
state aid, though under the new Research Framework this may partly be
considered non-economic knowledge transfer if profits are re-invested as has been
discussed in Chap. 3 Sects. 3.2.4.2 and 3.3.5.2 above.

Generally, it would appear that the Member States under scrutiny have become
somewhat more aware of state aid rules in the last couple of years and execute
more caution when it comes to statements in guidelines or on information sites.
For example, in the Netherlands, previous versions of legislation (e.g. Article 41
Kaderbesluit EZ subsidies) only required full costs (rather than market prices or
full cost plus) to be charged from the private sector (rather than from any
undertaking). Now, the *Kaderbesluit* avoids such specific statements (Article 41
has been repealed) and generally repeats or points to the EU state aid rules.
Further, while the *Kaderbesluit* already previously contained the EU definition of
'undertaking', the webpage containing definitions for TKI subsidies seemed to
have used the terms 'industrial partners', 'private contributions' and 'undertaking'
interchangeably and defined 'private contribution' as a monetary contribution
which is not received from a research organisation, the NWO, KNAW, public
bodies or third sector organisations thereby apparently not considering them
undertakings per se.[239] These definitions have now disappeared from the new site
on TKI subsidies.[240] Similarly, as regards providing additional public funding to a
collaboration with industry, the BMBF used to generically point to EU guidelines

[237] C-280/00 *Altmark*, Research Framework para 32 seq. See also Chap. 3 Sect. 3.3.5.2 above.

[238] Directive 2014/24 on public procurement and repealing Directive 2004/18/EC OJ [2014] L
94/65 contains specific provisions about how and when research needs to be procured and the
creation of the new innovation partnership broadens the set of tools that the State can use to
procure innovation. See also Chap. 2 Sect. 2.3.4 above.

[239] Agentschap NL, 'Definities TKI-toeslag' (English translation: Definitions TKI award)
(EZ Topkonsortia voor Kennis en Innovatie 2013) http://www.agentschapnl.nl/programmas-
regelingen/definities-tki-toeslag. Accessed 1 May 2013. This website does not exist anymore.

[240] RVO (2016) Definities bij TKI-projecttoeslag 2015 en 2016 (English translation: Definitions
for TKI award 2015 and 2016). http://www.rvo.nl/subsidies-regelingen/definities-bij-tki-
projecttoeslag-2015-en-2016. Accessed 14 August 2016.

mentioning that undertakings must contribute their own assets to a collaboration without providing any details of how this is done. It also appeared that the term 'undertaking' was used interchangeably with 'private sector entity'.[241] While the link still exists the site has changed now and points to the definitions in EU law. Further, in the Netherlands, the *Regeling nationale EZ subsidies* now also provides specific rules on certain forms of subsidies (e.g. on secondment in Article 3.4.16 or on research infrastructure in Article 3.17.9).

4.5.2 Exemptions

As has been discussed in Chap. 3 (Sects. 3.3.2 and 3.3.5), Article 101 and 107 TFEU and secondary legislation provide for exemptions for certain breaches of competition law, which could be relevant for HEIs, many of which depend on market share or the amount of the aid. It would thus be impossible to assess in how far they are generally applicable without further knowledge. Article 102 TFEU does not include such exemptions. If the service qualifies as a service of general economic interest (SGEI), Decision 2012/21/EU[242] exempts aid below €15 M per annum. Finally, the research activities of HEIs might more generally be exempted as SGEIs under Article 106(2) TFEU. As discussed in Chap. 3, for a service to qualify as an SGEI it has to qualify as a public service obligation and has to be entrusted to the undertaking in question. For the exemption under Article 106(2) TFEU it would also be required that the SGEI is then be obstructed by the application of the competition rules in a disproportionate way. Whilst in Germany and the Netherlands legislation is making research a statutory task of HEIs, this might in itself not be sufficiently precise to be regarded as an entrustment act. Whether or not the service in question is in the general interest, the application of the competition rules does obstruct it and the question of whether this is proportional would have to be looked at in the individual case.

4.6 Conclusion

The systems investigated differ in a variety of ways from the general national expenditure on research and the overall character of the system to the importance of individual sectors and the extent to which the recent trend of commodification

---

[241] BMBF, 'Förderung in der Forschung' (English translation: Research Funding) (2012) http://www.bmbf.de/de/1398.php. Accessed 2 August 2012. This website has now been changed.

[242] Commission Decision 2012/21/EU on the application of Article 106(2) of the Treaty on the Functioning of the European Union to State aid in the form of public service compensation granted to certain undertakings entrusted with the operation of services of general economic interest OJ [2012] L 7/3.

has influenced the research systems. Germany has constantly increased research expenditure coming close to reaching the 3 % goal of the Europe 2020 Strategy. Spending in the Netherlands has gone down from 2004 to 2008, but steadily increased since. The UK has had rather stable expenditure on R&D which has remained below 1.75 % of its GDP over the last ten years. Germany is traditionally characterised by a great extent of academic freedom of the individual which is even represented in its constitution and the federal structure also plays a significant role in the character of the system. England's research system is organised in a much more centralised and top-down fashion with strong elements of a liberal market economy. The Netherlands have a centralised, but very consociational research system. These characteristics are, to a certain extent, still visible in the respective research policies, despite all three systems having recently undergone changes towards external steering, funding on the basis of achievement and commodification.

In all three countries the private sector is the biggest research funding provider. However, this is most pronounced in Germany were the private sector contributes two thirds of all R&D spending, in the Netherlands the contribution is just over half of all research spending and it is even slightly less in the UK. The second biggest spender is congruently the public sector providing about a third of all research spending in all three countries. Differences are very pronounced when it comes to research financed by foreign sources and the third sector. The UK relies heavily on foreign investment in R&D with almost 18 % of all research being financed this way. In the Netherlands foreign contributions amount to nearly 13 % and in Germany to only 5 %. In all countries the third sector plays a small role; in the UK the third sector provides about 5 % of all research spending, in the Netherlands about 3 % and in Germany it is virtually non-existent in overall research funding.

Public sector research is also organised rather differently across the three systems. The German public research sector consists (mainly) of HEIs and four other public research organisations with clearly defined tasks. In both the Netherlands and England, HEIs are the most important public research providers. Nevertheless, the Dutch research system has also a wide and constantly increasing/changing variety of other research organisations, including many PPPs. In England there are hardly any public research organisations alongside HEIs, but there are relevant third sector providers. The latter play no significant role in Germany and the Netherlands.

When it comes to HEI funding, a large amount of public funding is still provided generically without recourse to competitive factors such as performance or focus on government priorities in Germany and in the Netherlands. In England the generic funding allocation in the REF always involves competitive factors based on quality, impact and environment. An attempt to introduce such a system early on in the Netherlands was prevented by strong resistance from the universities, while HEI resistance in England did not lead to the same result. This can be explained through the nature of the research systems as consociational and top down liberal systems respectively.[243] Despite these differences, an increase in the importance of non-generic funding (public competitive as well as non-public) can be observed in all systems. This kind of funding is often provided for particular aims and thus poses threats for the academic freedom of the individual researcher. Due to the changes in funding, all three systems have introduced or are in the process of introducing full costing methodologies. While in England this has been done centrally through the TRAC, it is undertaken on an individual HEI basis in Germany and the Netherlands. England is the first of the studied systems to have introduced full costing, followed by the Netherlands and, only recently and tentatively, Germany. In all three systems, however, it does not seem to be the case that all non-generic research funding is provided at levels covering the calculated full costs.

From a competition law perspective, generic public funding in all three systems would probably not have to be regarded as economic in nature. Public competitive and third sector funding could possibly be classified as economic in nature in certain cases and thus competition law would have to be applied. This would depend upon whether the activities funded could be classified as, as the Research Framework phrases it, 'independent R&D for more knowledge and better understanding' or would amount to a service which could be provided on a market. Private sector funding could in many cases constitute an economic activity, particularly with regards to contract research, research services even if they are labelled as collaborative research and the renting out of infrastructure. Other forms of collaboration will have to be assessed on an activity by activity basis. If an activity is classified as economic the HEI would have to comply with EU competition and state aid rules. It has been shown that in all three systems potential tensions could arise from this with national research policies/practices. However, the more economically oriented the system, the more frequently this may happen. The next chapter will empirically study in detail how far the established concerns might materialise, how far differences can be observed in the systems in this respect and how far HEIs are aware of possible consequences.

References

Abreu M et al (2008) Universities, business and knowledge exchange. The Council for Industry and Higher Education and the Centre for Business Research (University of Cambridge), London

Adams J, Gurney K (2010) Funding selectivity, concentration and excellence—how good is the UK's research? Higher Education Policy Institute, Oxford

Albrecht C (2009) Die Zukunft der deutschen Universität (English translation: the future of the German University). Forschung Lehre 2009:8–11

Andersen C (2010) Vollkostenrechnung in Hochschulen zur Erfüllung der EU-Anforderungen (English translation: Full costing in higher education institutions to meet the EU requirements). CöV Heft 10:1233–1248

---

[243] See also Becker 2009, p. 167 seq.

Arnold E et al (2006) Four case studies in university modernisation: KU Leuven, Twente, Manchester and Loughborough. Technopolis. http://www.technopolis-group.com/resources/downloads/reports/595_Final_060315.pdf

Astor M et al (2014) Wissenschaftliche Untersuchung und Analyse der Auswirkungen der Einführung von Projektpauschalen in die BMBF-Forschungsförderung auf die Hochschulen in Deutschland (English translation: scientific investigation and analysis of the impact of the introduction of project allowances into BMBF research funding on higher education institutions in Germany). Prognos AG, KPMG AG, Joanneum Research Forschungsgesellschaft mbH, Basel

Becker RFJ (2009) States, markets and higher education reform: the Netherlands and England. In: Zajda JI, Rust VD (eds) Globalisation, policy and comparative research. Springer, Dordrecht, pp 157–170

Berry DC (2010) Gaining funding for research. OUP, Berkshire

BIS (2015) Fulfilling our potential—teaching excellence, social mobility and student choice. Williams Lea Group on behalf of the Controller of Her Majesty's Stationery Office, London

BIS (2016) Success as a Knowledge Economy. Williams Lea Group, London

BMBF (2014) The new high-tech strategy-innovations for Germany. BMBF, Berlin

BMBF (2016) Bundesbericht Forschung und Innovation 2016 (English translation: Federal report research and innovation 2016). BMBF, Berlin

Braun M (2006) Country profile: the Netherlands. Proneos, Bad Camberg

Candemir B, Meyer M (2010) Grossbritannien (English translation: Great Britain). In: Simon D et al (eds) Handbuch Wissenschaftspolitik (English translation: Handbook Science Policy). VS Verlag für Sozialwissenschaften, Wiesbaden, pp 494–513

Centraal Bureau voor de Statistiek (2011) Herkomst en bestemming middelen voor research en development (R&D) (English translation: Origin and destination of resources for research and development (R & D)). Centraal Bureau voor de Statistiek, Den Haag/Heerlen

Centraal Bureau voor de Statistiek (2016) Research en development; financiering uitgaven per sector van uitvoering (English translation: Research and development; financing expenditure by executing sector). Centraal Bureau voor de Statistiek, Den Haag/Heerlen

Chiong Meza C (2012) De Nederlandse universiteiten (English translation: The Dutch universities). Rathenau Instituut, The Hague

Clare P et al (2014) Intellectual asset management for universities. Intellectual Property Office, Cardiff

Claßen U et al (2009) Stiftungsprofessuren in Deutschland (English translation: Endowed chairs in Germany). Stifter Verband für die deutsche Wirtschaft, Essen

CMA (2015) An effective regulatory framework for higher education: A policy paper. Crown Copyright, London

de Boer H et al (2015) Performance-based funding and performance agreements in fourteen higher education systems. CHEPS, Enschede

De Weert E, Boezerooy P (2007) Higher education in the Netherlands. CHEPS, Enschede

den Hertog P et al (2012) Science, technology and innovation indicators 2012. OCW, Utrecht

Directie Kennis (2012) Trends in beeld (English translation: Trends in focus). OCW, Kelpen

Edler J, Kuhlmann S (2008) Coordination within fragmentation: governance in knowledge policy in the German federal system. Sci Publ Policy 35:265–276

Elsevier (2011) International comparative performance of the UK research base—2011. Department of Business, Innovation and Skills. http://www.bis.gov.uk/assets/biscore/science/docs/i/11-p123-international-comparative-performance-uk-research-base-2011.pdf

Enders J (2007) Reform and change of German Research Universities. High Educ Forum 4:19–32

Entschließung der 2. Mitgliederversammlung am 27.11.2007 (2007) Zur Einführung der Vollkostenrechnung an deutschen Hochschulen (English translation: Regarding the introduction of full cost accounting at German universities). Hochschulrektorenkonferenz, Bonn

Esping-Andersen G (1990) The three worlds of welfare capitalism. Princeton University Press, Princeton

Estermann T, Claeys-Kulik A-L (2013) Financially sustainable universities—full costing: progress and practice. EUA, Brussels

EUA (2008) Financially sustainable universities—towards full costing in European Universities. EUA, Brussels

EUA (2015) Public funding observatory 2015. EUA. http://www.eua.be/Libraries/governance-autonomy-funding/november-2015.pdf?sfvrsn=0

European Commission (2012) Revision of the state aid rules for research and development and innovation. European Commission, Brussels

European Commission (2015) European Research Area—Facts and Figures 2014—The Netherlands. European Commission, Brussels

Farrington DJ, Palfreyman D (2012) The law of higher education. OUP, Oxford

Ferragina E, Seeleib-Kaiser M (2011) Welfare regime debate: past, present, futures? Policy Politics 39:583–611

Filippakou O et al (2010) Compliance, resistance and seduction: Reflections on 20 years of the Funding Council Model of Governance. High Educ 60:543–557

Friedl G et al (2008) Konzeption eines Kostenrechnungsmodells an Hochschulen zur Ermittlung von Gemeinkostenzuschlägen für EU-Forschungsprojekte am Beispiel der Universität Mainz (English translation: Design of a cost accounting model for universities to determine overhead rates for EU research projects using the example of the University of Mainz). Beiträge zur Hochschulforschung 30:86–113

Gideon A (2015) Blurring boundaries between the public and the private in national research policies and possible consequences from EU primary law. J Contem European Res 11:50–68

HEFCE (2009) A guide to UK higher education. HEFCE, Bristol

HEFCE (2012) Higher education—business and community interaction survey 2010–11. Bristol

HEFCE (2015) Higher education—business and community interaction survey 2013–14. HEFCE, Bristol

HEFCE (2016a) Guide to funding 2016–17—how HEFCE allocates its funds. HEFCE, Bristol

HEFCE (2016b) Memorandum of assurance and accountability between HEFCE and institutions—terms and conditions for payment of HEFCE grants to higher education institutions. HEFCE, Bristol

Herlitschka S (2009) Diversified funding streams for university-based research: impact of external project-based research funding on financial management in universities. Office for Official Publications of the European Communities, Luxembourg

Hetze P, Mostovova E (2013) Wie Hochschulen mit Unternehmen kooperieren (English translation: How universities collaborate with companies). Stifterverband für die Deutsche Wissenschaft, Essen

Hinze S (2010) Forschungsförderung in Deutschland (English translation: Research funding in Germany). In: Simon D et al (eds) Handbuch Wissenschaftspolitik (English translation: Handbook Science Policy). VS Verlag, Wiesbaden, pp 162–175

Horowitz DL (2006–2007) The many uses of federalism. Drake L. Rev 55:953–966

Howells J et al (1998) Industry-academic links in the UK. HEFCE/University of Manchester, Manchester

Internationale Expertenkommission Exzellenzinitiative (2016) Endbericht (English translation: Final report). Institut für Innovation und Technik, Berlin

J M Consulting Ltd (2005 (last updated 2012)) Transparent Approach to Costing (TRAC) Guidance. Joint Costing and Pricing Steering Group. http://www.jcpsg.ac.uk/guidance/index.htm

Jaeger M, In der Smitten S (2010) Indikatorenbasierte Modelle der Hochschulfinanzierung—wie wirksam sind die wettbewerblichen Anreize? (English translation: Indicator based models for university funding how effective are the competitive incentives?). HIS Magazin 2010:6–7

Jansen D (2010) Von der Steuerung zur Governance: Wandel der Staatlichkeit? (English translation: From control to governance: Change of public character?). In: Simon D et al (eds) Handbuch Wissenschaftspolitik (English translation: Handbook Science Policy). VS Verlag, Wiesbaden, pp 39–50

Jongbloed B (2010) The Netherlands. In: Dill DD and van Vught FA (eds) National innovation and the academic research enterprise: public policy in global perspective. Johns Hopkins University Press, Baltimore, pp 286–336

Kehm BM, Pasternack P (2009) The German "excellence initiative" and its role in restructuring the national higher education landscape. In: Palfreyman D, Tapper T (eds) Structuring mass higher education. Routledge, New York/London, pp 113–129

Kelly U et al (2014) The impact of universities on the UK economy. Universities UK, London

KNAW et al. (2014 (updated 2015)) Standard evaluation protocol 2015–2021. KNAW, VSNU, NWO, Amsterdam/Den Haag. vsnu.nl/files/documenten/Domeinen/Onderzoek/SEP2015-2021.pdf

Koier E et al (2016) Chinese borden (English translation: Plate spinning). Rathenau Instituut, Den Haag

Leisyte L (2011) University commercialisation policies and their implementation in the Netherlands and the United States. Science and Public Policy 38:437–448

Leisyte L et al (2008) The freedom to set research agendas—illusion and reality of the research units in the Dutch Universities. High Educ Policy 21:377–391

Matthijs J et al (2016) RIO Country Report 2015: the Netherlands. Joint Research Centre (European Commission), Seville

Mostert B (2012) Country Fiche Netherlands. ERAWATCH

Nurse P (2015) Ensuring a successful UK research endeavour. BIS. https://www.gov.uk/government/publications/nurse-review-of-research-councils-recommendations

OECD (2002) Frascati Manual. OECD, Paris

Office for National Statistics (2016) UK gross domestic expenditure on research and development: 2014. Office for National Statistics. http://www.ons.gov.uk/economy/governmentpublicsectorandtaxes/researchanddevelopmentexpenditure/bulletins/ukgrossdomesticexpenditureonresearchanddevelopment/2014

Office of Fair Trading (2014) Higher education in England. Crown Copyright, London

PACEC (2012) Strengthening the contribution of English higher education institutions to the innovation system: knowledge exchange and HEIF funding. PACEC, Cambridge

PACEC and the Centre for Business Research (University of Cambridge) (2009) Evaluation of the effectiveness and role of HEFCE/OSI third stream funding. HEFCE, Bristol

Palfreyman D (2003) The English chartered university/college: how 'autonomous', how 'independent' and how 'private'? Educ Law 15:149–156

Pirovano H (2015) Richtlijn Jaarverslag Onderwijs—Toelichtende brochure (English translation: Directive annual report education—explanatory brochure). OCW. www.rijksoverheid.nl/onderwerpen/financiering-onderwijs/toezicht-en-verantwording-in-het-onderwijs/richtlijnen-jaarverslag-onderwijs

RCUK/UUK Task Group (2010) Financial sustainability and efficiency in full economic costing of research in UK higher education institutions. UUK, London

Research Information Network (2010) Government and research policy in the UK: an introduction—a guide for researchers. Research Information Network, London

Rohrbeck R (2010) F+E Politik von Unternehmen (English translation: R&D policies of companies). In: Simon D et al (eds) Handbuch Wissenschaftspolitik (English translation: Handbook Science Policy). VS Verlag, Wiesbaden, pp 427–440

Schneider H et al (2009) Crossing borders—frontier knowledge. Maastricht University, Maastricht

Schreiterer U (2015) Deutsche Wissenschaftspolitik im internationalen Kontext (English translation: German science policy in an international context). In: Simon D et al (eds) Handbuch Wissenschaftspolitik (English translation: Handbook Science Policy). VS Verlag, Wiesbaden, pp 1–15

Schubert T, Schmoch U (2010) Finanzierung der Hochschulforschung (English translation: Funding of university research). In: Simon D et al (eds) Handbuch Wissenschaftspolitik (English translation: Handbook Science Policy). VS Verlag, Wiesbaden, pp 244–261

Scott P (2009) Structural changes in higher education—the case of the United Kingdom. In: Palfreyman D, Tapper T (eds) Structuring mass higher education. Routledge, New York/London, pp 35–55

Seckelmann M (2010) Rechtliche Grundlagen und Rahmensetzungen (English translation: legal foundations and frameworks). In: Simon D et al (eds) Handbuch Wissenschaftspolitik (English translation: Handbook Science Policy). VS Verlag, Wiesbaden, pp 227–243

Speth R (2010) Stiftungen und Think Tanks (English translation: Foundations and think tanks). In: Simon D et al (eds) Handbuch Wissenschaftspolitik (English translation: Handbook Science Policy). VS Verlag, Wiesbaden, pp 390–405

Statistisches Bundesamt (2015) Bildung und Kultur—Monetäre hochschulstatistische Kennzahlen 2013 (English translation: Education and Culture—Monetary statistical university indicators 2013). Statistisches Bundesamt, Wiesbaden

Statistisches Bundesamt (2016) Bildung und Kultur—Finanzen der Hochschulen 2014 (English translation: Education and culture—finances of HEIs 2014). Statischtisches Bundesamt, Wiesbaden

Stern N (2016) Building on success and learning from experience. BEIS, London

Tweede Kamer der Staten-Generaal (2000) Verantwoording en toezicht bij rechtspersonen met een wettelijke taak, deel 2 (English translation: Accountability and oversight of legal persons with statutory tasks, part 2). Sdu Uitgevers, The Hague

UCU (2013) The Research Excellence Framework (REF)—UCU survey report. UCU, London

UCU (2014) Seeing the bigger picture. UCU, London

Umbrella Committee for the Evaluation of the Bonus Incentive Scheme 2009–2010 (2010) Evaluation of leading research schools 2009–2010. NWO, The Hague

Universities UK (2012) Higher education in facts and figures. Universities UK, London

van der Meulen B (2010) The Netherlands. In: Simon D et al (eds) Handbuch Wissenschaftspolitik (English translation: Handbook Science Policy). VS Verlag, Wiesbaden, pp 514–528

VSNU (2012) Prestaties in perspectief—Trendrapportage universiteiten 2000–2020 (English translation: Performance in perspective—Trend report universities 2000–2020). VSNU, The Hague

Williams N (2004) Research costing plans raise fears. Curr Biol 14:731–732

Willmoth H (1995) Managing the academics: commodification and control in the development of university education in the UK. Hum Relat 48:993–1027

Wissenschaftsrat (2007) Empfehlungen zur Interaktion von Wissenschaft und Wirtschaft (English translation: Recommendations concerning the interaction between science and industry). Wissenschaftsrat, Oldenburg

Zoontjes PJJ (2010) Protecting 'university' as a designation—analysis and comparison of the legal position in several countries. Edu Law J 11:117–131

Chapter 5
Empirical Study

Abstract This chapter contains an in-depth empirical study of three countries (England, the Netherlands and Germany) exploring how far the competition law influences on research in universities might materialise, in how far differences can be observed between the systems in this respect and in how far key actors in HEIs are aware of possible consequences. It begins by setting out the methodology detailing, inter alia, how the universities under scrutiny have been chosen, how the interview questions have been drafted and how the interviews will be analysed. The latter is achieved by employing a framework developed on the basis of the results of Chaps. 3 and 4. This is followed by a subchapter on each country discussing the results of the empirical study. It will be shown that in all three countries interviewees expected the commodification tendencies in HEI research to continue and there was some criticism for this development. However, the more detailed sentiments about the research systems as well as the awareness of competition law of the interviewees differed between the countries which seems to correspond with the general character of the research systems. On the basis of the information received from the interviewees, a more in-depth appreciation of the question in how far competition law becomes applicable could be provided, but, as will be seen, this remains a difficult question. While some potential tensions with competition law discussed in previous chapters did not materialise based on the empirical information gathered, some in fact could cause concerns and others have been detected. Of course, there may still be the possibility of the application of exemptions, but these might not capture every situation and, in any case, might make the conduct of HEIs increasingly complicated from a legal/administrative perspective. Given the current situation, HEIs are thus advised to pay increasing attention to competition law.

Keywords Methodology of legal empirical study · Qualitative expert interviews · University research in England, the Netherlands and Germany · Framework for state aid for research and development · General Block Exemption Regulation · Research and EU competition law · Full costing of research · Commodification of university research

© T.M.C. ASSER PRESS and the author 2017
A. Gideon, *Higher Education Institutions in the EU: Between Competition and Public Service*, Legal Issues of Services of General Interest, DOI 10.1007/978-94-6265-168-5_5

Contents

5.1 Introduction

The preceding chapter established how the turn towards commodification of HEIs has been manifested in the three national research systems under scrutiny. Furthermore, it explored how far this can make research in HEIs susceptible to EU competition law. The purpose of this chapter is to study in detail how far the established concerns might materialise, how far differences can be observed in the systems in this respect and how far key actors in HEIs are aware of possible consequences.

The historical and theoretical background laid out in Chap. 1, the general legal and policy developments regarding HEIs (Chap. 2), the investigation of EU competition law effects on HEIs (Chap. 3) and the respective national legal frameworks for research in public universities (Chap. 4) led to the expectation that exposure to EU competition law might be greater in the UK, where commercialisation of the HEI sector had progressed the furthest (indicated by numerous competitive elements in allocating public research funding and pronounced encouragement of universities to engage in collaboration with business). It was equally expected that this might have resulted in both a higher awareness of this exposure and the ability to circumvent it through either compliance (an indication of which could be seen in the early introduction of a full costing methodology) or utilisation of relevant exemptions. Germany, with only modest steps towards commodification of HEIs, on the other hand, might suffer less from economic constraints and competition law exposure and, equally, HEIs might be less aware of it.

This chapter will, firstly, explain the methodology used for the empirical study (Sect. 5.2). It will give reasons for the techniques employed (interviews, focus groups), introduce the strategic sample and elaborate upon how the interview questions were established and how they will be analysed, namely through a framework based on the competition law problems identified in Chaps. 3 and 4. This will be followed by a subchapter for each country reporting the outcomes of the empirical study (Sects. 5.3–5.5). Finally, the results will be brought together in the conclusion (Sect. 5.6).

5.2 Methodology

The research required specific insights about the universities (e.g. on research funding and collaboration strategies) to establish whether or not the potential competition law constraints can materialise. These insights had to be gained from experts in the field; i.e. those responsible within the universities for these activities. In-depth answers were required and the opportunity to elaborate on these further needed to be given in order to fully understand research funding in the individual universities. Only through this approach could a substantiated assessment of potential competition law problems be made. Qualitative expert interviews[1] which employed a format between 'interview guide' (or semi-structured interview) and 'standardised open-ended interview' (or structured interview)[2] were, therefore, the most appropriate design for the research.

5.2.1 Strategic Sampling

Besides being limited to research in HEIs in three Member States, as explained in Chaps. 1 (Sect. 1.2) and 4 (Sect. 4.1), the sample had to be further condensed within the frame of an empirical qualitative study. Therefore, firstly, only public non-specialised universities, as the traditional publicly funded, research intensive HEIs,[3] are examined. In England where a binary system no longer exists post-1992 universities[4] have not been considered in order to maintain comparability with the other two countries which retain binary systems. Within these limitations an attempt was made to include a wide spectrum of universities. At least three universities have been identified for each country one of which had to fall within each of three categories established according to placement in international rankings and age of the university.

The categories were:

1. 'ancient': founded in the 16th century or earlier and usually ranked within the top 25 % in national comparison,
2. 'well-established': founded before the First World War and usually ranked within the top 60 % in national comparison,

---

[1] On expert interviews see Mangen 1999, p. 110; Patton 2002, p. 401; Littig 2008 p. 3 seq.

[2] An interview guide 'involves outlining a set of issues that are to be explored' while a standardised open-ended interview 'consists of a set of questions carefully worded and arranged with the intention of taking each respondent through [them]' (Patton 2002, p. 342 seq, quotes on p. 342). See also Yin 1994, p. 84 seq.

[3] On the traditional mission of HEIs see Chap. 1 Sect. 1.3.1 above.

[4] See Chap. 4 Sect. 4.2.1.1 "Public Research Organisations".

3. 'new-coming': founded in the second half of the 20th century and usually ranked below the top 60 % in national comparison, but present in the important rankings.

The Shanghai, Leiden, THE and QS rankings in the years 2008–2013 have been evaluated for the selection, as these are the most internationally recognised (though not uncriticised)[5] rankings.[6] The selection of universities also attempted to represent a geographical spread of institutions within the three countries. In Germany, the biggest of the three countries and the only federal system, two universities from category 1 could be included which also allowed a wider geographical spread and to represent more *Länder*.

Since there might be differences regarding funding situations between academic subjects, experts from different subjects were interviewed, if the structure of the relevant research office allowed. For this purpose, a variety of subjects needed to be identified from which to recruit the experts. This identification incorporated the in popular debate increasingly relevant distinction between applied and basic research[7] as well as the academic discourse which generally categorises disciplines in accordance with subject matter and methods. Thus a distinction is made between 'formal sciences' based on objective laws (e.g. mathematics, computer sciences), 'humanities' which employ methods of critical and speculative analysis (e.g. history, literature) and 'empirical sciences' based on empirical methods. The latter category is divided further into 'natural sciences' studying natural phenomena (e.g. biology, chemistry) and 'social sciences' focussing on human society and individuals (e.g. sociology, psychology). Sometimes further subcategories are made and for certain subjects the categorisation is controversial, especially between humanities and social sciences (law, for example, is mostly regarded as a humanity, while it is sometimes seen as a social science).[8] Humanities and social

---

[5] One of the criticisms is that they focus too much on research. However, this is an advantage for the purposes of this study, which equally focuses on research. On criticism see CHERPA-Network 2010, p. 62 seq; Lange 2010, p. 324 seq. See also the contributions to Erkkilä 2013.

[6] CHERPA-Network 2010, p. 6 seq; Lange 2010, p. 324. Note that these publications still refer to the combined THE/QS ranking. Since 2010, however, THE and QS publish separate rankings (Baty P (2009) New data partner for World University Rankings. THE, 30 October 2009 https://www.timeshighereducation.com/news/new-data-partner-for-world-university-rankings/408881. article. Accessed 16 August 2016).

[7] Politicians frequently distinguish between applied and basic research. Former BIS Secretary of State, Vince Cable, for example, stated that more applied subjects, especially in the category of STEM (science, technology, engineering and maths), have a particular value for the national interest and should thus enjoy differential funding based on excellence (Cable 2010). We have also seen in the previous chapters that international organisations place emphasis on this distinction (see definition in OECD 2002). Finally, it has also begun to inform academic debates in the last decades (Kuhn 1991, p. 146 seq).

[8] On the academic classification of sciences see Carnap 1991, p. 394 seq; Burschel et al. 2004, p. 194; Koller 2009, p. 179 seq.

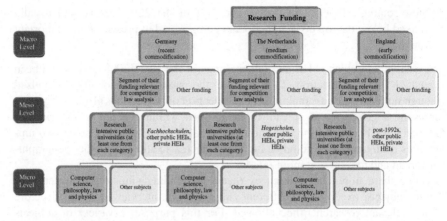

Fig. 5.1 Sample for the empirical study. The areas relevant for the research are *shaded dark*

science have therefore been merged here leaving three categories: formal sciences, natural sciences and social sciences/humanities. At least one subject from each category representing, at the same time, two more and two less applied sciences have been identified. These subjects are computer science (a more applied formal science), law (a more applied science from the group of social science/humanities), philosophy (a less applied science from the same group) and physics (a less applied natural science).[9] Figure 5.1 graphically illustrates the sample for the empirical study.

5.2.2 Interviews

This section explains how the interview guide was established and how access to the interviewees was gained and elaborates upon the interview situation.

5.2.2.1 Interview Guide

The aim of the empirical study to analyse exposure of HEI research to EU competition law as an example of exposure to economic constraints has been prepared by discussing potential competition law constraints for HEIs generally in Chap. 3. In Chap. 4 the HEI research systems of the countries under scrutiny have been introduced and a tentative competition law analysis has been conducted. Accordingly, potential issues which could arise under Article 101 TFEU were related to price

---

[9] This is not to say that the chosen less applied sciences cannot sometimes also be applied and vice versa.

fixing, market foreclosure (e.g. denying certain undertakings market access), market division (e.g. specialisation agreements, geographical division), anti-competitive research cooperation (e.g. limitations beyond research, limitations towards exploiting results), vertical cartels (e.g. special agreements with some research users) and limiting markets (e.g. limit on economic research). As exemptions for Article 101 TFEU depend mainly on market share it is impossible to find out about potential application of the exemptions in general questions. Article 102 TFEU could give rise to potential problems regarding non-economically justified contract conditions, output limitation, refusal to enter into contractual relations or provide licenses, the insistence on long-term licenses, price discrimination, technical restrictions, predatory pricing or abuse of (legal) monopolies. Unlike Article 101 TFEU, Article 102 TFEU does not contain exemptions. State aid could potentially be given if full costing is not adhered to, if economic activities are not commissioned according to the *Altmark*[10] criteria (or the alternatives set out in the Research Framework)[11] or if publicly generated knowledge is exclusively transferred to one undertaking. Here exemptions could apply for *de minimis* aid, for transparent aid for projects exempted by the General Block Exemption Regulation (GBER)[12] or for aid of up €15 M per annum for services of general economic interest (SGEIs). In addition, certain potentially anti-competitive research under all three provisions might more generally be exempted as SGEIs.

The interview questions were drafted according to the identified potential issues as outlined in Table 5.1. For example the question 'Are there any limitations as to the amount of research, in particular privately funded research your organisation may conduct?' aims to determine whether there might be a limitation of outputs. Some additional general questions on economic constraints for research were asked in order to be able to contextualise potential competition law constraints. The questions were thus mainly factual while a few questions also enquired about the opinion of the experts on the current situation or future developments.[13] As the tentative competition law analysis in Chap. 4 has shown, anti-competitive behaviour under the various provisions can partly overlap. If universities, for example, do not use a full costing system in areas of economic research, this can potentially be problematic in state aid terms. At the same time, if they agree on overhead rates, this could constitute price fixing. Finally, if a dominant university asks for prices that are abusively low, this might be regarded as predatory pricing under Article 102 TFEU. Some questions, like those on full costing methodologies, thus cover a range of competition law issues.

---

[10] C-280/00 *Altmark* (Judgment of 24 July 2003, EU:C:2003:415).

[11] Commission Communication 'Framework for State aid for research and development and innovation' OJ [2014] C 198/01.

[12] Commission Regulation 651/2014/EU declaring certain categories of aid compatible with the internal market in application of Articles 107 and 108 of the Treaty (General Block Exemption Regulation) OJ [2014] L 187/1.

[13] For more on question types see Patton 2002, p. 348 seq.

Table 5.1 Analytical framework. The below table demonstrates how the potential competition law constraints on HEIs identified in Chaps. 3 and 4 have been turned into interview questions and how the answers will be analysed to verify potential constraints

Issues identified in Chaps. 3 and 4	Interview question	Explanation
Economic activity	4, 7, 8	These questions aim to discover when research is, or could be, offered as a service on a market and may thus be an economic activity
Market definition	–	It would go beyond the scope of this study to conduct market definition for all potential problems which could arise
Price fixing (Article 101 TFEU)	20, 21	Questions 19–21 evaluate costing and pricing. Amongst them, question 20 and 21, inter alia, clarify if there might be price fixing which could be seen in cases where it is agreed on how full costing is applied or, generally, if prices are agreed upon
Market foreclosure (Article 101 or 102 TFEU)	22	This question attempts to find out if a collusion of undertakings denies market access to other undertakings or if a legal monopoly is being abused (e.g. by insisting on it despite not being able to fulfil demand). After studying the systems in Chap. 4, this does, however, seem unlikely
Refusal to enter into contractual relations with certain undertakings (Article 101 or 102 TFEU)	9, 10	These questions try to establish whether networks or any other kind of collaboration exist from which certain undertakings are excluded without justifiable cause since this could constitute a collusion hindering competition or the abuse of a dominant position, depending on the details of the case
Economically unjustified contract conditions (Article 101 or 102 TFEU)	11	This question tries to find out if any economically unjustified contract conditions are used, as these could hinder competition. Depending on the case such conditions could be part of a collusion or be imposed on other undertakings by a dominant undertaking
Refusal to provide licenses or unreasonably long duration (Article 101 or 102 TFEU)	17, 18	Questions 15–18 aim to establish whether intellectual property rights are used in a way that infringes competition law. Amongst them, questions 17 and 18 try to establish, if a license is not given to certain other undertakings or unreasonably long durations are attached to licenses. Depending on the case this could be an anti-competitive collusion or the abuse of a dominant position
Anti-competitive research co-operation (Article 101 TFEU)	13	This question aims at finding out if a co-operation has been initiated shortly before the discovery would have been made individually since this could constitute an anti-competitive collusion
Market division (Article 101 TFEU)	25, 26	Questions 25 and 26 aim to establish if any market division is taking place either by subjects (specialisation agreements) or geographically

(continued)

Table 5.1 (continued)

Issues identified in Chaps. 3 and 4	Interview question	Explanation
Limiting markets (Article 101 or 102 TFEU)	23	This question evaluates if there are limitations to the amount of economic research an HEI conducts (through legislation, collusion or by artificially limiting outputs unilaterally) since this could be seen as 'limiting markets'. Depending on the circumstances of the case this could infringe Article 101 or 102 TFEU
Price discrimination or other discrimination (Article 102 TFEU)	12	Question 12 aims to find out if there are advantages which are given to certain research users, but not to others. If conducted by a dominant undertaking this could constitute an infringement of Article 102 TFEU
Predatory pricing (Article 102 TFEU)	19–21	Questions 19–21 evaluate costing and pricing. Inter alia, it is aimed to find out if there might be predatory pricing. Prices are reasonable if they have been calculated transparently including all costs and reasonable profit
Mergers	–	Due to the very high annual turnover requirement it is unlikely that HEIs will come into conflict with the Merger Regulation
Hidden State Aid (Article 107 TFEU)	19–21	Questions 19–21 evaluate costing and pricing. Inter alia, an HEI might provide state aid if it offers services at an unreasonably low prices. In economic research the costs must thus be calculated transparently including all costs and reasonable profit
Applying the *Altmark* principles (Article 107 TFEU)	5	This question tries to establish whether calls from public funding agencies which are inherently commissioning a service (the existence of any such calls is established in question 4) are open to everybody. If not, this might infringe the *Altmark* principles
State aid through commercial use of licenses (Article 107 TFEU)	15, 16	Questions 15–18 aim at establishing whether intellectual property rights are used in a way that could infringe competition law. Amongst them, question 15 and 16 evaluate if a right is exclusively given to one undertaking without reasonable consideration, since this could be regarded as state aid
State aid through staff knowledge (Article 107 TFEU)	14	This question is tries to discover whether there are any limitations for staff working part-time or during leave in the private sector (or third sector) regarding the use of knowledge they generated during their work in the public sector
Exemptions Article 101 TFEU	–	The Block Exemption Regulations (BERs) depend on the market share an analysis of which would go beyond the scope of this research. Generally, the four conditions (efficiency gain, fair share for the consumer, necessity and no total prevention of competition) need to be fulfilled. Too much depends on each individual case to establish this in comparable questions
Exemptions Article 107 TFEU	6	This question tries to find out whether there is room for an exemption from state aid law

(continued)

Table 5.1 (continued)

Issues identified in Chaps. 3 and 4	Interview question	Explanation
SGEIs	24, 27	Article 106(2) TFEU exempts infringements of competition law if the service in question is of general interest and has been entrusted to the undertaking in question, the application of competition law would obstruct the performance of the service and the development of trade is not affected to an extent which would be contrary to the EU's interests. These questions ask the expert's opinion as to whether the research is in the general interest and if it has been entrusted to the HEI
	1–3	Introductory questions
	28–32	Considering that this study focuses on exposure of HEI research to EU competition law as an example of exposure to economic constraints, these last questions were asked in order to gain an overall assessment from the expert of economic constraints beyond competition law constraints

Having developed the questions this way initially led to a structure according to topic areas, which, however, turned out not to be ideal for the conversation flow (e.g. questions jumped between public and private funding requiring the expert to switch constantly between the different funders to answer the questions). After interviewing experts in the first couple of universities, the questions were, therefore, restructured into the following sections:

1. Introductory questions
2. Publicly funded research
3. Cooperation with the private sector
4. Full costing
5. Market entry, limitations of research
6. General opinion on funding situation.

Some questions which appeared to be repetitive (i.e. leading to the same answers as previous questions) were removed or merged. Aside from this, the questions remained the same for all interviews except for minor system-specific alterations (e.g. adapting the terminology to the relevant system or omitting superfluous questions such as questions on full costing in England where TRAC is compulsory). The final interview guide can be found in Annex I.

5.2.2.2 Access and Interview Situation

The interviewees were identified through researching the universities' research offices and/or general organisational forms in order to establish who could most suitably answer the questions (i.e. questions on public funding streams, private sector collaboration, intellectual property rights (IPR), costing and overall strategy). Since research offices are quite differently organised within universities, the position of the interviewees varies. Some offices are organised into subject areas whereby one person has an overview of everything related to the subject they are responsible for. Other offices are organised according to tasks with, for example, one person being responsible for IPRs, another for external contracts and another for public funding streams. Sometimes the relevant persons were not even located in one research office, but in various departments across the university (e.g. legal or finance departments in addition to research offices). These differences can be explained by the fact that these offices developed relatively recently and that there is no strict model to be followed. Instead universities have to find their own ways to establish suitable structures.[14] In each university the persons were chosen solely on their ability to answer the questions. If offices were structured according to subject areas, the persons responsible for the subjects identified above were asked all the questions. In other cases where offices were structured according to tasks, it was usually the public and private funding officers, the IPR officer and sometimes a legal or policy officer who were interviewed and the experts were only asked those questions which related to their respective responsibilities. In offices where it was difficult to identify the relevant interviewees, interviews were conducted with the head of the research office or in a focus group[15] containing all potentially relevant persons.

The interviews generally took place in a friendly, professional atmosphere with the interviewees seeming keen to help, provide information and showing an interest in the project and its outcomes. One exception occurred in the very first university visited where, in one focus group, one interviewee was unhappy with the information provided to her and with the questions asked, since she did not feel she could relate them to the overall project even after further explanation. This interviewee withdrew her consent at the end of the interview. Anything said by this interviewee therefore had to be disregarded. The other participants of the focus group, however, gave their consent, so the remainder of what had been said in the focus group could be used. A review with other, more senior researchers, has been conducted after this incident and it was agreed that the interview questions were appropriate and necessary, but that future interviews should adhere more closely to the guide rather than being conducted too freely which may have partly contributed to the problem. The more structured approach[16] as well as the increasing

---

[14] For more on this see Locker-Grütjen et al. 2012.

[15] On focus groups see Patton 2002, p. 385 seq.

[16] Despite using a more structured approach after the mentioned incident, the questions were not always asked in the same order, since they were split between different interviewees or the conversation flowed in different directions leading to proceeding to a different topic and returning to the other questions later. Sometimes interviewees had also already answered a question with a previous answer or less important questions needed to be skipped due to time constraints.

experience and ease of the researcher may have played a role in the much improved results thereafter. For future researchers following a similar structured approach it may thus be advisable to, at least initially, stick close to the guide and perhaps to prepare some more detailed examples of how questions relate to the project. It may, in cases of researchers who conduct empirical research for the first time, also be helpful to explain this to the experts to be interviewed (at least in the first couple of interviews) and to ask them to appreciate that this is a novel situation for the researcher as well. However, if an individual interviewee nevertheless feels that they do not wish to participate after all, this simply has to be respected and information needs to be gained as best as possible from other interviews or alternative sources (if at all applicable).

5.2.3 Ethics

Since the research consisted of expert interviews in EU countries and therefore neither contained vulnerable groups nor any potential risk for the researcher or the interviewees, there were no particular ethical concerns. The interviewees had been informed that they would be interviewed in their capacity as experts in the field and had been provided with a description of the project as part of the requesting letter and an abstract of the thesis in advance. They had to sign a consent form (including a brief description of the project) in which they gave their general consent for the interview and could choose between three options regarding consent for direct quotes under their name (consent, consent if seen in context, no consent for direct quotes). Despite most interviewees choosing the second option, it was later decided to keep the interviewees anonymous to avoid any potential confidentiality issues considering that HEIs increasingly compete and may wish to keep a closer lid on any information regarding their research policies.

5.2.4 Data Analysis

The interviews were recorded, except for a couple of interviews where recording was not or only partly possible due to technical problems and notes had to be taken which were transcribed more extensively immediately afterwards. The recordings have been transcribed and the answers have been analysed using the framework set out in Table 5.1.

This resulted in the following structure for the results subchapters:

0. Commodification constraints faced by the universities
1. Awareness of competition law
2. Economic Activity
3. Full costing

4. Market foreclosure
5. Refusal to enter into contractual relations and preferred partners
6. Economically unjustified or discriminatory contract conditions
7. Anti-competitive use of IPRs
8. Anti-competitive research co-operation
9. Market division
10. Limiting markets
11. Commissioning of research
12. State aid through staff knowledge
13. Exemptions
14. SGEIs
15. Interim conclusion

As mentioned above, an attempt was made to achieve a balanced sample of universities. As regards the topic of this study, this did not, however, lead to largely different results between the individual universities. If any peculiarities have been detected this has been made clear in the results chapters.

5.2.5 *Interim Conclusion*

Qualitative expert interviews which employed a format between 'interview guide' and 'standardised open-ended interview' were the most appropriate design for the research. The study has been limited to a small number of universities and subject areas (if appropriate) which have been chosen in an attempt to achieve a balanced sample. The questions were designed according to the results of the competition law analyses in Chaps. 3 and 4 and the experts were selected based on their ability to answer these questions. Generally, the interviews took place in a professional and friendly atmosphere. As only experts in their official role have been interviewed, there were no specific ethical issues. The interviews have been recorded and transcribed and were then analysed according to the same framework which had been used to establish the questions.

It is expected that the interviews have a high level of validity, since the experts are reporting about their everyday tasks and do not have any incentive to give false answers. The only concern could be that experts might be worried that their university is engaging in anti-competitive conduct and therefore attempt to cover this up. This, however, seems unlikely, since, different to, for example, a breach of criminal law, a potential breach of competition law is not necessarily an imminent threat. Firstly, HEIs would have to be regarded as undertakings to fall under competition law in the first place. Secondly, if competition law did apply and a breach was detected, there are a number of potential justifications. Thirdly, there have so far been no major investigations at the EU level which would lead one to think that this is currently a focal point of the enforcing authorities and that a study pointing to potential problems would lead to immediate action. The research thus did not try to uncover a clear breach of law which would lead to definitive action, so that interviewees should not have felt any need to disguise anything. Instead it aimed at uncovering potential tensions which it would be in the interest of the HEIs to know about in order to circumvent them. The interviewees seemed to widely understand this, found it helpful and were interested in the results.

The research is also expected to have a high degree of reliability. The questions have been designed to find out about specific situations in order to gain an insight into potential problems and they will be analysed in accordance with a framework set out in advance. As is general with more structured approaches, it is expected that similar results would have been obtained if the research had been conducted by another researcher and that the data gained can thus be regarded as relatively reliable. However, the research is a qualitative empirical study and as such has certain limitations. Only a small number of universities in three Member States have been studied at a certain point in time (2012/13). Whilst the sample has been strategically selected in order to present various types of universities, it can still only give an impression. The results are therefore not representative for all HEIs in Europe, but they do give an important insight into potential tensions between HEI policies and EU competition law.

5.3 England

In discussing university research in general, many interviewees expressed the view that there was increasingly less money available for curiosity driven basic research due to the increasing importance of non-public funding and government priorities and impact playing a role in public funding. Potentially resulting from this there was increasing emphasis on larger, collaborative, interdisciplinary research and the professionalization of researchers. Whilst the interviewees seemed to generally sympathise with the reason for these policies from government and the tax payer perspectives, many also expressed the worry that this could go too far and threaten the traditional mission of a university for which basic research was still regarded as academically the most valuable. Additionally, despite competition for funding having become generally fierce, differences between subjects were detected with subjects such as medical sciences, engineering and chemistry attracting funding more easily whilst the humanities, pure mathematic and astrophysics found it more difficult. Whilst this could partly stem from government priorities and the emotive character of medicine, differences in culture between disciplines might also facilitate this divide, with researchers in the social sciences and humanities being less eager to apply. An interviewee from a newcomer university, however, also mentioned that it depended somewhat on the university's strength making it easier for certain universities to attract funding in areas generally regarded as diffi-cult. Within subjects, as many interviewees remarked, certain topics would always be preferred (e.g. connective community, digital economy, climate change and renewable energy).

Regarding university culture, it was felt that there have been significant changes in recent years. Whilst TRAC fEC[17] was generally regarded positively by the interviewees, since it helped to achieve financial sustainability, one interviewee from a university in the North of England mentioned that the application of TRAC fEC could lead to inequality between universities as costs drivers such as buildings and salaries varied significantly between universities. Additionally, full costs were not always paid requiring research offices to look out for a healthy mix of funders with at least some paying more than full cost, something which could influence the decision whether or not to apply for a grant. Equally, other conditions (e.g. ethics, required partners and legal issues) could determine whether or not a project could take place. Researchers would also occasionally be encouraged, or even required, to find university-wide collaborations on interdisciplinary themes, since otherwise their topic might find funding difficult to obtain. On the other hand, universities also occasionally actively encouraged academics to apply for certain grants. Another pressure regarding research council funding, mentioned by many inter-viewees, would arise when research councils limit the number of applications uni-versities could submit thereby making the whole process less transparent due to incoherent internal pre-selection. A few interviewees expressed their feeling that generally universities were expected to do more for less and to strict deadlines. Such deadlines would also often require the subcontracting of elements of a pro-ject not conducted by the principal investigator (PI) rather than employing another researcher due to the high administrative requirements in universities for personnel appointments. A few interviewees mentioned that these changes were 'quite a cul-ture change for academics' who, in particular, felt that their academic freedom would be limited.

Overall the interviewees expected public funding to decrease further in the future with impact, performance indicators and priority areas gaining in impor-tance.[18] Some feared this might increase the divide between institutions as well as subjects. Such concentration could narrow opportunities, as the current govern-ment had

> a very narrow view of what the universities can do in terms of helping the British econ-omy. It's very focussed on technology and innovation and I don't think it's, even then, a particularly expansive view of what innovation is. And the danger is that in their despera-tion to resolve the economic crisis that they're in, they will just narrow it down more and more and more [...] [thereby weakening Britain's] position of influence and contribution, because some of the areas where we have expertise will, without appropriate funding, will just be lost.

---

[17] TRAC fEC is the full costing element of the Transparent Approach to Costing implemented in England. See further Chap. 4 (Sect. 4.2.2.4) above.

[18] The interviewees seem to be proven true in this respect considering the recent policy develop-ments, in particular the review of the research councils (Nurse 2015) and the White Paper (BIS 2016).

Many interviewees believed, therefore, that EU funding and other non-public funders, including third sector organisations and foreign funding, would gain in importance. English universities would become gradually more eligible for the latter, since funders would increasingly want to fund cutting edge research wherever it took place and foreign researchers would bring such grants with them. Such funding would, however, also increase risk and administrative difficulties due to different languages and jurisdictions.[19] Finally, many interviewees expected open access and new media technology to gain in importance. Concerns were raised with regards to the former, as it would, again, be more difficult in the arts as well as being costly for universities and mainly benefit the publishers.

5.3.1 Awareness of Competition Law

Most interviewees were not aware that EU competition law might play a role in their job. Some said that it could indirectly influence their work as it could be relevant for contracts or tendering. One interviewee whose work concerned commercialisation activities remarked that, in such activities and with non-standard contracts, care had to be taken that the market was not distorted. Generally, however, areas of concern seem to have been implemented into university policy or would be dealt with by a separate legal/contracts team or even external solicitors who could be consulted if necessary. One interviewee mentioned that senior management made the final decision, if a problem was detected. Research offices would normally not apply competition law directly themselves and are thus often 'not necessarily aware of what the competition rules are'.

5.3.2 Economic Activity

As has been explained in Chaps. 3 (Sect. 3.2.4) and 4 (Sect. 4.5), HEIs would have to be conducting an economic activity in order to fall under the competition rules. It was concluded that this is not likely to be the case regarding generic funding

---

[19] These problems may, in the future, also play a role as regards EU funding or funding from other EU Member States with the UK withdrawing from the EU. On such concerns see Cressey D (2016) UK government gives Brexit science funding guarantee. nature, 15 August 2016 http://www.nature.com/news/uk-government-gives-brexit-science-funding-guarantee-1.20434. Accessed 17 August 2016, Matthews D and Morgan J (2016) Brexit: growing numbers of UK academics face EU funding worries. THE, 5 July 2016 https://www.timeshighereducation.com/news/brexit-growing-numbers-uk-academics-face-eu-funding-worries. Accessed 17 August 2016, Toor A (2016) UK scientists face an uncertain future after Brexit vote. The Verge, 24 June 2016 http://www.nature.com/news/uk-government-gives-brexit-science-funding-guarantee-1.20434. Accessed 17 August 2016.

provided by HEFCE despite the recent impact agenda. The interviewees explained that research council funding can generally be divided into two categories; the responsive mode whereby the academic can apply at any time with any project falling into the remit of the respective council[20] and themed calls where a subject and a deadline for application is set. These still seem to be broad calls allowing the academic to decide about the exact project. An interviewee from a category 1 university explained this as the aim of the research councils being to strengthen the knowledge base and, ultimately the economy, generally rather than serve a more immediate goal. The academics would therefore compete on an academic level and the research council would pick the proposal most valuable for the public good. From this description, it does not generally seem to amount to a service which could be provided under market conditions and research funded this way would thus probably generally also not amount to an economic activity. One interviewee, however, mentioned that very large grants would sometimes be quite specific and come closer to a tender, something which might change this assessment.

Government departments usually have, according to the interviewees, very specific calls essentially commissioning research which would also often be classified as such and require declarations to be signed giving assurance that no anti-competitive behaviour is taking place. These calls, therefore, seem to be economic in nature. Other public funders might have specific as well as broader calls. With regards to third sector organisations, how specific the calls usually are would depend on the raison d'être of the organisation. The WELLCOME trust, for example, would 'come out with these really quite broad themes, but then the smaller charity that has been set up to look into a particular type of malignant tumour will have quite a narrow focus'. Judging from these descriptions, decisions would need to be made on a case by case basis on whether or not a call would amount to a service which could be provided under market conditions and thus as an economic activity.

In relation to collaboration with the private sector, the interviewees mentioned that all forms identified in Chap. 4 (Sect. 4.2.2.3) existed. They did not elaborate further on science parks which is perhaps explicable by this being a loose form of collaboration essentially amounting to a space where research takes place. As has been mentioned in Chap. 4, these would, in themselves, probably not constitute an economic research activity. Many interviewees talked about other looser arrangements for 'keeping in contact' including industry days, enterprise boards and research networks. More institutionalised forms of such arrangements might also provide funding to facilitate new collaborations. Some interviewees also mentioned strategic partnerships in which work was conducted collaboratively with a company on a regular basis which might go beyond research and also include employment schemes for graduates or access arrangements for technology. Research co-operations were described as general co-operations whereby research

---

[20] Within the responsive mode there would, however, sometimes be 'highlight notices' giving preferential treatment to certain themes.

is conducted jointly in the longer term and the private sector contributes financially (e.g. through staff time or use of their equipment). Sometimes these would
be supported by EU or national public funding sources, for example by the
Technology Strategy Board[21] or the research councils. Collaborations increased
through user-partners being required on 'the impact side'. Networks, strategic
partnerships and research co-operations would have to be regarded as undertakings
conducting an economic research activity if the research could have been conducted on a market. Judging from the descriptions, this would, again, need to be
assessed on a case by case basis with the stage of the research, openness of direction and predefinition of targets playing a role in such an assessment. The
Commission has made very clear in the review process of the Research
Framework that mere labelling of research as collaborative does not make it a non-
economic activity.[22]

The universities rely on academics to report innovations which they then
exploit, often through especially established companies. Sometimes this might
occur through spin-offs which, as some interviewees explained, initially will only
exploit one patent, but they eventually added to their portfolio. Occasionally, venture capital firms invest in such spin-offs. In para 19b of the Research Framework,
the Commission explains that licensing and spin-off creation are to be considered
as non-economic if they are of an internal nature and profits are reinvested. As we
have seen in Chap. 3 (Sects. 3.2.4.2 and 3.3.5.3) the combined reading of para 19
and para 15 of the Research Framework leave some confusion as to when exactly
knowledge transfer is non-economic in detail. It has been argued there that the
conception of competition law and the declared intention of the Commission in the
Issue Paper[23] would indicate a narrow reading here requiring also that the knowledge has arisen out of non-economic research and is being exploited non-exclusively. If these conditions are not fulfilled the activities can be of an economic
nature. According to the descriptions, both non-economic and economic exploitation seem to occur; the latter being especially the case where venture capital firms
are involved. With regards to spin-offs and start-ups, whether or not their behaviour or university interaction with them amounts to an economic activity for the
university, would also depend on how closely affiliated they still are with the university, how much private capital is involved and on the exact nature of their
activity.

According to the interviewees, the universities would also have privately
funded chairs, fellowships, post-docs or Ph.D. researchers. The interviewees
explained that the latter can be fully funded, if the company had a specific project
it wanted to be conducted. They might also be co-funded with additional research

---

[21] Now called Innovate UK and envisaged to become part of United Kingdom Research and
Innovation (UKRI). See further Chap. 4 Sect. 4.2.1.1.1 above.

[22] See Chap. 3 (Sect. 3.2.4.2).

[23] European Commission 2012, p. 7 seq.

council funding. As part of such a project the Ph.D. researcher would then also sometimes be seconded to the company. Such Ph.D. studentships would be especially common in the (natural) sciences. If staff or Ph.D. researchers are essentially conducting a pre-described service for the private sector, this could amount to an economic activity. From the explanations provided by the interviewees, this might occasionally be the case, especially in some of the Ph.D. studentships. If the private sector is simply donating money to a chair in an area of interest and the holder of the chair can still determine the direction of teaching and research, this would probably not amount to an economic activity.

Finally, the universities conduct some activities which are more obviously economic in nature. In this respect the interviewees mentioned contract research, consultancy,[24] the leasing of research infrastructure, material transfer agreements when the university has created materials which a company is interested in (e.g. cells or compounds) as part of their research and data access agreements if companies want to access university data sets. Interviewees from two universities mentioned that such activities are mostly conducted through separate technology transfer companies owned by the universities. The universities might equally, require such activities from private sector undertakings.

5.3.3 Full Costing

As has been explained in Chap. 4 (Sect. 4.2.2.4), English universities are using TRAC as a costing methodology and this seems to be unproblematic from a competition law perspective (Sect. 4.5.1). Nevertheless, pricing could be anti-competitive if, in areas of economic activity, neither market price nor full costs plus reasonable profit nor the at arm-length negotiated maximum economic benefit which at least covers marginal costs are charged. The interviewees explained that the full cost methodology is always used, but that there are very few sponsors paying full costs and the universities would need to underwrite many projects. Research councils would pay 80 %, charities only direct costs and with the private sector and other public funders (government departments, local government and quangos) it would be a matter of negotiation. The problem would then, as emerged from a focus group, be that they have, in advance, set aside a sum they are willing to pay for a certain piece of research. Therefore, the universities would have to go backwards to see how they could fit the project into the price. Especially with the private sector, the universities would attempt to receive 100 % fEC and, when an activity is classified as contract research or consultancy (which some interviewees mentioned was a 'commercial activity') or less beneficial research, an attempt would be made to generate an additional profit. This would be reinvested into

---

[24] On the economic nature of consultancy see also Chap. 3 Sects. 3.2.4.2 and 3.3.5.3 above.

activities which are not funded at 100 %. If 100 % fEC could not be achieved, universities would be more restrictive with other terms of the agreement, in particular, the partners would have to share IPRs. Generally, the question of whether or not less than 100 % fEC is acceptable for the universities would also depend on the strategic importance of the project and the partner in question. One interviewee working in the area of formal sciences mentioned that universities would not like to go below 90 % with these funders. This would be hard to explain to academics who believed that the 80 % the research councils were paying was a generally acceptable level. Some interviewees expressed that negotiations would be made more difficult by academics promising to do more than is possible for the price. This would also be facilitated by government departments and local authorities constantly expecting more for less and other universities accommodating this tendency by undercutting prices.

Some interviewees mentioned the 'public benefit test'[25] which is applicable to all charities in the UK, an organisational form often taken by UK universities including the ones under scrutiny. Accordingly, universities would not be allowed to trade and work for profit, but would have to further their charitable goals by conducting tasks for the public benefit. The test would establish if a certain activity serves the public benefit. If this was not the case for a certain research activity it could still be conducted, but usually as part of a university trading company. However, as an interviewee from the area of social sciences explained:

> It's still actually then delivered by the same academics, but that work would attract the VAT and there's an extra charge for doing it, and we would have to make sure that we were covering all our costs, so there's no way we'd be able to subsidise it in any way. It's quite rare for things not to pass, and usually we'd try and renegotiate the terms to make sure that things did pass.

The public benefit test under national law does not necessarily seem to be congruent with the question of whether an economic activity is taking place. As has been explained above (Sect. 5.3.2) and more extensively in Chap. 3 (Sect. 3.2.4.2), an economic activity is taking place if goods and services are or could potentially be offered on a market. It is irrelevant whether or not they are in the public interest. The latter might only play a role when it comes to exempting certain activities as SGEIs. Research which constitutes an economic activity has to be provided at market prices, for full costs and reasonable profit or at the at arm-length negotiated maximum economic benefit. The impression gained from the interviewees leads to the conclusion that currently this might not always be the case. Market prices

---

[25] The test entails that there must be clear benefits and that these 'must be to the public'. Whilst this excludes organisations that are run for profit, it does not mean that organisations cannot charge fees. Organisations must pass the test to be registered as a charity and registered charities have to make sure that their activities fall within the test. See Edwards and Stockwell 2011, p. 205 seq; Martin 2012, p. 458. According to the former, this means for research that it should be 'useful' and that 'some provision for the information gained to be disseminated and made available for study' should be made (ibid p. 211). It is thus a rather wide definition capable of capturing most research conducted by HEIs.

or full cost plus certainly do not always appear to be charged and neither do there always appear to be fierce arm-length negotiations considering what has been said, for example, about academics keen to do a certain piece of research promising more for less before the research departments could even start negotiations. It would thus appear that there might be occasionally instances of potential state aid. The fact that some universities are (consciously) undercutting prices could simultaneously be regarded as predatory pricing if they were dominant and could be challenged by competitors.

5.3.4 Market Foreclosure

Market foreclosure takes place if a collusion of undertakings, national legislation or a dominant undertaking denies market access to other undertakings. No signs of this could be detected for research in England.

5.3.5 Refusal to Enter into Contractual Relations and Preferred Partners

Whilst particular factors might facilitate certain collaborations,[26] partners are, according to the interviewees, usually chosen by the academics, occasionally assisted by research offices and driven by research interests. In this respect, future prospects of collaboration or the question of whether the collaboration was in an area of research strength or in a niche area in a currently relevant topic might play a role in deciding which partners to approach. Whether additional funding was available for certain forms of collaboration or if a certain call required a certain kind of partner are also factors. In so far government priorities might be taken into consideration. However, the interviewees seemed to agree that the main point was whether or not there was a 'good match' and the universities under scrutiny would not change their research strategies around government priorities[27] or apply for calls where the cooperation was not genuine even if partners could be added 'on paper'. Equally, an interviewed head of a research department mentioned that if they were approached by private sector entities to do work in an area that was simply not conducted by any of the academics and had no relation with anything they would do, they would not become involved solely for the purpose of catering for the market.

---

[26] Larger enterprises might more often attend conferences making it easy to establish relations. Common events or fieldwork could be easier conducted with local companies. Contractual negotiations could be facilitated by existing relationships.

[27] Yet, one interviewee mentioned that she knew about a university other than those under scrutiny which had a very strong 'working locally' policy.

The only reason for exclusion of partners, aside from reasons intrinsic in the research, would, according to the interviewees, be that a partner does not fulfil certain standards. Before a collaboration is begun, certain checks (e.g. credit and ethics) would be conducted and/or the external funder might have certain requirements regarding project management, auditing, quality assurance or the experience of the PI. Many interviewees mentioned, for example, that they would not work with tobacco companies due to ethical considerations and, as an interviewee in a category 2 university pointed out, this could potentially lead to the withdrawal of funding from charitable organisations. With regards to financial requirements, however, usually companies would not necessarily be excluded, but payment for their contribution might only be made after the contribution was received. Another interviewee from the same university spoke of cases where a university requires research work to be conducted by another party. Here the work would be commissioned under normal purchasing rules which, depending on the value of the work, would entail comparing prices, tendering or even Europe wide procurement. However, the commissioning of external research would not occur too often.

Given that the universities do not appear to exclude partners, there does not generally appear to be a general problem from a competition law perspective. The exclusion of partners due to ethical considerations does not generally pose a problem unless it is conducted by a collusion of universities or dominant university in a way that has a negative impact on competition. The exclusion of or the imposition of additional conditions upon certain companies for economic reasons would probably also have to be seen as reasonable commercial practice. One interviewee mentioned that there are also policies in place to avoid anti-competitive behaviour at the level of the individual academic. The behaviour could be anti-competitive through constantly working with or subcontracting work to the same company. This would be especially problematic if the academic held shares in that company or had any personal ties. Pre-project questionnaires and annual reviews attempted to detect such links which were prohibited if applicable.[28]

5.3.6 Economically Unjustified or Discriminatory Contract Conditions

The interviewees suggested that difficulties in contractual negotiations with private sector entities arose if the company desired to keep certain information secret whilst the mission of a university is to disseminate research results. Another issue

---

[28] The interviewee did state that at one occasion a contract to be given to another company which usually would have had to be prohibited 'was managed in a way that we set a price that was being payable to this company and it was a lot lower than had we gone somewhere else'. If this was the best price for that piece of research, the practice not a recurring constellation and the company not a dominant undertaking, this would probably not be problematic from a competition law perspective. The question whether or not this would be consistent with other areas of law would go beyond the scope of this study.

in the more open forms of collaboration was that companies often wished to agree upon milestones and deadlines which could be difficult in academic research where the outcome of the research and the timing of any results were not known in advance. Furthermore, issues would often arise as regards liabilities as well as IPR ownership and access. Universities would also oppose contractual terms that prevented them from working with other companies in the sector. Finally, universities had a variety of terms and conditions (e.g. financial regulations on travel, ethics etc.). Usually any issues arising could be resolved in the negotiations. Conditions might also be imposed by the entities providing additional funding for collaborations regarding ownership and backflow of IPRs or whether or not subcontracting is permissible. Some funders would make provisions for the results of a collaboration to be made publicly available if they were interesting to other companies as well. An interviewee from a category 2 university explained this as institutions being 'increasingly conscious about state aid rules and not using public money to support just one company's development'. She expressed that public funding rules would be welcomed since they would make certain terms clear before starting negotiations.

As mentioned in the last section, the exclusion of certain companies might be regarded as anti-competitive. Therefore, opposing conditions requiring universities to do so would be in line with competition law and universities might be able to utilise competition law in this respect. That publication requirements avoid state aid accusations, as mentioned by an interviewee, might be occasionally the case, since wide dissemination is often a condition for exemptions in the state rules. In other circumstances it might, however, constitute an anti-competitive condition if an economic activity is taking place, such requirements are not reasonable commercial practice, full costs are charged and such publication requirements are dictated upon an undertaking by a collusion of universities or a dominant university. Only the occasional condition that subcontracting was not permissible imposed by funders might in some cases cause concern, if an economic activity is taking place, since this could be seen as excluding other undertakings. This is not withstanding the possibility that there may be exemptions applicable in individual cases.

5.3.7 Anti-competitive Use of IPRs

As has been discussed in Chap. 4, the employer owns the inventions made by its employees. The interviewees explained that the academic therefore informs the university or the exploitation company respectively about a potential invention. The academics would be motivated to do so, since they might get generous returns from licensing in addition to their salary, since exploited IPRs created impact and since it was regarded as prestigious to have a patent on one's curriculum vitae. Patent searches and market evaluation would then be conducted to see if the innovation is exploitable. The registration and licensing or sale is often conducted by an exploitation company or an external agent, but the universities (and academics) received revenues. If the potential market is considered large enough a spin-off might be created which, as a head of department mentioned, was often the academics' preferred choice. The university and the academic would hold equity in the spin-off and sometimes venture capital firms would be taken on-board diluting the equity shares. The latter would sometimes be complicated, according to an interviewee working in the area of commercialisation, due to the value of the company being difficult to estimate. He also mentioned that there are preferred investors whereby the equity split is known in advance.

According to this interviewee, there are a variety of special conditions universities might impose when exploiting IPRs. Generally, unlike private companies who might hold back a patent in order not to dilute their market, universities would have to ensure that patented innovations are being used. In this respect it would also occasionally be discussed whether certain innovations (e.g. cancer therapeutics) should be 'open source'. However, considering the expense required to bring initial results to a marketable product (e.g. through clinical trials), commercialisation would mostly be the best route because companies would not be willing to make these investments if 'other companies can just come in and take the market from them'. It would therefore always be necessary to consider the best way to achieve the desired impact from an IPR. Unlike private sector companies, universities would also only give limited warranties on licenses (i.e. ownership and that no other commercial arrangements in relation to that IPR are known, but no guarantee that nobody else's IPRs are infringed), as any further warranties would require more market research than a university can reasonably conduct. Furthermore, sub-license partners need to be disclosed with universities retaining the right to object to inappropriate partners (e.g. the tobacco industry or military applications in certain countries). Since university research is often not complete when the IPR is created, partners could also benefit from IPR improvements for reasonable commercial terms, in particular as universities would not be free to exploit improvements with another party anyway. Finally, as it is often beneficial for partners, especially for small and medium sized enterprises (SMEs), to use a university's name when exploiting an IPR, universities would require knowledge about and, if applicable, object to the usage of their name.

With regards to externally funded research, some interviewees mentioned that charities would increasingly oblige universities to exploit in their funding conditions in order for the research to get 'out there'. External funders (charities and, especially, the private sector) would also increasingly require royalties. In private sector collaborations, who acquires ownership of IPRs would be contractually agreed. Since private sector companies might sometimes be better placed 'to take it through to the marketplace', the company might patent and thence provide the university with an academic license and royalty returns. Alternatively, if a higher rate is paid, the company might own the patent. Such routes could be desirable for the universities because the company would then take over the high costs associated with patenting. In other situations, where the research is mainly publicly funded, the university patents and provides the company with an option right and, if applicable, a license for reasonable commercial rates. In both cases, the universities would require the IPR to be exploited to its full potential and if a partner does not commit to this, the partner might only acquire the right in particular fields or the university might 'take back rights in particular fields [...] [to] exploit the IP with other interested parties'. In determining which route to go, the stage of the innovation might also play a role, since certain results are at a stage too early to be interesting for private sector partners. One interviewee additionally mentioned that universities needed to retain the right to publish, either independently or with the funder, and therefore needed to be cautious about restrictions to this (delays or complete denial) in prior negotiations.

If internally managed, knowledge transfer in the form of IPR exploitation has to be regarded as a non-economic activity according to the Research Framework if the profits are reinvested into the primary activities of the universities. This means the rules around direct exploitation efforts by universities will mostly not create competition law concerns. IPR exploitation could be classified as economic if venture capital firms have co-invested or, it is argued here,[29] if the IPRs arise from economic research or if the transfer is exclusive. If IPR exploitation is of an economic nature, special conditions or favourable prices granted to certain undertakings, be it to make innovation accessible, could be regarded as state aid if it does not pass the private investor test. However, the possibility of exemption according to Articles 107, 106(2) TFEU or secondary legislation remains. Contractual conditions, such as the limitation of sublicensing, could equally be regarded as anti-competitive if economically unjustified and thrust upon undertakings by a collusion of HEIs or a dominant HEI. Notwithstanding any potential exemptions, an economically unjustified contract condition could potentially be identified in the requirement to exploit to the full potential of the IPR. In order for IPR transfer in collaborations not to be regarded as state aid universities, according to para 28 of the Research Framework, would have to demand compensation equivalent to market prices[30] for any rights the partner obtains unless they just reflect the work packages the partner has delivered or unless all the costs for the research have been taken over by the partner entirely. If the partner has not paid the entire costs of the research collaboration, but contributed beyond its own costs, such contributions can be deducted from the market price.

5.3.8 Anti-competitive Research Co-operation

According to some interviewees, collaborations can start at any stage from the initial idea up to further development of already created IPRs. Inter alia that would depend on if there were existing relationships leading to the partner being

---

[29] See Sect. 5.3.2 above and Chap. 3 Sects. 3.2.4.2 and 3.3.5.3 above.

[30] Compensation is equivalent to market prices if the price has been established through an open sales procedure or through expert evaluation or through arm length negotiation or, if right of first refusal exists, the possibility to get other offers which have to be matched is existent.

involved early on or whether relationships needed to be constructed at a later stage where involvement of a partner seemed indicated or if it was the company which approached the university. Attempts to involve partners would generally be made as early as possible and, if the project was externally funded, the partner had to be already established at the application stage. Taking these explanations into consideration, there thus does not seem to be any indication that research was begun at an unreasonably late stage which could be in breach of Article 101(1) TFEU, as discussed in Chap. 3 (Sect. 3.3.2.4).

One might also wonder if the topic of the collaboration itself could be anti-competitive in nature. One interviewee mentioned that they were involved in a research council funded collaboration where the university was working with a company 'to help increase their market share of a product and looking at the social aspects of what that product's about'. While the latter part seems to be unproblematic from a competition law perspective, a university helping to increase a certain company's market share appears questionable as one may consider it state aid[31] or abuse of dominance if the university is in a dominant position.

5.3.9 *Market Division*

The interviewees in a focus group in a category 1 university suggested that their university prefers to have everything 'in house'. A head of department in another university explained that occasionally national archives are hosted by a university as is the case with her institution. However, she neither mentioned any specialisation or facility sharing agreements beyond this. Likewise, most interviewees in a university in the North of England were unaware of such arrangements. Only two interviewees here mentioned that this was a new endeavour in which an equipment database had been established which was being linked to the N8 (eight universities in the North of England). These universities could then share equipment something that was encouraged by the research councils. As stated in Chap. 4 (Sect. 4.5.1), the latter could potentially cause competition law concerns if other universities who would be willing to be involved are excluded and if market prices for the use of infrastructure are not paid for economic activities. One interviewee mentioned that they currently feared that VAT might become applicable to such

---

[31] However, the elements of Article 107(1) TFEU, of course, still have to be fulfilled. Thus arguably the topic as such does not change this, but just makes it more likely that this could be regarded as economic in nature and, if not paid for appropriately, as state aid.

activities[32] which might discourage universities from collaborating. This might indicate that, so far, market prices (including taxes and profits) have not been charged for such activities.

5.3.10 Limiting Markets

Generally, there do not appear to be any artificial restrictions in place as regards the amount of research, although some interviewees mentioned natural limitations (a member of staff can only commit to a maximum of 100 % fte and schools equally need to assure the necessary teaching capacity). However, thresholds where this would cause concerns are not normally reached and, instead, an increase in externally funded research projects is generally attempted. However, the interviewees in two universities mentioned the importance of the public benefit test in this respect. Research which passed the test could be conducted without restrictions. Research which did not pass could still go ahead, but this had to be accounted for separately. One interviewee stated that only 10 % of such research could go through the university books. The interviewees from the other university explained that such research could not be classified as research income. The interviewees from both universities explained that such research could instead go through the universities' trading companies. However, they all also mentioned that such research was very rare since the academics would not be interested in doing research which had no academic or broader interest. Additionally, as this would be a purely commercial transaction, they would also not be able to use any of the results thus reducing the output of high quality publications, in turn causing constraints regarding the Research Excellence Framework (REF).[33] None of this appears to be an artificial limitation on outputs which could be regarded as limiting markets from a competition law perspective.

5.3.11 Commissioning of Research

The funding agencies determine who can apply for a call which, according to the interviewees, varies between calls. Some interviewees mentioned that regarding the research councils, it is mostly only UK publicly funded universities and

---

[32] The Commission had made HMRC (Her Majesty's Revenue and Customs) aware that the VAT exemption for research was not in line with Directive EEC/77/388 on the harmonization of the laws of the Member States relating to turnover taxes—Common system of value added tax: uniform basis of assessment OJ [1977] L 145/1 as interpreted by the Court in case C-287/00 *Commission v Germany* (Judgment of 20 June 2002, EU:C:2002:388). HMRC has thus withdrawn the exception since 1 August 2013 making VAT applicable on 'business research' while 'non-business research' remains to be outside the scope of VAT. See further HMRC 2013.

[33] On the REF see Chap. 4 Sect. 4.2.2.2 "Public Generic Funding".

pre-recognised research centres that are eligible to apply. Sometimes they would be encouraged or required to have other partners which would, however, usually not be directly sponsored. Other funders would generally have broader eligibility requirements regarding the lead institution and would also partly fund other partners. In addition to defining the eligibility of organisations to apply, the funder rules often stipulate requirements as to the person of the PI (e.g. length of employment in the applying institution), the number of applications from one institution and the total value of the application. Government departments and local authorities would issue a request to tender. In these scenarios tendering organisations would need to sign declarations that they will not behave anti-competitively by exchanging information or deterring others from bidding. To an extent it would be possible to tender to become a preferred provider in which case, calls would then occasionally only be issued to the preferred providers. According to an interviewee working in social sciences, the conditions for contracts with the latter group of funders would become increasingly hard. She even mentioned one example where a local council contractually required the contract price to be decreased during the duration of the project, even though that had never been invoked.

If the research conducted under public calls can be classified as economic activity, it would need to be commissioned according to the *Altmark* criteria (i.e. usually as a public procurement procedure in line with the relevant directives)[34] or following the rules set out in para 31 seq of the Research Framework (Chap. 3 Sect. 3.3.5.2 above). Usually this would mean that calls need to be open to any willing provider, including foreign providers, and either market prices or full costs and reasonable profit need to be charged and, as regards the rules under the Research Framework, wide dissemination must be possible, for it not to be state aid. As has been mentioned above (Sect. 5.3.2), the majority of research conducted with research council funding might not be of an economic nature. If it or research conducted with funding from other public sources would have to be classified as such, the limitations in eligibility would probably need to be regarded as discriminatory and thus potentially as state aid to certain providers. Furthermore, whilst government departments and local authorities would usually tender, the fact that they often do not pay 'full costs plus' in the end and that they employ contract conditions forcing the contract price to decrease during a project, might have to be regarded as anti-competitive.

5.3.12 State Aid Through Staff Knowledge

According to the interviewees, staff members, especially post-docs, would occasionally be seconded to the private sector during a leave of absence or on a part time basis. Such practices had become more common in recent years. The

---

[34] Now Directive 2014/24/EU on public procurement and repealing Directive 2004/18/EC OJ [2014] L 94/65.

interviewees elaborated in this respect about the previously mentioned fully privately funded Ph.D. studentships and those which involved secondment to the private sector as well as about industrial fellowships for academics in which the funder (e.g. the Royal Society) would pay the salary for the fellow for a period of time allowing them to work in industry. One interviewee even mentioned that her university used to have a formal secondment programme with a private sector company. According to the interviewees, the advantages and disadvantages of such a secondment would first need to be weighed. Some interviewees mentioned that this would take place at school level. Then research offices would need to cooperate with human resources, legal services and other university departments to negotiate the secondment agreements in order, inter alia, to protect the individual, the university and deal with IPR issues and confidentiality questions. In particular the latter two issues would be problematic, since it would be difficult for researchers to 'forget' something they have learned especially if it was vital to their research. An interviewee in a focus group thus mentioned that, in her opinion, companies should not share highly confidential knowledge during such an exchange, as requiring that the researcher kept this information confidential would reduce the benefits of the exchange.

From a competition law perspective, provided an economic activity is taking place, problems could occur if advantages are given to companies through staff knowledge, particularly through IPR creation without appropriate consideration or public funding paying for an employee in a company. Also, Ph.D. studentships could amount to state aid where a company essentially defines a research task to be undertaken by the student because, even if the researcher is fully funded by the company, the researcher will still receive academic support and be registered as student with all the associated benefits rather than being a fully paid company employee. Of course, there may be potential for exemptions (Sect. 5.3.13 below) in particular if the circumstances can qualify as innovation aid for SME.

5.3.13 Exemptions

Potential exemptions for anti-competitive behaviour under Article 101 TFEU must be assessed on an individual basis, in particular the exemptions provided for in BERs, as they often involve market shares. Regarding state aid, as discussed in Chap. 3 (Sect. 3.3.5), the *de Minimis* Regulation[35] excludes aid below €200,000 and the *de Minimis* SGEIs Regulation[36] aid below €500,000 respectively over any period of three fiscal years to any one undertaking from the ambit of Article

---

[35] Commission Regulation 1407/2013/EU on the application of Articles 107 and 108 of the Treaty on the Functioning of the European Union to de minimis aid' OJ [2013] L 352/1.

[36] Regulation 360/2012/EU on the application of Articles 107 and 108 of the Treaty on the Functioning of the European Union to de minimis aid granted to undertakings providing services of general economic interest OJ [2012] L 114/12.

107(1) TFEU. The GBER exempts aid for basic research of up to €40 M per project with 100 % aid intensity, applied research of up to €20 M per project with 50 % aid intensity and experimental development of up to €15 M per project with 25 % aid intensity as well as certain amounts of aid with certain intensities for various forms on non-project aid if the relevant conditions, in particular as regards transparency[37] and incentive effects,[38] are complied with.[39] Finally, Decision 2012/21/EU[40] provides an exemption for aid below €15 M per annum for SGEI provision. Outside of these exemptions, aid would need to be notified and could potentially be exempted according to Article 107(2) or (3) TFEU. As regards Article 107(3)(b) and 107(3)(c) guidance is provided in the Commission Communication on import projects of common European interest[41] and the Research Framework respectively. The latter, in particular, removes the ceilings of the GBER for research and development if the aid contributes to a well-defined objective of common interest, there is a need for state intervention, the measure is appropriate, has an incentive effect and is proportionate, undue negative effects are avoided and the conditions on transparency are adhered to.

According to the interviewees, the amount of funding provided through public calls varies significantly. Whilst the smaller grants (e.g. for travel) might only be a few hundred pounds, the highest calls could be up to £10 M for the research councils' centres of excellence and networks of excellence calls which are often collaborative. Some interviewees also mentioned, however, that with certain grants, researchers could ask for as much as they needed to do the project which could technically be any value. A few interviewees remarked that recently there was a tendency towards calls for larger and longer projects. Smaller projects, if qualifying as economic in nature, might, due to the *de mimimis* rules, not fall under Article 107(1) TFEU in the first place, though they could, of course, cumulate over three years and thereby reach the €200,000 or €500,000 (in cases of SGEIs) threshold. Most projects which could be considered as infringing state aid law might be able to benefit from the exemptions in the GBER provided that it is

---

[37] See Article 5 GBER para 17 of the preamble on transparent aid and Article 9 (1) on requirements of the Member States to publish information about aid measures.

[38] Article 6 GBER and para 18 of the preamble. This means in particular that aid is not exempted if work has commenced before the application for aid was made to the Member State in question.

[39] See further Chap. 3 Sect. 3.3.5 above.

[40] Commission Decision 2012/21/EU on the application of Article 106(2) of the Treaty on the Functioning of the European Union to State aid in the form of public service compensation granted to certain undertakings entrusted with the operation of services of general economic interest OJ [2012] L 7/3.

[41] Commission Communication Criteria for the analysis of the compatibility with the internal market of State aid to promote the execution of import projects of common European interest OJ [2014] C 188/44.

transparent aid and that the aid intensities are adhered to. If projects can be classified as providing an SGEI (discussed further in Sect. 5.3.14 below), they are also likely to fall under the €15 M threshold in the SGEI Decision, since there rarely seem to be projects with a higher value in England. Individual cases need to be evaluated to determine whether these conditions are fulfilled or, alternatively, the measure could be exempted after notification according to Article 107(2) or (3) TFEU. As has been discussed in Chap. 3 (Sect. 3.3.5.1), it seems questionable, in how far any exemptions can apply to hidden aid.

5.3.14 SGEIs

For potentially anti-competitive activities by the universities to be exempted as SGEIs they would need to be in the general interest, be entrusted to the university, the application of the competition rules would have to obstruct the service in question and the development of trade must not be affected in such a way that it would be contrary to the EU's interests. When asked whether they believed the research in their institution to be in the public interest, many interviewees mentioned high impact research on topics regarded to be of societal importance which seems to indicate that research based purely on the researchers' curiosity is less seen as being in the general interest. Interestingly, it could, however, be argued that the English impact agenda is geared towards creating any impact on anyone which could favour particular interests, while one might argue that curiosity driven research for the development of science, as such, is in the interest of everyone. Nevertheless, the interviewees also emphasised that the research had to pass the public benefit test. Such research would then involve some sort of public interest and, as previously mentioned (Sects. 5.3.3 and 5.3.10) this encompasses the majority of the research conducted by the universities. In line with what has been discussed in Chap. 4 (Sect. 4.2.2.1), the interviewees did not believe research to be a statutory task of HEIs, but a task they could conduct and could receive funding for. However, as one interviewee pointed out, if universities did not conduct research they would have significantly less income due to lack of external grants as well as less generic funding which is partly based on research quality and contains a bonus for externally generated research income.

Except for research which has not passed the public benefit test, a general interest might thus be assumed. However, the concept of SGEI seems, as we have seen in Chap. 3 (Sect. 3.2.3.3), in addition to the general interest, to require a 'uniform' and 'binding nature' which might not always be applicable. At the same time, Member States have a fair amount of discretion in this respect, as long as they do not use the concept of SGEI to avoid the competition rules. As for the question of whether the SGEI is entrusted to the universities, research, unlike in the other two countries, does not appear to be a statutory task. However, grant agreements with public bodies might be regarded as acts that entrust universities with the specific task in question. To achieve more clarity on the question as to how far potentially anti-competitive research could classify as an SGEI and thus utilise the exemption of Article 106(2) TFEU and related secondary legislation, the interpretation of the Court would have to be awaited. Whether, as required by Article 106(2) TFEU the application of competition law would obstruct a potential SGEI, proportionality and effects on trade would have to be evaluated on an individual case basis.

5.3.15 Interim Conclusion

Overall, the funding situation was viewed critically by the interviewees, as public funding was conceived both shrinking in general and increasingly concentrated on research with impact and research in certain areas. It was mentioned that, in particular, academics perceived this as creating unnecessary administrative hurdles and causing tensions with academic freedom. The interviewees expected further concentration of public funding in certain topic areas and institutions making it necessary to look for alternative funding sources. Additionally, the interviewees saw the importance of open access publishing and new media technologies as becoming increasingly relevant for research in the future.

The interviewees overall were not particularly aware of competition law themselves, as this would have been implemented into university policy and they would just follow the policy as such. If any problem would come to their attention they would consult separate units or external solicitors rather than dealing with the issue themselves. They thus would also not themselves make a distinction between economic and non-economic activities.

In areas of economic activity, market prices or full costs plus profit would usually need to be charged which, in reality, despite the use of TRAC fEC to calculate the costs, does not always seem to be the case. Therefore, there might be instances of state aid or predatory pricing, if HEIs were dominant. Furthermore, the exclusion of partners (be it for ethical reasons), the imposition of publication requirements and the prohibition of subcontracting by funders might potentially be regarded as anti-competitive if in an area of economic research, imposed onto partners and if it creates anti-competitive effects. If IPR exploitation is of an economic nature, any economically unjustified advantageous conditions for undertakings, be it to make innovation in the public interest accessible, could be regarded as state aid. Also, contract conditions dictated upon undertakings such as the limitation of sublicensing could be regarded as anti-competitive and universities would have follow the Research Framework as regards the acquisition of IPR by the partner which usually means demanding market prices for any rights the partner obtains or exploits. Another issue which came up in an interview is the question of whether the topic of a certain piece of research could, in itself, be anti-competitive. Generally market division seemed not to be present in England, however, envisaged facility sharing endeavours might be regarded as anti-competitive if certain partners were excluded discriminatorily and/or market prices were not paid. State aid law could also be infringed if public calls are classified as economic activities and have not been commissioned according to the *Altmark* criteria or the rules in the Research Framework. Finally, if advantages are bestowed upon companies in areas of economic activity through staff knowledge, in particular IPR creation or Ph.D. students essentially conducting a study for the private sector, this could potentially be regarded as state aid.

However, depending on the individual case, there might be exemption possibilities for some of these practices under Article 101(3) TFEU or Article 107(2) and (3) TFEU and the related secondary legislation. If the undertakings in question have a low market share and the infringement in question is an effect restriction or the amount of aid received by an undertaking is below €200,000 (€500,000 for SGEIs) over three fiscal years the infringements may also not fall under Article 101(1) and 107(1) TFEU in the first place, as they would not be deemed appreciable. Projects infringing the state aid rules, which could be classified as SGEIs, could mostly benefit from Decision 2012/21/EU, as projects seem to be (almost) always under the €15 M threshold. More generally, it might be possible to exempt some potential breaches of competition law as SGEIs under Article 106(2) TFEU, but that would require that a SGEI had been entrusted to the undertaking in question.

5.4 The Netherlands

In the Netherlands, many interviewees expressed the view that overall public funding, especially generic funding, was decreasing, which made the other funding streams more important. The interviewees generally described that, while basic research (especially research funded through the *Vernieuwingsimpuls*) is academically most prestigious, government policy (especially top sector policy) increasingly steers towards impact oriented and applied research. As regards academic disciplines, the interviewees expressed that generally the natural sciences, life sciences and medicine are more easily funded and arts, humanities, law and social sciences have more difficulties. However, there are exceptions such as astronomy, for which it is harder to find funding, and archaeology and economics which are relatively successful. Whilst all subjects can still be funded in the *Vernieuwingsimpuls*, other funding options for certain subjects are declining which increases competition in the *Vernieuwingsimpuls*. An interviewee working in the field of business collaboration expressed his belief that certain subjects might ultimately die out or would only be offered in a few universities in the country, in Europe or even worldwide. The tendency in government policy, but (influenced by this policy) also within universities themselves to focus on certain research areas, would, according to the interviewees, also influence research priorities within subjects. Many interviewees were critical of this as basic and curiosity driven research was needed 'to get these really big changes that you need as knowledge economy', to maintain a high academic standard and to provide high quality, research informed teaching. However, while many academics would thus attempt to utilise the open funding streams as much as possible and, as an interviewee from a category 1 university mentioned, even private sector voices were calling for retaining sufficient space for basic research in universities, there would not be any real resistance. Instead universities would just adapt to the changes in research funding.

Commodification tendencies have thus led to certain changes in university culture. The feeling that a lot of pressure is created, when universities constantly have to compete for everything, was expressed in a focus group. A few interviewees mentioned that due to the increasing importance of the *tweede* and *derde geldstroom*[42] and of impact and performance indicators generally, universities had begun to focus on non-generic funding (providing internal incentives for this) and to work on their visibility to justify to the public their receiving of funding. This required a careful balancing act between following official policy, attracting sufficient funding and providing sufficient freedom to researcher to do their work. EU funding, especially, was seen by many as increasing in importance, but a few interviewees also mentioned the need to utilise the *vierde geldstroom* (philanthropic donations) further to achieve a certain independence. In the course of these developments, research support offices became increasingly important in helping to attract and administer research funding, including its legal aspects. One interviewee working on legal aspects specifically mentioned competition law in this context and expressed that he finds certain Technology Foundation (*Stichting voor de Technische Wetenschappen*, STW) schemes questionable from that perspective. Many also mentioned the importance of attracting funding at full cost levels to achieve financial sustainability which would not always be the case in many of the collaborative schemes. Another concern expressed was the fear to be losing talent. Since the open talent funding schemes like *Vernieuwingsimpuls,* but also European Research Council funding, often require certain career stages for researcher eligibility, researchers, especially early career researchers, from a subject area in which not many funding alternatives are present, may, according to a focus group, find it too hard to find funding and decide against an academic career.

When asked about their expectations for the future, a few interviewees expressed that they believed that these developments will continue and universities would become more commercial. A few mentioned that they believed that the Netherlands is following the same path as the UK but are about ten years behind. Additionally, some interviewees flagged up as a likely future development an increase in cooperation with emerging economies (e.g. China and Brazil) as funders and partners in research as well as the establishment of subsidiaries in these countries. At the same time, increasing local clustering of research specialities was something that an interviewee in a category 1 university saw as likely. Another interviewee from the same university suggested universities might need to get more creative as regards accessing or generating funding. For example,

---

[42] Second and third funding stream; referring to funding from specific intermediary organisation (*tweede geldstroom*) and other non-generic funding (*derde geldstroom*). See further Chap. 4 Sect. 4.3.2.2 above.

they could offer fee-based continuing education courses to pensioners to generate income which could then be used for research projects. An interviewee from a category 2 university even speculated that research funding might, in the future, be provided as loans rather than grants, to be paid back with interest.

5.4.1   Awareness of Competition Law

All interviewees seemed aware of competition law and most stated that competition law plays a role in their job to a varying extent depending on their exact position. It was frequently stated that they would obtain advice from legal officers if needed. An interviewee working as legal officer described EU competition law and the Research Framework as paramount.[43] Whilst the university would sometimes have a vertical relationship with companies (and hardly ever a horizontal one), it was more common that it would act as the state, making state aid law particularly important. This view was shared by many interviewees who saw state aid law as the main concern, as it would, inter alia, assert influences on access conditions (exclusivity, option periods, price) for IPR generated in publicly funded research and the levels of financial participation in public-private partnerships (PPPs). It was also stated that competition law would prohibit discriminatory contract conditions. Generally, it would appear that the awareness for EU competition law amongst research office staff in the Netherlands is quite advanced and comprehensive in comparison to England.

5.4.2   Economic Activity

As in England, research conducted freely with generic funding is not likely to be regarded as an economic activity. With regards to funding provided through the *tweede geldstroom,* the interviewees confirmed that the *Vernieuwingsimpuls* in NWO (Nederlandse Organisatie voor Wetenschappelijk Onderzoek; Netherlands Research Council) funding is a completely open talent funding scheme given mainly for basic research. It would therefore, probably also not amount to an economic activity. Another part of NWO funding would go towards bottom up ideas provided by senior researchers for projects of varying kinds and sizes. Open calls like these where researchers enjoy a large amount of freedom to conduct independent research and which, according to the interviewees, also existed in other intermediary agencies like STW, would probably also not have to be regarded as an economic activity. However, an increasing amount of public funding is themed.

---

[43] Then still in the previous version (Community framework for state aid for research and development and innovation OJ [2006] C 323/01).

Two interviewees considered that themed calls would represent more than half of the non-generic public funding overall, especially since the introduction of the top sector policy discussed in Chap. 4 (Sect. 4.3.1.1 "Public Research Organisations"). Some themed calls are, according to the interviewees, very detailed with exact descriptions to be followed, especially the public funding provided for bigger co-operations or public-private funding for Ph.D. projects. Similar to what has been discussed for England (Sect. 5.3.3), this might be considered as an economic service that could be commissioned on a market. As regards the top sector funding, as an interviewee explained, the private sector and academia must come up with a research agenda within the field of the top sectors and then receive public funding to set up the co-operation as well as most of the academic funding. Here the classification as an economic activity, would therefore depend on the research agenda as will be discussed further below (in this section) for public-private co-operations.

As mentioned in Chap. 4 (Sect. 4.3.2.2), the *derde geldstroom* consists of funding from a variety of providers. Firstly, there is contract research for the government which will have to be regarded as an economic activity. Secondly, there is EU and international funding which will not be looked at in this study. Thirdly, there is funding provided by charities. According to the interviewees, funding from charities would usually only set out a subject area within which researchers freely apply with any kind of projects. As this is difficult to replicate under market conditions, it seems unlikely that this amounts to an economic activity. Finally, collaborations with the private sector fall under the *derde geldstroom*. Here a variety of collaborative forms have been identified in Chap. 4 (Sect. 4.3.2.3) which all seem to be present in the universities under scrutiny. The interviewees described contract research as delivering certain results with little or no freedom for researchers. This form of collaboration is clearly an economic activity.

Like in England, the interviewees did not elaborate further about science parks (or *innovatiecampussen*) which could equally be explained by the loose form of the collaboration which in itself will probably also not have to be regarded as an undertaking. In PPPs, the universities would, according to the interviewees, look for companies to collaborate with which would then pay cash or contribute in kind, while additional public funding is often also available from the government or the EU. In such co-operations work packages are agreed and the main point is joint research and mutual learning. The parties in the co-operation share intellectual property with each other in order to do further research (not to exploit). Commonly generated IPRs will be allocated according to previously agreed contracts which also set out the other terms of the co-operation. There are standardised templates, but especially the negotiation of IPR issues could be lengthy. This form of collaboration would currently be pushed by both the government, especially through the top sector policy, and by the EU. It is difficult to make a general statement about the economic nature of this collaborative form. If the research takes place freely with the aim of generating knowledge and disseminating it at a pre-competitive stage and the universities have sufficient influence on the directions of research, the collaboration might be non-economic in nature. If the cooperative project essentially amounts to conducting a research service for the private sector partner or the partners are, in essence, cooperatively conducting a research service for the government, as the description of the calls for some collaborative projects given by some interviewees indicate, this could amount to an economic activity.

IPR exploitation was regarded as very important by the interviewees. Firstly, the commercial interest and exploitability of the research would be assessed and then there would be a search for partners to develop the research further and exploit the results. The exact deals in this context would be negotiated. These could either be with existing companies or a spin-off would be created specifically for the exploitation. The latter is preferred if the potential IPR is 'disruptive' technology significantly different from what companies are currently doing and there is little synergy to integrate it into an existing company. Start-ups beyond spin-offs were not mentioned by interviewees. As, discussed above (Chap. 3 Sects. 3.2.4.2 and 3.3.5.3 as well as Sect. 5.3.2 for England), IPR exploitation has to be regarded as non-economic activity if, according to the Research Framework, it has an internal character and profits are reinvested and, as is argued here, it arose from non-economic activities and is non-exclusive. Judging from what has been said, there appears to be economic as well as non-economic IPR exploitation. As regards newly founded companies, whether or not they constitute an economic activity for the university depends on the activity and on how affiliated they still are.

The *vierde geldstroom* contains purely philanthropic donations without any consideration. An interviewee responsible for charitable donations explained how in his university a charity as a separate legal entity is established to collect donations and then pass them on to the university thereby allowing for the donations to be tax deductible. The charity is also utilised if calls in the *tweede* or *derde geldstroom* require a charity to be involved. The interviewee gave the example of the Coca-Cola Foundation which would only accept applications from charities and wherein the university fund would then submit the application for the researchers. The money generated by the fund would mainly go to research projects, but also to educational activities and community projects. The persons or institutions providing the funding can chose between general donations or donations for a specific fund dedicated to scholarships or chairs. Higher donations can also be named funds which can be dedicated to specific kinds of research. Generally a committee in the university fund chooses which project is to be funded, but occasionally donors would want to be involved. This can even go as far as donors prescribing a very specific project, although this would be exceptional. The interviewee mentioned the example of an individual donor requesting a rather specific project be undertaken on rehabilitative medicine for work-related physical problems of certain professionals. Sometimes the university fund also approaches philanthropists who are known to be interested in a specific topic with an already existing project requiring additional funding. A donor may also approach the fund wanting to donate to a specific project. Generally, the described situations where money is provided in a purely charitable fashion to the university in general or even for research in specific areas could not be regarded as buying a market service. However, in the exceptional cases where a very specific project is demanded, this could probably be seen as being able to take place under market conditions. The fact that the commissioners of such research are neither using the results themselves nor making an economic profit from them, does not change the possibility that such studies could be commissioned on a market from private providers. It might therefore be regarded as an economic activity.

5.4.3 Full Costing

While, as discussed in Chap. 4 (Sect. 4.3.2.4), all Dutch universities have an individual full costing system, a financial officer interviewed explained that most of the systems ended up being relatively similar. He further explained that in his university a 'profit and loss account' was in place. They would therefore know the income and the costs from their annual report. From the total costs specific education related costs would be deducted and the remainder would then be divided by the number of fte and then by 1600 h per year. This would result in the cost rate per fte per year. On this basis the university had created 70 categories of salaries with the equivalent full cost rates. Researchers could simply look up their salary in the list to know their full cost rate. The project costs are then calculated by the full cost rates of the hours of the staff members working on it which already includes all the hidden costs (e.g. for infrastructure or electricity). Common rules for universities would not exist, as universities had not been able to agree on them.

According to the interviewees, the funder usually determines the pricing rules in public funding.[44] NWO would only pay direct costs with occasionally a small overhead, as it had been agreed between government, NWO and universities that a part of the *eerste geldstroom* is intended to match NWO funding. There are, therefore, incentive payments for every fte created from NWO funding.[45] Some funders have fixed hourly rates which do not always cover full costs. Others allow for fullcost calculation. For the EU a simplified full cost method has been used. Things could get particularly complicated, as a few interviewees mentioned, if a number of funders contributed to a project, as then the funding rules would have to be made compatible. The big PPPs especially were described as administratively complicated regarding costing. Interviewees from one university mentioned that, partly, universities even created a private sector entity to avoid risk and make cost calculation easier as well as fulfilling the requirement of some calls to have a private sector partner. One interviewee also talked about the danger of providing state aid through PPPs and pointed out that intellectual property is, therefore, only made

---

[44] It is assumed that this is also true for charity calls. However this was not explicitly mentioned.

[45] It was not entirely clear whether these incentives are provided through internal funding allocation or directly through the *eerste geldstroom* (generic public funding) or both, as the statements of the interviewees differed in this respect.

accessible for partners in PPPs for the duration for the project rather than being transferred. Beyond that, universities would only grant an option right to negotiate commercial access and potentially a discount equal to the company's contribution to the overall project. Furthermore, the universities seemed very aware that publicly funded projects are often costing them money. Whether or not to utilise this funding, would therefore be a strategic decision which depended on their matching capacity, the importance of the project and also on whether 'in kind' or 'in cash' matching would be required, wherein the former would be preferable. It was often mentioned how prestigious NWO funding is and a few interviewees pointed out that this funding would always be matched in their universities.

Companies are usually, particularly in contract research, asked for full costs and a surplus for profit, risk and capital investment (the rates for this varied between universities). An interviewee responsible for policy and funding mentioned that if clear market prices were accessible, these would be applied as a reference point. Interviewees seemed very aware that this could otherwise infringe competition law. However, according to the interviewees, strategic decisions for lower prices could be made for strategically important partners or based on past agreements. One interviewee explained: 'It can be worth to put your own money in that project. That is also what companies do in general.' However, there would be guidelines in this respect and full costs at least should be covered. He also pointed out that, to retain financial sustainability, this cannot be done too extensively. Furthermore, the faculty board or board of directors would have to co-sign the contracts and would not do so if pricing was completely disproportionate. Simultaneously, a few other interviewees explained that due to the public funding rules being limited to direct costs or certain hourly rates, researchers would often think those were the actual costs or that full cost plus prices would be too high and thus offer arrangements below full cost prices to companies. They would then thereby sell themselves under-price and companies would also, despite being aware of that, try to negotiate prices as low as possible. The assumption that matching might thus still occur was therefore expressed.

IPR exploitation follows different rules entirely. Here the universities operate on a risk sharing basis with the private sector, since it would be very difficult to assess the value of an IPR and companies would also not be keen on making huge investments up-front for an uncertain development trajectory where the technology could simply fail. Given this, the agreements would provide for the university to share some of the success through royalties on sales and milestone payments (e.g. for a successful clinical trial or drug approval). The royalties and milestone payments are calculated based on the plans of the company and the market forecast regarding revenue as well as comparable deals (i.e. a fair market rate). Regarding charitable donations, research could only be supported with what has been provided. There is, therefore, no full costing. Potentially, matching has to take place or additional funders have to be found.

The full costing methodologies generally seem to comply with competition law as they are based on actual costs and there do not appear to be fixed profit rates or other anti-competitive agreements. Competition law problems could thus only occur if, in an economic activity, market prices, full costing plus profit or the maximum economic benefit negotiated at arm-lengths is not applied. The greatest risk here could be public calls not using full costing despite being an economic activity, given that, as discussed in the last section, some of these calls might potentially be considered as an economic activity. The rules regarding PPPs seem in line with competition law requirements and risks in this area seem low. The rules described for contract research or IPR seem generally unproblematic from a competition law perspective since they charge full costs and are oriented along market prices. However, if incidents occur where full costs plus profit (or the relevant alternatives) are not applied this could constitute state aid or predatory pricing (if the HEI is a dominant undertaking). Finally, charitable donations are, as explained in the last section, generally unlikely to be an economic activity and therefore full costing would not be required. In the exceptional cases where a study on a subject is essentially commissioned, this might be regarded as state aid.

5.4.4 Market Foreclosure

As in England (Sect. 5.3.4), no signs of market foreclosure could be detected for research in the Netherlands.

5.4.5 Refusal to Enter into Contractual Relations and Preferred Partners

All the interviewees stated that the universities, as such, do not exclude partners. An interviewee working on business collaborations mentioned this would amount to anti-competitive discrimination. He explained they would like to 'collaborate with as many parties as we can', as that would be beneficial for the university. Even collaboration in one project with companies which are competitors would, from the university's point of view, be welcome. Essentially, as many interviewees stated, it would depend on the researchers and the research question. Nevertheless, some interviewees stated that they might have preferred partners for certain subjects due to existing relationships, geographical proximity, a company being the producer of high-end equipment and therefore the natural choice or, when it comes to other HEIs, due to the fact that they are in an association or strategic partnership. One interviewee, for example, stated that in the area of food and agricultural research they would often look for local partners, since in their area many companies are working in this field. Funding agencies would, on the other hand, sometimes insist on certain partners; regional agencies are aimed at economic prosperity in the region and thus require regional partners, national funding is partly for national partners only,[46] other programmes might require the involvement of SME and the Coca-Cola foundation would only fund charities. A few interviewees mentioned, however, that fulfilling these conditions is not always possible or appropriate, especially in basic research, and might lead to the university not applying for a call. As the universities do not appear to exclude willing partners, there does not seem to be a problem from a competition law perspective. Only the public funding rules might potentially be regarded as anti-competitive, something which will be discussed further below (Sect. 5.4.11).

5.4.6 Economically Unjustified or Discriminatory Contract Conditions

The interviewees saw the major contractual problem which needed to be solved to be the desire of some companies for secrecy versus the aim of the university to disseminate knowledge through publication, further exploration of results and research informed teaching. Additionally, as an interviewee working on business collaborations mentioned, it was a concern for the university that research needed to be 'result-open' rather than geared towards making a specific invention. An invention should always be an added bonus that occurred in 'result-open' research. Another interviewee mentioned that universities, in his opinion, should exclude ethically questionable research. He mentioned that he had heard that companies had specifically come to Dutch universities to undertake animal testing as animal protection laws in other countries would be stricter. He found this especially controversial if the testing is merely standard not containing any scientific interest. Beyond that, interviewees did not know of any particular conditions for partners. Generally, however, as the business collaboration officer stated, it is important for universities to establish strategic long-term relationships due to the benefit gained from increasingly substantial knowledge which is created in a line of common projects. Therefore, it was an aim in contract negotiations to find solutions both sides can benefit from.

This would sometimes be difficult, according to a legal officer due to the expectations which companies have and which would differ between companies. As an example he mentioned the general culture of 'BV Nederland'; namely the view of the Netherlands as a trading nation where the assumption is commonly held that if one supports Dutch industry the whole nation will prosper. Due to this mind-set Dutch companies expected to gain advantages. This would be especially true with regards to publicly funded universities as the companies, as tax payers, expected returns. According to him this mind-set had led to many incidents of

---

[46] An interviewee mentioned that this is not the case in top sector funding where international cooperation is possible and even foreign partners can receive the subsidy.

210 5 Empirical Study

anti-competitive behaviour in the past in other sectors. More generally, there might potentially be other issues that needed to be resolved in the negotiations.

As explained for England (Sect. 5.3.6), generally requirements on dissemination, leaving research 'result-open' and, perhaps, ethics will not cause any concerns, unless perhaps if dictated upon undertakings by a collusion or dominant undertaking in the area of economic research in a way that causes anti-competitive effects. However, even then there may be possibilities to exempt this. If companies, due to a specific corporate culture in a country or sector, try to impose anti-competitive conditions on HEIs, as they partly at least appear to attempt, HEIs may also be able use competition law to their advantage by reference to the relevant provisions of national and EU competition law in contract negotiations or even by relying on their rights in enforcement.

5.4.7 Anti-competitive Use of IPRs

As mentioned in Chap. 4 (Sect. 4.3.2.3), IPRs created by employees are usually owned by the employer. The interviewees explained that employees report their inventions. They are then reviewed to determine how far the university is free to exploit (i.e. potential rights of other parties are scrutinised) and the potential for exploitation is evaluated. If applicable, rights are registered which are often managed by a university holding. The universities do not exploit IPRs themselves, but look for partners for exploitation or found spin-offs. If a spin-off is created the holding company might hold equity in it or assist with other IPR related activities. The preference would be towards conferring licenses rather than the assignment of IPRs. As has been mentioned above (Sect. 5.4.3), royalties and milestone payments at market rates are received for licenses. Next to compensation, another important factor for universities is the limitation of restrictions regarding future research based on the IPR. In particular, if Ph.D. researchers are involved in the creation of the IPRs, they are eventually required to publish their theses. Additionally, as universities aim at making knowledge publicly accessible (be it through a product created by a company), the agreements would contain an anti-shelving clause. If no partner willing to exploit the IPR could be found, the application would, according to a legal officer, usually be dropped after 30 months. He mentioned that there used to be patent targets in some Dutch universities which had led to unexploited patents, but such policies have been abandoned.

As it is sometimes difficult to find partners for exploitation (for example the invention might still be at too early a stage to be attractive to private sector partners (knowledge gap)), another interviewee explained that his university would sometimes lend money from a fund established for this purpose to companies in order to jointly bring the invention to a prototype stage which can then be further developed. At that stage, except for receiving royalties from the license, the university would leave the collaboration. The company would also need to invest during the common phase and sometimes additional public funding is available.

The interviewees explained that, in PPPs, the agreements would contain rules concerning sharing IPRs and future income. According to an interviewee working on business collaborations, the rule 'ownership follows inventorship' would apply in his university. Thereby, jointly made inventions would be jointly owned, those made by the company are owned by the company and if university staff made the invention, it is owned by the university. Another interviewee mentioned that his university would try to negotiate that the IPRs would generally belong to the university as far as possible. If the university has the rights, the procedure as outlined above is followed. Companies might additionally want a first option clause, so 'they can be sure that if they want they can get access to the technology', but reasonable commercial rates would still need to be paid.

From a competition law perspective, the rules seem generally unproblematic. If anything, demanding anti-shelving clauses might be regarded as anti-competitive if imposed on undertakings in a way that is not reasonable commercial practise, but there may be room for exemptions. A legal officer explicitly mentioned the potential of IPR assignment or licensing agreements to constitute state aid. Interestingly, he mentioned that companies would be equally aware of this, but would nevertheless try to negotiate advantages, as they would assume that the amount would usually be below the *de minimis* threshold and that interstate trade would, in most cases, be unaffected. Even if that was the case, the university would, however, nevertheless not agree to anti-competitive arrangements because Dutch competition rules would still apply.[47] The subsidies/loans provided through public funding or through the university, mentioned by one interviewee, might, however, qualify as state aid if they cannot pass the private investor principle or could be exempted.

5.4.8 Anti-competitive Research Co-operation

There did not seem to be any indication that research was begun at an unreasonably late stage which could be in breach of Article 101(1) TFEU, as discussed in Chap. 3 (Sect. 3.3.2.4).

5.4.9 Market Division

The interviewees explained that in national (NWO, national infrastructure roadmap) and European (European Strategy Forum on Research Infrastructure)

---

[47] However, as we have seen in Chap. 3 Sect. 3.3.5.3 above with regards to the case T-488/11 *Sarc* (Judgment of 12 June 2014, EU:T:2014:497), some Dutch universities seem rather generous towards their own spin-offs which one may assume to be anti-competitive even if the General Court here dismissed the case due to limited standing of the competitor who had brought the case before the General Court.

funding policy strong attempts are made not to duplicate expensive research equipment. Thus if such equipment already exists it is often not funded again in another university, unless there is a particular reason for it. The universities would also be discussing to share facilities beyond that; amongst each other as well as with the private sector (which also sometimes contributes to the equipment). Furthermore, an interviewee from a category 1 university explained that universities would be expected to give start-ups (not just their own) access to costly equipment as it would be too expensive for the start-ups to maintain this themselves. Specialisation would also occur, to some extent, mainly regarding patient care due to reimbursement issues, since health insurers determine what and where is acceptable treatment. From a competition law perspective, one might wonder if the placement of infrastructure into only one or a few universities could be regarded as anti-competitive if it involved areas of economic activity. Firstly, this might amount to state aid as it provided one institution with an advantage over others particularly if it can then charge others rent for use of the infrastructure. Secondly, it might place the organisation into a dominant position in a certain research market which it could abuse should it not provide (equal) access to the essential facility. If voluntary facility sharing between HEIs or between HEIs and other parties makes economic sense, no party is discriminatorily excluded from it and, if the equipment is co-financed, all parties receive reasonable economic rates when letting the infrastructure out, this would, however, probably not constitute anti-competitive behaviour. Access to equipment for start-ups would probably only amount to state aid if no adequate consideration was paid. Other areas of specialisation like the example of health insurers deciding about specialities in universities and university hospitals might cause constraints because it could be regarded as a vertical cartel.

While institutions need no accreditation to research and the research market, as such, is thus open, the public HEI market is widely foreclosed by government. Interviewees in a category 3 university described the difficulties their university had to establish itself as a university because the government was of the opinion that the public HEI market was sufficiently saturated and did not want a new public university to be established. This university was only able to be founded, because it argued that it was focussing on the international market rather than the local one and would have a different, problem-based teaching philosophy. The other interviewees confirmed that it is almost impossible to establish a new university and receive public funding. An interviewee in a northern university described how Friesland recently failed in its endeavour to establish a publicly funded university, despite having argued that they would cater only for the local market where need had apparently increased. The same would be true for new courses or research areas within a university. Indeed, all the interviewees pointed out that the government now expects universities to pick focus areas and to concentrate on them, which are then also supported through extra funding. Some interviewees were rather critical of that, as they saw their university as a comprehensive research university which carries a certain prestige. Attempts would thus be made to attract non-public funding in order to continue to excel in all areas. One interviewee mentioned that he believed it would make interdisciplinary research more complicated, if not every area was researched intensively in-house. Aside from these concerns, it also seems possible that, if and in so far as universities can be regarded as undertakings, these government policies would amount to market division and state aid for existing universities to the detriment of those trying to establish themselves or establish a new area. Interestingly, we have seen in Chap. 3 (Sect. 3.3.2.3) the reforms the current government in the UK is aiming to bring into place for England would make access for new providers easier (inter alia due to reports by the national competition authorities) which indicates how competition law can contribute to accelerate commodification. This may be something that could become equally relevant for the Netherlands in the future, especially if they move forwards on the path towards commodification of HEIs.

The universities would, according to some interviewees, also often collaborate more extensively with each other in an inner state region (Twente, Nijmegen, Groningen and Wageningen or Leiden, Delft and Rotterdam), across borders (Northern Netherlands and North Germany) or Europe wide (Gent, Groningen, Göttingen and Upsalla) in strategic partnerships. Particularly in these partnerships, but also beyond, according to one interviewee working on policy aspects, it is attempted not to double-up in research specialisation or duplicate equipment. Thus if one of the partners has a chair in a certain area the other partner would not employ a professor with the same speciality. This would enhance cooperation. Even if universities retained all subject areas, concentration would take place within specialities. Another interviewee described an internal research policy in his university which provides that they would not compete with local companies. Investment was therefore only supposed to go to such spin-offs and start-ups deriving from unique research in the university. In particular, infrastructure was not to be exploited if it would lead to competition with local companies. An example was also provided of a scheme between a universities, the local *Hogeschool* and one in a different location. In this scheme, the two HEIs in the first location would stick to one area of research, while the other HEI would investigate, together with private sector entities, whether the waste from the former could be utilised to make certain products. The former HEIs refrained from investigating what could be done with the waste. Depending on the exact details of the cases, (particularly on the question as to whether it is normal market behaviour to offer a slightly different product or if behaviour amounts to actual collusion) all these policy examples risk being regarded as infringing Article 101(1) TFEU, though there may be exemption possibilities, especially under the Specialisation BER,[48] if they do not involve hardcore restrictions and stay within the market share thresholds.

---

[48] Regulation 1218/2010/EU on the application of Article 101(3) of the Treaty on the Functioning of the European Union to certain categories of specialisation agreements OJ [2010] L 335/43.

5.4.10 Limiting Markets

The interviewees stated that there were no quantitative restrictions on the amount of research generally and on privately funded research in particular. On the contrary, as public generic funding decreased there would be a strong desire to attract more privately funded research, in particular private funding for full costs. However, as two interviewees pointed out, there might be reservations as to the content. If a project has little academic value or it excessively limits academic freedom, universities might refrain from conducting it. Yet, in a focus group the concern was expressed that the decreasing public funding might, in the future, also lower the threshold with regards to content. Content restrictions, do not generally appear to pose an issue, unless perhaps the university thereby denies access to an essential facility or there is a collusion on the matter which could cause anti-competitive effects. However, if that was the case, there may still be possibilities for exemption.

5.4.11 Commissioning of Research

The funding agencies determine who can apply for a specific call which, according to the interviewees, varies. An interviewee working on public funding streams mentioned that most calls are for universities and, depending on the call, partners. Only few schemes have a reverse approach. If partners are allowed or even required, there are, as has been mentioned above (Sect. 5.4.5), occasionally limitations/requirements as to which kind of partner organisations need to be involved. As discussed in Chap. 3 (Sect. 3.3.5.2) and more specifically for England earlier in this chapter (Sect. 5.3.11), if public calls can be classified as economic activities, they would need to be commissioned according to the *Altmark* criteria or the rules set out in the Research Framework which contain that calls need to be non-discriminatory and that prices reflecting market value usually need to be charged for it not to constitute state aid.

5.4.12 State Aid Through Staff Knowledge

In the Netherlands, according to the interviewees, university staff do sometimes work in the private sector. In these cases academics would still have to follow the national code on academic integrity which researchers needed to sign and which require them inter alia to behave ethical, trustworthy and carefully. Sometimes, staff work in their own companies spun out of the university. This would be a preferred situation, as staff can retain their employment within the university whilst experimenting with the setting up and running of a company. It was mentioned by some interviewees, that such constellations became problematic if staff were in managerial positions and able to sign contracts for both sides. This would be a concern because the university could not be certain that these members of staff represented the university to its best interest. One interviewee working on legal aspects specifically mentioned, as an area for concern, the potential of favours given to spin-offs led/owned by employees because this could constitute state aid. He said that this is difficult for the research office to scrutinise since academics are managed by line management not by the research offices and the former are not involved in the spin-offs activities. However, such constellations would be rare, as most companies would quickly spin out properly and very close ties are only maintained with few. Generally, the interviewees also mentioned IPR issues which needed to be negotiated as regards ownership and publication of results as a concern in cases where staff worked in the private sector. Beyond these issues, as one interviewee working on policy pointed out, there is not much concern as regards staff knowledge being used in the private sector. Instead, the exchange would be regarded as mutually beneficial. From a competition law perspective, provided an economic activity is taking place, such arrangements could be problematic, if advantages are bestowed on companies through staff knowledge, in particular IPR creation or favourable contract conditions given to staff owned companies. There may be exemption possibilities, as we will see in the next section (Sect. 5.4.13), especially if the circumstances can qualify as innovation aid for SME which specifically involves staff exchanges.

5.4.13 Exemptions

As has been discussed in relation to England in Sect. 5.3.13, it is impossible to make a general determination of the potential for exemption under Article 101 TFEU, as this would depend too much on the individual cases and, in the case of BERs, on market shares. We have, however, seen (Sect. 5.4.9) that the specialisation BER could be particularly relevant. As in England, the amount of funding provided through public calls differs, according to the interviewees, significantly from a few thousand Euros to up to €30 M per collaborative project or even €40 M for institutional funding through the gravitation programme. As regards state aid, smaller projects could thus equally benefit from the *de minimis* rules if they do not accumulate to above €200,000 over three fiscal years (or €500,000 if an SGEI is given), the exemptions in the GBER and, if projects can be classified as providing an SGEI (Sect. 5.4.14 below), from the €15 M threshold in the SGEI Decision. The amounts of funding provided through public calls are much higher than in England, though. Therefore there is more room for potential aid falling outside of the exemptions. The measures, if classified as infringing the state aid provisions, might then still be able to utilise Article 107(2) and (3) TFEU as an exemption generally, which would need to be evaluated in the individual case taking into account relevant guidelines, especially the guidelines in the Research Framework as regards Article 107(3)(c) TFEU.

5.4.14 SGEIs

Some of the exemptions mentioned in the last section (e.g. exemption of SGEIs below €15 M in the SGEI Decision) require the services in question to be SGEIs. Further, there may be potential to exempt services as SGEIs more generally if the exemptions above do not apply or in the case of potential infringements of Article 102 TFEU. As we have seen above in the relevant section (Sect. 5.3.14) for England services need to be in general interest, be entrusted to the university, the application of the competition rules would have to obstruct the service in question and the development of trade must not be affected in such a way that it would be contrary to the EU's interests for them to qualify for exemption under Article 106(2) TFEU. In the Netherlands, the interviewees generally believed that the research conducted in their university was in the general interest. A few interviewees mentioned that academics were divided into those who believed impact-focussed and applied research would be more in the general interest, while others believed that curiosity driven, basic research would, in the long term, serve the general interest better and had more academic integrity. It was noted that a scientific interest was needed in both cases, though. A few interviewees, however, pointed out that occasionally there might be an economic necessity for conducting research for particular interests even without a scientific interest (e.g. contract research for a company for full costs) even though currently that was seldom the case. One interviewee in a category 1 university mentioned that if research seemed too far removed from the universities conception of what it should be doing or was unethical or illegal, they would not conduct it.

From these statements, it seems as if the universities would only pursue research if there is a scientific interest, unless they felt economically required to do other research to attract income. Except for the latter cases a general interest (i.e. the advancement of science) might thus be assumed. As with England, more than just such a general interest might be required for research to be an SGEI, however, and clarity can only be achieved through a ruling by the Court. As regards the question of whether the SGEI is entrusted to the universities, the interviewees named the WHW (Wet op het hoger onderwijs en wetenschappelijk onderzoek; Higher Education and Research Act) as an act entrusting universities with the task of research. While this tasks them with research in general, this might not be precise enough to fulfil the conditions on entrustments acts in the post *Altmark* legislation.[49] Grant agreements from public bodies might, in that case, be regarded as acts entrusting universities with the specific task in question. If the application of competition law would obstruct a potential SGEI, proportionality and effects on trade would have to be evaluated on a case by case basis.

---

[49] See, for example Article 4 of Decision 2012/21/EU. See also generally on the post *Altmark* legislation Chap. 3 Sect. 3.3.5 text surrounding n 268–272.

5.4.15 Interim Conclusion

Overall the funding situation was viewed critically since public funding was conceived as shrinking and increasingly concentrated only on certain areas and for research with impact. This was regarded as being potentially limiting to academic freedom and basic research. Despite the widespread criticism, the interviewees expected this development to continue and for the Netherlands to follow the path taken in England. Unlike in England, all interviewees were aware of competition law and seemed to have a relatively comprehensive knowledge of it. In government policy there are rules referring to, in particular, EU state aid law which seem to indicate that there is awareness that these might be economic activities. The main areas which might be erroneously classified as non-economic could be themed public calls and charitable donations which could in particular circumstances amount to commissioning a service.

If areas are erroneously identified as non-economic and no full costs are applied, this could amount to state aid or be regarded as predatory pricing. The rules on IPRs seem to be generally unproblematic. Only anti-shelving clauses if imposed on undertakings or subsidies to companies willing to exploit university IPRs might potentially be regarded as anti-competitive, but there may be exemption possibilities. Unlike in England there seemed to be rather strong indications for potential market division. The placement of infrastructure in only one or a few universities, health insurers determining specialisation in university health research, limitations on the establishment of new universities, division of research specialisation and no competition policies or agreements might be regarded as problematic from a competition law perspective. Tensions might also occur if public calls are economic activities and have not been commissioned in a non-discriminatory way for prices reflecting market value. Finally, if advantages are given to companies through staff knowledge, in particular IPR creation or favourable contract conditions given to staff owning companies, this could potentially be regarded as anti-competitive, if an economic activity is taking place.

As in England, depending on the individual case, there might be possibilities of exemption. As regards restrictions of Article 101(1) TFEU, the Specialisation BER in particular may be applicable. However, this would depend on market shares. The sums provided for public research are much higher than in England and thus there is more room for certain potentially anti-competitive public calls to fall outside the scope of the *de minimis* rules, the GBER and the SGEI legislation. While the thresholds in the new GBER are much higher now, certain conditions would have to be fulfilled, especially as regards transparency. When it comes to SGEIs (in the specific legislation or generally under Article 106(2) TFEU), these would require a service of general interest to be entrusted to the undertaking in question. Whilst the WHW might not be precise enough to serve as entrustment act, individual grant agreements by public funders might fulfil this requirement.

5.5 Germany

As has been mentioned in Chap. 4 (Sect. 4.4), the overall climate for investment in research is good in Germany, something which benefits universities. One interviewee expressed this by saying: 'Academic research is prospering, quite unlike France, Italy or Great Britain... That's a catastrophe [there].' Generic funding and DFG funding under which researchers are free to pursue any direction of research comprises the majority of research funding. Interviewees also felt less pressure from performance indicators implemented into generic funding distribution. Most interviewees, therefore, felt that there was still significant academic freedom in Germany. In thematic calls some interviewees deemed that there was a push towards applied, collaborative and economically impactful research. These programmes would also be influenced by, and merge with, the aims of Bologna and Lisbon/Europe 2020.[50] This was viewed critically by interviewees from two universities since they felt that big collaborations can be suffocated by administrative requirements and communication problems, can require too much to be achieved by a single project and nobody ever seemed to research whether the assumed added value is actually achieved. Most interviewees felt that there was more funding for subjects such as engineering and information technology and less for the humanities. It was also mentioned that inter-disciplinary research sometimes found funding hard to come by as experts from one subject when evaluating a study from another employing their methodology might easily find it lacking. However, a couple of interviewees mentioned that the preferential situation of some subjects could also be explained by different needs (e.g. humanities and social sciences inherently needing lesser resources than human medicine), less of a culture of applying for *Drittmittel*[51] in certain subjects or simply due to a lack of interest in the topics of the calls. It might thus not (entirely) be the result of intentional governmental steering. Most interviewees mentioned that, within subjects, calls are often issued in particular fashionable areas (e.g. climate change, electronic cars) which might be explained by the accessibility of certain subjects to the public (e.g. curing cancer or preventing climate change is more obviously desirable than studying the Merovingians).

Despite the mentioned criticism, economic constraints and culture changes did not appear to be seen as significant as they were in the other two countries. In particular, it was felt that the situation did not (yet) require researchers to apply for *Drittmittel*, that through creative proposal writing one could draft applications in a way to fit one's agenda into a variety of only loosely related calls and that academics had the chance to influence the thematic areas. The latter was viewed critically by one interviewee because the researchers may have personal motives (e.g. trying to continue their research area until retirement). It was also mentioned

---

[50] See further on the Bologna Process and the Lisbon 2020 Strategy Chap. 2 Sects. 2.2.2 and 2.2.3 above.

[51] *Drittmittel* refers to all non-generic funding. See Chap. 4, Sects. 4.4.1.1 and 4.4.2.2 above.

that young researchers particularly might be influenced by extrinsic pulls of thematic calls. Despite being encouraged to collaborate more with the private sector, private funding was still regarded as playing a minor role in German universities. An interviewee from a category 1 university, however, mentioned that universities are not at an eye to eye level with private sector partners in contract negotiations. In particular, companies would still try not to pay full costs and, especially if the researcher negotiates and signs agreements without the involvement of the relevant research offices, they may succeed in this. More generally it was feared that relying strongly on *Drittmittel*, particularly if not provided at full cost levels, might be financially unhealthy for universities. Especially in a category 1 university, it was felt that success in attracting *Drittmittel* was, in this way, being punished. At the same time, it was for certain situations seen as bizarre to ask for full costs. An example given was a funder providing full costs for a visiting researcher, as this would amount to the visitor (or the funder on the visitor's behalf) paying to come and work at the university. This seemed to collide with the general self-perception and university culture of universities in Germany.

When asked for an opinion on how research and research funding will develop, an interviewee from a category 1 university expressed that generally too much is expected from universities. They were required to do basic research leading to new ideas in all subject areas, innovate, excel in topical subjects, identify a unique focus, provide research informed teaching which also focussed on employability and student satisfaction, engage internationally, attract external funding and perform well in rankings with a variety of parameters. This would lead to a mission overload. Universities would currently have to find their place in all this, also considering their own understanding of their role. The same interviewee said that, despite the generally positive research funding situation in Germany, he believed public research would continue to be underfunded. Especially there was insufficient generic funding which, combined with the fact that non-generic funding is not provided at full cost levels, might lead to insufficient infrastructure. Another problem identified was that the programmatic calls, even though they are supposed to encourage innovation, would often lag behind 'real cutting edge' research since once an idea is through the administrative process and a call is issued, research has already developed beyond that. Therefore, innovation can actually be hindered by increasing competitive programmatic calls and, for an institution which invested highly in an area which is discontinued after one call, this may also have significant financial consequences. A focus group expressed their fear of certain subjects being destroyed and that teaching and research could be increasingly separated, something which collides with the traditional German understanding of university education.

5.5.1 Awareness of Competition Law

Concerning the relevance of competition law for research, all interviewees were aware of the Research Framework[52] and its requirement to distinguish between economic and non-economic activities as well as to apply full costs to the former. Beyond that most interviewees were not generally aware of competition law problems or had not yet come across competition law in their everyday tasks respectively. Only two interviewees mentioned IPRs and one interviewee mentioned procurement as areas where competition law becomes relevant. This does not necessarily mean the other interviewees are not aware of competition law beyond that if prompted further, but it was very clear that the Research Framework and full costs were the first things that came to mind for all interviewees.

5.5.2 Economic Activity

As in the other two countries, research conducted independently with generic funding will probably be a non-economic activity. As regards public competitive funding the interviewees pointed out that DFG funding is mostly open subject-wise and provided for basic research. Funding by the Federal Ministry of Education and Research (*Bundesministerium für Bildung und Forschung*, BMBF) and other ministerial funding, if applicable, would implement research policy in areas which are 'fashionable'. Here universities/researchers could lobby in advance for their subjects, but, once the calls are out, they have to apply within set limits which differ between calls. The majority of the interviewees stated that calls can be very specific. Sometimes the creation of a prototype in a certain area is required or a specific study commissioned whereas, on other occasions, programmes just generally encourage entrepreneurship, co-operation or offer institutional funding. Some of the larger programmes were offered for collaborations between companies, HEIs and others which were then supposed to work together and utilise synergies from basic research up to the final product stage. Situations where the funders are essentially commissioning a prototype or a study would probably have to be regarded as economic in nature, as they could be provided under market conditions. The responses from the interviewees seem to indicate that such calls exist. The universities under scrutiny, however, seemed to regard any public funding as non-economic in nature. Only the interviewees in one category 1 university made a specific point of declaring that they do assess public funding for its economic nature. That assessment would usually lead to the result that they considered it non-economic.

All the universities under scrutiny seemed to be involved in (almost) all the co-operation forms of non-public funding described in Chap. 4 (Sect. 4.4.2.3).

---

[52] Then in its previous version (see n 43).

A cluster was described as an area where many public and private sector research organisations are located which all work on a few subject areas. They do not collaborate in an institutionalised way, but instead create synergies and can lead to smaller co-operation on project basis. Sometimes there are also shared laboratories in a cluster. With the exception of renting out infrastructure or when common projects are agreed upon, which could be economic activities, clusters themselves, as has been discussed for the other two countries (there referred to as science parks),[53] would probably not be regarded as undertakings because they are essentially just a space in which separate entities are located. Also, privately funded chairs are probably mostly not an economic activity. The interviewees explained that these are often not entirely privately funded. Instead, it was, in their experience, more common that private or third sector partners only contribute to existing chairs in a subject area. Even if they do help create a new chair, the academic is free to decide how to proceed within this area. This kind of institutional funding appears to enable independent research for better knowledge rather than being a service which could be commissioned on a market. It therefore seems likely to be non-economic in nature.

Research co-operations have been described as 'eye to eye' co-operations in which outcomes are shared fairly by providing the private partner with know-how and the researchers with publications. The project theme is decided upon between partners and researchers from both parties working together, often in the facilities of the universities. The details of such co-operations are agreed upon in contracts, in particular, who receives ownership of which results. Sometimes co-operations are co-financed through additional public funding. Yet, an interviewee from a category 1 university expressed that he is doubtful if it really is always a 'win-win' situation, as the private partners are sometimes overly influential in deciding the direction of research due to their financial investments and the involvement of their staff. They would also profit significantly from use of the infrastructure and from receiving the results. It is for this reason, as well as because the companies do not want their competitors to know with whom they cooperate, that these co-operations are sometimes kept at a low profile. He considered this as being potentially at odds with the mission of a university which involved disseminating research results and sharing research experiences with students. PPPs are, according to the interviewees, co-operations with the private sector for a longer term. They have been described as forums for intellectual exchange, common projects, reciprocal support and advancement to new areas. Such collaborations have framework agreements in place. Equally, they often receive additional public funding. University-industry research centres (*Universitäts-Industrie-Forschungs-Zentren*) were described as innovation centres with common infrastructure. Accordingly, they seem to be something in between PPPs and a cluster, sometimes with a special focus on entrepreneurs.

---

[53] See Sects. 5.3.2 and 5.4.2 above.

All these forms of collaborations need to be assessed on a case by case basis as to the question of whether an economic activity is taking place. If the research is taking place freely with the aim of generating knowledge and disseminating it at a pre-competitive stage and the universities have sufficient influence on the directions of research, the collaboration would be of a non-economic nature. If essentially the cooperative project is conducting a research service for the private sector partner, if the partner gets to use the university infrastructure beyond the level necessary for the projects or receives all the IPRs, it might be of an economic nature. This did not necessarily seem to be clear to the interviewees. Whilst a few interviewees pointed out that a differentiation between economic and non-economic activities needs to be made and that it can be difficult, many interviewees seemed to assume that co-operations are usually non-economic in nature (with which they also seemed to be more comfortable) and that in particular the involvement of additional public funding would automatically take the co-operation out of competition law.[54] One interviewee also said he assumed that the fact that one institution is particularly chosen because it might be the only university conducting a certain type of research, and therefore had no competitors, would mean that any involvement with them would not take place on a market which corresponds with the approach taken in public procurement law. As previously mentioned (Sect. 5.5.1) the interviewees in one category 1 university seemed to be the clearest on the fact that the economic nature of an activity need to be assessed for every individual activity. They pointed out that, in cases of doubt, they would assume it was an economic activity. In accordance with the Research Framework they would only assume a non-economic co-operation if both partners contributed equal amounts of work and when success and risks are shared and every partner owns their results. If one party retains all the results this would be an indicator of an economic activity and they would then apply full costs. However, while the Commission indeed declares in para 28 seq of the new Research Framework[55] that under such conditions it does not consider a collaborative project to constitute hidden state aid for the private sector partner, this does not necessarily mean that in such a case no economic activity is taking place and that other provisions of competition law cannot apply. This would still rely on the question if it was independent research for 'more knowledge and better understanding'.

An-Institute have been described by the interviewees as small entities which are independent, but with which the university keeps a close relationship and partly does cooperative research with. Often they are led by university academic staff, but without the university having supervisory powers over the staff in their managerial capacity in the *An-Institut*. Sometimes they were described as service sector

---

[54] This is in line with what the Commission assumed Member States would think (see European Commission 2012 p. 8) and thus attempted to clarify this in the new Research Framework in in para 15(h) and para 27. See further Chap. 3 Sect. 3.2.4.2 above.

[55] Then similar in Sect. 3.2.2 of the previous version of the Research Framework.

companies, sometimes as public entities. Spin-offs and other start-ups were also described as independent companies in which the universities might have shares but in which private partners are also involved. Often they are led by, or employ, university staff and they also often receive additional public funding. It was recognised by the interviewees that such entities need to differentiate between economic and non-economic activities. However, as they are independent entities, this was not necessarily regarded as a problem for the university. The universities could, however, conduct an economic activity, provided the external entity is doing so, through holding shares in them, through common projects as outlined above and through the process of spinning out and/or transferring IPRs in particular if private money is invested and not all income is reinvested into the primary activities.

As has been previously mentioned, contract research is clearly an economic activity of which the interviewees were also very aware. According to the interviewees, companies prefer this way of co-operation because it allows them to keep all the research results and it is therefore most common among the various collaboration forms.

5.5.3 Full Costing

The interviewees realised that full costing needed to be used in areas of economic activity. The interviewees also mentioned that the implementation period for full cost systems of the previous Research Framework had expired.[56] As some of the interviewees explained, to enable a real full costing method, the universities would need to change from governmental accountancy (*kameralistische Buchführung*) to double entry book keeping (*Doppelte Buchführung*) which would allow them to simulate an economic accounting system. This would, however, be both very difficult to achieve and a significant change for public accounting in universities in Germany. The universities were currently working on financially simulating a private sector company for the areas identified as economic in nature, using full costs for them and adding VAT. However, none of the universities under scrutiny had, at the time of the interviews, implemented a real full costing methodology. Instead they were using overhead rates in addition to direct costs which usually differed between subjects. Partly they were already able to prove the full costs for some of their activities the results of which had informed the overhead rates and they generally aimed at having real full costing systems in the future. Many stated that they often needed to sign a clause in agreements stating that they comply with state aid law.

---

[56] The previous Research Framework (n 43) in Section 10.2 compelled Member States to introduce changes to their costing and accounting systems of research organisation until 1 January 2009 which allowed them to separate costs of economic and non-economic activities in order to avoid cross-subsidisation.

Full costing is, according to the interviewees, not defined by a common approach or guidelines at the federal level or in three of the four *Länder* under scrutiny (Bremen, Baden-Württemberg and Berlin).[57] Bavaria seems to be the exception since a state working group has agreed a framework of how to separate accounts and calculate costs which formed the basis for the individual models. Some interviewees stated that they exchange information about their methodologies/rates with other organisations and that the approach used needed to be approved by a certified accountant. The accountants would generally approve the approach/rate rather than the price for every individual contract. The information exchange and the approval required may, according to some interviewees, have led to similar approaches and rates because the accountants usually approved systems for a number of universities and it was easier to suggest using the same scheme. Also accountants may be worried that it could look 'suspicious' if they approved rates which varied extensively between universities.

Conflicts with competition law in this respect could mainly occur if an area is erroneously classified as non-economic and costs and accounts are not separate and/or market price, full costs plus or the maximum economic benefit are not used. This could amount to hidden state aid or competitors could challenge unreasonably low prices as being predatory pricing. Also, publicly funded research might potentially be economic in nature and it would then not generally be sufficient that the public funder only covers the direct costs. Additionally, as many interviewees stated, the costing systems might not be completely sound yet. While the universities are currently working on this, it could in the meantime lead to unreasonable prices. Finally, if overhead rates are agreed upon between universities or are discussed to an extent beyond discussing which factors need to be included, this might potentially be regarded as anti-competitive in itself.[58]

5.5.4 *Market Foreclosure*

As in the other two countries (Sects. 5.3.4 and 5.4.4), no signs of market foreclosure could be detected for research in Germany.

---

[57] On the federal system as regards research policy see Chap. 4 Sect. 4.4.1.1 "The Governmental Structure".

[58] On anti-competitive information exchange systems see, for example, case C-7/95 P *John Deere* (Judgment of 28 May 1998, EU:C:1998:256). See also the English private school case discussed in Chap. 3 Sect. 3.3.2.1 above.

5.5.5 Refusal to Enter into Contractual Relations and Preferred Partners

The interviewees stated that partners are usually found through relationships of the researchers and that it is also topic dependent (i.e. who works on the subject at all). Generally, the universities would not have particular preferred partners nor exclude certain entities as potential partners. Some interviewees talked about the knowledge transfer chain whereby a researcher has an invention, for which the university gets an IPR, which then turns into a business idea and a spin-off in the region, ideally even in their own cluster. This would then be supported by receiving a preferential start-up license. Once it has grown, it offers internship opportunities, part time jobs for students and later employs graduates and gives research contracts to the university. Such a regional focus appears to be something that is theoretically aspired towards. However, this ideal chain would, according to the interviewees, rarely occur in practice because all sides will look globally for the best partners, especially in cutting-edge areas. In a focus group the issue was raised as whether co-operation with two or more competitors would be possible. Although interviewees were themselves unsure, as they were yet to experience the situation, they assumed if a certain amount of secrecy was adhered to this should still be possible. However, this would need to be carefully considered with an eye to the public mission of the university to disseminate knowledge. The only situation interviewees described in which the choice of partners may be limited or certain partners (regional or SMEs) compulsory were collaborations receiving additional funding, since this may be required by the funding rules. The only influence the universities have in this respect is pre-call lobbying. An interviewee working on aspects of knowledge transfer stated that this, to a degree, influences their co-operations because they like to cooperate with partners with whom they will receive additional public funding since this makes co-operation more attractive for the private partners.

The universities do not generally appear to anti-competitively exclude partners. Limitations seem to only derive from the public funding rules which will be discussed below (Sect. 5.5.11). Public regulations might also potentially be regarded as anti-competitive if they are based on a recommendation by a committee of experts from within the sector, unless the experts acted independently from interested undertakings and suitable governmental review took place.[59] The lobbying of, or advice for, the government regarding which areas to have calls in might potentially be viewed critically in this respect. Whilst it might also appear somewhat controversial that many co-operations are apparently based on personal

---

[59] See C-185/91 *Reiff* (Judgment of 17 November 1993, EU:C:1993:886) para 14 seq on the question of when expert committees can be regarded as an anti-competitive collusion under Article 101 TFEU. See also case C-35/99 *Arduino* (Judgment of 19 February 2002, EU:C:2002:97) para 34-37. For more see Chap. 3 Sect. 3.2.2 above.

relationships, this would probably not constitute a competition law infringement if no other potential partners are excluded, no preferential conditions are provided and full costing is adhered to. As one interviewee reported, the actual extent of relationships is also partly tested through questionnaires in order to avoid the impression of corruption or collusion.

5.5.6   *Economically Unjustified or Discriminatory Contract Conditions*

The interviewees explained that the universities try, as far as possible, to negotiate the right to publish results and to use experiences to inform teaching. Furthermore, they would insist on the right of the researchers not to be obliged 'to do anything they do not want to do' which according to some interviewees is also foreseen by statute. Otherwise they do not generally have any conditions. The private sector, on the other hand, might prefer to keep certain things secret and to retain IPRs. The exact details are then always negotiated in agreements which can vary. An interviewee from a category 3 university stated that he would find it helpful if they had standardised conditions or legislation prescribing details of university-private sector collaboration because the negotiations can prove very difficult and certain universities might give in more easily to private sector requests which provide them with a competitive advantage. Some interviewees mentioned that the rules of public funders might sometimes dictate conditions, for example, it might be required that the outcomes of a project will be brought to the market in the end and that this is done by an SME involved in the co-operation. There might also be different funding rates depending on whether the SME wants to retain the IPR. Other programmes may be tailored to regional co-operations. The universities themselves, in attempting to provide a good climate for entrepreneurs might offer special conditions in this respect, for example, for spin-offs.

From a competition law perspective, the condition that results should usually be made publicly accessible through publication or in teaching might technically qualify as anti-competitive if it cannot be considered normal business practise and is imposed by a collusion of HEIs or a dominant HEI upon other undertakings. However, there may be possibilities to exempt this or it may qualify as an 'ancillary restraint'[60] in particular as EU policy encourages wide dissemination. HEIs may also be able to use competition law against the private sector if it attempts to impose secrecy or other conditions upon them if this could be regarded as anti-competitive. Public funding rules might be more problematic. If the funded activity can be classified as economic in nature, rules providing advantages for certain undertakings or excluding certain undertakings from a collaboration could be

---

[60] See Chap. 3 (Sects. 3.2.2, 3.3.2 and 3.3.2.1).

regarded as anticompetitive behaviour or as state aid (Sect. 5.5.11 below). The same might be true for advantages provided by HEIs to start-ups if this happens selectively in an area of economic activity.

5.5.7 Anti-competitive Use of IPRs

As discussed in Chap. 4 (Sect. 4.4.2.3) inventions belong, according to the *Arbeitnehmererfindungsgesetz* (Employee Invention Act), which now also applies to HEIs, to the employer. The process in the universities is, according to the description of the interviewees, similar to the processes in the other two countries; researchers need to report inventions even if made in their spare time or while working in the private sector. The latter would, of course, be difficult to control, but such scenarios would also not occur that frequently. Some interviewees said that this may have occurred more often in the past before *Arbeitnehmererfindungsgesetz* applied to HEIs. Inventions are then assessed as to their suitability for exploitation and an IPR (usually a patent) is registered if applicable. The IPR is then sold or licensed to partners by contract which can take various forms from a patent pool and geographic licenses to having very small non-exclusive patents. Occasionally funding rules, specific laws or ethical considerations would lead the universities to give licenses for free to certain organisations or to everyone who wants it. In this respect an interviewee from a category 1 university described a project funded by a charity where the funding rules required that a license for a special food related invention would go to all third sector organisations who wanted it free of charge. The universities assign the right or licence it rather than exploiting it directly, except perhaps through a spin-off. They receive an income of which the inventor and the relevant school get a share or they might hold equity in spin-offs which are often founded by the relevant researchers. Some of the universities under scrutiny use an exploitation company to transact IPRs. Generally, IPR exploitation would still not be very common and could mostly be found in the natural and life sciences. Copyrights would, as mentioned in Chap. 4, always remain with the author, although certain exploitation rights might be with the employer.

In collaborations, universities have to negotiate IPR ownership and conditions which can, according to some interviewees, become rather tedious. It emerged from a focus group that large companies often want to receive all IPRs, register them themselves and keep them with related ones in 'patent families'. SMEs, on the other hand, are very keen to obtain the intellectual property without necessarily registering the right and they like to keep their research quite secretive until they have an actual product. Excepting contract research, where it is accepted that the partner gets the IPRs, the universities generally try to negotiate ownership of all the rights in order to be able to publish, use the knowledge in teaching, for financial benefits and to avoid state aid accusations. These aspects are more important in negotiations than the durations of licenses. Finally, funders may also have rules on the use of IPR.

As explained above (Sect. 5.5.2), the procedures of IPR exploitation in the universities as such would partly be of a non-economic and partly an economic nature. If the latter is the case, competition law problems might arise should universities offer special conditions or advantages to certain undertakings. However, there was no general indication for this, except for the afore-mentioned cases based on charitable considerations. These could perhaps be regarded as non-economic in nature in the first place or, if considered as problematic from a competition law perspective, there may be room for exemptions. With regards to IPRs generated in any form of collaborations, any economically unjustified limitations as to the use of generated IPRs could fall under competition law if an economic activity takes place. The universities insistence on being able to publicise the results may potentially be regarded as such if it is not common business practise and is imposed on other undertakings but, again, there might be exemption possibilities in particular considering that EU policy (e.g. in the Research Framework) encourages wide dissemination. When it comes to state aid law, whether or not the conditions of the Research Framework are fulfilled will have to be assessed on a case by case basis. In particular, universities may not transfer IPRs without receiving appropriate consideration reflecting market value as discussed in Chap. 3 (Sect. 3.3.5.3). While some of the interviewees mentioned that they are aware of this and negotiate accordingly, there might still be a risk that this is not always assessed correctly by referring to public funding rules and the assumption by some universities that additional public funding automatically makes a collaboration a non-economic activity.

5.5.8 Anti-competitive Research Co-operation

As in the Netherlands (Sect. 5.4.8), there did not seem to be any indication that research was begun at an unreasonably late stage which could be in breach of Article 101(1) TFEU, as discussed in Chap. 3 (Sect. 3.3.2.4).

5.5.9 Market Division

Some interviewees mentioned that the universities do coordinate to an extent regarding rare subjects. Accordingly, one university might continue to teach and research in one rare subject which another ceases to offer. The second might instead focus on another rare subject that the first university ceases to offer. This would be an economically more efficient use of decreasing resources. If there are economic activities within such a subject division and the 'coordination' amounts to an agreement or concerted practice this might constitute market division. However, if this would produce efficiency gains, there is, of course, the possibility of exemption under Article 101(3) TFEU and the relevant secondary legislation.

5.5.10 Limiting Markets

All interviewees stated that there are no quantitative restrictions to the amount of economic research their universities can conduct. Many interviewees expressed they would be concerned if too much economic research would be conducted because they did not regard this as the role of a university. They also pointed to the restriction inherent in the Framework Act for Higher Education (*Hochschulrahmengesetz*, HRG), discussed in Chap. 4 (Sect. 4.4.2.1), which states that there must still be sufficient capacity for research and teaching in the public interest. However, they also believed that the universities are still far removed from a stage where this would become a problem because universities have only started to generate private sector income and it does not yet account for a large percentage of all research. Limitation of markets, therefore, does not seem to be a problem in the universities under scrutiny and if, as some interviewees suggested, this should become necessary in the future to protect the capacity of public research and teaching as required by the HRG, this would firstly, only be an issue if agreed upon by universities or decided by a dominant university and secondly, could probably be covered by the exemption in Article 106(2) TFEU if there would be an appropriate entrustment act.

5.5.11 Commissioning of Research

The interviewees explained that there is much variation between calls from public funders as to who can apply. Sometimes they are limited to universities and sometimes a consortium of partners is required and they may even stipulate what kinds of partners need to be involved. Within a call, the rules applicable to the individual partners might also vary. Universities might only be allowed to apply for direct costs for their share of the research, while private partners apply with full cost, but do not get 100 % of them funded. Non-HEI research organisations can only apply under limited conditions. Some calls would also be clearly marked as commissioning research, are open to industry and those who tender are specifically alerted to the state aid rules.

If public calls constitute economic activities, they would need to be commissioned according to the *Altmark* criteria or the rules set out in the Research Framework which require them to be generally non-discriminatory and reflect market value. While this is apparently the case with some calls which are also clearly marked as contract research, other calls could potentially also be classified as economic in nature. An interviewee working on legal aspects also pointed out that the university is sometimes just given research contracts and that they would not examine whether this should have been commissioned as they assume this to be the responsibility of the public authority. As the university would potentially have to pay back illegally obtained aid, this could, however, also put universities at risk. In this respect more caution might thus be indicated.

5.5.12 State Aid Through Staff Knowledge

While, according to the interviewees, there are staff working in the private sector during research leave or a sabbatical and there are funding programmes for
such staff transfers between the universities and the economic sector for a limited
period of time, this is rather rare because, inter alia, a public interest in doing this
has to be proven and that is difficult. It is more common, though not frequent, that
members of staff have a side job in the private sector or work as entrepreneurs
having established their own companies out of the universities, often with the help
of the university or public funding initiatives. One interviewee, for example, mentioned state funding which pays half the salary of the member of academic staff
to allow them to work part time in the start-up. Some interviewees mentioned that
the universities may help through initially providing infrastructure or giving contracts to the start-ups or spin-offs, but with a view to the companies eventually
becoming economically self-sustainable. Often such support would be regarded as
starting help without returns being required, but if the investments are more significant, the universities attempt to agree some kind of payback to be received in due
course. The spin-offs/start-ups could also be beneficial for the university because
they may later involve them in common projects. Finally, Ph.D. researchers would
sometimes write their theses in co-operation with a company. In the latter case the
companies would often pay a scholarship and direct costs which, according to one
interviewee, allows them very cheap access to research results.

The interviewees explained that if staff work in the private sector they have to
notify the universities of the private sector role and its extent. For civil servants,
approval must be sought which may be denied if there is a conflict of interest (i.e.
if the work for the private sector is something which should be done in their main
activity). According to an interviewee working on business collaboration, this
assessment had been more relaxed in the past and has recently become stricter.
Since the employers own any inventions, companies may try to argue that they
own an IPR if it was made during the researcher's working time at the company.
As mentioned above, the universities will, however, always argue that any invention should belong to them as the invention could not have been made without
the expertise acquired during staff's public sector work. In some universities this
would also be contractually agreed and the *Arbeitnehmererfindungsgesetz* would
support this assessment. The private sector company may, however, get an option
right towards receiving a license for the usual fee. As regards general experience
and knowledge, staff can bring this freely into their private sector work without
any further obstacles because the main focus here is the transfer of knowledge and
the bringing of academic results to the market as actual products.

Universities try to protect themselves from private sector exploitation of IPRs
which could only be generated through the knowledge by seconded staff acquired
in the universities. This would, however, obviously, require the universities being
notified about IPRs which might not always be the case, since the universities
rely on inventions being reported by employees. Furthermore, knowledge is being

transferred beyond actual inventions leading to IPRs through staff or Ph.D. students working in the private sector and, additionally, there are even public initiatives supporting this. While the creation of a spin-off by the universities itself and with the sole aim of reinvesting all income into the primary activities is regarded as a non-economic activity by the Commission, this might end if the spin-off becomes privately owned. Additionally, all knowledge transfer beyond this may potentially be regarded as state aid, subject to the possibility of exemption especially as regards innovation aid for SME, because the private sector company in question exclusively benefits from the researchers knowledge and potentially from additional funding.

5.5.13 Exemptions

As has been discussed for the other two countries (Sects. 5.4.13 and 5.5.13), it is impossible to make a general determination of the potential for exemption under Article 101(1) TFEU, because it depends too much on the individual cases and, with regards to BERs, on market shares. Yet, as we have also seen in Chap. 3 (Sect. 3.3.2), especially the Technology Transfer, Research and Development and Specialisation BERs might be applicable.

As in the other two countries, the amount of funding provided through public calls differs, according to the interviewees, significantly from a few thousand Euros to up to €8 M per annum or even €20 M per annum for institutional funding through the Excellence Initiative.[61] As regards state aid, smaller projects could benefit from the *de minimis* rules unless aid cumulates above the relevant thresholds, the exemptions in the GBER and the SGEI Decision. As regards the SGEI Decision and the SGEI *de minimis* rule, the service in question would, of course, have to qualify as an SGEI (Sect. 5.5.14 below). When it comes to exemptions under the GBER the relevant conditions discussed in Chap. 3 (Sect. 3.3.5) would have to be fulfilled, especially as regards transparency. In Germany, as in the Netherlands, the amounts of funding provided are higher than in England and, therefore, there is more scope for potential aid falling outside of the exemptions. However, such measures, if classified as infringing the state aid provisions, might then still be able to utilise Article 107(2) and (3) TFEU as an exemption generally. As regards the especially relevant Article 107(3)(c) this would need to be evaluated in the individual case according to the guidelines in the Research Framework.

---

[61] On the Excellence Initiative see further Chap. 4 (Sect. 4.4.2.2 "Public Competitive Funding").

5.5.14 SGEIs

As mentioned in the previous section (Sect. 5.5.13) for some of secondary legislation to apply the services would have to qualify as SGEIs. In addition, potential
infringements might be exempted as SGEIs more generally under the conditions
mentioned above in the relevant sections for the other two countries (Sects. 5.3.14
and 5.4.14). The general opinion in the universities seemed to be that if the public
funder decides to fund a project it is therefore in the general interest. This would
be particularly so since the main outline of the programmes would need to be
agreed on by parliament and could be lobbied by researchers, even though a few
interviewees said that they did not necessarily always agree with the funders'
assessment of what was in the public interest. Research funded by the private and
third sectors was regarded by some as being in the funders' interest, even though
this could simultaneously also be in the public interest. From these statements, it
thus seems as if the universities would pursue research in the public interest as
well as in particular interests. Only the former could qualify as an SGEI. However,
as we have seen with the other two countries, it might require more than just such
an interest and clarity can only be achieved through a ruling by the Court. As
regards the question of whether the SGEI is entrusted to the universities, the interviewees named the HRG, the respective state laws, the constitution (with the academic freedom) and EU law, especially the Research Framework,[62] as acts
entrusting universities with the task of research. However, they only entrust them
with research in general rather than with specific tasks which they might conduct
as part of a research project and it may be questioned if this fulfils the requirements in the relevant SGEI legislation.[63] Potentially the grant agreements by public funders could be seen as such acts, though. Whether the application of
competition law would obstruct a potential SGEI, whether this would be proportional and whether the development of trade would be unduly effected, would
depend on the individual case.

5.5.15 Interim Conclusion

Since investments are high in Germany, the research funding situation was generally seen more positively compared to other countries. However, whilst generic
and DFG funding remain the most important sources and these allow researchers
to unfold their academic freedom, the increasing importance of steering calls was
regarded as somewhat problematic. It was also felt by some interviewees that universities suffer from a mission overload and that the current problems may lead to
less innovation, the extinction of certain subjects and a separation of teaching and

---

[62] Then in its previous version (see n 43).

[63] See n 49 above.

research. All interviewees were aware of competition law, however, the focus here was mainly the previous Research Framework's requirements of full costing and separate accounting for economic activities. The interviewees all explained that their universities differentiated between economic and non-economic activities. However, this determination might potentially not always be in accordance with competition law particularly since the involvement of public funding seemed to be regarded as automatically making an activity non-economic in nature.

If areas are erroneously identified as non-economic and thus are not appropriately accounted and/or neither market price, full costs or maximum economic benefit negotiated at arm-length are applied, this could amount to state aid or be regarded as predatory pricing. Exchange about costing systems, depending on what kind of information is exchanged, could also be anti-competitive. Universities do not seem to prefer partners in an anti-competitive way, even though public calls seem to sometimes require certain partners. In addition to this, lobbying attempts for certain calls might potentially be regarded as anti-competitive in some cases unless the 'procedural defence' discussed in Chap. 3 (Sect. 3.2.2) can be applied. The universities under scrutiny also do not seem to impose special duties, except, usually, a requirement to make results publicly accessible which, if regarded as anti-competitive at all, is likely to be exemptible considering that this is encouraged in EU policy such as the Research Framework. If other undertakings require universities to act in a way they do not wish to act, they may also be able to use competition law to their advantage. Public funding rules as well as universities providing advantages for certain undertakings or excluding certain undertakings from a collaboration, could potentially be regarded as anticompetitive behaviour or as state aid if in an area of economic activity. The procedures of IPR exploitation in the universities as such do not seem problematic from a competition law perspective. With regards to IPRs generated in collaborations, any economically unjustified limitations as to the use of generated IPRs could potentially fall under competition law. When it comes to IPR and state aid law, the conditions of para 28 of the Research Framework need to be adhered to in order to avoid state aid accusations. Problems with competition law could also occur, if universities divide workload along subject lines (some indication of which was found), if this amounts to an agreement or concerted practice in an area of an economic activity. Furthermore, if public calls are economic activities, they would need to be commissioned according to the relevant rules which in particular involves non-discrimination. Finally, special support for certain privately owned spin-offs or knowledge being transferred exclusively to one entity in an area of economic activity might potentially be regarded as state aid.

As in the other two countries, there might be exemption possibilities for potential infringements depending on the individual case. As regards Article 101(1) TFEU, especially the Technology Transfer, Research and Development and Specialisation BER may be useful, but there may also be exemption possibilities under Article 101(3) TFEU beyond this if there are efficiency gains. When it comes to state aid law, the sums provided for public research are higher than in England and thus there is more room for certain, potentially anti-competitive, public funding to fall outside the scope of the *de minimis*, GBER and SGEI legislation. As in the other two countries, it might also more generally be possible to exempt potential breaches of competition law as SGEIs under Article 106(2) TFEU. In this respect, as in the Netherlands, research is a statutory task, but the legislation establishing this might, in itself, not be precise enough to be regarded as an entrustment act. This might, however, be achieved by public grant agreements in some cases.

5.6 Conclusion

The chapter has shown that when it comes to the overall estimation of the research systems, the opinions of the interviewees differed. However, there were some common tendencies. In Germany there was a generally positive opinion of research funding, although the increasing importance of steering calls was regarded as somewhat problematic and it was felt that universities are suffering under a mission overload which could ultimately lead to less innovation, the extinction of certain subjects and a separation between teaching and research. The interviewees in the Netherlands, were more pessimistic as it was felt that public funding was shrinking and increasingly concentrated on certain areas and for research with impact. This was seen as causing tensions with academic freedom and as unduly limiting basic research. The problem of shrinking public funding, a strong focus on impact and concentration on certain institutions and areas, was expressed even more strongly in England. Whilst the interviewees in the latter country seemed to be understanding of the government's approach in general, it was said that it might be taken too far and that, academics especially, perceived this as creating unnecessary administrative hurdles and causing tensions with regards to academic freedom. In all three countries it was expected that the tendency towards more economically based approaches in research funding would continue.

The awareness of competition law also differed in the three countries under scrutiny. Whilst the interviewees in Germany were very aware of the necessity to implement full costing methodologies according to the previous Research Framework, the Dutch interviewees and the relevant legislation (Chap. 4, Sect. 4.3.2.4) presented a broader awareness of potential competition issues. The English interviewees, on the other hand seemed less aware of competition law themselves, but the policies followed seemed to have taken many aspects of potential issues into consideration. This seems to correspond with what has been discussed as regards the research systems in Chap. 4 (Sect. 4.6) more generally. In England, a more commercialised top-down system, it might have been required for certain adaptations to happen early on whilst not necessarily communicating the reasons to employees at every level. The Netherlands, being a consociational system with a medium degree of commodification, are increasingly considering competition law and involving these legal aspects into the research offices. Germany, which has only taken the first steps towards commercialisation of HEI research, is only just coming to grasp with competition law implications. Thus far this is limited to the most pressing concern of full cost calculation of which the research officers were, however, very aware drawing the distinction between economic and non-economic activities independently.

Generic public funding and most calls from public funders would probably be non-economic in all three systems. However, public funding which essentially is paid for a commissioned service, irrespectively of whether it is classified as a call or as the commissioning of a service, would be economic in nature. While contract research, consultancy and similar activities are arguably an economic nature, the differentiation between economic and non-economic activities would need to be made on an individual case basis in other collaborative forms with the private or third sector. These forms were relatively similar in the three countries. Whilst England and the Netherlands have advanced costing methodologies which in themselves do not pose competition law issues, German universities appear to mainly still use overhead rates. Nevertheless, in all three countries it appeared as if there were cases which would need to be classified as economic in nature and where full costs plus profit were not charged which could potentially be regarded as state aid or predatory pricing unless an argument could be made that this was the maximum economic benefit that could possibly be achieved in arm-length negotiations and it at least covered marginal costs.

Other potential constraints also seemed to be similar in the three countries. Universities do not seem to exclude partners unless, perhaps, due to ethical considerations or the rules of funders which might be regarded as anti-competitive if applied in an area of economic activity and imposed on undertakings by a collusion of universities or a dominant university, though there may be exemption possibilities or the former may be regarded as ancillary restraint. In Germany one might also wonder if governmental consultation of stakeholder when it comes to determining research agendas could be anti-competitive. Whilst it was also occasionally mentioned that lobbying took place in the other two countries, this appeared to take a less organised form. The universities in all three countries do not seem to impose any uneconomically justified contract conditions on partners, except perhaps for the requirement to allow them to publish. The latter seems generally unlikely to be regarded as anti-competitive, but, if it was, it could possibly be exempted especially as this is something that is required in EU policy, in particular in the Research Framework. If other undertakings require universities to act in a way they do not wish to act, they may also be able to use competition law to their advantage to fend this off. Generally, the procedures for IPR exploitation in the three countries seem to be unproblematic from a competition law perspective. Only anti-shelving clauses, the limitation of sublicensing or subsidies to companies willing to exploit university IPRs might be regarded as anti-competitive, but at least as regards the former there may be exemption possibilities. In collaborations, universities have to be careful to demand prices reflecting market value for any rights the partner obtains or exploits and neither side may impose economically unjustified limitations as to the use of generated IPRs. An issue that only came up in England was the question of whether the topic of a research project as such might be anti-competitive as an advantage would be conveyed on a particular company selectively by helping it to improve its market share.

There were also different degrees of potential market division. While this does not appear to be present in England, though certain infrastructure sharing arrangement might in some circumstances be problematic, there was some division in Germany, even though this might not actually amount to collusion captured by Article 101(1) TFEU. In the Netherlands, however, there seems to be a high degree of government supported concentration. Problems might also occur in all three systems if public calls would need to be classified as economic in nature, but do not fulfil the rules on commissioning which at least require non-discrimination and payment reflecting market value. Finally, if advantages are conveyed to companies through staff knowledge (in particular IPR creation), favourable contract conditions are given to staff owning companies or Ph.D. students are essentially conducting a study for the private sector, this could potentially be regarded as anti-competitive, if the activities in question are economic in nature.

The assessment of the potential of exemptions would have to be made on an individual case basis. Generally, as we have seen in Chap. 3 (Sect. 3.3.2) the Technology Transfer, Specialisation and Research and Development BERs could be useful, though the applicability of these would depend on market shares. Further exemptions according to Article 101(3) TFEU may be possible beyond that, if there are efficiency gains from the collusion. Regarding state aid, generally, many smaller projects in Germany and the Netherlands and most projects in England (as the funding levels are lower), might be able to benefit from the *de minimis* rules (unless aid accumulates beyond the thresholds), from the GBER (if the corresponding aid intensities and other conditions, especially on transparency, are adhered to) or from the SGEI Decision (if the projects could be classified as providing SGEIs). More generally, it might be possible to exempt some potential breaches as SGEIs under Article 106(2) TFEU. What seems most problematic in this respect may be that in England research is not a statutory task and in the other two countries, where it is, this may not be sufficient to qualify as an entrustment act. When it comes to public funding the individual funding agreements may, however, do qualify as such in some cases.

The next and final chapter will connect these results to the previous chapters and the overall situation of HEIs in Europe. It will then proceed to draw some further conclusions and discuss some future prospects.

References

BIS (2016) Success as a knowledge economy. Williams Lea Group, London
Burschel C et al (2004) Betriebswirtschaftslehre der nachhaltigen Unternehmung (English translation: Business administration tenet of sustainable enterprise). Oldenbourg Wissenschaftsverlag, München
Cable V (2010) Higher education speech. Gov.UK, London. https://www.gov.uk/government/speeches/a-new-era-for-universities

Carnap R (1991) Logical Foundations of the Unity of Science. In: Boyd R et al (eds) The philosophy of science. MIT Press, Cambridge (Mass)/London, pp 393–404

CHERPA-Network (2010) Design Phase of the Project 'Design and Testing the Feasibility of a Multi-dimensional Global University Ranking'. http://www.cheps.org/UMR_IR_0110.pdf

Edwards R, Stockwell N (2011) Trusts and equity, 10th edn. Pearson Education, Harlow

Erkkilä T (2013) Global University Rankings. Palgrave Macmillan, Basingstoke

European Commission (2012) Revision of the state aid rules for research and development and innovation. European Commission, Brussels

HMRC (2013) VAT: Supplies of research between eligible bodies 11/13. HMRC, VAT Info Sheet. https://www.aber.ac.uk/en/media/departmental/finance/pdf/VAT_+supplies+of+resea rch+between+eligible+bodies.pdf

Koller H-C (2009) Grundbegriffe, Theorien und Methoden der Erziehungswissenschaft: Eine Einführung (English translation: Basic concepts, theories and methods of educational science: an introduction). W. Kohlhammer Verlag, Stuttgart

Kuhn T (1991) Scientific Revolutions. In: Boyd R et al (eds) The philosophy of science. MIT Press, Cambridge (Mass)/London, pp 139–158

Lange R (2010) Benchmarking, Rankings und Ratings (English translation: Benchmarking, rankings and ratings). In: Simon D et al (eds) Handbuch Wissenschaftspolitik (English translation: Handbook Science Policy). VS Verlag, Wiesbaden, pp 322–333

Littig B (2008) Interviews mit Eliten - Interviews mit ExpertInnen: Gibt es Unterschiede? (English translation: Interviews with elites—Interviews with experts: Are there differences?). FQS 9:1–17

Locker-Grütjen O et al (2012) Definition für optimales Forschungsmanagement (English translation: Definition for optimal research management). Wissenschaftsmanagement 18:34–38

Mangen S (1999) Qualitative research methods in cross-national settings. Int J Soc Res Methodol 2:109–124

Martin JE (2012) Hanbury & Martin Modern Equity, 19th edn. Sweet & Maxwell/Thomson Reuters, London

Nurse P (2015) Ensuring a successful UK research endeavour. BIS. https://www.gov.uk/government/publications/nurse-review-of-research-councils-recommendations

OECD (2002) Frascati Manual. OECD, Paris

Patton MQ (2002) Qualitative research & evaluation methods, 3rd edn. Sage, Thousand Oaks/London/New Delhi

Yin RK (1994) Case study research, 2nd edn. Sage, Thousand Oaks/London/New Delhi

Chapter 6
Conclusion: Higher Education Institutions in the EU Between Competition and Public Service

Abstract The aim of this last chapter is to connect the results of the empirical study with the previous chapters thereby assessing how applying the EU's economic constitution to HEIs may lead to unforeseen consequences including further commodification which could endanger the traditional non-economic mission of European HEIs. The constraints faced by the sector are then contextualised in the wider debate and some recent attempts by the Commission to align EU research policy with competition law are critically discussed. It is concluded that these attempts seem equally insufficient, as they do not necessarily clarify the legal position, are still fragmented, are decided upon entirely by the Commission and do not appear to necessarily reflect the views of the general public or stakeholders in HEIs. Therefore, an outlook is given of potential alternative strategies, as unlikely as their realisation in the current Eurosceptic climate may be, for a more coherent EU level policy on HEIs which moves away from the current tendency towards commodification and truly clarifies the legal position of HEIs under EU law.

Keywords Economic and social integration in the EU · Commodification of higher education institutions · EU higher education and research policy · Universities and EU law · Spill-over · Competition law and higher education institutions · Services of general economic interest · Framework for state aid for research and development · General Block Exemption Regulation · University research in England, the Netherlands and Germany

Contents

© T.M.C. ASSER PRESS and the author 2017
A. Gideon, *Higher Education Institutions in the EU: Between Competition and Public Service*, Legal Issues of Services of General Interest, DOI 10.1007/978-94-6265-168-5_6

6.1 Introduction

This book has provided an in-depth appreciation of EU law constraints on European higher education institutions (HEIs) as an example of tensions between EU economic and social integration. It has been argued that exposure to EU (economic) law may compromise the wider aims that European HEIs traditionally pursue in the public interest. The analysis has been conducted using an interdisciplinary approach combining legal doctrinal and empirical research with insights from other disciplines such as political science and education studies; thereby contributing a distinctive legal dimension to existing research which is nevertheless grounded in research in other disciplines and in empirical study.

Chapter 1 illuminated the background of the tensions between economic and social integration as regards HEIs by explaining the traditional mission of European HEIs and by situating European HEI policy within the context of European integration theories. Chapter 2 then investigated the position of HEIs in European (EU and beyond) policy and the potential of spill-over from seemingly unrelated provisions of EU law. It has been shown that there is a tendency towards commodification of HEIs, inter alia, influenced by research and education policies at the European level. Nevertheless, despite increasing EU level activity in these policy areas, the main competences for research and education remain with the Member States. At the same time, their policy choices have to comply with directly applicable EU law which might cause spill-over potentially leading to more commodification. The first two chapters thus related the discussion of EU law constraints from potential spill-over of constitutionalised provisions of EU law to European integration theory explaining the theoretical foundations of such potential spill-over and linked the discussion of EU law constraints on HEIs to the discussion on the position of HEIs in Europe which takes place more widely in other disciplines, but had received only limited attention from a legal studies perspective, despite legal consequences having the potential to significantly influence the relevant policy areas.

In order to illuminate the potential constraints the subsequent chapters were dedicated to analysing this issue specifically for the area of competition law. As a first step in this endeavour Chap. 3 explored potential EU competition law spill-over on HEIs, a thus-far largely unexplored area, in an in-depth legal doctrinal analysis. Furthermore, the project included a comparative empirical study to test the findings of the legal doctrinal analysis on the systems of HEI research in three Member States chosen on the basis of their varying degree of commodification. As part of this study the research systems of England (UK), the Netherlands and Germany have been detailed and doctrinally analysed for their susceptibility to EU competition law in Chap. 4. This has then been complemented by an empirical phase in which the potential problems were tested against realities described by experts in research offices in a variety of universities chosen from three categories established on the basis of age and international ranking positions. To conduct the empirical study a novel framework had been developed based on the results of the general competition law analysis in Chap. 3 as well as on the results of the tentative competition analysis for the three countries in Chap. 4. Additionally, the interviewees were also questioned as to their awareness of competition law and on other constraints they might experience or foresee. The developed methodology of the empirical study and the results were presented in Chap. 5. The conclusions of the book are thus not only drawn from legal doctrinal analysis, but are also based on the realities of research funding in the institutions studied. Therefore, although a qualitative study is not representative, it does provide some insight into the problems universities actually face. This is not only interesting from an academic point of view, but might also make policy makers and professionals in HEIs aware of the potential consequences of the current developments. Additionally, the results and, in particular good practices, could be utilised by policy makers at national and at the EU level in order to circumvent potential problems in future policy settings. As such the findings have relevance beyond the universities and countries under scrutiny.

This last chapter will bring together the results from all previous chapters (Sects. 6.2 and 6.3), highlight more specifically the potential consequences and set these into the wider context (Sect. 6.4) thereby answering the research question of how EU law and policy (could) impact on the HEI sector with a specific focus on potential constraints from EU competition law on research in HEIs as an example of exposure to economic constraints. It will then proceed to briefly assess how more recent tentative attempts to align policies at the EU level affected the situation (Sect. 6.5) and discuss alternatives (Sect. 6.6) before a final conclusion (Sect. 6.7).

6.2 European HEIs and EU Law

As shown in Chaps. 1 and 2, European HEIs were first established in the Middle Ages as centres of learning and teaching which were later nationalised and, in the Humboldtian era, succumbed to a strong research mission. In recent decades HEIs have, again, undergone changes due to the introduction of mass higher education, increasing commodificaton and a stronger focus on internationalisation. The latter two trends have not gone unnoticed by policy makers at the EU level who originally had not concerned themselves with HEIs as the European project had started as an economic integration endeavour and the economic value of HEIs had not been initially apparent. At the same time, potentially due to the important value of HEIs in national culture and them being maintained by public funding, the Member States seemed reluctant to provide far reaching competences to the EU level and only equipped them with a supplementary competence in education and a shared competence in research, the latter only having been extended recently with the Treaty of Lisbon 2007 and containing a caveat in Article 4(3) TFEU. These limited consequences did not lead to, and in the case of education, indeed, explicitly prohibited, harmonisation. As this, nevertheless, appeared to have been

desired (to a certain extent), the Member States in cooperation with European
third countries agreed on the Bologna Process for the harmonisation of higher education systems. As regards research, despite the extended competences since the
Lisbon Treaty 2007, the main EU instruments remain funding and the Open
Method of Coordination (OMC).[1] Here, research and the role of HEIs for the
'knowledge based economy' have become increasingly important in the framework of the Lisbon/Europe 2020 Strategy with which the Framework Programmes
have now been streamlined in Horizon 2020. The soft law mechanisms (the
Bologna Process and the OMC) have attracted a variety of criticisms including the
legal and democratic concerns of the Bologna Process pointed out by Garben.[2]

At the same time, HEIs need to comply with other seemingly unrelated directly
applicable provisions of EU law such as those on Union citizenship, the fundamental freedoms, competition and state aid. As in other more social policy areas,
the retaining of competences at national levels with the simultaneous requirement
of abiding by EU (economic) law may thus lead to spill-over, as neo-functionalism
explains, of these provisions and influence national policy concepts on HEIs. This
assumption seems to have already been proven true by the citizenship cases of
Austria and Belgium,[3] discussed in Chap. 2 (Sect. 2.3.1.2), where the large net
influx of foreign students created pressures on the free and open access policies of
those Member States.[4] The possibility of HEIs coming within the ambit of the
more economic free movement provisions or competition and state aid law
increases with ongoing commodification and might in turn require even further
commodification. In the cases *Schwarz, Jundt* and *Neri*,[5] for example, the fundamental freedoms have already been applied to educational activities and required
changes in national tax policy in the former two and a change in diploma recognition policy in the latter case.

As explained in Chap. 3 (Sects. 3.2.1 and 3.2.4), for the competition and state
aid law provisions to be applicable to HEIs the latter would need to conduct an

---

[1] See also Ulnicane 2016, p. 229 seq.

[2] Garben 2010.

[3] C-147/03 *Commission vs Austria* (Judgment of 7 July 2005, EU:C:2005:427), C-65/03 *Commission vs Belgium* (Judgment of 1 July 2004, EU:C:2004:402).

[4] However, in C-73/08 *Bressol* (Judgment of 13 April 2010, EU:C:2010:181) the Court accepted seemingly unrelated concerns about the health care system as a justification, while keeping its general approach towards free movement (i.e. equal treatment with regards to access and the pos-sibility of differentiation as regards maintenance) intact. This was possible as in this case the free moving students were mainly studying medical subjects which, assuming they would return to their home states, could lead to a shortage of medical professionals. See further on citizenship and HEI policies Chap. 2 Sect. 2.3.1 and on *Bressol* Sect. 2.3.1.2 above.

[5] Cases C-76/05 *Schwarz* (Judgment of 11 September 2007, EU:C:2007:492), C-281/06 *Jundt* (Judgment of 18 December 2007, EU:C:2007:816) and C-153/02 *Neri* (Judgment of 13 November 2003, EU:C:2003:614).

economic activity.[6] The Commission recognised in Decision 2006/225/EC[7] and in a Communication on state aid and services of general economic interest (SGEIs)[8] that 'public institutions can also offer educational services which, due to their nature, financing structure and the existence of competing private organisations, are to be regarded as economic'.[9] In the Research Framework[10] the Commission provides guidance as to when research amounts to an economic activity. Accordingly, in particular, 'independent R&D for more knowledge and better understanding' is a non-economic activity, while, in particular, 'renting out equipment or laboratories to undertakings, supplying services to undertakings and performing contract research' are activities of an economic nature no matter as what they are labelled by the Member States. Therefore, HEIs in systems with a higher degree of commodification are more likely to conduct an economic activity and fall under the competition rules.

As regards EU competition and state aid law, there has so far only been a single case regarding HEIs which has not received full scrutiny due to the limited standing of the competitor who had brought the case before the General Court. The analysis here (Chap. 3 Sect. 3.3) thus had to be conducted mainly from a theoretical legal doctrinal perspective. This analysis resulted in the conclusion that, whilst the application of the competition rules might occasionally aid 'consumers' (students) or HEIs themselves, there are situations where they might have a detrimental effect on (social) national or HEI policies. The scholarship scheme which was challenged as price fixing in an US American case[11] discussed in Chap. 3 (Sect. 3.3.2.1) might be such an example, even though a compromise was found in the end and the case settled. It might also be conceivable that competition law will require national bodies distributing study places to be opened to institutions from other Member States of which the systems might not be capable. As regards research HEIs must, in particular, be careful to demand market prices, full costs plus profit or to negotiate at arm-length the maximum economic benefit in areas of economic activity to avoid state aid or predatory pricing accusations. Furthermore, public funders might have to commission research, if it had to be regarded as economic in nature, according to the *Altmark*[12] case law or the relevant rules in the Research Framework which both, at a minimum, seem to require non-discrimination and prices reflecting market values.

---

[6] C-41/90 *Höfner* (Judgment of 23 April 1991, EU:C:1991:161) para 21.

[7] Decision 2006/225/EC on the aid scheme implemented by Italy for the reform of the training institutions OJ [2006] L 81/13.

[8] Commission Communication on the application of the European Union State aid rules to compensation granted for the provision of services of general economic interest OJ [2012] C 8/02.

[9] Ibid para 28.

[10] Commission Communication 'Framework for State aid for research and development and innovation' OJ [2014] C 198/01.

[11] *United States v. Brown Univ.*, No. 91-CV-3274.

[12] C-280/00 *Altmark* (Judgment of 24 July 2003, EU:C:2003:415).

While arguably certain case law[13] might indicate some leniency of the EU institutions towards areas of primary responsibility of the Member States,[14] it is the national competition authorities who are now investigating most competition law cases and the national cases on educational institutions discussed in Chap. 3 (Sects. 3.3.2–3.3.4) seem to indicate that they are not reluctant to open proceedings. If HEIs would have to pay fines for the infringement of competition law, the question would also arise how or by whom these would be paid. On the other hand, strict compliance with the competition rules might commercialise the activities of HEIs even further. For example, if HEIs cannot fix tuitions fees at a low level, less well-off students might not be able to get into certain universities and if HEIs have to compete on a full cost level, those located in parts of the country with higher salary levels or those owning antique buildings would have a competitive disadvantage which they could not rationalise in a way private companies could whilst at the same time retaining their heritage and traditions. There are, of course, still exemption possibilities for infringements of competition law under Article 101(3), 107(2) and (3) and under Article 106(2) TFEU as well as the relevant secondary legislation. These might, however, not capture every situation and, in any case, it might make the conduct of HEIs increasingly complicated from a legal/administrative perspective.

6.3 Competition Law Constraints on Research in Germany, the Netherlands and England

In Chap. 4 we have seen that the research systems of Germany, the Netherlands and the UK differ in a variety of ways. The UK is a devolved state with four separate countries. England, which has been the focus of attention, is organised in a centralised and top-down fashion with strong elements of a liberal market economy. The UK's research spending has been relatively stable and below 1.75 % of its GDP over the last ten years. The private sector provides less than 50 % of all research funding which, nevertheless, makes the sector the largest funder. Whilst the public sector is the second largest funder, as in the other two systems, the UK relies to a larger extent on foreign funding. HEIs are by far the most important public research organisations in regards to which England is, in comparison with the other two countries, most progressed on the path towards commercialisation.

The Netherlands are a centrally governed, yet consociational system. Research spending has gone down from 2004–2008, but steadily increased since and is

---

[13] T-289/03 *BUPA* (Judgment of 12 February 2008, EU:T:2008:29), C-113/13 *Spezzino* (Judgment of 11 December 2014, EU:C:2014:2440), but potentially also cases like C-523/12 *Dirextra* (Judgment of 12 December 2013, EU:C:2013:831) in the area of free movement law.

[14] Similar Hatzopolous 2009, p. 236 seq; Sauter 2015, p. 142 seq; Gideon and Sanchez Graells 2016, p. 42 seq, 53.

now around 2 % of its GDP. The private sector is the largest research funder and conductor, followed by the public sector which contributes around a third of all research funding. Foreign and third sector spending plays a smaller role than in England, though together they still amount to around 15 %. While publicly funded research is mainly conducted by the 14 universities, there are also a variety of other research organisations including many collaborative organisations. The Netherlands have equally begun to introduce steps towards a more commercial system, but, as some interviewees expressed, they are some years behind England in this endeavour.

Research in Germany is characterised by a strong constitutional protection of academic freedom. As a federal republic, the states as well as the federal level play a role in devising research polices and providing research funding. Research spending is comparably high and has increased consistently over the last decade nearly meeting the 3 % target of the Europe 2020 Strategy. With about two thirds of funding coming from the private sector, the private sector is by far the biggest contributor of funding most of which is, however, also used for research conducted by the private sector. Publicly funded research is undertaken in four major non-HEI research organisations with clearly defined tasks and in HEIs. While these are still significantly publicly funded, first steps towards commodification have recently been introduced.

In Germany and the Netherlands, a large amount of public funding for HEIs is still provided generically without recourse to competitive factors such as performance or focus on government priorities. As generic HEI funding is a state competence in the former it differs between states to what extent performance indicators are used. In the Netherlands, consecutive governments have tried to make generic research funding allocation more reliant on performance indicators which, however, has continually met with resistance by the universities. In England generic funding allocation is conducted competitively on the basis of the REF (Research Excellence Framework) which systematically measures research quality, impact and environment. In all three systems non-generic funding (public as well as non-public) has increasingly gained in importance. While all three countries offer open public competitive funding, themed calls and priority areas have started to play a significant role and non-public funding is dependent on the intentions of the funder. The increase of such funding methods might thus pose a threat for purely curiosity driven research and academic freedom. Due to increasing non-public funding and requirements in the EU Framework Programme 7,[15] all three countries have begun to introduce full costing methods. While this is well developed in England where TRAC fEC[16] has been systematically introduced, the

---

[15] Decision 1982/2006/EC concerning the Seventh Framework Programme of the European Community for research, technological development and demonstration activities (2007–2013) OJ [2006] L 412/01.

[16] The full costing element of the centrally introduced Transparent Approach to Costing (see Chap. 4 Sect. 4.2.2.4).

introduction has taken place later in the Netherlands and every university has found its own system. In Germany many universities still do not seem have real full cost methodologies and are using overhead rates instead. Despite the differences regarding the introduction of full cost methods, universities in all three systems seem to struggle to actually receive funding at full cost levels from many funders.

As reported in Chap. 5, the attitudes of the interviewed experts (officers working on funding, policy and legal aspects of HEI research) towards the current state of the research systems in the three countries differed. While the interviewees in England generally seemed to be sympathetic to the idea that publicly funded research needs to be justified as to its use for society, it was expressed that current policy with shrinking public funding, its focus on impact and priority areas and concentration of funding might be taking this too far and that especially academics perceived this as creating unnecessary administrative hurdles and causing tensions with academic freedom. The interviewees in the Netherlands equally felt that public funding was shrinking and increasingly concentrated on certain areas and research with impact. This was regarded as causing tensions with academic freedom and limit basic research unduly. Interviewees in Germany generally saw the research funding situation more positively, as investments are high. However, some regarded the increasing importance of steering calls as problematic when it comes to academic freedom and it was felt that universities are suffering from a mission overload which could ultimately lead to less innovation, the extinction of certain subjects and a separation between teaching and research, despite these developments contradicting strongly how universities are traditionally conceived in the country. Many also felt that the growing importance of non-generic funding combined with the fact that such funding is mostly not provided at full costs levels, financially punishes successful institutions. In all three countries it was expected that the tendency towards more economic approaches in research funding would continue.

The awareness of competition law as a potential constraint for HEIs also differed in the three countries under scrutiny (Chap. 5 Sects. 5.3.1, 5.4.1 and 5.5.1 respectively). While the awareness of the interviewees in Germany seemed to focus on the necessity to implement full costing methodologies according to the previous Research Framework,[17] the Dutch interviewees and the relevant legislation (Chap. 4 Sect. 4.3.2.4) presented a broader awareness of potential competition law issues. The English interviewees, on the other hand, seemed less aware of competition law themselves, but the policies followed seemed to have taken many aspects of potential issues into consideration. This seems to correspond with the fact that England has a more commercialised top down system which might have required certain adaptations earlier while not necessarily communicating the reasons to staff in research offices. The Netherlands, being a consociational system

---

[17] Community framework for state aid for research and development and innovation OJ [2006] C 323/01.

with a medium degree of commodification, are increasingly considering competition law involving these legal aspects into the research offices. Germany, which only took first steps towards commercialisation of HEI research, is only coming to grips with the competition law implications. Thus far this is limited to the most pressing concern of full cost calculation of which the research officers were, however, very aware, drawing the distinction between economic and non-economic activities independently.

From a competition law perspective research conducted freely financed from generic public funding in all three systems would probably not fall under EU competition law as it constitutes 'independent R&D for more knowledge and better understanding' and it is difficult to imagine how this could be replicated under market conditions. Competitive public calls equally would probably not amount to an economic activity if they are completely open or just establishing a broad area of research. According to the interviewees, this appears to be the case for most public calls. However, there also appear to be calls in all systems which are very specific, essentially prescribing a service for which a provider is sought and which could be commissioned under market conditions. The latter could amount to economic activity and partly such research is also officially procured. A similar distinction would need to be drawn for third sector funding or private philanthropical contributions.

The forms of private sector collaboration are quite similar in the three systems. Some research funded by the private sector, such as contract research or renting out infrastructures, would have to be regarded as economic in nature. With other forms of private sector collaboration such as research co-operations, private funding of academic staff or Ph.D. researchers the lines are less clear cut and the distinction would have to be made on a case by case basis by asking if the research is amounting to a service which could be conducted under market conditions rather than as what it is labelled.[18] As regards the knowledge exploitation, the Commission in the Research Framework (para 19(b)) states that it will consider this as non-economic if handled by, with or on behalf of a research organisation (here HEI) and all income is reinvested. As we have seen in Chap. 3 (Sect. 3.2.4.2) the combined reading of para 19(b) and the definition of 'knowledge transfer' in para 15(v) is somewhat confusing and could potentially be understood as taking a vast amount of knowledge exchange out of the scope of competition law. As has been argued,[19] case law, other Commission documents[20] and the general conception of competition would indicate a narrower reading, however, including as non-economic activities only transferred knowledge that has resulted from non-economic research, is exploited non-exclusively by with or on behalf of the research organisation and the profits of which are reinvested. Thus this would in

---

[18] The Issue Paper (European Commission 2012) makes this particularly clear by pointing out that mere labelling of an activity as collaborative research does not necessarily make this non-economic in nature.

[19] Chapter 3 Sects. 3.2.4.2 and 3.3.5.2 above.

[20] E.g. European Commission 2012.

particular mean that the exploitation of IPRs, including by own spin-offs, resulting from non-economic research would be non-economic in nature under these conditions, while a consultancy contract conducted on request of an undertaking is not. In any case, exploitation that is not conducted by, with or on behalf of the HEI and where profits are not entirely reinvested, for example, in cases where venture capital firms are brought on-board, is economic in nature.

Whilst the advanced full costing systems in England and the Netherlands themselves do not pose competition law issues, the overhead rates used in Germany could potentially cause constraints, if they did not separate accounts and capture the actual full costs and thus left room for state aid through cross-subsidy and for predatory pricing. Furthermore, exchange about costing systems, depending on what information is being exchanged or commonly set rates, might be regarded as price fixing. More importantly, universities in all three systems do not necessarily appear to be charging full costs plus profit in areas of economic activity which (in the absence of market prices for that activity) could constitute state aid. The new Research Framework, alternatively, allows to charge the maximum economic benefit achievable which at least covers marginal costs. This may cover some of these cases. However, even then it is required that research organisations negotiate at arm length and make an effort to gain the maximum economic benefit rather than just submitting to the funders demands as appears to be partly the case. In particular, it was often mentioned that academics would too easily submit to such demands by companies as they are not necessarily aware of the implications. It has also been mentioned in England that some universities[21] would consciously try to undercut prices to gain research contracts to the detriment of others (universities or other research providers) which are unable or unwilling to do so which thus could be regarded as predatory pricing if the universities are dominant.

While the exclusion of partners from economic forms of collaboration might be regarded as anti-competitive, there were generally no signs of this in the three systems except for ethical considerations or funders rules. In Germany, there seemed to be rather extensive governmental consultation of stakeholders when it comes to determining research agendas which one might wonder if could be anti-competitive. In the other two countries lobbying research funders or policy makers also seemed to take place, but to a less organised extent. The universities in all three countries do not seem to impose any economically unjustified contract conditions on partners, except perhaps for the requirement to allow publication. The latter, if it was to be regarded as anti-competitive at all, could probably be exempted, in particular since EU research policy (e.g. in the Research Framework) regularly requires wide dissemination. As regards IPR exploitation the universities in all three systems generally do not seem to act anti-competitively. Occasionally, conditions such as anti-shelving clauses or the limitation of sublicensing could be regarded as unduly limiting the companies behaviour and thus as anti-competitive

---

[21] This has been remarked about competitors rather than the universities under scrutiny themselves.

or subsidies to companies willing to exploit university IPRs might be regarded as state aid. However, it might be assumed that at least the former could potentially be exempted, if one considers the general aim of research policy at national and EU levels to actually bring research to the users. When it comes to the exploitation of IPRs generated as part of a co-operation, the Research Framework determines that compensation at market price levels has to be paid for all IPRs which are retained by the private sector partner[22] which generally seems to be the case in the universities under scrutiny.

In England one interviewee mentioned that the topic of an envisaged co-operation was to increase the market share of a certain company. In this respect one might wonder if the topic as such makes this co-operation anti-competitive, as it could be regarded as selectively conveying an advantage on an undertaking from state resources at least if there was no compensation. In Germany and the Netherlands, on the other hand, there were signs for potential market division. While division of the subject market in Germany might not actually amount to an agreement or concerted practice under Article 101(1) TFEU, market division seems rather common in the Netherlands and is officially supported by the government which might become problematic. Problems might occur in all systems if the *Altmark* criteria or the rules laid down in the Research Framework are not adhered to when the state is commissioning economic research. As the eligibility criteria appear to differ between calls and funders, this would need to be assessed on a case by case basis. Finally, if advantages are being given to companies through staff knowledge, in particular IPR creation, favourable contract conditions given to staff owning companies or Ph.D. students essentially conducting a study for the private sector, this could potentially be regarded as anti-competitive, if economic in nature. In Germany protection against this appeared to be highest by, in particular, prescribing that any IPRs created in such a relationship would belong to the universities, whilst in England especially certain externally funded Ph.D. studies seemed questionable. Overall, there are thus areas in the three systems where spill-over from EU competition and state aid law may occur.

In cases of potential infringements, there is still the possibility of exemption according to Articles 101(3), 107(2) and (3) and 106(2) TFEU and the relevant secondary legislation. The assessment of this would have to be made on a case by case basis. As regards potential infringements of Article 101(1) TFEU, especially the Technology Transfer, Research and Development and Specialisation Block Exemption Regulation can be considered, if the market share thresholds are not met and the infringements do not fall under the excluded hardcore restrictions. When it comes to potential infringements of state aid law, generally, many smaller projects in Germany and the Netherlands and most projects in England (as the

---

[22] The private sector partner could also pay for the entire collaboration or receive IPRs reflecting the work packages conducted by the private sectors partner.

funding levels are lower), might be able to benefit from exemptions/exclusions such as the *de minimis* rules, the GBER[23] or the SGEI Decision.[24] However, in the case of the general[25] or SGEI *de minimis* rule,[26] the aid to one undertaking must not accumulate above the thresholds of €200,000 and €500,000 respectively over any period of three fiscal years. As regards the GBER the relevant conditions have to be fulfilled; in particular the corresponding aid intensities have to be adhered to and rules on transparency followed. The latter might make it unlikely that hidden aid through inappropriate costing can be exempted. For an exemption of aid under the SGEI Decision and the SGEI *de minimis* rule as well as for an exemption under Article 106(2) TFEU generally, the projects would have to be classified as providing SGEIs. For this, in addition to a general interest, there would need to be an entrustment act. While there is legislation making research a statutory task in Germany and the Netherlands, this legislation might be too general to fulfil the requirements for entrustment acts set out by the Commission.[27] In all three countries, entrustment acts might be seen in the actual call or agreement if the funder is a public sector institution. However, overall, the exemptions might not capture every situation and, in any case, might make the conduct of HEIs increasingly complicated from a legal/administrative perspective.[28]

6.4 Constraints Faced by the HEI Sector

Whilst the results of the empirical study, of course, just give an impression (as, being a qualitative study of a small number of universities, the study cannot be representative for all HEIs in Europe), the observation of the interviewees mentioned earlier do match the general tendency towards commodification regarding

---

[23] Commission Regulation 651/2014/EU declaring certain categories of aid compatible with the internal market in application of Articles 107 and 108 of the Treaty (General Block Exemption Regulation) OJ [2014] L 187/1.

[24] Commission Decision 2012/21/EU on the application of Article 106(2) of the Treaty on the Functioning of the European Union to State aid in the form of public service compensation granted to certain undertakings entrusted with the operation of services of general economic interest OJ [2012] L 7/3.

[25] Commission Regulation 1407/2013/EU on the application of Articles 107 and 108 of the Treaty on the Functioning of the European Union to de minimis aid' OJ [2013] L 352/1.

[26] Regulation 360/2012/EU on the application of Articles 107 and 108 of the Treaty on the Functioning of the European Union to de minimis aid granted to undertakings providing services of general economic interest OJ [2012] L 114/12.

[27] See, for example Article 4 of Decision 2012/21/EU. See also the secondary legislation referred to in Chap. 3 Sect. 3.3.5 text surrounding n 275–279.

[28] This is exemplified by, for example, compliance in the form of beginnings to introduce full costing and separate accounting in Germany in line with the previous Research Framework despite this being difficult to be combined with public accounting in that country.

HEIs examined generally in Chap. 1 (Sect. 1.3.3) and for the three systems in Chap. 4. This tendency has been reinforced through EU policy on HEIs; especially regarding research policy and since the alignment of Europe 2020 and the Framework Programmes in Horizon 2020.[29] The consequences (aside from potential legal consequences) have been analysed and been regarded critically by many, often in line with what the interviewees expressed. Enders, for example, assumes an increase in productivity (measured in publications and patents). At the same time, he also assumes that the relative homogeneity of (in his analysis German) universities will change towards more differentiation and that there will be a stronger divide or even competition between research and teaching.[30] Jansen also sees the differentiation amongst HEIs, especially the concentration of resources in already strong HEIs as problematic, as these strong HEIs make it increasingly difficult for others to survive and for newcomers to enter the 'market'. Furthermore, Jansen points to the fact that certain areas of research are more favoured than others and that this will affect the directions of research traditionally decided autonomously by the researchers.[31] Schubert and Schmoch as well as Albrecht fear that while research might become more economically efficient, the market-like structures could lead to subjects regarded as less relevant dying out and a strong tendency towards applied research, which might restrict future long term innovation.[32]

This tendency might actually go so far that basic curiosity driven research becomes a luxury that needs to be earned as advocated by De Fraja[33] who develops a model where HEIs are to receive a governmental block grant for which they need to conduct a certain amount of applied research. Only if funding remains after having done so, they may use the surplus for basic research. If the 'social value of applied research is sufficiently high'[34] HEIs can receive more funding for additional applied research which will, however, always be provided below full-cost levels and thus require HEIs to match. The latter is to encourage HEIs to also use their 'savings' for applied research as that would be co-funded whilst basic research would not. This model seems precarious not only because of the overwhelming limitation of basic research, but also from a competition law perspective as it is

---

[29] See, for example, Communication from the Commission to the European Parliament, the Council, the European Economic and Social Committee and the Committee of the Regions 'Research and innovation as sources of renewed growth' COM/2014/0339 final. See also Chap. 2 Sect. 2.2. above. Similar also Garben 2012, pp. 6, 20 seq; Beech 2013; Ulnicane 2016, pp. 331, 334, 336 seq.

[30] Enders 2007, p. 27 with further references, similar Holmwood et al. 2016 p. 26 seq.

[31] Jansen 2010, p. 45 seq; similar Holmwood et al. 2016, p. 26 seq.

[32] Albrecht 2009, p. 8 seq; Schubert and Schmoch 2010, p. 252 seq; similar Holmwood et al. 2016, p. 26 seq.

[33] De Fraja 2011.

[34] Ibid p. 4.

generally advocating to '"co-fund" [...] in contrast to the "cost-plus" approach'[35] without differentiating between economic and non-economic activities.

Another worrying aspect is the increasing use of targeted calls imposing certain research themes currently deemed relevant, as this seems to infringe the academic freedom. In Germany, where academic freedom is even to be found in the human rights catalogue of the constitution (Article 5 *Grundgesetz*), one might wonder if such developments might at some point become unconstitutional. Furthermore, one might wonder more generally if such steering policies are steering in the right direction and if short term political goals should be imposed upon academic research which develops over decades rather than until the next election, as this might, again, hinder innovation long-term. After all, as Beech phrases it, 'scientists throughout European history have traditionally been driven in their work by curiosity [...] [and] it is this blind and often serendipitous pursuit of knowledge that has been behind many of the greatest scientific breakthroughs of the modern world'.[36] Additionally, the research by Leisyte, Enders and De Boer might question the effectiveness of steering policies, as their empirical research suggests that creative proposal writing allows researchers to do the research they would have done anyway just with a much higher administrative effort.[37]

Some interviewees had also pointed to the negative effects on employment situations and opportunities for early career researchers. Accordingly, it was often easier to hire external companies than employing a research assistant for short term assistance and funding opportunities for post-docs are rare which leads young researchers to leave academia. These concerns link to a general debate on the divide between management and academic staff.[38] In this respect the proposal in the Stern Review that research stays with the university may be noted which is intended to diminish staff poaching before the REF cut off days,[39] but thereby arguably removes ownership of academic staff of their research and thus limits their bargaining power. Furthermore, commercialisation of HEIs can also lead to other issues in the relationship between staff or between staff and students in that unacceptable behaviour might not always lead to appropriate consequences if the individual in question has a good research track record or a large grant income.[40]

---

[35] Ibid p. 4.

[36] Beech 2013.

[37] Leisyte et al. 2008. See with respect to the REF in England similar Holmwood et al. 2016, p. 31 seq.

[38] Catcheside K, 'The growing divide between academic, administrative and management staff' guardian.co.uk (23 June 2011) http://www.theguardian.com/higher-education-network/higher-education-network-blog/2011/jun/23/ucu-sally-hunt-academic-admin-divide Accessed 11 July 2011.

[39] Stern 2016, p. 34.

[40] Weale S and Batty D (2016) Sexual harassment of students by university staff hidden by non-disclosure agreements. The Guardian, 26 August 2016 https://www.theguardian.com/education/2016/aug/26/sexual-harassment-of-students-by-university-staff-hidden-by-non-disclosure-agreements. Accessed 15 September 2016.

All this is shows that commodification of HEIs is problematic as HEIs as institutions are fundamentally different in nature to businesses. It is difficult for them to rationalise in the same way private companies could and to remain true to their mission and history. Increasingly commercialised research might also be questionable as it might hinder free, unbiased innovation. An example would be the increasing focus on generating intellectual property when the use of patent law as an incentive to innovate has generally been questioned.[41] As regards non-public funding there is, additionally, the concern about conflict of interest. Friedman and Richter,[42] for example, found a strong correlation between conflict of interest (i.e. financial relationships with companies)[43] and publication of findings in favour of said companies in their study on medical research and Lemmens and Dupont have pointed to the questionability of commercial cooperation in the alcohol or illegal drug business.[44]

Whilst the above was focussed on constraints regarding research in HEIs, as this aspect was the focus of this book, there are also questionable points in the commercialisation of the education aspect of HEIs, some of which have been discussed in Chap. 1 (Sect. 1.3.3). As with research, the commodification of the educational aspect of HEIs is taken especially far in England. Here the debate if the customer-provider relationship is suitable for higher education has already been raised in the popular debate after earlier policy changes.[45] We have also seen that in this country the tensions with competition law may be particularly strong (Chap. 3 Sects. 3.3.2–3.3.4) which seems verified by the fact that the competition authorities have already shown an interest for the sector.[46] In the competition authorities' reports it has, for example, been raised that there should be a baseline level of quality for all providers which should be kept to a minimum (including mainly information requirements to inform the student consumer) to allow entry of new competitors and create a level playing. It has further been recommended that there should be risk based review (thereby de-regulating the system), equal sanctions for all providers and an exit regime since exit has to be an option in a competitive market.[47]

In addition to general policy ambitions existing in that direction anyway, the assessments of the competition authorities now played a role in the new legislative proposals where many of the recommendations seem to have been included[48] and which will take the HEI system even further in the direction of commodification;

---

[41] Thambisetty 2013.

[42] Friedmann and Richter 2004.

[43] For the exact definition used see ibid p. 52.

[44] Lemmens and Dupont 2012.

[45] See, for example, Coughlan S, 'Is the student customer always right?' BBC News (28 June 2011) http://www.bbc.co.uk/news/education-13942401 Accessed 11 July 2011.

[46] OFT 2014; CMA 2015.

[47] OFT 2014, p. 72 seq; CMA 2015 para 5.24 seq.

[48] BIS 2015, p. 42 seq; BIS 2016b, p. 21 seq.

exemplifying the circle of commodification in national policy, application of and therefore spill-over from (EU) economic law and more commodification as a result. That many stakeholders have voiced negative opinions during the consultation on the Green Paper, especially on the market based approach including, for example, the negative academic consequences of letting non-teaching bodies validate as suggested,[49] seems to have been widely ignored.[50] Instead, the new White Paper makes clear reference to HEIs as part of the economy and students as future workforce and sees any problems in the system as due to insufficient competition and choice, inter alia, referring to the CMA report.[51] Furthermore, it aims to introduce a similar competitive generic funding allocation system as the REF for teaching (Teaching and Excellence Framework, TEF) which will be based, to a large extent, on metrics such as student surveys, proportion in employment and high skilled employment.[52] These rather drastic changes (on top of previous ones) have been considered 'a major assault on'[53] or a 'degeneration of'[54] the idea of the university due to the vast commodification envisaged, the arbitrary metrics considered for the TEF (e.g. graduate employment has also to do with factors as gender and ethnicity leaving HEIs with a more diverse student body potentially with less funding), the precarious situations which students may face in cases of market exit of an HEI, the resulting inequality, high levels of debt through the loan system, the power shift from academics to management and the fact that the role HEIs traditionally pay in a local community cannot be fulfilled by private providers.[55]

Whilst the tendency towards commodification is especially pronounced in England, measurability, standardisation, homogenisation and commodification of higher education have been recognised as general global trends.[56] In Europe after the financial crisis there has, in addition, been criticism of reductions in public investment into education, especially as regards tertiary education, and a limited interest/not sufficient attention for the subject matter at the EU level.[57]

---

[49] BIS 2016a, pp. 5, 31, 34, 39, as regards research see pp. 51, 53 seq. It is also interesting to note that, while responses could be sent by anybody, the focus groups do not seem to have included students or academics (ibid p. 4).

[50] The White Paper seems to have largely taken over the proposals in the Green Paper (see BIS 2015, p. 42 seq; BIS 2016b, p. 21 seq).

[51] BIS 2016b, p. 7 seq, 15, 23.

[52] BIS 2016b, p. 40 seq.

[53] Holmwood J (2016) HE White Paper plans place the market, not students, at the heart of the UK HE. THE, 20 May 2016 https://www.timeshighereducation.com/blog/he-white-paper-plans-place-market-not-students-heart-uk-he. Accessed 23 May 2016.

[54] Holmwood et al. 2016, p. 22.

[55] Boxall M (2016) Higher education white paper: the big changes. The Guardian, 16 May 2016 https://www.theguardian.com/higher-education-network/2016/may/16/higher-education-white-paper-the-big-changes. Accessed 23 May 2016, Holmwood (n 53), Holmwood et al. 2016.

[56] Kamola and Noori 2014, p. 600 seq.

[57] Vandenbroucke and Vanhercke 2014, pp. 9, 11, 22, 102.

The legal constraint arising from directly applicable EU economic law discussed previously in this book for both aspects (research and education) might reinforce the commodification tendencies, something that, as just observed, seems to have already taken place in England.[58] This tendency can go beyond European or national economic law. Education already falls under the General Agreement on Trade in Services[59] and might be affected by other international trade laws which, again, might have unforeseen consequences and could further commodification. In this respect, concerns have especially been raised with regards to the Transatlantic Trade and Investment Partnership which has been described as a 'profound threat to public services in general, including education, leaving them wide open not only to greater privatisation but making it harder for any future government to regulate'.[60] Arguably the new discourse around free trade as a result of the BREXIT decision in the UK will also open up a new discussion on the role of education as a service.[61]

6.5 Tentative Alignment of Research Policy and State Aid Law as a Way Forward?

This book has analysed the (potential) tension between national policies and EU law; notwithstanding the observed (Sect. 6.2), more recent, tendency of the Court to be slightly more lenient in areas of primary responsibility of the Member States. In particular, it has been observed that, when Member States start implement commodification policies, the economic provisions of EU law become more readily applicable and may lead to further commodification. Furthermore, it has been discussed (Chap. 2 Sect. 2.2) that the EU has limited competences in research and education and that therefore policies in this area seem to be additional and next to the national policies and other areas of EU (hard) law. In this regard the new Research Framework and GBER appear to be somewhat of an exception in that they are more aligned with EU research policy. This might be due to the fact that the EU has slightly broader competences in research policy after the Treaty of Lisbon. It may have also to do with the fact that a more market based approach in research is advocated in the EU's own research policy and, therefore, it is felt

---

[58] The national competition authorities appear to have considered the situation generally under competition law not making a specific difference between national and EU law since they essential prohibit the same kind of practices (anticompetitive collusion and unilateral conduct) and national competition authorities are also responsible for the enforcement of EU competition law as we have seen in Chap. 3 Sect. 3.3.2 above.

[59] Kamola and Noori 2014, p. 599.

[60] UCU (2016) Fighting privatisation in tertiary education. https://www.ucu.org.uk/stopprivatisation. Accessed 11 March 2016.

[61] However, this may not be a clear cut approach, since it is goes alongside discussions to limit the number of non-EU (possibly in the future non-UK) students admitted to UK universities.

that this needs to be taken into consideration to a greater extent when assessing if a certain conduct infringes the state aid rules. In the following we will have a brief look at this tentative alignment in these two instruments.

The new Research Framework (in para 2) makes an explicit connection to Article 179 seq TFEU and in para 3 to the Europe 2020 Strategy. It is remarked that the Europe 2020 Strategy identified 'research and development ("R&D") as a key driver for achieving the objectives of smart sustainable and inclusive growths' and that it is further noted 'that State aid policy can "actively and positively contribute … by promoting and supporting initiatives for more innovative, efficient and greener technologies, while facilitating access to public support for investment, risk capital and funding for research and development"'.[62] The Commission also explicitly made clear that redistributive Union research policy is to be regarded as *lex specialis* and thus does not need to be exempted from the state aid rules (para 9). The same is included in para 26 of the preamble of the GBER. As we have already observed (Chap. 3 Sect. 3.3.5), both instruments broaden the exemptions from the state aid rules. In particular, the exemption thresholds have doubled in the new GBER and it includes various new aid categories (e.g. process and organisational innovation aid, aid for innovation clusters and aid for research infrastructures).[63] Further, it does not exclude ad hoc aid for large enterprises anymore and commercial revenues from prototypes no longer need to be offset with the aid. In addition, under both instruments prototypes might be classified as applied research rather than as experimental development, thereby allowing higher aid levels for prototype production. The new Research Framework is equally more generous than its predecessor, as it, for example, allows broader evidence for market failure and assumes fulfilment of certain conditions if the project is co-funded by the EU. Finally, unlike the old Research Framework, the new Research Framework has no expiry date, but can be reviewed by the Commission at any time for any justified reason (para 129) allowing the Commission more flexibility in changing and adapting the new framework.[64]

---

[62] Such alignment with the Lisbon 2020 aims as well as consideration of the financial crisis has already been foreseen in the Mid-Term Review (European Commission 2011, pp. 1, 8). It has also been said that the Member States should be encouraged to utilize the exemptions provided in the Research Framework and the GBER further (ibid p. 7). Equally the Issue Paper envisaged alignment with Europe 2020 and Horizon 2020 declaring the intention 'ensure that it [the new Research Framework] sufficiently caters for the Europe 2020 objectives' (European Commission 2012, pp. 2, 6 seq).

[63] Article 4(1)(j), (k) and (m) GBER.

[64] This might have been due to the experiences during the long revision process. The Research Framework was due to expire on 31 December 2013, however, in Commission Communication concerning the prolongation of the application of the Community framework for State aid for research and development and innovation OJ [2013] C 360/1 the Commission extended its applicability until 30 June 2014 to allow more time for revisions.

This then leads to the question whether such an alignment as in these two instruments is indeed the way forward? While the new rules are providing more leeway to HEIs when it comes to exempting potential state aid in line with the aims of European research policy which advertises public-private cooperation and increasing innovation and exploitation of research results, this does not appear to necessarily have made things easier for HEIs. In particular, to delineate between economic and non-economic activities seems rather complex as has been discussed in detail in Chap. 3 (Sect. 3.2.4.2). While there was confusion, in this respect before, which might in fact have been clarified by the new Research Framework making clear that research services are economic in nature no matter as what they have been labelled, other areas (e.g. the new ancillary activities and knowledge transfer) still seem far from clear. Further, while it is helpful that the new Research Framework clearly states that economic research needs to be procured and provides more leeway in costing by allowing an at arm-length negotiated price covering marginal costs rather than insisting on full cost plus, the interpretation of the details of these rules are left to the HEIs. Especially the determination of when a negotiation can be seen as having been held at arms-length might in fact be more complicated than simply insisting on full-costs plus.

HEIs are required to make these assessments in order to decide whether they need to notify any financing they provide or receive. Despite the state being responsible for notifying aid in the latter case in the first instance, HEI should also have an interest therein as they are the ones who have to pay any unduly obtained aid back. As we have seen (Sect. 6.3 and Chap. 5 Sects. 5.3.1, 5.4.1 and 5.5.1 respectively), the awareness of competition law as a potential constraint for HEIs generally differs in different countries depending on the general governance systems employed and the new rules can lead to confusion here or may potentially even discourage HEIs from entering into a collaboration. The latter point had been addressed by the OFT (Office of Fair Trading, previous UK competition authority) who had, despite not having found sufficient evidence of actual anti-competitive behaviour (though the OFT had not investigated state aid), noticed fears and uncertainty about applicability of competition law and when a practice may be anti-competitive.[65] This underlines what has been found in Chap. 5 (Sect. 5.3.1); namely that there appears to be little awareness/understanding for competition law in England and it may be assumed that England is not the only EU Member State where this is the case. Yet, especially with further commodification, such assessments may more frequently have to be made. To stay within the rules may also require further commodification (e.g. through procurement of more research services where commercial providers can participate).

---

[65] Suarez 2014.

In addition, it still seems a very fragmented approach to rely on individual pieces of secondary legislation. While, as Szyszczak observes,[66] this tendency towards fragmentation of policy in areas of EU social law may be the only pragmatic way towards firming up a harder policy, it arguably lacks a coherent strategy when it comes to the applicability of EU law to HEIs.[67] Furthermore, the approach is also questionable from a democratic perspective as currently the balancing seems to have been made entirely by the Commission, since the two pieces of secondary legislation discussed are a Commission Communication and a Commission Regulation. As regards the Research Framework, it has to be noted that a Commission Communication is obviously only soft law. However, that does not necessarily resolve the concerns. As Ştefan[68] explores Commission soft law can create perceived binding effects or even binding effects and is indeed more difficult to challenge in the Court. While the Commission did have a consultation procedure,[69] this is arguably an insufficient replacement for rule-making under a proper legislative procedure, in particular if one considers the various voices in and outside academia raising concerns against the current more economic tendencies in EU research and education policy as discussed above (Sect. 6.4). The present situation with legal constraint arising from directly applicable EU law discussed in Chaps. 2–5 as well as the limited attempts to align the EU research policy (which in itself promotes commodification) with directly applicable EU law reinforce these criticised commodification tendencies.

6.6 Towards an EU Level HEI Policy Beyond Economic Integration

As mentioned above (Chap. 1 Sect. 1.3.4 and Chap. 2 Sect. 2.2.1), European integration began as an economic integration project, as it was assumed that this would automatically also lead to 'an increase in stability, an accelerated raising of the standard of living and closer relations between the states belonging to it' (Article 2 EEC). If, however, economic integration was seen as a means to an end in that sense, there is no necessity to limit EU law to economic competences.[70]

---

[66] Szyszczak 2013.

[67] This also raises questions such as the relationship between various areas of social services and coherency amongst them. Would, for example, university-funded healthcare research be treated differently from other forms of research and, as has been discussed, for example, with reference to C-113/13 *Spezzino* (Chap. 3 Sect. 3.3.5) can developments in other areas, such as healthcare, always be applied to HEIs?

[68] Ştefan 2012 pp. 8, 15 seq, 24 seq, 232, 235.

[69] On the limits of these procedures see Ştefan 2012 p. 234.

[70] Schiek 2012, in particular Chapters 1 (pp. 13–52) and 5 (p. 216 seq). Similar Vandenbroucke and Vanhercke 2014, p. 7.

Additionally, even when insisting on narrow boundaries for integration, these are hard to be contained, as integrated areas tend to spill-over with unforeseeable and possibly undesirable consequences. Having conducted an in-depth analysis of seven years of case law, Schiek observes that 'a slight bias in favour of economic freedoms emerges in the frequency with which economic freedoms prevail over either national policy or social policy'.[71] She thus concludes that it becomes increasingly impractical to limit the social to the national level while the economic is being efficiently integrated.[72]

From what has been set out above, this seems particularly true in the area of HEIs. Not only might the application of directly applicable EU law deconstruct national policy concepts as has been shown in Chaps. 2–5, but also the concerns about the Bologna Process and the Lisbon/Europe 2020 Strategy set out in Chap. 2 (Sect. 2.2.4) would advocate for a coherent policy at the supranational level.[73] Furthermore, as explored in the previous section (Sect. 6.5), the attempts of the Commission to align the aims of competition law and research policy in the Research Framework and the GBER show that the balancing between letting activities fall under EU law and exempting them, if regarded necessary (as many of them have previously been encouraged by the EU's own policy), makes the whole area immensely complicated and uncertain and this Commission driven policy equally raises democratic concerns. In addition, if commodification continues and HEIs (and their spin-offs) essentially become (nearly) fully commercialised entities, but benefit from generous exemptions, a point may be reached where this undermines the whole idea of the competition rules and competitors are, understandably, likely to feel disadvantaged, as was the topic in the case *Sarc* discussed in Chap. 3 (Sect. 3.3.5.3) above.[74] Finally, there are various indications that European civil society and stakeholders are unhappy with the current policy developments towards ever more commodification of public services in general and of HEIs in particular. Regarding the former, one example is the first European citizen initiative (ECI) to ever succeed in collecting the necessary number of signatures

---

[71] Schiek 2012, p. 213. Sauter equally finds that the 'mixed economic constitution' favours the market, but believes that there are sufficient exemptions (Sauter 2015, pp. 35, 222, 224).

[72] Schiek 2012, p. 242; Schiek 2013.

[73] Similar Garben 2012. See also Prosser 2005, who generally points to the problem of hard law integration in more economic areas (competition law) versus soft law integration in the area of public services.

[74] Commission attempts to align different policies in secondary legislation have also been criticised in other area as creating incoherent results. See, for example, Sauter's criticism of the Broadband Guidelines (Sauter 2015, p. 151 seq).

which requires halting privatisation of water supply and sanitation.[75] As regards
the latter, there has equally been an ECI to exclude public spending on education
from calculation of deficits and imposition of austerity measures, though it did not
reach sufficient support in the relevant time period.[76] Another example, though
from the sub-national level, would be the abolishment of tuition fees by the state
government in Bavaria after a successful citizen initiative on the matter at state
level.[77] Furthermore, protests against Bologna style reforms mentioned in Chap. 2
(Sect. 2.2.4) and the critical voices in academic writing mentioned there and above
in this chapter (Sect. 6.4) as well as what many interviewees expressed (Chap. 5
Sects. 5.3, 5.4 and 5.5) indicates that stakeholders are equally unhappy with the
current commodification policies regarding European HEIs.

Even though, as discussed in Chap. 1 (Sect. 1.3.4), a currently negative attitude
towards the EU might make this difficult,[78] a more coherent policy for HEIs at the
supranational level thus might seem timely. The alternative, namely the cutting
back of EU competences, is extremely unlikely, as we are talking about spill-over

---

[75] ECI 'Water and sanitation are a human right! Water is a public good, not a commodity!'
Commission registration number: ECI(2012)000003. More information available on http://
ec.europa.eu/citizens-initiative/public/initiatives/successful/details/2012/000003. The Commission
has since answered to the ECI in a Communication (Communication from the Commission on
the European Citizens' Initiative "Water and sanitation are a human right! Water is a public good,
not a commodity!" COM(2014) 177 final), but aside from a consultation on the Drinking Water
Directive (Directive 2000/60/EC 'establishing a framework for Community action in the field of
water policy' OJ [2000] L 327/1) the Commission does not appear to be planning much concrete
action. This has been criticised by the European Parliament which approved a report requesting
the Commission to do more than just reiterating existing commitments; in particular to exclude
water and sanitation services from trade agreements (see European Parliament (2015) Right2water
citizens' initiative: Commission must act, say MEPs. Press Service, http://www.europarl.europa.
eu/news/en/news-room/20150903IPR91525/right2water-citizens%E2%80%99-initiative-com-
mission-must-act-say-meps, Accessed 26 August 2016). The limited results of successful ECIs
and the complicated process have also led to the European Parliament requesting a reform of the
ECI which, however, seems to equally be stalled by the Commission (The ECI Campaign (2016)
Commission Unlikely to Revise ECI Regulation This Year. http://www.citizens-initiative.eu/com-
mission-unlikely-to-revise-eci-regulation-this-year/. Accessed 11 April 2016).

[76] ECI 'Do not count education spending as part of the deficit! Education is an investment!'
Commission registration number: ECI(2013)000006. More information available on http://
ec.europa.eu/citizens-initiative/public/initiatives/obsolete/details/2013/000006.

[77] Zeit Online (2013) Landtag beschließt Ende der Studiengebühren in Bayern (English translation: State Parliament decides the end of tuition fees in Bavaria). Zeit Online, 24 April 2013
http://www.zeit.de/studium/hochschule/2013-04/studiengebuehren-bayern-abschaffung.
Accessed 1 September 2015. See also Holmwood et al. 2016, p. 4 with regards to results from a
national survey showing discontent of civil society with the UK government's commodification
policies.

[78] On the negative attitudes towards the EU since the finical crisis see also Vandenbroucke and
Vanhercke 2014, p. 7. Sauter equally expresses some doubt that social integration generally can
catch up with economic integration due to insufficient will of the Member States and public opinion (Sauter 2015 pp. 34, 230).

from the core provisions of primary law (i.e. competition law, but also citizenship and free movement law) here. The abandonment of competences in these areas thus seems impossible without an abandonment of the whole European project. In the area of competition law Swennen has raised the question as to whether competition law as a whole should be differently drafted/applied, as currently it conceivably favours a specific kind of undertaking. In a completely different competition law the problems arising from application on public services might become irrelevant.[79] While this could be an interesting solution, it might be a too ambitious endeavour to depart from decades of practice and case law. Therefore, the best that could be likely be achieved with a view to retaining national competence are more encompassing and clearer exemptions. Here, it is submitted, that rather than just redrafting the Research Framework and the GBER to find an acceptable place for HEIs in state aid law and leaving the other areas to be decided upon on a case by case basis, there could at least be scope for a more general block exemption regulation from competition law specifically on HEIs setting out their position more clearly and comprehensively. Such a regulation could next to state aid issues involve issues like allowing price fixing at low levels for social purposes if competition on the merits would still be possible[80] and setting out when and if the limitation of outputs is considered abuse of dominance.

However, despite this not seeming likely in the current political climate, a more comprehensive EU policy seems preferable. Firstly, as Schiek establishes and as we have already briefly seen at the beginning of this section, economic integration was initially considered a means to an end and European integration thus does also aim at social integration; something which (at least rhetorically) has been strengthened with the Treaty of Lisbon (e.g. through the 'horizontal social clause' in Article 9 TFEU).[81] Secondly, it has been stressed that the current 'muddling through' approach towards social integration is simply not sustainable in time of crisis, but that comprehensive social integration with mainstreaming into all areas is required.[82] Thirdly, and for the area of HEIs possibly most importantly, simple exemptions would not remove the possibility of continuing commodification policies through soft law in Bologna and Lisbon with all the concerns, especially democratic concerns, this involves which have been discussed in Chap. 2 (Sect. 2.2.4).[83] Therefore, alternative bases for regulating more social policy areas at the European level have already been explored in literature. Garben[84] has, for example, explored various options and, while remaining doubtful that a stronger

---

[79] Swennen 2008/2009, p. 279.

[80] Similar to T-289/03 *BUPA* (Judgment of 12 February 2008, EU:T:2008:29) and the US case *United States v. Brown Univ.* discussed on in Chap. 3 Sect. 3.3.2.1 above.

[81] Schiek 2013 in particular p. 85 seq. Similar Vandenbroucke and Vanhercke 2014, p. 14 seq.

[82] Vandenbroucke and Vanhercke 2014, pp. 16, 22.

[83] Beyond these two mechanisms nation states are arguably generally 'vulnerable to economic globalisation' (Schiek 2013, p. 85).

[84] Garben 2011, p. 184 seq; Garben 2012, p. 24 seq.

primary law competence can be achieved, suggested alternative measures for 'a stronger base in EU law' for education policy. More generally, conceding that it seems unlikely that it will be used in the near future, others have pointed to the new legislative competence in Article 14 TFEU for the regulation of SGEIs.[85] There may thus be avenues, even without the extension of competences for research and higher education, especially given that research already is a shared competence, to establish a coherent legislative framework at the EU level.

While it would go beyond the scope of this study to offer a solution as to *how* to regulate HEIs at the supranational level, we can start to identify issues which would have an important impact on potential solutions. In developing stronger EU policies the question of how far these could be regarded as a *lex specialis* to other areas of EU law would need to be addressed in order to avoid strategies, laws and policies to conflict.[86] Given the problems identified as regards commodification of HEIs and the mentioned critical voices, an alternative direction might be considered consulting stakeholders and allowing public debate.[87] Furthermore, ideally, the ordinary legislative procedure should be followed for such legislation (e.g. on the basis of the new competence for research in Article 4(3) TFEU in conjunction with article 182 TFEU or utilising Article 14 TFEU) rather than leaving such legislation entirely to the Commission. This could remedy (at least some of) the democratic concerns, since the European Parliament is not only directly elected but also more susceptible to citizens' wishes.[88]

Additionally, it might be desirable to decrease the administrative efforts involved in applying for EU research funding if truly efficient research is envisaged, as currently, as some interviewees mentioned, these have deterred researchers from applying and it may arguably also favour certain institutions. Yet, despite the administrative hurdles, national budget cuts in some Member States and the increasing encouragement of applying for non-generic funding may nevertheless lead to an increase in applications for EU funding, as, if the impression gained from the interviewees is more widely true, many HEIs are increasingly looking

---

[85] Schiek 2013, p. 81 seq; Sauter 2015 pp. 27, 177 seq, 222, 241.

[86] As mentioned above, the new Research Framework and the GBER have in fact treated EU funding policy as such by explicitly declaring that EU funding is excluded from the state aid rules.

[87] Schiek (2013 in particular p. 76 seq) submits that the 'constitution of social governance' and especially Article 2 TEU can be interpreted as an acknowledgement for societal activity. She thus argues that this should play a role when the Court interprets exemptions and rules on area where such societal activity has taken place. It may also be conceivable that this could strengthen the argument that civil society's wishes should be further regarded in law making, especially when they have already widely been expressed through citizen initiatives at various governance levels as is the case as regards commodification of HEIs. See also Vandenbroucke and Vanhercke 2014, p. 23 who equally argue that social integration should not take place 'top-down'.

[88] See, for example, the different reactions to the water ECI mentioned in n 75 above.

towards Europe for research funding.[89] Therefore, whilst, in contrast to the EU budget in general, funding for research and innovation seem to be an area for which there is a willingness to invest,[90] there might be the necessity for even further research funding. Within the competences available, there could also be more initiative and funding for education, especially considering that, unlike research, funding in this area has generally decreased.[91]

6.7 Final Conclusion

This work has assessed EU law constraints on HEIs. It has used a socio-legal approach including an empirical study by, first, placing the legal assessment in the wider context of the historical mission of HEIs and of European integration theory. It has then assessed the political and legal situation of HEIs in Europe before conducting a comprehensive competition law analysis, until now a largely unexplored area. Following this, the research systems of Germany, the Netherlands and England (UK) have been explored and analysed as to their potential for tensions with EU competition law. These potential tensions as well as the awareness of experts in research offices for competition law and their overall estimation of the research situation have then been empirically examined. Due to the differences in the systems the awareness and potential conflicts with competition law differed, but in all systems a susceptibility to competition law has been detected which may require further commodification. Having set the observations from the empirical study into the wider context in this chapter (Sect. 6.4), it became clear that they mirror critical voices in literature as regards economic constraints generally and that certain developments beyond what has been found in the empirical study (e.g. the currently debated changes as regards education in the UK (English) Higher Education and Research Bill) could be regarded as a case in point for the potential of spill-over from economic law.

This study concludes that the constitutionalised provisions of EU law can indeed spill-over, as neo-functionalism explains, into policies for the HEI sector and constraints may arise, especially with further commodification, and can indeed require even further commodification potentially endangering the traditional non-economic mission of European HEIs. While the Court has recently shown some restraint in areas of primary responsibility of the Member States, this is still does not generally negate the possibility of spill-over from directly applicable law and,

---

[89] Indeed, Ulnicane reports that HEIs in many countries 'are expected to supplement decreasing national funding with EU funding' despite the latter being unfit for this purpose and that in 'its first year, Horizon 2020 experienced a "tsunami of proposals" and low success rates leading to questions [if it] […] is destined to be an underfunded and oversubscribed programme' (Ulnicane 2016, p. 336).

[90] Ulnicane 2016, pp. 330, 332, 335.

[91] Vandenbroucke and Vanhercke 2014, pp. 9, 11, 22.

in the area of competition law, it is the national competition authorities who would be responsible for enforcement. Current limited attempts by the Commission to align policies seem equally insufficient, as they do not necessarily clarify the legal position, are still fragmented, are decided upon entirely by the Commission and do not appear to necessarily reflect the views of the general public. It might thus be time to implement a more coherent EU level policy on HEIs which moves away from the current tendency towards commodification and truly clarifies the legal position of HEIs under EU law. However, while raising some points to be taken into consideration, the details on how this can be achieved will need to be left to future research. In the meantime the book offers a comprehensive discussion of the topics and constraints. As such it can be utilised by policy makers and staff in research offices to become aware of potential constraints in order to circumvent these and instead chose the best practises.

References

Albrecht C (2009) Die Zukunft der deutschen Universität (English translation: The future of the German University). Forschung & Lehre 2009:8–11
Beech DJ (2013) The European Research Area: beyond market politics. Europe of Knowledge, 5 October 2013. http://era.ideasoneurope.eu/2013/10/05/the-european-research-area-beyond-market-politics/. Accessed 7 October 2013
BIS (2015) Fulfilling our potential—teaching excellence, social mobility and student choice. Williams Lea Group on behalf of the Controller of Her Majesty's Stationery Office, London
BIS (2016a) Summary of consultation responses. BIS, London
BIS (2016b) Success as a knowledge economy. Williams Lea Group, London
CMA (2015) An effective regulatory framework for higher education: A policy paper. Crown Copyright, London
De Fraja G (2011) A theoretical analysis of public funding for research. University of Leicester Department of Economics Working Paper 31:1–27
Enders J (2007) Reform and change of German Research Universities. Higher Educ Forum 4:19–32
European Commission (2011) Commission Staff Working Paper: Mid-Term Review of the R&D&I Framework. European Commission, Brussels
European Commission (2012) Revision of the state aid rules for research and development and innovation. European Commission, Brussels
Friedmann LS, Richter ED (2004) Relationship between conflict of interest and research results. JGIM 19:51–56
Garben S (2010) The Bologna Process: from a European Law Perspective. ELJ 16:186–210
Garben S (2011) EU Higher Education Law—The Bologna Process and Harmonization by Stealth. Kluwer, Alphen aan den Rijn
Garben S (2012) The future of higher education in Europe: the case for a stronger base in EU Law. LSE 'Europe in Question' Discussion Paper Series 50:1–44
Gideon A, Sanchez-Graells A (2016) When are universities bound by EU public procurement rules as buyers and providers?—English universities as a case study. Ius Publicum 2016(1):1–58
Hatzopoulos V (2009) Services of General Interest in Healthcare: an exercise in deconstruction? In: Neergaard U et al (eds) Integrating Welfare Functions into EU Law—from Rome to Lisbon. DJØF Forlag, Copenhagen, pp 225–252

Holmwood J et al (2016) The alternative White Paper for higher education. Convention for Higher Education

Jansen D (2010) Von der Steuerung zur Governance: Wandel der Staatlichkeit? (English translation: From control to governance: Change of public character?). In: Simon D et al (eds) Handbuch Wissenschaftspolitik (English translation: Handbook Science Policy). VS Verlag, Wiesbaden, pp 39–50

Kamola I, Noori N (2014) Higher education and world politics—introduction. PS: Polit Sci Polit 47:599–603

Leisyte L et al (2008) The Freedom to Set Research Agendas—Illusion and Reality of the Research Units in the Dutch Universities. High Educ Policy 21:377–391

Lemmens P, Dupont H (2012) "Onder invloed": is samenwerking met commerciële partijen te verantwoorden? (English translation: "Under the influence": is collaboration with commercial partners justifiable?) Verslaving 3:67–72

Office of Fair Trading (2014) Higher education in England. Crown Copyright, London

Prosser T (2005) Competition Law and Public Services: from Single Market to Citizenship Rights? European Public Law 11:543–563

Sauter W (2015) Public Services in EU Law. CUP, Cambridge

Schiek D (2012) Economic and social integration—the challenge for EU constitutional law. Edward Elgar, Cheltenham

Schiek D (2013) Social Services of General Interest: The EU Competence Regime and a Constitution of Social Governance. In: Neergaard U et al (eds) Social Services of General Interest in the EU. T.M.C. Asser Press, The Hague, pp 74–94

Schubert T, Schmoch U (2010) Finanzierung der Hochschulforschung (English translation: Funding of university research). In: Simon D et al (eds) Handbuch Wissenschaftspolitik (English translation: Handbook Science Policy). VS Verlag, Wiesbaden, pp 244–261

Ştefan O (2012) Soft Law in Court: Competition Law, State Aid and the Court of Justice of the European Union. Kluwer, Alphen aan den Rijn

Stern N (2016) Building on success and learning from experience. BEIS, London

Suarez C (2014) Competition in the HE Sector. Competition in the Higher Education market

Swennen H (2008/2009) Onderwijs en Mededingsrecht (English translation: Teaching and competition law). Tijdschrift voor Onderwijsrecht en Onderwijsbeleid 4:259–280

Szyszczak E (2013) Soft Law and Safe Havens. In: Neergaard U et al (eds) Social Services of General Interest in the EU. T.M.C. Asser Press, The Hague, pp 317–345

Thambisetty S (2013) Why Patent Law Doesn't Do Innovation Policy. LSE Law, Society and Economy Working Papers 20:13

Ulnicane I (2016) Research and innovation as sources of renewed growth? EU policy responses to the crisis. J Eur Integr 38:327–341

Vandenbroucke F, Vanhercke B (2014) A European Social Union: 10 tough nuts to crack. Friends of Europe, Brussels

Annex
Interview Questions

Section 1: Introductory Questions

1. Could you please first state your name and task within the university?
2. Does EU competition and state aid law play a role in your everyday tasks?
3. Which measures, if any, have been undertaken to adhere to legal requirements and what consequences has this had on research funding?

Section 2: Publicly Funded Research

4. This question concerns funding awarded from public budgets and not-for-profit organisations for which your organisation competes with other organisations. Is such funding awarded to any type of research or any type of research in a specific field? Or are the calls very detailed and you have to adjust the research very much according to what is wanted in your application? Can you give examples of the latter?
5. Are you aware of any limitations as to who can apply in any of these calls? In particular, can the private sector and the third sector also apply for such calls? Can you give examples of cases which are limited to certain organisations?
6. Subject to confidentiality, what is the highest amount of funding you received from public sources in a competitive way?

Section 3: Cooperation with the Private Sector

7. In addition to contract research, what kind of collaborations/knowledge exchange/interaction with the private sector is your organisation involved in (e.g. research co-operations, patenting and spin-offs, setting up new

© T.M.C. Asser Press and the author 2017
A. Gideon, *Higher Education Institutions in the EU: Between Competition and Public Service*, Legal Issues of Services of General Interest, DOI 10.1007/978-94-6265-168-5

companies, individuals working in undertakings next to their HEI task, privately financed chairs, science parks/clusters, etc)?

8. Subject to confidentiality, can you give some details of the named collaborations? In particular, who contributes in which way (financially)? Who decides what will be researched?

9. How is it decided in these forms of collaboration with the private sector (or third sector) who can join such a collaboration/apply? Can anyone join who wants to?

10. Are there any kind or undertakings (e.g. SME or local undertakings) whom your organisations prefers to cooperate with? If yes, what are the reasons for this?

11. Are there any networks/collaborations with special conditions/duties for participating parties? Please specify any conditions which are imposed upon your organisation or which you require from others (e.g. limitations beyond the research, limitations towards using the results)?

12. Are there any advantages in such networks/collaborations in terms of prices or contract conditions for any undertakings? Do you give advantages to any research users? Examples in both cases could be advantages for SMEs or local undertakings.

13. If you are planning to enter into a research co-operation, what conditions your decision? Is this usually something that is done at the beginning of a project/ an idea or at a later stage? Are research co-operations also entered into, if the research is almost finished (shortly before a breakthrough)?

14. If you have staff partly working for the private sector or who can take leave to work in the private sector, what are the conditions? Is it a concern to share publicly generated knowledge or to make sure not to do so?

15. What arrangements are made in respect of intellectual property rights? How are these used (directly, in spin-offs, leave it for the public)?

16. Do the arrangements regarding IPRs differ according to who is funding the research (public funding, private sector funding, third sector funding)?

17. Do you have a practice of giving licenses for IPRs? If yes, how does this work? Do you give licenses for the use of IPRs (e.g. patents) to anyone who wishes to use them?

18. Are there any limitations or conditions regarding licenses? What is the usual duration of a license? Is that what is the common duration in the sector?

Section 4: Full Economic Costing

19. Has your organisation adopted full economic costing?

20. How are the full economic costs calculated? Are there any agreements/guidelines which apply to universities in this respect?

21. How are costs calculated in cases where full economic costing does not apply?

Section 5: Market Entry, Limitations of Research

22. Having studied the research systems, I do not think this is the case, but for the sake of completeness; are there any limitations as to who can conduct research (e.g. through national legislation or due to having to be accredited in any way)?
23. Are there any limitations as to the amount of research, in particular privately funded research your organisation may conduct?
24. Are you aware of any legislation or other act entrusting your organisation with the task of research?
25. Do you have any specialisation agreements with the private sector or other HEIs? A specialisation agreement is an agreement between two or more entities which contains that rather than both/all conducting a variety of tasks/services, one undertaking is conducting one task/service and the other another. They then receive the task/service which they stopped conducting from each other.
26. Now, again, having studied the systems, I do not believe there is anything of the kind, but for the sake of completeness; do you have any arrangements for geographical division of workload with other parties?
27. In your opinion, is the research your institution is conducting in the general (public) interest? Can you think of examples of research which was mainly for the benefit of particular interests? If yes, how is such research funded?

Section 6: General Opinion on Funding Situation

28. Do you think that your organisation is expected to increase specific kinds of research (e.g. applied research, research that generates impact, basic research)?
29. Are there any differences between subjects (i.e. is it easier to generate funding for certain subjects rather than for others)? If yes, which subjects are easily funded and for which is funding more difficult to be obtained?
30. What consequences have the general developments in regards to funding streams over the last decades had in your institution?
31. Do you think legal requirements and your responses to them, if applicable, have resulted in limitations on academic freedom?
32. What do you expect to be the trends in research funding and research policy in the next 10 years?

Index

© T.M.C. ASSER PRESS and the author 2017
A. Gideon, *Higher Education Institutions in the EU: Between Competition and Public Service*, Legal Issues of Services of General Interest, DOI 10.1007/978-94-6265-168-5

Printed by Printforce, the Netherlands